How to Release Fear-Based Thinking and Feeling

D1640480

How to Release Fear-Based Thinking and Feeling

An In-depth Study of Spiritual Psychology Volume 1

Dr. Joshua David Stone

Writers Club Press
San Jose New York Lincoln Shanghai

How to Release Fear-Based Thinking and Feeling
An In-depth Study of Spiritual Psychology Volume 1

Writers Club Press
an imprint of iUniverse.com, Inc.

For information address:
iUniverse.com, Inc.
5220 S 16th, Ste. 200
Lincoln, NE 68512
www.iuniverse.com

ISBN: 0-595-17227-X

Printed in the United States of America

Contents

The Key Fundamental Spiritual Question of Life Explained from the Perspective of Soul and Spirit

My Beloved Readers, this chapter I now share with you is one of the most profound and crucial understandings in this entire book. For it goes right to the core of the negative ego and Spiritual thought system and asks the fundamental key question of life, which must be answered and understood to fully transcend the negative ego/fear-based/separative thought system. Without understanding what I am about to share in this chapter, the negative ego thought system cannot be fully undone. With this you will be able to completely undo the negative ego thought system at its very core and you will never be the same again! On this Spiritual note I will now begin!

I share this for we are all literally incarnations of GOD, Eternal Selves, Christs, Buddhas, Atmas—literally Gods. As the Bible says, we are made in the image and likeness of GOD! The Bible says, "Ye are

Gods and know it not!" I share this key to God Realization with you, for by helping you I help GOD, you and myself, for there is, in truth, only one infinite being in the universe and that is GOD! There are no separate beings outside of GOD. So, in truth, in this moment, God is helping God, in service of a greater vision of GOD! This is why in GOD there is never any lack of love, separation, competition, comparison, envy or jealousy! For why would God create separation from him or herself? To have all, one must "Give all to all!" That which one holds back from a Brother and Sister is that which, in truth, one back from oneself! The negative ego thinks it gains by holding back' however, the truth is your Brothers and Sisters are only a mirror or screen for your own consciousness! You and your Brothers and Sisters are God whether you like it or not! You have no choice in the matter because you did not create yourself, GOD created you! What you gain in life is literally what you give! Since your true identity is God, and not your physical body, then, in truth, you literally are and have everything! However, the law of the mind is that whatever you think is the reality you live in. So if you think you are just a body and are separate from everyone and at war and competition with everyone else is illusion, however, you will live in the nightmare illusionary dream of your own thought creation thinking separation is real. When the truth is you are God, you always have been and always will be! Everyone and every-thing is a part of you in truth, and you are a part of them! My Beloved Readers, we all share the same identity in GOD! So of course I give freely to you my Beloved Brothers and Sisters, for to hold anything back from you is to hold it back from my self and GOD! A lot of peo-ple think when they help someone they are giving "charity" to them. In truth, my Beloved Readers, this is illusion! In truth, if you really see clearly and with GOD's eyes you are giving charity to yourself! For any-thing you hold back from a Brother and Sister (who is God), you hold back from yourself. Your Brother and Sister literally are yourself, in truth! GOD, in truth, has only one Son or Daughter, and we all share in this one Sonship or Daughtership! So in truth, when you give to your Brothers and Sisters you are giving charity to yourself. You need the blessing more than they do. You literally cannot achieve God Realization without it. The negative ego would have you think that by giving something you are losing it. As with everything in life, the negative ego has it completely backward. Giving to your Brothers and Sisters is how you are gaining God Realization for yourself. This is also why if you steal from your Brothers and Sisters on any level you are literally stealing from yourself. For you would be stealing from GOD, and stealing from your Brothers and Sisters who are God. The negative ego believes giving is losing and stealing is gaining! GOD would have you know in this moment that nothing could be farther from the truth. To steal from a Brother or Sister on any level is to steal God from yourself. To give to a Brother and Sister is literally gaining GOD for yourself. You are not literally giving anything away, for you are giving to God, which is yourself. All of Creation, is a part of you and you are a part of all Creation for we share with our Brothers and Sisters the same identity as Gods or Sons and Daughters of GOD! Are you beginning to see now, my Beloved Readers, the full profundity of that which I speak? Do you see now the absurdity of negative ego thinking and feeling? The negative ego's main premise is that it thinks you are a physical body, and it only sees with physical eyes, not Spiritual or Christ/Buddha eyes! If you are just a physical body, then death is real. Physical bodies are separate! The negative ego has confused your identity! It is from this faulty premise that this whole illusionary thought and feeling system began! You have been unloving, had separative feelings and emotions, held back giving, competed, compared, and/or been jealous and envious because you have not seen your self and your Brothers and Sisters as the Gods you and they are! Now it is important to understand that it is not enough to just see yourself as God, for you will not Realize God unless you also see your Brothers and Sisters as God as well! This is regardless of their level of evolution. Everyone is God, period, end of discussion! However everyone also is in an evolutionary process which is part of GOD's grand experiment of Creation! So just because you or your Brother's and Sister's, mental, emotional or physical body does not always reflect your true identity this, does not change the truth of your being or their being! This is why I also like to say at times, on the Realization level of things we are apprentice Gods growing up to be like GOD as well! Just because we have not Realized God fully in our Spiritual, mental, emotional, or physical bodies does not change the fact in the slightest that we are Gods! Half the battle to Realizing God is first realizing your identity as God! How can you achieve God Realization if you don't accept the truth that God is your true identity? Do you see how simple it all is? All that has happened is that we have fallen into mass consciousness and negative ego/fear-based/separative thinking and feeling that we are all physical bodies and not Gods living in physical bodies. Now if you prefer to call this Christs, Buddhas, Eternal Selves, Atmas, or Sons and Daughters of GOD, that is fine! The names, terms, religion or Spiritual path does not matter! The first key to successful inner and outer living begins with the simplest question of all, which is the one most people forget or do not ask. What is your true identity? The key fundamental question of life that everyone for-gets to ask is "Are you a physical body, or are you God living in a phys-ical body and using a physical body for Spiritual growth and service?" This one fundamental existential choice will determine all other choices. It is from that "choosing to think of yourself as a physical body" that all negative ego thinking and feeling stems from. It is the overidentification with matter! Some have called it materialism! It is not that matter is bad, for it is not! It is one of the Four Faces of GOD! However, we were never meant to so identify with it that we forgot who we really are. We are supposed to be in this world but not of this world! Involved but detached! My Beloved Readers, in the history of the Earth, Sons and Daughters of GOD became overidentified with matter to the point of forgetting who they really were! There is no harm done in this, for as *A Course In Miracles* says in its introduction, "Nothing real can be threatened and nothing unreal exists! Herein lies the peace of GOD!" Just because you thought you were a physical body and not God, did not change the truth of your being! Just as going to sleep at night and having a bad dream does not change the truth of your being in daily life when you wake up from that dream! The only difference is that this dream of thinking you were a physical body, instead of God living in a physical body, lasted a little longer! From GOD's perspective and infinite expanse of time it lasted a second or two! All that matters now is that you have awakened! The negative ego's fear-based, separative thought and feeling system has now come to an end! Now that you fully recognize that you and your Brothers and Sisters are God living in physical bodies, you can also choose to think only with God consciousness, which is also known as Spiritual/Christ/Buddha consciousness! Do you see how God consciousness must first stem from owning the truth that you and your Brothers and Sisters are Gods? Do you see how simple it is? Do you see how easily the negative ego thought system is now falling away? After understanding this truth as fully as you are right now, the negative ego thought and feeling system will never be able to get a hold of you again. This is because you are now seeing through your "God eyes" and "Spiritual eyes" as well as your physical eyes! From this moment forward you will always see and know yourself and your Brothers and Sisters as God! I emphasize that one last game the negative ego might try to play in its last ditch effort for power is to say "Okay, you are God, but your Brothers and Sisters aren't." Sorry negative ego, that illusionary game is now "busted" as well! My Beloved Readers, listen closely. You cannot realize God unless you also see your Brothers and Sisters as God! Every encounter with a Brother and Sister is a Holy encounter! God meeting God! Christ meeting Christ! Buddha meeting Buddha! Atma meeting Atma! Eternal Self meeting Eternal Self! Son and Daughter of GOD meeting Son and Daughter of GOD! My Beloved Readers, your Brother and Sister is God, as you are whether you believe it or not! Again I remind you that you have no choice in this for you did not create yourself, GOD created you and your Brothers and Sisters! So my Beloved Readers, I am happy to say, "We are all Gods whether we like it not!" The negative ego can rant and rave and scream all it wants to, but this fundamental truth of GOD is the truth. We can choose to think anything we want because GOD gave us free choice, and the law of the mind is that whatever we think is the thoughtform world we will live in. If you think the glass of water is half empty then that is the thinking and feeling world you will live in. If you think you and your Brothers and Sisters are physical bodies and not Gods, this is your right! However, my Beloved Readers, let me make you aware that you do have the right to think whatever you want and you do have the right to live in whatever thought and feeling creation you choose, but your thinking does not create truth! It just creates the mental and emotional world you live in! The book *A Course In Miracles* calls this the "Authority Problem"! The key question you must ask yourself is "Did GOD create you or did the negative ego create you?" This of course is almost comical! The truth is that GOD created everything and everyone! The truth also is that you created the negative ego by thinking out of harmony with GOD! This is the eating of the Tree of Good and Evil that the Bible speaks of! Before we ate the apple we lived in this world thinking only with God's mind and feelings! When we used our free choice to eat the apple we thought out of harmony with GOD! This is where this illusionary thought system of negative ego/fear-based/separative thinking and feeling began. It never existed until we made this choice! Now the comical part of this whole story is that GOD created us and we created this illusionary thought and feeling system called negative ego or fear-based thinking! However, the negative ego is going around acting like GOD saying that GOD doesn't exist, that we are not God, but actually just a physical body, and that the only thing that is real is separation, fear, attack, war, competition, and death! The negative ego, believing that you are just a physical body, tells you that there is no GOD, and that separation from your Brothers and Sisters is your true reality. It tells you that you die at death, for you are not an eternal soul or God being! So the negative ego believes only in itself, and is self-centered! God Consciousness sees you and your Brothers and Sisters as God, and all of Creation as GOD! It recognizes that you and your Brothers and Sisters are a part of all Creation! God consciousness recognizes that GOD has stated that you are and have everything in all Creation, for it is literally a part of you and your Brother and Sister. Your identity does not exist like a fence around you, as the negative ego would have you believe. You and your Brothers' and Sisters' identity as God are as big as all Creation! We are all part of each other! We all share the same identity in GOD!

So my Beloved Brothers and Sisters, do you see how incredibly delusionary the negative ego thought system is? It would be comical if so many people were not caught up in it! The crazy thing is they can let go of it anytime they want; for it has never been real, is not real right now, and never will be real! It is just a bad dream! It is just a massive negative hypnosis! The truth is GOD created us. We have free choice in how we think and cause or create our own reality, however we do not have free choice as to who created us! GOD created us whether we like it or not! So we are Gods whether the negative ego thought system likes it or not! This is a fact, and all the negative ego thinking in the infinite universe will not change the fact that GOD created us and we are Gods! This is a fact and this is why the Bible states, "We are made in the image of God and that we are Gods and know it not"!

The truth is, whether the negative ego likes it or not, that GOD created us, we are Gods, and we created the negative ego thought and feeling system by using our free choice to think out of harmony with GOD! The negative ego's delusionary and disturbed thought system is not real! It has never been real, is not real now and never will be real! It is nothing more than faulty thinking! It is nothing more than glamour, illusion and maya! It is time that this delusionary and disturbed thinking and feeling system be stopped! The negative ego delusionary and disturbed thought system is the cause of all problems in people and the cause of all problems in the world. The negative ego's belief that GOD does not exist, that you are a physical body and not God living in a physical body, that separation is real, that fear is real, that death of you as a God being is real, that competition is real, that your only purpose should be for yourself and that this so called self is contained by some imaginary fence in the physical body, is total delusion, disturbance and illusion. The negative ego's belief that there is no purpose to life, except to indulge lower-self desire, hedonistic tendencies, and thirst for power, fame, money and sex as its reason for living, is downright sick when you see the negative ego for what it is. The negative ego's belief that life is war and an ego battle, and that the best way to get what it wants is to attack, be angry, judge, hold grudges, manipulate, cheat and steal, is delusionary as well. The game of being superior or inferior, and being jealous and envious of other God beings' success, is also where the negative ego lives and is stuck in. The negative ego is unable to transcend this superior/inferior, top dog/underdog thinking. It is endlessly stuck in superior, top dog aggressive thoughts and feelings and inferior, underdog, depressed, sad, hurt, guilty, regretful, rejected, abandoned feelings! My Beloved Readers, it is only when you embrace your and your Brothers' and Sisters' identity as God beings, and embrace God consciousness, Spiritual consciousness, Christ consciousness and Buddha consciousness, which are all the same thing, that this nightmare of the negative ego/fear-based/separative thinking and feeling will end!

My Beloved Readers, I apologize for being a little serious towards the end of this chapter, however I felt inwardly guided to finally call a spade a spade, and call the negative ego on what it really is! I felt inwardly guided to fully let you see in clear and no uncertain terms how disturbed and sick the negative ego thought system really is. Is it no wonder there are so many Sons and Daughters of GOD in this world, suffering, abused and unhappy? It is nothing more than a byproduct of the negative ego/fear-based/separative thought system that has corrupted this world and created a negative dream reality that a great many people are living in! After reading this chapter you will never be the same, and this was my purpose for writing it! You now see the negative ego/fear-based/separative thought system for the true delusion, disturbance, and illusion that it is!

My Beloved Readers, to put this in perspective for you, however, you have absolutely nothing to be concerned about for the negative ego has absolutely no power over you! That is why I have written this chapter! Once you see what the negative ego really is as I have described, and see how delusionary and illusionary its thought system is, and you compare it to God consciousness, it really just disappears. I humbly suggest that you will never be the same after reading this chapter! The negative ego has been undone by the Grace of GOD and Spirit! The negative ego's nightmare dream has now ended! You have seen in clear and no uncertain terms how delusionary and disturbed the negative ego's thought system really is! You have seen the core premises of the negative ego and it has now been caught in the act, where before it was sneaking around creating its negativity and disturbance without you fully being able to get a 100% handle on it. My Beloved Readers, by the Grace of GOD and the Masters now you have! Your eyes have been opened and the "Truth has set you free"!

The negative ego is easily transcended for all the negative ego is are some thoughts in your mind and you are now the master of your thoughts! The key is to do what *A Course In Miracles* says, "Deny any thought not of GOD to enter your mind"! It is really so simple! There are only two ways of thinking in the world, and only two philosophies in life. Every person on Earth either thinks with their negative ego/fear-based/separative mind or with their God/Spiritual/Christ/Buddha mind! All you have to do to stay centered, clear, unconditionally loving, forgiving, nonjudgmental, happy, joyous, peaceful, and evenminded all the time and to push the negative ego thoughts and feelings out of your mind and immediately switch them to your God/Spiritual/Christ/ Buddha interpretation and attitude and feeling system! By not giving energy to the negative ego way of thinking and feeling it withers and dies from lack of energy, like a plant from lack of water. The God/Spiritual/Christ/Buddha thought system will expand and grow because you are focusing on it! It is just a matter of where you put your attention! What manifests in life is where you put your attention and focus! It is also a psychological fact that it only takes 21 days to create a new habit in the subconscious mind! You can get rid of the negative ego instantly and forever by just choosing in this moment not to think that way. Remember it is your thoughts that create your feelings and emotions. This is another psychological law! You cause your own reality by how you think! So just push the negative ego thought and feeling system out of your mind when it arises, and switch it and keep it focused at all times on the God/Spiritual/Christ/Buddha thought and feeling system. You do this by owning your 100% personal power at all times, which allows you to remain in a state of self-mastery and be the cause of your reality at all times instead of being a victim of your negative ego thoughts and feelings!

So, it is really so simple my Beloved Readers, when you really understand! There is really nothing to be concerned about! I have been serious only for the important point of showing you how disturbed and negative the negative ego thought system really is and to show you what its true motivations and purpose was and is at its core. It is absolutely essential that you understand this. If you do not understand this truth, you will not demonstrate the proper "Spiritual Vigilance" to not go on automatic pilot and let the negative ego try and sneak back in! By the Grace of GOD and the Masters I humbly believe that I have succeeded in my purpose!

So, my Beloved Readers, we come to the moment of truth that we all have been waiting for! In this "Holy Instant" Spirit and the Masters now ask you two key existential questions that will determine your existence for the rest of Eternity!

The first is "What is your true identity?" Are you God living in a physical body as GOD states is the truth whether your negative ego believes it or not, or are you just a physical body? Spirit and the Masters humbly request that you make a 100% decisive decision in this moment as to if you believe GOD's answer or the negative ego's answer to this question. Please choose!

Secondly, this being your choice from this moment for the rest of your life, Spirit and the Masters now ask you to choose in a 100% decisive manner, God/Spiritual/Christ/Buddha thinking and feeling or negative ego/fear-based/separative thinking and feeling.

Congratulations on your choice for GOD and God consciousness! Welcome Home! You are now living in Heaven within your own consciousness!

There is, of course, only one choice that can be made, for one is GOD and one is illusion, and a choice for illusion is not even a choice, for negative ego and illusion do not even exist! This last statement I made is very profound and bears repeating! The negative ego and its thought and feeling system do not really exist! This is why there is nothing to be too serious about. I was serious only as a temporary and important step to help you transcend the entire thought system all together! The negative ego thought and feeling system is nothing more than faulty thinking! It is nothing more than a bad dream, which you have now awakened from by the Grace of GOD and the Masters! Peace has come at last! The nightmare and bad dream of the negative ego is now over! Joyous Spiritual vigilance will always be needed even after it becomes a Spiritual habit to think with your Spiritual/Christ/Buddha thoughts and feelings. After reading this book and practicing and demonstrating that which is contained here, you will very shortly have developed a Spiritual habit of thinking and feeling from God consciousness. The subconscious mind, having no reasoning, plays back whatever you program into it. It is like a tape recorder! You have in this moment transcended negative ego thinking and feeling! Within two months it will with joyous Spiritual vigilance, practice and demonstration, start really becoming a habit. It will actually start becoming hard to think and feel any other way. You will look back and say, "How could I have possibly thought and felt with my negative ego mind?" You will say, "It is so simple, how could I have not seen this before. I wish I would have read this book 20 years ago."

One last reminder, my Beloved Readers, is that you have transcended the negative ego thought and feeling system and changed to the God/Spiritual/Christ/Buddha thought and feeling system already in this moment. Nothing will change this as long as you choose to own your personal power, self-mastery, and Spiritual joyous vigilance. Within two months or much less, maybe even within 21 days, it will really start becoming a Spiritual habit. However, even once it becomes a Spiritual habit you must always remain "joyously vigilant", for the negative ego is always capable of returning! This is nothing to be concerned about, for as long as you maintain your personal power, self-mastery, and joyous vigilance it cannot and will not return! However, some light-workers can fall into the trap of being overconfident, or go too much back into automatic pilot, or be too prideful which of course is the negative ego. As the Bible says, "After pride cometh the fall"! So as long as you remain in your personal power, self-mastery, unconditional love and wisdom, and maintain humbleness and humility, and don't go back into automatic pilot, and maintain your joyous vigilance, you will be fine and the negative ego will never return! For no matter how far one Spiritually and/or psychologically evolves, it is always possible to take a tumble down the Spiritual mountain and/or fall from Grace! This is because GOD has given us free choice and it is always possible to misuse your free choice again! So keeping this in mind and keeping this in proper perspective, Spirit and the Masters wish to congratulate you on taking this most important step on your Spiritual journey! They wish you to know that you will hear them and the "still small voice within" much clearer now that the static and noise of the negative ego mind has been decisively transcended! By the Grace of GOD and the Masters you have now returned to your original Edenic state of consciousness before the illusion of negative ego and separation began! You have now returned to the state of consciousness that can be most aptly described as a "Peace that passeth understanding"! By the Grace of GOD and the Masters the "Truth has set you free"! This is also why the Bible says, "Seek ye the Kingdom of GOD and all things shall be given unto thee"! I think after reading this chapter you can see another level and deeper truth of this statement. By choosing GOD instead of negative ego you have reclaimed your Spiritual inheritance! You literally are and have everything! The Prodigal Son and Daughter of GOD have now returned home in consciousness!

So let it be Written! So let it be Done!

CHAPTER 2

The Importance of Learning to Balance Your Three-Fold Flame

We on the Spiritual path recognize the importance of the proper balance of the Three-Fold Flame. The Masters have guided me, however, to look at this subject from a more in-depth perspective for it is an issue that a great many lightworkers are struggling with. All of us on the Spiritual path certainly recognize the importance of unconditional love. The ability to demonstrate this however is easier said than done. The only way a person can be unconditionally loving at all times is if they have completely transcended the negative ego and all negative ego thinking and emotions. They secondarily must at all times think and process their reality from the Melchizedek/Christ/Buddha attitude system. There is also, in truth, no way a person can be unconditionally loving at all times if they do not 100% own their personal power at all times. The owning of your personal power is what allows you to maintain self-mastery and vigilance over your thoughts, feelings, emotions and energy. Most lightworkers do not fully understand how intricately tied together these two Christ/Buddha qualities are. You will never ever learn to be unconditionally loving if you do not learn to own your personal power. Without your personal power you will be a victim of your subconscious mind, emotional body, inner child and negative ego. There is no way you can be a Master instead of a victim or a cause instead of an effect in life if you do not own your personal power. There is no way you can control the negative ego and remain in Melchizedek/Christ/Buddha consciousness if you do not own your personal power.

On the other side of the coin, without unconditional love personal power becomes a total agent of the negative ego and becomes a corruption of the highest order. This is the masculine and feminine and/or Yin and Yang aspects of life working together in perfect balance and harmony. The third aspect of this trinity is wisdom. Wisdom is an essential ingredient and quality in the process of Self-Realization and successful living. We have all heard the expression "A little knowledge is a dangerous thing." We have also seen many people exemplify this most true full proverb. To use your personal power always in an appropriate manner in every situation of life takes much wisdom. To remain unconditionally loving at all times and in all situations takes enormous wisdom. To constantly monitor one's every thought, feeling, word and deed and to keep your energies and Three-Fold Flame always appropriately balanced takes enormous Spiritual wisdom, psychological wisdom and physical/earthly wisdom. To be joyously vigilant over one's every thought and impulse to make sure that one's motivations are always of the highest order and not tinged by the selfish desires and personal agenda's of the negative ego and self-centeredness takes enormous wisdom.

It is only when these three Melchizedek/Christ/Buddha qualities are perfectly balanced within self and within the sacred chamber of your own heart that true Self-Realization and full-fledged integrated ascension can take place. My beloved readers, strive at all times to keep these qualities and your own sacred Three-Fold Flame in balance, for it is truly one of the sacred keys to the path of God Realization and successful living!

CHAPTER 3

The Eight Point—21 Day Program for Creating Unconditional Self-love and Self-worth

One of the single most important Spiritual qualities to develop in life is unconditional self-love and self-worth! This chapter is dedicated to simply and easily explaining this process and sharing with you a very practical program to achieving this and/or increasing your present unconditional self-love and self-worth to the highest and most Spiritual/Christ/Buddha level you can achieve! It is actually a very simple process to achieve this once you understand it, how-ever it is one of those things that is sometimes like not being able to see the "forest for the trees"!

There are eight basic things one must understand to master, achieve, and then practice this program! The first key to developing unconditional self-love and self-worth is that you must own your 100% personal power, unconditional love and wisdom in life at all times! This, of course, is your own personal Three-Fold Flame! You can't achieve true lasting unconditional self-love and self-worth if you don't fully 100% claim your personal power and self-mastery at all times! If you don't own it, then you give it away to other people and/or your own subconscious mind, negative ego, and emotional body, which will "run you into the ground." This is not because they are inherently bad, it is just because they have no reasoning. They were never created to cause and create your life. You were! You cannot do this if you do not fully 100% claim your personal power, self-mastery and be the captain of your ship! You cause your own reality by how you think. To remain the cause and creator of your reality you must remain in your personal power and Spiritual vigilance at all times; in regard to keeping out negative ego/fear-based/separative thinking and feeling, and always maintaining Spiritual/Christ/ Buddha thinking! Secondly, you must claim your 100% unconditional love towards self and others at all times. To maintain unconditional self-love and worth you must maintain the attitude of unconditional love at all times, in general not only to yourself but others! You cannot maintain unconditional love towards self if you do not give it to others as well. Thirdly, you must 100% claim your wisdom at all times! For unconditional self-love and self-worth cannot be maintained if you do not do this as well! It takes great wisdom to properly parent your inner child and yourself, and maintain the perfect balance of this Three-Fold Flame in your daily life! So part of this first lesson again is keeping the negative ego/fear-based/separative thoughts and feelings out of your consciousness and mind, and constantly affirming the Spiritual/Christ/Buddha thoughts and feelings instead. The constant process of doing this will reprogram your subconscious mind and lay the foundation for creating unconditional self-love and self-worth within yourself!

The second key point is that you do have an inner child! The first key to developing unconditional self-love and self-worth is learning to parent your inner child properly. The key here is to parent your inner child with "firmness and unconditional love!" Just like in real life, some parents are too firm, critical and judgmental! On the other side of the coin some parents are too spoiling and permissive! The ideal is the proper balancing of masculine and feminine energy here! Either extreme of criticalness or spoiling will cause the development of lack of self-love and self-worth in the inner child and in your self! If you are too critical, the inner child will feel beaten down, rejected, and psychologically abused! If you are too permissive, your inner child will act out, become spoiled, rebellious, and overindulgent. It is your job to always be unconditionally loving to it, but very firm and disciplined with the inner child and self! This is the ticket to create a balanced, healthy inner child and personality development!

Now, the third key point to developing unconditional self-love and self-worth has to do with the understanding that there are two levels or two kinds of unconditional self-love and self-worth! There is the "form" level and the "essence" or Spiritual level! You cannot develop true unconditional self-love and self-worth unless you work on both levels! Let me begin with the "essence" or Spiritual level! The essence of the Spiritual level of unconditional self-love and self-worth is that you have are unconditionally loveable and have worth because GOD created you! You are a Son and Daughter of GOD. You are the Christ, in truth! You are the Buddha, in truth! You are God, in truth! You are made in the "image and likeness of GOD!" The microcosm is like the macrocosm. "As within, so without. As above, so below"!

My Beloved Brothers and Sisters, of course we have unconditional self-love and self-worth because GOD created us and we literally are incarnations of God! We could have a choice in the matter as to our self-love and self-worth if we created ourselves, however we did not, although the negative ego mind would like to think so. We did not create ourselves; GOD created us! Of course we have unconditional self-love and self-worth. When we raise a real child we make a distinction between the child and their behavior. We sometimes do not like their behavior, but we always unconditionally love the child. This same applies towards the inner child. The inner child or self may do things we don't like, and there may be lessons to learn and/or mistakes to adjust or correct; however, we always unconditionally love ourself, we may just not like our behavior. This is a very important distinction here. The inner child and inner self is always worthy and lovable, for we are, in truth, incarnations of God in the process of fully Realizing GOD! We are incarnations of God, this is a fact, however we have not yet fully Realized GOD consciously on all 352 levels of integrated initiation, which is what the process of evolution is all about! At the end of this chapter I will be providing you with specific affirmations for developing this "essence" level of unconditional self-love and self-worth to practice for 21 days!

The fourth key point to developing unconditional self-love and self-worth is to understand that there is not just an "essence" level to life where we are unconditionally loveable and worthy, there is also a "form" level of life that must be addressed as well. We must feel good about ourselves on this level as well. If all we did all day long was take drugs and drink alcohol, watch television, indulge our lower-self and sleep, and did not even try to be Spiritual in our daily lives and try to accomplish anything, we would still have "essence" level unconditional self-love and self-worth; however, we would not have a "form" level of self-love and self-worth! Now it is important to understand here that "Righteousness in the eyes of GOD is trying!" GOD expects us to make an effort in life to try and live a Spiritual life with honesty and integrity! GOD is less concerned with the outcome as He is the effort! Even if you are making mistakes, this is fine with GOD as long as you are trying to practice the Presence of GOD in your daily life. Said another way, trying to be of a Spiritual/Christ/Buddha consciousness in your thoughts, words and deeds!

Now most people in life do "try," yet many do not have unconditional self-love and self-worth! Why is this? This is because they are not affirming the lovableness and worthiness on the "essence" level. They are not recognizing that "Righteous in the eyes of GOD is trying!" Thirdly, on the "form" level they are not recognizing in their own consciousness the successes and progress they are making! They are instead listening to the negative ego/fear-based/separative mind that is being critical, or having them compare and compete with others. We all know how the negative ego mind can turn gold into garbage. It turns diamonds into mud! Even though, in truth, from GOD's objective perspective you are doing wonderfully and GOD and your own Mighty I Am Presence and Higher Self are totally pleased with your progress and efforts, your own negative ego mind is having you "forget" all of your successes and efforts on a "form" level. There is a very easy remedy for this called a "Victory Log" and a "Gratitude Log"! The Victory Log is the key to developing unconditional self-love and self-worth on the "form" level. What you do is just make a list for your entire life of all the reasons you feel good about yourself. You list everything you can possibly think of. List Spiritual things, mental things, emotional things, energetic things, physical things, actions you have taken, Spiritual achievements, earthly achievements, social achievements, books you have read, every possible thing you have accomplished that you feel good about. This first Victory Log is one for your whole life.

Then make a second Victory Log for everything you have been doing recently in the past year, past six months, past month and past week. Remember your thoughts create your reality! Is the glass of water half empty or half full? We often, because of the negative ego mind, look at ourselves as half empty instead of half full! The Victory Log is one of the most profound Spiritual tools ever invented, which hardly anyone knows about on Earth! It will immediately bring you back to a "half full" perspective! You will see the donut instead of the hole! You will be taking the optimistic view of self rather than the pessimistic view of self. You will be taking GOD's view of self rather than the negative ego's view of self!

Then after doing the first two Victory Logs do one more which is a future Victory Log, and list all the things you are planning to accomplish and achieve that you really feel good about! Then do one last log or list, which really is a gratitude list! Make a list of everything in your life you have to be grateful for! We often do this at Thanksgiving time, and we always feel wonderful doing it, however we should be doing it everyday, or at least until it is a habit in our subconscious minds to think this way!

My Beloved Readers, if you will do these four types of Victory Logs and/or lists, I personally 100% guarantee you that you will feel like a million dollars! Be sure to be humble at the end and thank GOD and the Masters for all their blessings for as the saying goes, "But for the grace of GOD go I!" So feel like a million dollars as you should, and be grateful to GOD and the Masters for all the bountiful blessings they have bestowed upon you, including your health! There are plenty of people in this world who have it a lot worse off than you. Look at the freedoms you have living in the country you do. How about your physical health? There are people with missing arms or limbs, or are paralyzed, have AIDS, dying of cancer, and the list could go on and on! Thank GOD for your blessings and all you have going for you! I am sure you feel even better about yourself after just reading this chapter and you haven't even started your Victory Log yet! Do you see the power of the mind? The truth is, you never had to feel bad about yourself, and you could have done this process at anytime in your entire life and you would have felt a million times better. This is the kind of thing that should be taught in schools from first grade onward! Kids would do much better in school if they had more unconditional self-love and self-worth!

Do you see, my Beloved Readers, after doing this process with the "essence" level affirmations and visualizations I am going to give you, and the "form" level affirmations and visualizations I am going to give you, you are going to feel like a million bucks for the rest of your life, and if you ever start to slip you just go back to doing these practices and you will immediately get pumped back up again! The great secret of the universe is that your thoughts create your reality and that we as children, adolescents, and adults are not given all the proper insights and Spiritual and psychological tools we need to easily do these things. People are suffering all over the world for no reason, when it is completely unnecessary and could be remedied in moments! It is your job, once you master this 21 day program within self, to share it with family, friends and students, and spread it around the world. For lack of self-love and self-worth is one of the single most important psychological problems on this Earth and is the core cause of most problems along with not owning your personal power!

The fifth key point to developing unconditional self-love and self-worth is to recognize that everything that happens in life is just a lesson and not a sin. Mistakes occur in everyone and this is normal and unavoidable. You do not go out of your way to make them, but when they happen the key is to just learn from them and gain the golden nugget of wisdom, and then "forgive yourself!" You cannot develop unconditional self-love and self-worth without self-forgiveness, and forgiveness for others! I emphasize the point of "for others" as well, for the outside world is really a projection screen for your own thoughts. To insure that you are able to maintain unconditional self-love and worth over the long term you must forgive self and others for all of it is God, and you are God! So in forgiving others you are really forgiving yourself as well! This last thought is not something you will find in any "personality" level understanding book on understanding self-love! Yet it is an essential key ingredient to maintain self-love, otherwise the law of karma will bring those unforgiving thoughts towards others back to self, which will affect the personal level of self-love! In truth, you forgive others as well not as a charity to them, but as a charity to yourself! Your forgiving them has nothing to do with them, it has to do with correcting faulty thinking within yourself!

Many, however, on this earthly plane forgive others but do not forgive self. This is faulty thinking for everything is forgivable! This world is but a dream of GOD! There is no such thing as death! Earth is really just a Spiritual school to see if you can forgive self and others in all circumstances. If Jesus can do it on the cross while being crucified and physically killed, then you can forgive yourself and others for all your lessons! That is why he demonstrated this example! So your negative ego could not say my lessons are worse!

By forgiving self for all mistakes, all guilt is relieved as well as regret! By learning from the experience and making a specific Spiritual vow to never let that mistake happen again, you can let go of all guilt and all regret! To not forgive self is to just make another mistake that you will need to forgive yourself for! As *A Course In Miracles* says, "Forgiveness is the key to happiness"! There is no mistake in the history of the Earth, and of the history of this infinite universe that is not 100% forgivable by GOD, and this is a fact! It is only the negative ego mind that holds grudges. The Spiritual/Christ/Buddha conscious-ness sees nothing in life to even forgive for mistakes are positive not negative. Perfection is not, not making mistakes. Perfection is trying to not make conscious mistakes! Even the Ascended Masters make mistakes! This is how we learn! It is true. However, the more of a Spiritual Master you become the less mistakes you will make! As Paramahansa Yogananda said, "A Saint is a sinner that never gave up"!

The sixth key point to developing unconditional self-love and self-worth is the process of Spiritual Alchemy or turning negatives into positives. In GOD's eyes there is nothing that you have ever done in this life or a past live that cannot be turned into a positive, no matter how bad the mistake! The gaining of the golden nuggets of wisdom is of course a big part of this process. Also using that mistake and lesson to help others. Use any big mistakes you have made to become an expert in that area and then dedicate a part of your life to helping others not to make that same mistake. This is how lemons are turned into lemonade! If a person kills someone in a car crash because of drinking alcohol, they could, for example, then dedicate their life to educating people to not drink alcohol and drive. If you took drugs and lost all your money, destroyed your marriage and alienated your kids, you could then dedicate your life to remaining drug free and educate others about the danger of drugs, using yourself as an example. If you have been in prison, then educate adolescents about crime and prison so you may help another not suffer as you have! My Beloved Readers, "Grace erases karma!" Even King David in the Bible, who was "Beloved of GOD," lusted over another man's wife and had her husband sent to the front lines of the war so he would more likely be killed and David could have her. David repented for his sins, and became one of the greatest kings of Israel! GOD always welcomes his prodigal Sons and Daughters home no matter what they have done! It is true that all karma must be balanced! Karma can be balanced by grace, by learning and by service! Even Hitler is forgiven and, in truth, is an incarnation of God! He will have to achieve Spiritual/Christ/Buddha consciousness first and balance all his karma though before he will be allowed to return to his Spiritual home. This will happen, for the Divine Plan will not be complete until all souls return home! Again, I repeat, there is absolutely nothing in the history of the infinite universe that is not 100% forgivable! It is only the negative ego that thinks not. However, the definition of GOD is "GOD equals man minus ego"!

The seventh and final key point to achieving unconditional self-love and self-worth is the recognition that just as we are a Spiritual parent for our inner child and/or inner self, GOD and our Mighty I Am Presence and Higher Selves are our Spiritual parents! In the Huna teachings of Hawaii, the Higher Self is called the "Aumakua" or "utterly trustworthy parental self"! Just as our Higher Self is the "utterly trustworthy parental self for us," we must learn to be the "utterly trustworthy parental selves" for our inner child and/or inner self! So part of the process of achieving self-love is allowing yourself to receive unconditional love from GOD, Christ, the Holy Spirit, your Mighty I Am Presence, and your Higher Self! So you not only receive unconditional worth from GOD because GOD created you and you are an incarnation of God, but you also allow yourself to "feel" the flow of GOD's love for you! This way you as a Spiritual parent unconditionally love your inner child and self, and GOD, Christ, the Holy Spirit, your Mighty I Am Presence and Higher Self unconditionally love you! Through this process you also give unconditional worth to your inner child and self. Plus you receive the same unconditional worth from GOD! Plus, you are being firm and loving with your inner child and self, just as GOD is firm and unconditionally loving with us as a parent. For just as GOD is, of course, unconditional, He is firm in the sense that he does have universal laws He expects us to learn and to follow, and if we don't follow them and become obedient to them, we cause suffering upon our self. The suffering is not a punishment, it is just a reminder or a signal to seek truth and understand GOD's universal laws on a Spiritual, mental, emotional, etheric, physical and earthly level!

So by applying all the aforementioned things, you become right with self and right with GOD before entering into any other relationship! You are fully unconditionally loved and worthy before entering any other relationship! You are fully balanced within the masculine and feminine of firmness and love before entering any other relationship! In doing this you will not need to seek love outside of self or from other people, for you will be giving it to self and allowing yourself to receive it from GOD first! Hence, you go into life fully empowered because as we already spoke of you are going to be fully claiming your 100% personal power, unconditional love and wisdom! So you go into life fully empowered, fully loved, fully balanced, and fully whole and complete within self! This way you will not need to seek power, love, worth, approval, acceptance, or wholeness outside of self, for you will have found it within your relationship to self and relationship to GOD! Plus, you are fully owning that, in truth, "you are God!" So you will not seek false gods outside of self, or put things before GOD and your Spiritual path, for you fully know that you are God, you are the Christ, you are the Buddha, you are the Eternal Self, as are your Brothers and Sisters! You will hence not only see this within self, you will also see this in your Brothers and Sisters who are part of GOD with you! By seeing this in your Brother and Sister, it insures that you maintain this in yourself, for, in truth, they are part of your self in a Spiritual sense! You will have achieved unconditional self-love and self-worth within yourself and will be giving unconditional self-love and self-worth outside of self to others and to your greater and larger Spiritual self as the infinite God Being you truly are. So the circle will be complete, so to speak! Most important you will be right with self and right with GOD, which will allow you to be right with all other relationships in your life! For you cannot be right with others if you are not first right with self and right with GOD!

As the saying also goes, you cannot love others if you do not love yourself. If you do not love yourself you can still love others in a romantic relationship, however the type of love relationships you form will be an addictive love, a dependent or co-dependent love. It will be a complementary love of a mother/son or father/daughter psychological love, rather than a mutually independent or adult/adult love in regard to a romantic relationship!

So my Beloved Readers, you see how incredibly important developing this unconditional self-love and self-worth is, otherwise you will look outside of self for it rather than find it within your relationship to self and relationship to GOD!

The last key to this process of maintaining unconditional self-love and self-worth is maintaining your Spiritual vigilance and Golden Bubble of Protection at all times around yourself! This is important because there is a lot of negative energy in the world and a lot of people who are run by the negative ego! So it is not only important to be

Spiritually vigilant against allowing your own negative ego to try to enter your consciousness and mind; it is also essential to put your Golden Bubble of Protection up every day almost like a piece of clothing you put on every morning to keep out other people's negative energy! Because most people have no training in Spiritual psychology, even lightworkers are extremely run by the negative ego! They are very Spiritually advanced in their Spiritual bodies or "light bodies," but they have a lot of rough edges around their psychological selves and bodies from lack of proper Spiritual training which is not really their fault! This is something our society should provide in schools, but it does not. Because of this there are constant attacks, criticisms, judgements, put downs, self-righteousness, competitiveness, anger, intolerance, impatience, irritableness, and frustration, which of course are all negative ego qualities. If you do not keep your Golden Bubble of Protection up, these outside negative ego thought forms and energy can act as negative programming to try and counteract the Spiritual work you are doing. The key is to put this Golden Bubble of Protection on every morning from your "energetic or etheric wardrobe," and place it around yourself so that when other people are manifesting this type of negative energy it just slides of your bubble like "water off a duck's back"! Or it just bounces of your Golden Bubble like a "rubber pillow"! This, my Beloved Readers, is the final eighth point to insure that you will always have unconditional self-love and self-worth! You can see from my explanation that it is something that is really so very simple to understand once you "get it." However, it is one of these things if you try to figure it out yourself you can search for lifetimes and not be able to figure it out and get all the puzzle pieces to fit together. Well I am happy to say there is no reason to have to reinvent the wheel, for Spirit, the Masters, and I have been very happy to have the time to explain this most wondrous process to you!

Now since this "Eight Point Plan to Achieving Unconditional Self-love and Self-worth" has now been explained we will now move to the final aspect of this chapter, which is the "21 Day Program that Spirit, the Master, and I have put together to implement and cement in this program! As you all know it takes 21 days to cement any new habit into the subconscious mind. So practice everything I have said in this chapter and follow the program I am about to lay out for you, and within 21 days you will have developed a habit of having 100% unconditional self-love and self-worth! It will actually be a habit where it will actually be hard not to have! You will always have to be Spiritually vigilant against negative ego thinking from within and without, however as long as you do this you will be set for life on this most important Spiritual issue!

The 21 Day Program for Developing Unconditional Self-love and Self-worth

The first part of this 21 day program is to work with the personal power, self-love, invulnerability and Spiritual affirmations (also called my favorite affirmations) in the chapter in this book called "affirmations." These affirmations will help keep your Three-Fold Flame of power, love, wisdom and Spiritual attunement and protection working at 100%! Say these affirmations three times a day for about ten minutes each time, out loud, and anytime you feel yourself sinking mentally and emotionally and you need to get pumped up! Do this for 21 days, and longer if you like!

Secondly, work with the following "essence" affirmations I spoke about earlier in the chapter, for five minutes, twice a day, for 21 days!

- I have unconditional self-love and self-worth because GOD created me!
- I am blessed as a Son or Daughter of GOD!
- Be still and know I Am God!
- I am made in the image of God, so of course I am worthy and loveable!

- I am God and fully know it, and I am fully deserving of unconditional self-love and worth!

- I am, in truth, the Christ, the Buddha, the Eternal Self, so of course I have unconditional self-love and self-worth!

- I am literally an incarnation of GOD, and even though I make occasional mistakes, that does not affect my inherent unconditional self-love and worth!

The next Spiritual practice to develop unconditional self-love and self-worth is to do your four types of Victory Logs as described in the beginning of this chapter. The Victory Log or list for your entire life. The Victory Log or list of all your recent victories in the last month or week, no matter how small. Then the future victories you are planning on achieving. Then the Gratitude List for the entire past and recent past! Doing this will revolutionize your conscious-ness and completely reprogram your subconscious mind. Then every day, once a day, read this list over, out loud, for 21 days. Keep adding to the list each day as new things keep coming to mind! If ever you feel yourself sinking, either read the list or type it over! It is guaranteed to pump you back up mentally every time without fail!

The next Spiritual practice is to start your day by calling for a Golden Net from your Mighty I Am Presence to clear your energy fields. Then say the following mantra:

I am the Monad!

I am the Soul!

I am the Light Divine!

I am Love!

I am Will!

I am Fixed Design!

- Call to Archangel Michael and your own Mighty I Am Presence for a Golden Dome of Protection to be placed around you!

- Then call forth to GOD, Christ, the Holy Spirit, your Mighty I Am Presence, and your Higher Self, for help this day in developing unconditional self-love and self-worth!
- Then make a specific prayer to the Holy Spirit to "undo" and all conditional self-love and self-worth programming and to remove the cause 100%!
- Then call forth your Mighty I Am Presence, your Higher Self, the Ascended Master Djwhal Khul, Sananda, your Spirit Guides, your Guardian Angels, Healing Angels, and call forth the "Core Fear Matrix Removal Program"! Then ask them to remove all core fear programming in your subconscious mind, conscious mind and energy fields! Also then ask for them to remove all conditional love programming. Do this for 20 minutes every morning and 20 minutes before bed every night! As you go to bed at night ask them to continue working on you all night until all conditional love and fear-based programming is removed!
- Then ask them before bed to imprint into your subconscious mind unconditional self-love and unconditional self-worth programming, however make a statement that you will only accept this from your own Mighty I Am Presence and from the Ascended Masters of the Light of GOD and from no one else!

Continue these practices every day religiously for 21 straight days! If you do this you will be completely transformed after three weeks!

The next Spiritual practice is that on the first day you begin this program write out or type out on a piece of paper a specific Spiritual vow you make to your-self, GOD and your inner child that "From this moment forward you will 100% give yourself unconditional self-love and self-worth every moment of your life to the very best of your ability!" Then say, "So let it be written! So let it be done!"

- Call to the Divine Mother, Mother Mary, Quan Yin, Isis and the Lady Masters before bed and ask them for help as well in developing unconditional self-love and self-worth! Ask them for help in training you at night while you sleep, and helping you in any way they can during the day!

- Then for one minute, twice a day, call forth to GOD, Christ, the Holy Spirit, your Mighty I Am Presence, your Higher Self, the inner plane Ascended Masters and Angels for a "Love Shower"! Bathe in this Love Shower for one minute and then go about your business! Do this for 21 days!

Put your affirmations on an audiocassette tape and listen to it as background music while working around the house. Also play it very softly as you go to bed at night so it is barely audible, so the affirmations go into your subconscious mind as an autosuggestion or self-hypnosis type of method, taking advantage of your greater suggestibility as you fall asleep at night! You do not have to do this method, however if you want to try it is effective and quite comforting. Kind of like a lullaby of self-love and self-worth affirmations very softly putting you to bed for 21 days after your nightly prayers!

Then every other day, have a dialogue in your journal with your inner child. Talk to your inner child and ask it how it is doing! Then in your journal become the inner child and let it talk back! This is kind of like role-playing or a type of voice dialogue in your journal! Ask your inner child if there is anything it wants. Ask it how it feels about this new program you are doing. Ask it if it feels if you're striking a good balance of firmness and love in how you are parenting it. Ask it if there are any adjustments it would like to make. Ask it how it feels about your current life plan!

Then do the same thing with your own Higher Self and/or Mighty I Am Presence! Ask it if it has any further guidance for you on this 21 day program that you are doing! Does it have any other suggestions or adjustments it would have you make? Ask it how it feels about your current overall life plan and the direction you are going! Any changes or adjustments? Then become your Higher Self or Mighty I Am Presence and talk back to your self! This is good channeling practice as well! You will be surprised what comes through. Just do the process and do not filter it. It does not matter if you think you are not doing it right! Let go of all that! Just do the process and see what comes through! We are just trying to open the lines of communication a little more clearly and consciously between you, your Mighty I Am Presence and inner child! This process helps these three levels become more integrated and cohesive!

The next Spiritual practice to do for 21 days is to write out on a piece of paper the words, "personal love, unconditional love, wisdom, firmness with inner child, unconditional self-love to your inner child, spoiling your inner child, too self-critical to your inner child."

Then everyday, every morning and before bed give yourself a percentage score from one to one hundred on how you have been doing that last 12 hour period manifesting the qualities I have listed! The ideal, of course, would be to have 100% on everything except for "spoiling" and being "too self-critical." Those ideally would be zero! We, of course, are not expecting perfection but improvement! This is a psychological logging tool. Its purpose is to make you more conscious of what you are doing every moment. By keeping a log it is kind of a little game you are playing with yourself to see if you can raise the percentage of your scores! By doing this every day for 21 days you can raise your scores and see your progress! If your scores are ever too low then just write out a new specific Spiritual Vow on paper or just say it out loud that you will improve in that area! Work more closely with the affirmations that I have given you that apply to the quality you want to improve or make-up some additional ones that specifically fit the quality you need to develop!

Every morning when you get up and when you go to bed, put on your Spiritual, mental, and emotional clothing.

- First put on your personal power, which might be visualized as holding a blue flame sword of Archangel Michael.

- Then place a red or pink rose in your heart from the Divine Mother symbolizing unconditional self-love and unconditional love for others as well!

- Then place your Golden Bubble of Protection around you as mentioned earlier in this chapter!

- Then call forth a Tube of Light and Pillar of Light of Protection from GOD and your own Mighty I Am Presence! See and visualize a Tube and Pillar of White Light surrounding you from GOD and your own Mighty I Am Presence! Then placing around yourself the Mantle of Spiritual consciousness, Christ consciousness and/or Buddha consciousness! This can be visualized as some kind of Golden White Mantle that you take out of your closet! It can be visualized as a Golden White Robe. It can be visualized as a beautiful Golden White Dress. It can be visualized as a garment of Christ/Buddha light!

Just as they get dressed every morning with physical clothes, most people don't realize they need to dress themselves with Spiritual, mental, emotional, and energetic clothes! They will absolutely be amazed what a powerful and profound effect this simple exercise will have on you. Do this as you get physically dressed every day. When you finish dressing physically, then take one minute to dress yourself Spiritually, mentally, emotionally and energetically as well!

The last of the Spiritual practices in this 21 day program are creative visualization practices. In the first one, see and visualize yourself in the morning and before bed for one or two minutes as the true God being,

Christed being and Buddha being you are. See yourself in your mind's eye as GOD created you! You might see yourself in our Ascended Garment of Light! In a golden white robe! Again in a beautiful Christed dress! Imagine how you would look, and in truth, as you really are as an Ascended Master! Imagine how you looked upon your creation by GOD! Recognize fully that you are still that being! You are just that being living in a physical body! Visualize this! Then say to yourself again "I am an incarnation of God and so, of course, I am 100% deserving of unconditional self-love and self-worth!"

- Then visualize your inner child playing in a grassy field! See yourself as the adult you currently are, walking towards your inner child! See the inner child seeing and recognizing you, of course, and running towards you and leaping into your arms. See and visualize yourself giving it a gigantic hug and your inner child hugging and loving you! Tell the inner child in your mind's eye how much you love it! How you will always take care of it, protect it, be firm and disciplined with it, but always give it 100% unconditional love and forgiveness at all times! Tell the inner child that you and it will begin a new start of this day and this three-week period!

- Then see GOD, Christ, the Holy Spirit, your own Mighty I Am Presence and your Higher Self appear above you as a gigantic golden white light! See them wanting to join in this hug and see them pouring love down from Heaven upon the both of you! Totally receive this! Then both you and the inner child send love back up to GOD, Christ, the Holy Spirit, your Mighty I Am Presence and Higher Self!

- Then see the love flowing back and forth up a Tube of Light and Pillar of Light! Then see the Light of GOD descend and anchor itself on Earth, in you and the inner child, forming a perfect integration and harmony!

Conclusion

My Beloved Readers, I humbly suggest that this is one of the most profound Spiritually integrated programs ever put together to create "unconditional self-love and self-worth!" It is 100% guaranteed to work, for it is based not on whimsical things, but on GOD's laws on Spiritual, mental, emotional, energetic and physical levels! Integrate this within yourself and then share this information and book with your family, friends and students! The majority of the world is suffering from some form of lack of self-love and self-worth! There is absolutely no reason for this to be, for it can be easily remedied! Just the reading of this chapter without even starting the program has almost done it already! Once these principles are understood, and you see how easy they are to understand and how much sense they make, everything just starts to fit and come together! Share this information and book with as many people as you can, for these are, in truth, the nuts and bolts of the Spiritual path that our fellow Brothers and Sisters are crying out for the most! Working all together as fellow Sons and Daughters of GOD we shall transform this world and help to bring all Sons and Daughters of GOD "to the peace and love that passeth understanding"!

So let it be Written! So let it be Done!

CHAPTER 4

The Soul and Mighty I Am Presence 21-Day Program for Mastering Bad Habits and Addictions

The whole subject of addictions is a most interesting subject! It is actually a subject I have not written about as a chapter! After writing 27 books it is always fun to come up with new subjects for chapters which I have not specifically written about, in a totally focused manner where this was the only subject I was covering! I have referenced the subject in a general sense but not in a focused sense like I am planning to do in this chapter! So on this note I will begin!

To understand addictions it is first essential to understand that the sub-conscious mind can also be referred to as the habitual mind. The subconscious is where habits are stored. Now some may think that habits are a negative thing, however this is not true! One can have the habit of eating right, exercising, meditating, thinking with one's Spiritual mind rather than with one's negative ego mind! So, in truth, one of the main Spiritual practices of the Spiritual path is to fill one's subconscious mind with good Spiritual habits!

The problem is that in past lives we have had bad habits, and we bring these negative programs and bad habits with us when we incarnate into a baby's body. Second, when we incarnate into children's bodies we pick up both good and bad habits from our parents, family, school, television, peers, and mass consciousness!

An addiction is an "attachment" or "bad habit" on a thought, feeling or physical level. Now, most of the time we think of addictions as being focused on a physical or outer thing! For example, being addicted to cigarettes, alcohol, food, sex, drugs, painkillers, shopping, gambling, sugar, or even to a person. The truth is, even though all these things are physical in nature it is the "feeling" that is often addicted to! Let me give some examples of what I mean. The person who drinks too much alcohol to escape the pain or anguish they feel. They are trying to get a different kind of a feeling! The food, for example, may be used as a replacement for love, for greater protection, or to stuff feelings! Drugs may be used to get a certain kind of a feeling that the user is looking for. Shopping because of the feeling it gives one in the moment. Gambling, because of the high of winning. So we see that addictions are often to escape a negative feeling or to try and create a new one!

A person can actually be addicted to feeling! We have all heard the title of the book, *Women Who Love Too Much*. I have not read the book; however, the truth of the title is obvious in some cases. A person can be addicted to love, or addicted to power, or addicted to activity and cannot be still and meditate! This is kind of interesting for these are the first three Rays of God, (Power, Love, and Active Intelligence!) So we see people can be addicted to a Ray in its lower aspect! Each of the Seven Rays has a higher and lower aspect! So we are beginning to see here that a person can be addicted to an idea that goes along with a feeling as well. A person may be addicted to a group of ideas and feelings such as power, fame, material things, sex, or money!

Addictions can also be connected with energy. One example is people who are addicted to doing dangerous things like bungie jumping, sky diving, or hang gliding! They go from one dangerous activity to the next because they love the "energy rush!" They love the adrenaline and the fear and excitement!

So we see that addictions can occur on a mental, emotional, energetic and physical level. Most often, in truth, all these aspects of self are interconnected to addictions.

The next interesting thing to understand is that some addictions can have a physical component. For example, cigarette smoking serves an emotional and mental need, but also is addictive on a physical level because of the nicotine. I think it is pretty much common knowledge the cigarette companies look at cigarettes as nothing more than "nicotine delivery devices"! So, the addiction takes on a mental aspect because of the mental habit of doing it. It takes on an emotional addiction because of the feeling it gives the person when they are feeling nervous, uptight or anxious. It also satisfies the physical addiction. The more you do it, the more it becomes engrained like a tape recording in the subconscious mind, and the more the nicotine gets into the cells. The same is true of heroin, alcohol, sugar, drugs and so on! So what happens over time is the constant doing of these activities forms deeper and deeper grooves in the subconscious mind and a habit is formed and over time it becomes a very ingrained habit on a mental, emotional, energetic, and physical level. Even though it is totally poisonous to the soul, every part of these three lower bodies craves this poison! The mind, emotions and body actually crave toxicity because of the improper mental, emotional, energetic and physical programming!

So, the next key question we must ask ourselves is "What is the cause of addictions?" The original cause is always the same thing! It always begins with a negative/fear-based/separative thought instead of a Spiritual/Christ/Buddha thought! This leads to a negative/fear-based/separative feeling! The person in a past life, or as a child, adolescent or adult, does not know how to escape this negative thought, negative feeling, and suffering, and begins to try and use an "outside source" to solve the problem instead of Spiritual mastery and being trained in Spiritual psychology! If they were trained in how to master their thoughts, feelings, emotions, energy, physical body, negative ego, desire body, inner child and subconscious mind in service of GOD and Spiritual/Christ/Buddha consciousness, there would be no need to have to form addictions!

So addictions can be caused by a way to escape pain and suffering or they can be caused by not having a healthy psychology, philosophy and mind set! Let me explain this second cause of addiction. Because people are not trained in Spiritual psychology by their parents, or in school, or at church or temple, or by psychologists and counselors, or even in the New Age movement, they are off-center in this area. The person may be highly Spiritual, and even highly successful in an earthly sense, however, without proper training in Spiritual psychology, their psychologies and/or philosophies are off-center and off-kilter. For example, most people are not in control of their minds. Their mind or subconscious mind runs them; they do not run their mind. Another case is that most people are run by their emotional body. They are not masters and causes of their feelings and emotions. Third, most people are run by their desire body. This is an interesting one for the desire body is always connected with addiction. When you are run too much by your emotional body, you are also going to be to run by your desire body, for the desire body is connected to the emotional or astral body! When a person allows themselves to be too run by their mental and emotional body, they end up being run by their desires. When the mind and emotional body run you too much, the negative ego mind becomes the director and programmer by psychological law. If people allow themselves to become a victim rather than a master and cause, then the negative ego will program their emotional life. This causes negative feelings and emotions such as fear, worry, sadness, depression, hurt, abandonment, loneliness, anger, judgement, impatience, irritation, frustration, lack of love and lack of inner peace. These feelings of course can lead to addiction. Then what happens is because the emotional body is too much in control, the desire body automatically becomes too much in control. This is why in Buddhism and Hinduism they teach to abolish all desire as one of their main teachings! In truth, however, you don't want to abolish all desire, just all "lower-self" or negative ego desire! You want to channel all your desire into "Higher Self" desire which is desire only for Self-Realization, God Realization, Ascension, completion of your Twelve Levels of Initiation, Integrated Ascension, and so on! So what happens is people are not properly trained in how to do this, so the fact that they are too run by the feelings, emotions and negative ego also causes lower-self desire to be in control, which leads to overindulgence and getting involved with lower-self types of habits such as cigarettes, too much alcohol, drugs, overindulgence in sex, pornography, gluttony, sugar, junk food, drug addiction, recreational drugs, and an overly outer focus!

The lack of training in the difference between negative ego/fear-based/separative thinking and feeling and Spiritual/Christ/Buddha thinking and feeling, and not being able to demonstrate this self-mastery in their daily lives, is the biggest cause of addictions. Our thoughts cause our reality. If we don't think right then we will not be in control of our emotional bodies and desire body and we will have too many negative feelings and emotions and too much lower-self desire. This all leads to addictions and bad habits!

Then because people do not know how to master and control the subconscious mind, this causes all those aforementioned things to take place as well. The subconscious mind has no reasoning whatsoever. So if you let the subconscious mind run you in the slightest, the negative ego mind becomes your director, which leads to addiction. Then if you have not been trained in Spiritual psychology you have not been trained in how to properly parent your inner child. Most people either repress their inner child or are run by it. This causes the emotional body to run the person and causes the negative ego to become the programmer, and the desire body to take over which leads to addictive behavior and bad habits!

Then because of all these things going on, because of lack of training in Spiritual psychology, which is no real fault of the person, the negative ego causes people to have "attachments rather than preferences!" This again is because people are not trained in how to think properly! As Buddha said in his Four Noble Truths "All suffering comes from attachments"! All suffering comes from wrong points of view. Attachments and addictions are very interrelated. People get attached to alcohol, for example, instead of it being an occasional preference. People get attached to having to eat and have sugar, instead of it being an occasional preference. The negative ego mind causes the person to latch on and become attached or addicted to certain types of behavior which then form habits in the subconscious mind on a mental, emotional, energetic and physical level! A preference is an attitude that goes for what it wants, but if it doesn't get it, the person remains happy!

So my Beloved Readers, in truth, it is all these factors combined together that form the root cause of all addictions! Addictions are really deeply ingrained mental and emotional negative habits of faulty thinking and emotional patterns, which have moved from the mental and emotional plane also into the physical body and material plane! An addiction in essence is a mental, emotional, energetic and physical bad habit! An addiction is often a physicalized negative ego thought and emotional process, which has formed a bad habit and is usually focused on trying to seek happiness and inner peace through an outside source instead of through inner means. It is the direct result of lack of Spiritual mastery, victim consciousness, and lack of Spiritual and/or psychological understanding and demonstration. It is not a judgement to have addictions. Everyone has had them in past lives and this life. They are just signposts that more Spiritual and psychological mastery are needed! It is not the fault of people for having them, for, in truth, they are just caused by lack of proper training in Spiritual psychology as I have said. There are not that many people on the planet that, in truth, truly understand Spiritual psychology. Our parents did not understand it, schools don't, extended family doesn't, churches and temples don't, counselors don't, psychologists don't, social workers don't, psychiatrists don't, and most Spiritual teachers are just that, Spiritual teachers, not psychological teachers. Spiritual psychology is a tremendously in-depth science as you can see from reading this book and my other books. For the most part it is the weakest area in almost all lightworkers, Spiritual teachers, channels and healers. I do not mean this as a judgement, it is just a loving statement of fact. Lightworkers on the whole have very highly developed Spiritual bodies and even physical/earthly selves, however not as developed psychological selves. This is because there are not as many really good Spiritual psychology books, classes, workshops and seminars as there are Spiritual ones. Spiritual psychology, in truth, is the foundation of your Spiritual life! All Spiritual life will ultimately be corrupted if this level of God Realization is not addressed properly.

Addictions are very deeply ingrained mentally, emotionally, energetically and physically, however with the proper training can "easily" be overcome.

The other thing that can cause addictions is not being on a Spiritual path and not being connected to one's Higher Self and Mighty I Am Presence! The key question here is if your Higher Self, Mighty I Am Presence, and the Holy Spirit (Still, Small Voice Within) are not your guides, then who is? The answer is the negative ego, lower-self, emotional body and desire body! This will lead the person into negative thoughts, negative feelings, bad habits and addictions!

The proper way to live life is with "involvement, but to also be detached simultaneously!" The idea is to live in this world but not of this world! The ideal is to live in Heaven and Earth simultaneously. Kind of like straddling two dimensions simultaneously. The ideal is to bring your Heavenly consciousness to Earth in an integrated and balanced way. If one is not on a Spiritual path, which is a "higher life," then what is the other alternative?

The other alternative is a "low life"! We all know what that is. It is a life filled with low life or lower-self habits and addictions. Because people in this world have not been properly trained in Spiritual psychology, they do not realize that one of the premiere purposes of life is to master and get rid of the lower-self thoughts, feelings, emotions, desires, habits, attachments and addictions and completely reprogram your being into having only Higher Self or Spiritual thoughts, feelings, emotions, desires, habits and preferences! If you do not live to realize the soul and Spirit within you, then you live out of your "personality" instead of realizing you are a God incarnating into a body. You think you are just a person or physical body totally separate from GOD, if you even believe in one, and separate from your Brothers and Sisters and life! When you live out of your personality you can still strive for success and a type of self-actualization, however, it is a worldly success, not what is called "Soul Self-Actualization" or "Monadic (Spiritual) Self-Actualization"! Personality level self-actualization is good, but is only one third up the "Spiritual Mountain" or ladder you are here to climb. Most of the world is still either living out of their personality or a mixture of personality and soul! This is only because they have not been trained in Spiritual psychology! Can you imagine, my Beloved Readers, if the kinds of things I write about in this book and my other books were taught in school from the first grade onwards? Children and adolescents would be absolutely on fire for GOD! They would love to come to school! If people knew what they were supposed to do and understood clearly in very simple and easy to understand charts, books and explanations, who in their right mind would not choose a Spiritual path. I guarantee you almost no one. The reason being is "we each are God!" That is who we are! The only person who would not choose this is someone who still has too much disturbed programming in their subconscious and energy fields from past lives or this life, and this could be cured and healed in every case over time, with the proper unconditional love, nurturing and care!

So, my Beloved Readers, when a person lives out of their personality and not totally out of guidance and merger with the Soul, Spirit, Higher

Self, Monad, Mighty I Am Presence, Holy Spirit and your Spiritual/Christ/Buddha consciousness, then they may have some degree of personality level self-actualization such as a movie star, successful businessman, lawyer, professional person, or professional trade person for example. However, they are still going to have some negative thoughts, feelings, emotions, lower-self desires, bad habits, and addictions. Maybe not as many as the person who is totally run by the lower-self and negative ego, however some will still be there. The reason is that they have not totally switched over to "100% living out of the Soul, Spirit, and Spiritual/Christ/Buddha consciousness!" The only way Self-Realization, full Self-Actualization, Enlightenment, full Liberation, Resurrection, God Realization, Ascension, your Twelve Levels of Initiation, and Integrated Ascension will be achieved is if you live 100% fully out of the Spiritual! Most people on Earth and even lightworkers, my friends, are still split because of improper training in Spiritual psychology. They live half out the Spiritual/Christ/Buddha consciousness and half out of negative ego/fear-based/separative thinking! They live half out of personality level self-actualization and half out of Soul and Spiritual self-actualization! They live half out of the personality and half out of the Soul and Spirit! Now the key thing to understand is that this is not because they are not totally sincere in their Spiritual path, and it is not because they are not good people and totally dedicated to GOD and Spiritual growth or living a good life. It is because of this lack of proper training and understanding of what exactly they need to do. It is kind of like they have not been given the "Spiritual map, workbook, and directions." So, they are working to the best of their understanding and ability and are totally sincere in their efforts, however without the "Training Manual" I think you would agree progress is going to be slow and there is going to be much confusion! Lightworkers like to think they fully understand, but with no judgement intended, they don't. Spiritual psychology is an incredibly in-depth and complicated Spiritual science. Reading one book on the subject or taking one course does not make one a master. In truth, it is a lifelong study, and no matter how advanced you are, it is possible to lose it and become unclear in the a "twinkling of an eye"! The negative ego mind and the psychodynamics of thinking, feeling, desire, the subconscious mind, the inner child, inner parenting, the physical body, Spiritual development, Spiritual/Christ/Buddha Consciousness, and integrating and balancing all one's Seven Rays, Twelve Archetypes, Twelve Signs of the Zodiac, Twelve Sephiroth on the Tree of Life, all the cards in the Tarot Deck, three minds, four bodies, Four Faces of GOD, God/Goddess, feminine and masculine, Heaven and Earth, can be very complicated and a very intricate process. People and lightworkers have a lot of really crazy ideas that they think are true, but are not. There are also, as the Bible states, an enormous number of false prophets, cults, twilight masters, disintegrated Spiritual teachers, fragmented Spiritual teachers, personality level psychologists and counselors, channels that are not clear, people who claim to be God Realized and are not, and Spiritual and psychological teachers and counselors, who are very highly developed Spiritually or psychically, but not necessarily psychologically. There are enormous numbers of teachers, channels and healers who are extraordinarily gifted in one area, or even two, but very few are total Spiritual masters on a Spiritual, psychological and physical/earthly level, and very few are totally clear of all negative ego/fear-based/separative thinking, feeling, bad habits and addictions! Most are extremely highly developed in one area or maybe two, but weaker in the second or third! Lightworkers see these Spiritual teachers, channelers, psychics or healers and think that because they are so extraordinarily gifted in one area, they must be total Spiritual masters! They are Spiritual masters in one aspect or area of God, which is great! However, God Realization is much more complicated than that! You must be a master of all three levels (Spiritual, psychological and physical/earthly) and you must be the absolute master of all negative ego thinking, feeling, bad habits, and addictions to truly be a God Realized being. You must be able to totally ground your Spirituality on Earth and fulfill your Spiritual mission and puzzle piece on Earth! You must be able to do this in a totally balanced and integrated manner! You must be able to develop all your talents on a Spiritual, psychological and physical/earthly level. This is where the confusion lies. Lightworkers develop their Spiritual talents and gifts in one area like channeling, Spiritual teaching, healing, science, psychic work, clairvoyant work or psychology, for example, and this again is wonderful. The problem is if they don't do it on all three levels (Spiritual, psychological and physical/earthly) with no negative ego/fear-based/separative influence, and if they don't do it in a totally integrated and balanced manner, integrating the Seven Rays, twelve archetypes, balancing the vertical and horizontal planes of life, integrating and sanctifying the Four Faces of GOD (Spiritual, mental, emotional and material), God/Goddess, feminine and masculine, Heaven and Earth, balancing four bodies, three minds, properly parenting the inner child, mastering the subconscious mind, mastering lower-self desire, mastering the mind, mastering the feelings and emotions, totally mastering the physical body, mastering one's energy, just to name a few, then disintegration and fragmentation can and will take place! Limited lens seeing will take place. Faulty thinking and negative feelings and emotions will slip in. Wrong motives will be prevalent. Some bad habits will be prevalent. Health lessons will present themselves other than for reasons of just Spiritual mutation! Addictions will be prevalent as well! All these things will occur at times in even the most gifted Spiritual teachers, channels, healers, psychics, clairvoyants, Spiritual scientists, counselors and lightworkers! This occurs because most on Earth are developed in one area or at most two, but very, very rarely are they developed in all three in all the ways I am talking about in this chapter! So the key question now is what does this have to do with bad habits and addictions? What I have written here is absolutely essential to understand. For it is not just people who are totally run by the negative ego and lower-self who have bad habits and addictions. It is also Spiritual leaders, teachers, channels, psychics, healers, counselors, scientists, metaphysicians and lightworkers! This stems from either lack of full training in the area of Spiritual Psychology and/or because of this aspect of being extraordinarily highly developed in one area, or maybe at most two, but not in all three and not in a way that is totally free of all negative ego/fear-based/separative/lower-self influence. It also occurs because of lack of integration and balance of all the aspects I mentioned above! Also because they have developed their talents or came in with them in one area or level of God, however they have not learned to develop their talents on all levels of God!

This lack of total self-mastery and integration on all levels of God in all the things I have mentioned here causes there to be imbalances, weak spots, blind spots, and limited lens seeing in some areas, even though the person is so incredibly talented and gifted in one area or level of Self-Realization! Because of this, bad habits and addictions in some areas set in.

What I have shared here is incredibly important for Spiritual leaders and lightworkers to understand about themselves so they don't get overly comfortable in just being gifted and talented on this one level. Strive to develop yourself on all three levels in the way and manner I have described in this chapter. This is the key to getting rid of all negative thoughts, feelings, emotions, energy, health problems, bad habits, and addictions!

Second, this understanding is incredibly important to Spiritual leaders and lightworkers to be much more Spiritually discerning when dealing with other lightworkers, and to see that just because someone is extremely highly developed in one area, it doesn't mean they have achieved full God Realization, and this doesn't mean they do not have negative thoughts, feelings, emotions, health lessons, bad habits and addictions of some kind! This is why many Spiritual leaders and lightworkers who are quite highly evolved in a Spiritual sense still have bad habits and addictions!

Now my Beloved Readers, I contemplated about going over each addiction in infinite detail, however upon further attunement and contemplation I really find that this is unnecessary, for, in truth, all bad habits and addictions result from the dynamics I have talked about in this chapter. So instead, what I have been guided to do here is give you a program for mastering all bad habits and addictions, for, in truth, they all come from the same set of causes! So whatever bad habit or addiction you have; Spirit, the Masters and I have designed a 21 day program that is personally guaranteed to help you to master whatever bad habit or addiction you are trying to master and reprogram! I have been guided to set this program up for 21 days because it takes 21 days to fully cement any new habit into the subconscious mind. Even though I am setting this for 21 days, it is recommended that you continue the program for two months just to make sure that the bad habit and or addiction is 100% cleared and reprogrammed. The mastery of the bad habit and/or addiction will take place, however, within 21 days if you follow my guidance, directions and instructions exactly!

It is now my great joy, with the help of Spirit and the Masters, this day to show you how to get rid of all your addictions quite simply and easily! It is for all the aforementioned, reasons and more that Spirit, the Masters and I now bring up the Soul and Mighty I Am Presence 21 Day Program for mastering your Bad Habits and Addictions!

The Soul and Mighty I Am Presence 21-Day Program For Mastering Your Bad Habits and Addictions

- 100% fully claim your personal power and self-mastery over your every thought, feeling, word, deed, subconscious mind, desire body, physical body, inner child, and every aspect of self and earthly life!

- Write a Spiritual Vow out on a piece of paper that as of this moment, as GOD, the Masters, and the Angels are your witness, that you are going to officially stop this or these habits!

- Monitor and remain Spiritually vigilant over your every thought and feeling, and push out of your consciousness, in thought or feeling, that which is not of GOD and replace it with a thought and feeling of GOD!

- Deny entrance into your consciousness of any negative ego/fear-based/separative thought and feeling and replace it with the opposite Spiritual/Christ/Buddha thought or feeling!

- Do the affirmations in this book for personal power, self-love, Bubble of Protection, and Spiritual attunement for 15 minutes every morning and 15 minutes every night! Also do them any time you feel your energy attunement sinking or if you are being tempted!

- Write out a Huna Prayer, which is a letter to GOD, Christ, the Holy Spirit, The Mighty I Am Presence, your Higher Self, the Masters and the Healing Angels, for help in helping you to stop this bad habit and/or addiction! Say this prayer two times every morning and two times at night, out loud! If you feel so guided, at the top of the prayer the Masters or Saints you feel attuned to. For example: Jesus, Buddha, Moses, Mohammed, Mother Mary, Djwhal Khul, the Mahatma, Archangel Metatron, Archangel Raphael, Galactic healers, to name just a few.

- Call forth every morning and evening for fifteen minutes for 21 days, a short meditation where you call to God and all the aforementioned God Force and ask for them to officially anchor the Core Fear Matrix Removal Program! Ask Spirit, the Masters and the Angels to officially remove the bad habit and addiction from your energy field and subconscious mind. Spirit and the Masters will literally pull the bad habit out of your energy field like a gardener pulls a weed out of a garden. Spirit and the Masters will pull them right out of your Crown Chakra. Ask for this also every night before you go to bed and request that Spirit and the Masters pull this programming, all core fear programming and negative ego programming out of you all night long! Do this for 21 straight days!

- Every morning when you first awaken, pray to GOD, Christ, the Holy Spirit, your Mighty I Am Presence and your Higher Self, with all your heart and soul and mind and night, for their help in not indulging in that bad habit and addiction that day!

- Then make a second prayer directly to the Holy Spirit and ask the Holy Spirit to "undo" the original cause of this bad habit and addiction and to completely remove it from your energy field and subconscious mind! Do this every morning when you first get up and when you got to bed at night!

- If you are ever tempted, immediately pray to God, Christ, the Holy Spirit, your Mighty I Am Presence and your Higher Self to remove this temptation from your consciousness! Then visualize yourself taking the Blue Flaming Sword of Archangel Michael and slicing the cord to that temptation and say "Be still, and know I Am God!"

- Say a special prayer to Archangel Michael every morning when you wake up and before you go to bed every night, and ask him to cut all energetic cords within your being to this bad habit and addiction!

- Every morning when you first get out of bed, do a one-minute meditation where you put on your "Spiritual Armor of Protection"! Visualize that you are claiming your blue sword or Archangel Michael as your symbol of claiming your personal power, and see it in your right hand! Then place a pink or red rose in your heart for unconditional self-love and unconditional love for others. Then place around yourself a "Golden Bubble of Protection" that will keep all negativity of others out of your consciousness and energy fields all day long! Then visualize a tube of light going all the way up to your Higher Self,

Mighty I Am Presence and then all the way back to GOD! Then pray to GOD, Christ, the Holy Spirit, your Mighty I Am Presence and your Higher Self for a "Tube of Light and Pillar of Light" of protection to be placed around you all day long! Reinforce this every afternoon and before bed for one minute for 21 days!

- Do a one minute meditation every day for 21 days where you visualize and see your inner child and give it a big hug, lots of love, and tell it that you need to be very firm in regard to stopping this bad habit and addiction. Then ask you inner child for its cooperation for this is something you must do and are going to do no matter what, and it would be easier if you had the inner child's cooperation. Ask the inner child if there is anything it wants or needs! Tell the inner child you are going to raise it from now on with firmness and unconditional love and you are not going to spoil it or be too critical anymore!

- Call forth a "Golden Net" three times a day from your own Mighty I Am Presence and Higher Self to cleanse your energy fields!

- Go on a physical fast for two days on Bieler Broth and a little bit of protein. Steam a big pot of zucchini, green beans, with a little bit of celery and parsley. Put it in the blender with just a little bit of hot water from cooking and blend it up so it is like thick soup. Eat this for two days straight, if you feel a little weak and a little bit of protein. This will clean out your liver of any toxicity!

- Send a prayer request to the Academy for help for stopping the addiction and I will place it on our Interdimensional Prayer Altar!

- If you are so guided, order my Ascension Activation Meditation tape called the "18 Point Cosmic Cleansing Meditation" and listen to it once a day for 21 straight days! This will totally cleanse your energy fields! Not required in this program, but can be a helpful tool!

- Call to Spirit, the Ascended Masters and Healing Angels before bed every night for 21 days to remove all your negative implants and negative elementals from your energy field!

- Call to Spirit, the Masters, and Angels, to repair all your bodies and balance your chakras every night before bed for 21 days!

- Call to Spirit and the Masters to anchor into your field once a day for 21 days the "Prana Wind Clearing Device" which serves like an etheric fan which will blow all the negative or stuck energy in your meridians and acupuncture points right out so your energy will run smoothly! Do this for five minutes! It is quite enjoyable and you will definitely feel it!

- Once a day call forth from Spirit and the Masters for a "Light and Love Shower" for one minute! Ask for this as well if you are ever tempted!

- If you are ever tempted, say this mantra:

I am the Monad!
I am the Soul!
I am Light Divine!
I am Love!
I am Will!
I am Fixed Design!

This will immediately reconnect you to your Higher Self and break any lower-self or lower-self desire connection!

- Once a week put burning pots in all the rooms of your house to cleanse it. This is done using a metal pot with rubbing alcohol and Epsom salt. Put a plate under it so nothing catches fire. Put it in the middle of the room and light it with a match. It will burn for about five minutes. This will cleanse all the negative energy in the room so you are living in a clean Spiritual atmosphere!

- If you are ever tempted by the bad habit or addiction, immediately start chanting the name of "GOD" or any of your other favorite names of GOD or Mantra of GOD! No habit or addiction in this infinite universe can withstand the Name of GOD!

- Another good tool to battle any temptation is to say the "Lord's Prayer"!

- Upon getting up every morning for 21 days, call forth from Spirit and the Masters for an "Axiatonal Alignment"! This will balance your energy fields!

- Eat a good diet!

- Try to get a little physical exercise, fresh air and sunshine even if it is just a little bit of walking, every other day!

- Call to Spirit and the Masters before bed each night for 21 days, for the anchoring and activation of your "Anointed Christ Overself Body, your Zohar Body of Light, your Higher Adam Kadmon Body, and your Monadic Blueprint Body"!

- Ask that your entire house be also placed in a Pillar of Light and Ascension Column of Light!

- Call to Dr. Lorphan and the Galactic Healers and Angels to repair any physical or etheric damage that was done to these bodies from the past bad habit or addiction!

- While on this program and over the next two months read my books: *How To Release Fear-Based Thinking and Feeling: An In-depth Study of Spiritual Psychology, Soul Psychology, The Golden Book of Melchizedek: How To Be An Integrated Christ/Buddha In This Lifetime,* and *The Complete Ascension Manual!* All these book are available from the Academy!

- An idle mind is the devil's workshop, so keep your mind and actions totally focused on activities of GOD, your Spiritual path and positivity!
- Keep a positive mental attitude and feeling at all times!
- Keep your attention only focused on GOD and your Spiritual path at all times!
- Why worry when you can pray!
- Remain Spiritually vigilant for GOD and His Kingdom!

My Beloved Readers, if you follow this basic program set forth by Spirit, the Masters and I, I personally guarantee you that there is no bad habit or addiction in this infinite universe that can withstand your full personal power, the power of your mind as a Son or Daughter of God, and the love, wisdom and power of GOD, Christ, the Holy Spirit, your Mighty I Am Presence, your Higher Self, the inner plane Ascended Masters, the Archangels, and the Angels of the Light of GOD!

So let it be Written! So let it be Done!

CHAPTER 5

The Negative Ego and The Return of the Divine Mother and The Goddess Energies to Earth

My Beloved Readers, I consider the following chapter to be one of the most important chapters in this entire book! I have really been looking forward to writing this chapter since it is so incredibly important at this time! I have much I want to say and as the ancient Chinese proverb says, "The thousand mile journey begins with the first step"! It is and will be a most enjoyable thousand-mile journey indeed! On this note I will humbly begin!

There was a time on Earth during the time of the ancient civilization of Lemuria (which predated Atlantis) when the God/Goddess energies were in perfect balance! In the Bible this could be referred to as the time of the Garden of Eden, or first Golden Age on this planet! However, when there was the first eating of the fruit from the "Tree of Good and Evil," this Biblical story speaks to that time when man, for the first time on Earth misused his free choice and thought out of harmony with GOD! This, of course, was the beginning of negative ego/fear-based/separative thinking and feeling! This was the first time mankind thought out of harmony with GOD and out of harmony with the Spiritual/Christ/Buddha consciousness!

It was this choice of fear, separation, selfishness, lower-self desire, conditional love, judgement, anger, grudges, guilt, hurt, depression, sadness that also began the process of rejection and abuse of the Divine Mother and Goddess energies on Earth!

This misuse of free choice also began a process of mass consciousness on the Earth to identify with masculine energies over feminine energies! The mind over the heart! Thinking over intuition! Thinking over feeling! Thinking over psychic perceptions! Thinking and science over Spirituality! Thinking, selfishness and technology over anything in regard to Mother Earth and Nature!

My Beloved Readers, this caused an overidentification with the Patriarchy over the Matriarchy! Left brain became more important than right brain! Men began to control society and women were not seen as equals! This overidentification with masculine energy caused there to be too much aggressiveness, willfulness, loss of sensitivity, psychological and physical violence, inability to nurture, pridefulness, loss of compassion, jealousy, competition, loss of unconditional love, and a focus on war as a means to get what one wanted!

There became a focus on science and technology over Spirituality and Mother Earth. Nothing was real except if you could experience it with your five physical senses! Logic was favored over intuition, channeling or psychic perception! There was the rejection and disowning of the 22 Supersenses of GOD that go beyond the five physical senses!

Women were forced to become more subservient and lesser class citizens. Just think about it, my Beloved Readers, people have been on the Earth for 18.5 million years and even 20 years ago we were voting in the

United States for an equal rights amendment for women! What have we been doing for 18.5 million years?

Descartes, the famous philosopher, said, "I think therefore I am"! I ask you, my Beloved Readers, how come he didn't say, "I feel therefore I am," or "I intuit therefore I am"! Women were burned at the stake in the Middle Ages for just being mystics and channels! Women in the Orient are still brought up to be subservient!

In our modern day society women are often portrayed as sex objects! They do not get the same pay as men! There has never been a woman President of the United States, and very few women leaders in this world! There are still very few women members of the Senate and House of Representatives as compared to men!

It was only 150 years ago that women were even allowed to vote! Only men could vote up until that time! Again I ask, what has been going on for 18.5 million years? The cutting off of the Feminine also cut off Spirituality to a great degree. It caused a total disconnection from Mother Earth and the living Being that she is. There was the total disconnection from the Animal Kingdom, Plant Kingdom and Mineral Kingdom. Animals were seen as objects or just pets, not as younger brothers and sisters. They were and still are greatly abused by our society! They are used in the most abhorrent scientific experiments with no regard for the God Beings that they are! They trap and kill animals for furs in the most inhumane ways you don't even want to know about! I heard a report recently from China where they put bears in small little boxes for their entire life, unable to move so they can extract bile from their gall bladder for the bear's entire life! This is one of the most abhorrent things I have ever heard of! We all know about the experiments scientists do on animals.

We have the same disregard for plants! Plants are incarnations of GOD as well. They have consciousness and feelings! Maybe not in the same way we do, but they still have a form of consciousness! Yet we rip things out of the ground and just use this Kingdom for our purposes with total disregard! We have all heard about the book *The Secret Life of Plants*! Plants are living beings and must be worked with, not just used. We also tear down the rain forests and foul up the oxygen level on the planet all in the name of greed and technology!

My Beloved Readers, it was this same greed and technology which destroyed Atlantis! This disownment of the Goddess and the focus on the mind, science and technology, caused the civilization which followed Lemuria on the other side of the globe to eventually be destroyed in a series of massive catastrophic Earth changes which were basically caused by mankind's abuse of the Divine Mother, Mother Earth and their own Goddess energies!

Even the word mankind! How come we don't call mankind, "womankind"? Even our Spiritual books are all written in patriarchal language! Part of this is the problem of our language, however part of this is because it became the accepted norm of our society, so of course the inner plane Ascended Masters just had to follow the norms of our society to get their point across. Have you noticed how a great many of even our favorite Spiritual books have been written in patriarchal language? This is not a judgment upon these books, as much as a product of our society!

My Beloved Readers, the supreme example of this is that even GOD was seen as being masculine! When we referred to GOD we were taught to call "Him" the Heavenly "Father." The feminine aspect was seen as Mother Earth! The Divine Mother was completely rejected from Spirituality!

The Heavenly Father and the Earth Mother form the two sides of GOD's nature! Kind of like sitting on GOD's left and right side! The whole study of the Divine Mother is left out of most Spiritual training and schools of thought for it is not understood!

How come GOD was not portrayed as a woman in all the ancient artwork and in our books? Of course we are not looking to do a pendulum swing and overidentify with the Matriarchy, for that would be just as bad as overidentifying with the Patriarchy. It is balance we seek!

Here is another very interesting one, my Beloved Readers! Have you ever wondered why there is a negative stigma about a woman being a "feminist," however there is not a similar stigma of a man being a "masculinist"?

Women who don't have a husband are "old maids"! Men who don't have wives are eligible bachelors and "studs"! In Hollywood, men get more of the key roles! Our heroes are portrayed as these violent, egotistical protagonists on the side of good, having sex with beautiful woman after beautiful woman! There is the incredible focus on a woman's physical looks and not as much as on her Christed nature!

Even the Masters who formed our religions have all been men! This is not the Masters fault for they are not patriarchal, they just had to incarnate in male bodies otherwise they would not have been listened to by the unconscious mass consciousness! Even the Spiritual Hierarchy that governs our planet seems to be mostly men. This is not really true; this is just what mass consciousness through the lens of Patriarchy has allowed us to see! The Divine Mother and the Lady Masters basically had to back away!

My Beloved Readers, in a great many of our modern day religions women are not allowed to be priests or priestesses! In ancient times the priestesses were revered. With the eating of the fruit from the "Tree of Good and Evil," over time the priestesses had to go into hiding! This not allowing women to be priests occurs in Fundamentalist Christianity, Catholicism, and the Mormon faith! In the Jewish religion there is the Kabbalah of Jewish mysticism. Women, up until recently, were not allowed to even study the Kabbalah, only men were!

Then we see in our society all the spousal abuse, usually its' women! We also see this towards children as well! We also see how women have to put up with all the sexual comments and if they report it they lose their jobs because of a men's club who are in control! There are very few women corporate leaders or who really have the power in our world.

Have you ever asked yourself what our world would be like if women were in charge from the beginning? Would there be as much war? Would there be as much violence? Would Mother Earth be as abused? Would technology be put before Spirituality? Would the mind be made as more important than the heart? I think we all know the answer to these questions!

Getting back now to the Mineral Kingdom! Mankind has had no regard for the Mineral Kingdom. Minerals, gemstones, crystals and even rocks have a form of consciousness as well! All mankind has done is strip the Earth for greed and its energy concerns. Showing no appreciation or love for this kingdom! We strip mine and basically rape the Earth and leave it polluted, basically for money! We dump toxic waste into the Earth. We don't remediate our trash sites properly. We dump nuclear waste into the Earth! We pollute our oceans and rivers, air, and earth! We put gigantic gaping holes in the ozone layer. We create the "greenhouse effect"! We kill off animals to the point where they are extinct! We have as a species, greatly abused the Earth Mother. We have not cleaned up our "campsites" after we have left, so to speak. We have not given back to Mother Earth. We have not planted trees! We have gotten so disconnected from Goddess energies that we have lost all contact with Pan, the Nature Spirits, Plant Devas, Gnomes, Elves, Sylphs, Salamanders, Undines, Nature Elementals and all the Etheric Beings that overlight and live inside the flowers, plants, vegetables, shrubs and trees! It is these beings that create nature, and most of mankind has no idea they even exist. Instead of working in cooperation with these beings and nature, the rejection of the Goddess has caused us to use pesticides, chemicals, and treat nature as some kind of mechanical mechanism instead of the Divine process of GOD it is! We as a species, as part of this rejection of the Goddess, have driven the Nature Spirits, Devas, Elves, and Elemental beings from our farms and nature spots! Yet they have forgiven and waited patiently, as has the Divine Mother and Goddess energies, for the time of their return to Earth, to be honored and sanctified in their rightful place! My Beloved Readers, this time has come!

My Beloved Readers, you have all heard of the movie the *Return of The Jedi*! Well, I tell you, as we now enter this New Millennium, Aquarian Age and Seventh Golden Age, I say unto you that we have now entered the time of the "Return of the Divine Mother and the Goddess Energies to Earth," after 18.5 million years! Enough is enough!

There have been times in Earth's history where the Goddess energies made a slight comeback, however the negative ego minds overidentification with God energies over Goddess energies has always abused them in the end and driven them back out! As they say in the political speeches at the conventions, "It is time for this to end!" It is not only time for this to end, it is going to end, and we as the Spiritual leaders and lightworkers of this planet are going to make it end!

I just had another insight while writing this. Have you ever noticed how we make a special consideration to integrate the Goddess energy, but do not have to use the same special consideration for the God energies. Even the term is a foreign term! In truth, God energies should be both God and Goddess energies however, in our world it is not!

The word feminism exists, but there is no such word as "masculinism"! Our world is unbelievable. We as species have not fully recognized the degree to which we are seeing through a masculine lens.

My Beloved Readers, listen very closely to what I am about to say! God Realization, the Divine Plan and Integrated Ascension will not be achieved if the Divine Mother, the Goddess energies, the Lady Masters and Mother Earth, Pan, the Nature Spirits, Plant Devas and Elementals, are not brought back into their rightful Divine place within yourself and our society as a whole!

Even in the way Earthly and Spiritual history is recorded, women are not given their proper respect! We have all heard the saying, "Behind every great man there is a great woman"! This is true, but those great women have not been honored and recognized enough! Even in the way we describe Spiritual history, even as Spiritual leaders and lightworkers! Mother Mary for example, I don't believe she was given enough credit in the whole story of Jesus for the incredible demonstration of Godliness she lived out. What Jesus demonstrated was incredible, however, what Mother Mary demonstrated was also incredible and I don't think this is talked about enough.

Another interesting point is that one of Jesus' teachers, according to the Universal Mind channelings of Edgar Cayce ("the Sleeping Prophet"), was a woman by the name of Judy! This, of course, is not talked about!

My Beloved Readers, have you ever noticed that women usually make up 90% of every Spiritual workshop, seminar and lecture? I have been doing this work for almost 30 years and this never fails to be the case! Thank GOD for women who have "held up the flame" for Spirituality on this planet for 18.5 million years!

Have you also noticed in the New Age movement that there is a great focus on Spirituality but there is an overidentification with Heavenly energies and a lack of appreciation for the Material Face of GOD? The masculine path of GOD has stressed the Occult knowledge and understanding the Laws of GOD. It has also focused on the Heavenly and Celestial realms, the Ascended Masters, Archangels and Angels, Elohim, Christed Extraterrestrials, dimensions of reality, and the study of psychology! This is certainly all wonderful! However, the feminine path of GOD honors all this but also seeks to "feel life and fully embody life!" It seeks, of course, to always live in the Heart! It seeks not just deductive thinking, but also inductive knowledge and wisdom. This means asking Spirit and listening! The feminine path of GOD fully recognizes the Earth and the Material Universe as much a part of GOD as the psychological level and Heavenly or Spiritual level! The feminine path of GOD recognizes the need to master the Earth, totally love the Earth, and take responsibility for the Earth, in the form of honoring and sanctifying the Earth Mother and the Nature, Devic and Elemental Kingdoms and the Animal, Plant and Mineral Kingdoms, but also our Earthly civilization itself! The masculine path of GOD just seeks to use the Earth as a means to achieve liberation. It is the feminine path of GOD that teaches the purpose of life is not to "Ascend and leave the Earth" but rather "Descend and anchor God onto and into the Earth and Earth life!" The Four Faces of GOD are equally revered, "Spiritual, Mental, Emotional and Material"! The feminine path of GOD wants to bring Heaven to Earth! It loves our civilization as much as it loves Mother Earth and nature. The feminine path of GOD recognizes that your Spiritual path is not really complete unless you physically ground it into the Earth and Earth life. Your Spiritual path is not complete unless you demonstrate GOD on Earth! Your Spiritual path is not complete unless you complete your Earthly/Spiritual mission and purpose on Earth! Your Spiritual path is not complete unless you totally sanctify, revere, honor and appreciate the Material Face of GOD! The feminine path to GOD realizes we have contracts and Spiritual commitments to fulfill, which we made on the inner plane before we came. The feminine path of GOD wants to fully embody God on Earth! It wants to feel life to its fullest without getting into negative ego forms of feeling! The feminine path of GOD often experiences "Goddess Tears," which are not the negative ego's forms of tears, but more occasional "Spiritual tears" of unconditional love and Divine compassion! Men on a masculine path of GOD often do not understand this and judge this as just women being taken over by their emotional body and negative ego again! This is, of course, not true, and is even Spiritual men's limited lens patriarchal seeing!

Women, of course, have to be careful not to overidentify with the Goddess path and not become matriarchal in nature, feminist in the sense of anti-masculine, overemotional where they are victims of the emotional body, and negative ego mind. Women have to be careful to avoid being too right brain where they lose common sense or logic, and become too empathic. The true Goddess path does not try to oppose the masculine path of GOD, but to just properly integrate it. The same is true of the masculine path of GOD! In its truest form, it fully integrates the feminine path of GOD! So as to avoid confusion here, sometimes men and/or women in the past and very much presently as well, embrace a masculine path of GOD that is rejecting the feminine path to GOD. Sometimes as a counter balance or pendulum swing women, and sometimes men as well, have taken on a feminine path of GOD that has rejected the masculine path of GOD! Each side has thought their path to GOD was better! Both of these states of consciousness are illusion. The only true path to GOD is one of integration and balance! Please listen very carefully, my Beloved Readers, to what I am about to say. "No one on Earth will achieve true God Realization in the fullest sense of the term, which integrates all Four Faces of GOD (Spiritual, Mental, Emotional and Material), if they don't fully embrace the masculine path of GOD and the feminine path of GOD! It is only then that you will know the "Wholeness of GOD!" The problem is that in our Spiritual history and in our present day society, it is the masculine path of GOD that is being focused on, and the feminine path of GOD that is being rejected to a great extent!

Again, to avoid confusion and to explain my terms here clearly. In the true Goddess path there is no over- or underidentification with the God/Goddess energies! Equally as true, in the true God path there is no favoritism to God over Goddess energies. I am, for the sake of clarification of Spiritual principles, pointing out here how a masculine path of GOD can and is being overidentified in our past history and in our current civilization. I am also pointing out how the feminine path to GOD needs to be much more developed in people and lightworkers around the globe to hence then find the proper God/Goddess balance that true Gods and Goddesses both want! The feminine path to GOD has been disowned! Lightworkers on Earth and in the New Age Movement are extremely imbalanced! Their Spiritual bodies are highly developed, but their bank accounts are not! Their light bodies are highly developed but their love bodies may not be equally as balance! They may be communicating with the inner plane Ascended Masters, but they are not communicating enough with Mother Earth, Pan, the Nature Spirits, Elementals, and Plant Devas! Lightworkers may be achieving their higher levels of initiation but they are not grounding their Spiritual missions on Earth! They are also not loving Mother Earth and earthly civilization enough! They are also not taking enough responsibility for healing Mother Earth and healing our society! Lightworkers are taking Spiritual action, but not political and social action. Remember the Material Universe is one of the seven Heavens of GOD! The Divine plan is to bring Heaven to Earth! To create cities and countries of GOD on Earth! Lightworkers are enjoying their Spiritual life but not enjoying their Earthly life with the same fervor! Lightworkers are embodying Spirit, but they are not embodying Spirit on Earth! Lightworkers are becoming filled with love, wisdom and power, however are not demonstrating this enough on Earth! They are not living in the marketplace! Lightworkers are loving God and the Masters, but not loving their physical bodies enough!

My Beloved Readers, look at the reverence the American Indians have for the Earth and the Material Face of GOD! The Essenes at the time of Jesus had a similar type of reverence for the Earth and the Material Face of GOD and this was why Jesus was raised in an Essene community! My Beloved Readers, the Divine Mother and Goddess energy brings us not only a reconnection to our feeling nature but also the ability to "Ground our Spirituality!" The Divine Mother and Goddess energies help us also to fully Realize GOD through embodying God on the Earth! Lightworkers to a great extent have no idea of the profundity of God Realization they are actually "missing" by not fully embracing the Earth and material life! Fully embracing the Material and Earthly Face of GOD will add to your Spiritual path infinitely! Without doing this you will not really fully understand and appreciate the full profundity of GOD and the entire process of GOD's Divine plan! You will literally be missing a quarter or a third of GOD's complete Divine nature! Embracing the Material Face of GOD will open your eyes to GOD in a way that is just as rich as the Spiritual level and psychological level! It is only when you have all three levels of God Realization that you will truly know and Realize God!

The Divine Mother and the Goddess energies also give a deep and rich appreciation of the feeling nature. In the history of the Earth, what happened is when the negative ego/fear-based/separate mind took over, it caused the feeling and emotional nature to become filled with negative feelings and emotions! This then caused a process of shutting down the emotional nature, as a means of self-protection and as a means to stop suffering! Mankind not being able to recognize the true cause because of its lack of training in Spiritual psychology, just made the feeling nature of less importance and basically in a mass consciousness numbed it out! This caused a loss of love, joy, bliss, ecstasy, sensitivity, Spiritual enthusiasm, Spiritual passion, Spiritual compassion for our Brothers and Sisters and ourselves! It caused also a loss of love and enjoyment for Earth life! The integration of the Divine Mother and Goddess brings all these things back! My Beloved Readers, the Divine Mother and Goddess energies brings back now the final piece in the puzzle to regain our full "wholeness in God!"

The Divine Mother and Goddess energies bring back the profundity of the process of incarnating into a physical body into another of GOD's seven Heavens! The Divine Mother and Goddess energy brings back the proper integration of our inner child! This is what was truly meant in the Bible when it says, "to be like a child"! Not to be a victim of your inner child, but to have the wonder and joy of the inner child in the process of Spiritual mastery! Not to lose your inner child, playfulness, fun, excitement, wonder, curiosity even though you are a Spiritual master! The Divine Mother and Goddess energies help us to enjoy the process of Earth life to the hilt! Enjoying every precious second of it. Enjoying, sanctifying and appreciating the Material Face of GOD!

Lightworkers are paying their rent to the Spiritual Face of GOD and maybe the Mental Face or Emotional Face, but are not paying their rent to the Material Face of GOD. They are building the Spiritual knowledge and information banks, but are not building their psychological and earthly knowledge and information banks to the same degree. There is a subconscious belief that material energies are inferior to Spiritual energies! There is also one that says Spiritual energies are superior to psychological energies! Just as the negative ego overidentified with the mind over feeling and the heart! The negative ego also overidentified with Heavenly energies over material energies! These two choices were the rejection of the Divine Mother and the Goddess energies, and the Earth and its people have not recovered from this choice from 18.5 million years ago until now! By the grace of GOD, of the Masters and the Divine Mother, the Goddess energies are now finally returning to the Earth!

One other aspect of the return of the Divine Mother and Goddess energies to Earth, has to do with the return of the Archangels and Angels to Earth in a more open and pronounced way! Where as the Elohim or Co-creator Gods are the "Thought Attributes" of GOD, the Archangels and Angels are the "Feeling Tones" of GOD! This is why in esoteric thought it is known that there are three distinct lines of evolution. The Ascended Master line, the Elohim line and the Angelic line of evolution. Part of the process of Integrated Ascension is to integrate all three of these lines of evolution into your nature, even though each person is created by GOD upon one of these lines! Most on Earth are on the Ascended Master line of evolution, however, there are many who are not. It is very important, for example, if you are on the Ascended Master line of evolution that you integrate and incorporate psychologically the Elohim and Angelic aspects of your self! At the highest stages of evolution on a Spiritual level these lines of evolution integrate, blend and merge together! One of the reasons the Archangels and Angels are becoming more in the mass consciousness now is because of the return of the Divine Mother and Goddess energies to Earth!

One other interesting patriarchal ceremony in our society is how when a woman and man get married, the woman is given away to the man by the father, but the man is not given away by the mother. Interesting, wouldn't you say?

Another interesting phenomena is how people throw trash on the ground. Mother Earth is a living being. How would you like it if people threw garbage on your physical body or just threw garbage and trash on the floor in your home? My Beloved Readers, it is the same thing! The Earth is a living being! Even worse, we pollute her with industrial waste and nuclear waste, which enters her bloodstream and water systems, air, and the very earth itself. How would you feel if someone poured industrial and nuclear waste down your mouth and stomach? My Beloved Readers, this is what mankind has done to the Earth unconsciously! Mother Earth has lovingly said, "Forgive them GOD, they know not what they do!" However Mother Earth's physical body has become sickened by the toxic abuse of the people of the Earth!

I was watching one of the those news magazine shows and they showed how female babies were killed because they were not seen as having as much value as male babies. It was the most unbelievable thing I have ever seen. It was either in India or one of the Arab nations, I can't remember which!

Then we do see in some of the Arab nations how women are not allowed to have professions, reveal any skin, show their face, and for minor infractions they are even killed! Some of the things that are going on in this world are unbelievable!

Then we also see that when men have sex with a lot of different women they are called studs! Whereas women have sex once and they are called prostitutes! The patriarchal and macho energy that pervades our culture is unbelievable! This of course may not be the consciousness of lightworkers, but these subconscious patterns of belief are still in the deeper layers of people's subconscious minds.

Another example of patriarchal consciousness is that it is okay for older men to be with women a lot younger, however the reverse is not always the case in terms of what is seen as socially and politically correct!

In the Arab world as well, the men give the orders and women must follow! This consciousness pervades a great many of the religions and cultures over our world!

Women after dinner clean up and wash dishes. Men sit in the living room socializing. How come it isn't reversed!

What men must realize is that if they don't integrate the feminine and Goddess nature they will probably just have to incarnate as a women next lifetime which will force them to learn the lesson. The lesson is to learn the lesson in this lifetime by grace, so the laws of karma don't force you to do it this way next lifetime! Better yet, learn your lessons and become androgynous! This applies to men and women. Learn to balance and integrate your God/Goddess and you will achieve liberation and achieve enlightenment and you will not have to reincarnate at all unless you choose to!

Another very interesting lens of the Patriarchy on Earth is how we have called the Ascended Masters "The Great White Brotherhood"! My Beloved Readers, why have we not called it "The Great White Sisterhood"? I bring these points up to show how this patriarchal lens has even infiltrated religions and the New Age movement! Part of the transformation of the New Age will come in the reframing of our language to more properly describe the God/Goddess balance that lives throughout all Creation!

Another aspect that the Divine Mother and Goddess energies bring is the ability to physically manifest. This has been a real weak spot for lightworkers. They have been able to manifest on all levels but not as much physically! This has been because of the lack of proper integration of the Divine Mother and the Goddess energies. As these energies are properly integrated you will see your ability to manifest on Earth greatly increase as well! Hence people will become an integration of a "Visionary and Manifestor"! Lightworkers are very good at coming up with great ideas, however, they are not as good in putting them into physical manifestation! As the Material Face of GOD is integrated and the mastery and integration of the Divine Mother and Goddess energies is achieved, you will find yourself becoming a master of both! Your earthly bank account will also then begin to match your highly developed Spiritual bank account, which will allow you to do more on the physical/earthly plane! You will also find all the physical things you need coming much more effortlessly and easily!

Another aspect of the return of the Divine Mother and Goddess energies will be much greater Spiritual gifts and psychic abilities. Much greater intuition, channeling abilities, and subconscious mind abilities. The eating of the fruit of the "Tree of Good and Evil" or the choice to think with one's negative ego mind, cause a greater identification with the conscious mind over the subconscious and superconscious mind. This was good in terms of self-mastery and self-control, but also cutoff a great deal of our extrasensory perceptions. We are basically taught in school to use only our left brain, and there is absolutely no honoring of right brain methods of gaining knowledge and information. The negative ego hence chose science over Spiritual senses, even making decrees that the mind and five senses are all that exists! In making this choice, it basically cut off 22 of your Spiritual senses that GOD created you with! We are literally programmed by our parents and school that everything to do with our Spiritual senses is imagination and not real, and by the time we go through the indoctrination of traditional school which is basically souless and Goddessless, most of the abilities we came with have basically, systematically shut down! As we people reopen to the Divine Mother and Goddess nature, many of these abilities will open up again! For in returning, we now have the understanding that the Goddess energy integration does not mean being run by the negative ego! One is still a master of all one's thoughts, feelings, emotions, energy, physical body and the Earth! However, one also integrates unconditional love and the Goddess energies in the process! In not being run by the negative ego and not creating so many negative feelings and emotions, there is no more need to be so shut down in terms of one's feminine nature! This will allow some of the more feminine sub-conscious and superconscious senses to open up. There are more mas-culine supersenses as well! To learn more about this read my book *The Golden Book of Melchizedek: How To Become An Integrated Christ/Buddha In This Lifetime*, which is available from the Academy! This will allow the honoring and proper integration of the Occult path to GOD and the Mystic path to GOD! In the ideal state we need to inte-grate both the Occult path and the Mystic path within ourselves! Often among lightworkers there has been competition between the two, or judgment on both sides as to which one is better! Both sides are not right! Integration of both is the ideal within every person even if a per-son leans a little bit one way or the other because of how GOD created them or their Ray structure! Remember, the ideal is to properly inte-grate all seven Rays regardless of your Ray configuration. People tend to fall into patterns of Ray structure being 2/4/6, which are more feminine Rays, or 1/3/5/7 which are a little more masculine Rays. Part of the inte-gration of the God/Goddess within is to become a master of all Seven Rays and not let the Ray configuration you incarnated with, make you overidentify with you God/Goddess nature!

The negative ego/separative mind has created a seeming separation between Heaven and the Material Universe when, in truth, they are all the same energy! It is like water being boiled and becoming steam. Water is material, steam is Spiritual. It is the same energy! It just appears different to the five senses and negative ego mind, which has created a separation which is not there! To think one form of GOD is better than another form of GOD is total illusion. It is just energy or GOD sub-stance vibrating at different rates of speed. To the physical eyes matter appears dense. This is illusion as well, for it is not! There is space between the electrons, protons, neutrons and atoms! GOD's Divine plan is to outpicture His Divine idea into all aspects of His creation! We are incarnations of GOD who have volunteered to not only evolve back through the 352 levels of initiation, but also to do our part in creating

GOD's Divine plan on the Material Plane of existence. This is what we have contracted to do! This is our Spiritual mission and purpose. We each have a Divine puzzle piece to outpicture on the physical/earthly plane. We are not just here to do it on the Spiritual plane, or just the mental, or just the emotional plane, we are also here to do it on the physical plane! This means demonstrating God on Earth and also helping to create a Spiritual civilization on Earth that reflects a Godly/Christed/Buddha-like civilization on Earth! The integration of the Divine Mother and Goddess energies has been the last missing key ingredient to now make this full embodiment of God on Earth within each individual, which will then allow us as a civilization on Earth to embody God in terms of creating a true God society! The return of the Divine Mother and Goddess energies along with fully appreciating the Material Face of GOD, as an absolutely essential key ingredient in understanding the true nature of God Realization, will be, in my humble opinion, the final catalyst, along with learning to master negative ego/fear-based thinking and changing it to Spiritual/Christ/Buddha thinking that will allow us, society and our earthly civilization to fully realize the Seventh Golden Age!

One other very interesting aspect of the return of the Divine Mother and Goddess energies has to do with the reawakening of the Spiritual people of the Earth to the Presence of the Holy Spirit! The Holy Spirit is part of the Trinity of GOD! This Trinity is, of course, GOD, Christ and the Holy Spirit! One does not have to be a Christian to appreciate the Presence of the Holy Spirit. Whether you believe in Christianity or not is not even the point. I believe in all religions! I also believe in Brahma, Shiva, and Vishnu from Hinduism. I believe in anything that is true! Regardless of what religion you were brought up in or what you believe, the Holy Spirit does exist and can be of an absolute enormous amount of help! It is amazing to me that lightworkers do not call on the Holy Spirit more. The Holy Spirit is one of the most powerful forces in this infinite universe. Lightworkers call on their Higher Self and Mighty I

Am Presence, and even the Ascended Masters, Archangels and Angels, however, they do not call that much on the Holy Spirit! This is also part of the lack of integration of the Divine Mother and Goddess energies, for the Holy Spirit is part of the feminine aspect of GOD! The Holy Spirit is literally the Voice of GOD! When you pray to GOD it is the Holy Spirit who answers! The Holy Spirit is the answer to every question or problem you have! It has the ability to undo all mistakes on every level! The Holy Spirit is Omnipotent, Omnipresent and Omniscient! It is probably the most powerful force in this infinite universe! A lot of people go to the Ascended Masters or Angels for answers and help, which is great! Others go to their Higher Self and Monad, or Mighty I Am Presence, which is also an aspect of GOD! However it is also possible to go directly to the Trinity of GOD for help! Part of the return of the Divine Mother and Goddess energies is, in truth, also the return of the Holy Spirit to Earth! The Holy Spirit, of course, has always been here and never left, for it is the "Still small voice within!" However, even though it has always been here, it has not always been here in Earthlings awareness! Do call on the Holy Spirit for help, for it will astound you with its love, wisdom and miraculous powers!

Another aspect of misunderstanding among lightworkers that stems from this lack of proper integration of the Divine Mother and Goddess energies is, that they think Spiritual knowledge is better than psychological knowledge. They also think that Spiritual knowledge is much better then earthly knowledge. They actually believe that earthly knowledge does not have much value on a subconscious level.

Well, my Beloved Readers, this is another major block of negative ego faulty thinking. In this book I have talked extensively about how important an understanding of Spiritual psychology is! It is the foundation of your entire life! This also applies to a proper understanding of how to properly master yet integrate your feelings and emotions which is part of psychology! In truth, Spiritual psychology is the foundation of your Spiritual life. If it is not mastered and properly integrated it will not only completely corrupt one's Spiritual life, it will corrupt your physical/earthly life as well. It will affect your physical body in an adverse way and it will make you unsuccessful in earthly endeavors depending on how extensive the imbalance or lack of understanding is. In truth, the belief that Spiritual knowledge is more important than psychological knowledge is actually one of the most dangerous and disturbed beliefs of all of the negative ego, and it is one of the single biggest reasons 98% of lightworkers do not pass the advanced tests of Spiritual leadership and planetary world service. Without mastery and proper integration of Spiritual psychology and the negative ego/fear-based/separative mind not only will lightworkers not pass their lessons, the Spiritual work they are doing will become corrupted and they won't even realize it! Ponder deeply on what I have just said for it may be one of the most important things I have said in this book!

Taking this one step further, lightworkers also think that Spiritual knowledge is much better than earthly knowledge! This is equally as much a corruption of the negative ego mind! It is again a rejection of the Material Face of GOD! It is also one of the main reasons why they are unable to fully manifest their Spiritual mission, purpose and puzzle piece on Earth. It is why their Spiritual teaching and channeling remains on the Spiritual plane and never grounds itself! It never embodies into the physical body or serves Mother Earth in a complete sense. Lightworkers, to a great extent, don't realize that what is in your information banks both in a Spiritual, psychological and earthly sense, from past lives and this life govern all channeling. If there is no knowledge on an earthly level in your information banks, then you will not be able to channel helpful information that has any earthly practicality. Anyone who doesn't believe this is being deluded by the negative ego! Even the great Edgar Cayce, the "Sleeping Prophet," was told by the Universal Mind that it was his past life training that allowed him to channel the information he was bringing through! If you have no training in past lives or this life in astrology, for example, you will not be able to channel on astrology; this is a fact! If you have no earthly knowledge in your information banks because you spend all your time only studying Spiritual things or just psychological things, then you will not be able to channel anything of earthly use! My Beloved Readers, we are meant to be whole and complete on all 352 Levels of GOD like the Mahatma, not skipping the lower ones and saying only the higher levels are important. This is like saying that the upper part of the Cosmic Tree of Life is important and the lower Sephiroth or parts are unimportant. This is like saying the upper chakras are important and the lower ones are not important. My Beloved Readers, this is delusion! Do not buy into false illusionary separation of Spirit and Matter! This is why the educational system in our world is so unintegrated, for they have separated our educational system from the soul. They have separated Church and State! It is why the Earth has so much pollution. It is why our society, civilization and all its institutions are operating out of the personality and not the soul! My Beloved Readers, this all stems back to 18.5 million years ago of the eating of the fruit of the "Tree of Good and Evil" and the choice to think with the negative ego mind which chose the mind over the heart and Heaven over Earth for those who did believe in GOD! The negative ego has infiltrated every aspect of life including Psychology, Religion, Spirituality and the New Age movement! It creates separation, corruption, distortion, delusion, illusion, glamour, maya, and false divisions in every move it makes! Do not be deluded by the negative ego's deluded and corrupt thinking patterns. It is now time for you to develop 100% Mastery, Love and Wisdom on a Spiritual, Psychological, and Physical/Earthly level! Read the newspaper, watch the news, become socially aware, become politically aware, read books about the earthly things that interest you, learn about the people of the Earth you respect and admire. I personally love reading autobiographies of famous people on the Earth in all areas of life!

Become a master of Earth life as well. Become a master of gardening, nature, your business, economics, money, sexuality, your physical body, the arts, music, architecture, dance, culture, and the sciences. Become a master of civilization and society so you can help raise consciousness to change our world on the earthly level! If you want a quick crash course, read my book *Manual for Planetary Leadership*! Over two-thirds of the book focuses on the great philosophical, social, and political issues of our times, from the perspective of Spirit, the Soul, and the Ascended Masters. Contrary to popular opinion, Spirit, the Soul and the Masters are all 100% totally involved in these issues; it is just a great many lightworkers who are not! This all stems from the false separation that was made by the negative ego which mass consciousness and lightworkers have never fully recovered from! It is time to recover from this now! Become a master of Earth life. My Beloved Readers, listen very closely to what I am about to say, for it may be one of the most important things I say in this entire book! There is no feeling in the world better than the feeling of being a Spiritual Master, a Psychological Master and a Physical/Earthly Master all in proper integration and balance! In my own life I love the feeling of moving from one level to the next. After doing my Spiritual work I love to watch the news, work in the garden, or clean and fix-up our home and the Academy! I love politics, sports, gardening, business, all the sciences, astronomy, art, music, dance, spiritual architecture, Feng Shui, sacred sites, spiritually decorating our home and garden, physically helping people as well as spiritually and psychologically helping people. I love cooking, or watching news magazine shows like "60 Minutes". I learn incredible things. I learn a lot through educational television channels and the internet. I love mastering computer technology and having all the most advanced equipment in the Academy and Ashram. I love the science and art of wearing spiritual clothing! For Wesak I actually have seven different tuxedos I wear, some of which I have had specially made to look a lot like how the Masters sometimes dress on the inner planes. I love learning about holistic health, cultures, religions, and sociology. I like watching movies, videos, races, some of the talk shows occasionally, and learning about people. I love watching the Olympics and learning about the different athletes' lives and what inspires them. I love to study about Spiritual leadership, and the great leaders of our world in all aspects of life! Much can be gained from studying their lives and expertise. I love to master and study the many forms of healing so I can not just help heal people's Spirit, mind, and emotions, but also their physical bodies. I love studying nutrition and have even written a book called *How To Achieve Perfect Radiant Health From The Perspective of The Soul*! I love learning about things so I can raise consciousness to help heal the Earth and the society and civilization of the Earth! I love learning about the Earth so I can call in Spirit and the Masters to help heal and fix the things that are wrong! I love the feeling of actually making a difference in the world! I love manifesting Wesak on the Earth! I love writing books that actually get physically published. I love accomplishing things physically every day, not just Spiritually, mentally and emotionally. If you talk to anyone who knows me, they know that I can get more done physically than most people on the Earth. This is because I believe in "consistency"! This is the great problem with a great many lightworkers, they are not consistent. The ideal in life is that whatever you do, you do with all your bodies and all aspects of your Being! So whatever I do in life I do on all levels, or I don't do it at all. If I do it Spiritually, then I also do it mentally, emotionally, etherically, energetically, physically and on an earthly level! Whatever I do, I do with 100% consistency between my superconscious mind, conscious mind, subconscious mind, physical body and the Earth Mother! With no judgement intended, people on the Earth and lightworkers tend to be very inconsistent and fragmented. The superconscious mind does one thing, the conscious mind another thing, the subconscious mind another thing, and things never even get to the Earth! They are not consistent in all their chakras and not consistent in the mastery of all their Rays, and not consistent in honoring and sanctifying the Four Faces of GOD and their four bodies in a balanced manner!

I love to watch the awards shows and study and learn from the people who are the best in their fields. I study the science of how things work, on a Spiritual, psychological and physical/earthly level. One of the biggest reasons, I humbly suggest, why I have been successful, is my learning to understand the laws that govern this universe on a Spiritual, psychological and physical earthly level. I am not satisfied with just Spiritual success and psychological success, I want and have achieved physical/earthly success as well! That is what a Spiritual master does, they are successful on all levels of GOD! They don't reject levels of GOD and say one is more important than another is; or one is lesser than another is. This is total illusion of the negative ego, yet this is what a great many lightworkers believe on a subconscious level. My job is to bust the negative ego wherever it sticks its ugly little head! My job and mission is to write a book that leaves no stone unturned, to find out where the negative ego might be trying to hide! My Spiritual passion and mission here is to bring the Light of GOD and the Light of the Holy Spirit where others have not tread and where others have not looked!

I love studying all forms of psychology, physical sciences, and the mechanics of all things. It is why I like studying the book *The Keys of Enoch,* even though it is more of a science book rather than a self-help book! This is also why my writing is so easy to understand and practical. I am interested in making things work on Earth not just in Heaven! I love being a philanthropist to the best of my ability and helping out people and causes I believe in. I love trying to reform and reorganize our society along more Christed lines! My great Spiritual passion in life has been not only to bring Spirituality, Ascension and the Ascended Master Teachings into the areas of Spiritual psychology, marriage, family, and children, but also into every area of Earth life. This is what excites me the most! How does Spirituality translate into the mental body, emotional body, etheric body, physical body, social self, environment, and our earthly civilization? This is why the next book I am writing is *The Divine Plan for the Seventh Golden Age*! This is Spirit's and the Ascended Masters' plan for revamping our civilization and turning it into Spiritual/Christ/Buddha civilization!

So, my Beloved Readers, I have explained these things to try to give you a taste for the incredible richness of God's wisdom and knowledge on the physical/earthly plane! Don't just be a master of the Spiritual level and skip the psychological and earthly levels. Don't just be a master of the Spiritual and psychological and skip the earthly level. Be a full, absolutely 100% master on all levels! Educate yourself on all levels! Become a master of all seven Rays, all four bodies, all three minds, all 12 archetypes, all 12 signs of the Zodiac, all 12 Sephiroth of the Tree of Life, all Tarot Cards, all Four Faces of GOD, your Spiritual Self, your Psychological Self and your Physical/Earthly Self! Educate your self on all levels! Do not become so Spiritually or Heavenly focused that you are of no good use to GOD on Earth! Grounding your Spirituality into your physical body and into this Earthly world and civilization is the Spiritual battle cry and mantra for the New Millennium, The Aquarian Age and the Seventh Golden Age! Be consistent on "all" levels! Develop your talents and abilities on all levels: Spiritually, Psychologically and in a Physically/Earthly Sense! I tell you again, my Beloved Readers, there is absolutely no better feeling in this infinite universe than being a master on a Spiritual, Psychological and Physical/Earthly Level! Educate yourself and build your Spiritual information banks, your psychological information banks and your physical/earthly information banks with total knowledge and wisdom at each level! This way you will also be able to intelligently deal with every person you meet and converse with, no matter what their perspective and background! This also, my Beloved Readers, is the only way you can develop a "God Realized Full Spectrum Prism Consciousness" that is not filled with blind spots and limited lens seeing! This is also the way you will become knowledgeable and wise of both God and Goddess energies! Do not just focus on developing knowledge of God energies and not of Goddess energies! If you do this, it is you who will be the loser, for the negative ego will have bamboozled you into thinking you were realizing the fullness of GOD, and, in truth, you will have not! You will have missed half of GOD! In this existential moment and Holy Instant you have the Divine opportunity to humbly and egolessly rethink this decision that the negative ego may have unconsciously made and make a new choice and new decision right now in this moment to never ever let this happen! Do not settle for one third of GOD, or one half of GOD, or three quarters of GOD! Only accept and fully claim for yourself 100% of GOD! Do not settle for less! Become a 100% master on a Spiritual, psychological and physical/earthly level and fill your information banks with wisdom and knowledge on all three levels as well!

Another aspect of this return of the Divine Mother and Goddess energies will be the recognition that Mother Earth is a living Being, and as a race we have treated her as an inconsequential material object with no consciousness! Not only is Mother Earth a living Being, Mother Earth is in a state of evolution as well! Mother Earth is taking her initiations as well. Lightworkers at times unconsciously are kind of selfish and are only focusing on their evolution and do not care about the evolution of Mother Earth! This is why I am now, and have in the past, recommended that all lightworkers when they do any type of ascension activation work, do it for Mother Earth simultaneously as they do it for themselves! Also when you care for the Earth and sanctify the Earth and clean up the Earth in an ecological and societal sense, you are helping her evolution! It is time that lightworkers start thinking less about themselves and more about a bigger picture perspective as well! I am not saying that lightworkers should not focus upon their own Spiritual growth and initiation process, but they also need to focus much more on helping other people with theirs, and helping the Animal Kingdom, Plant Kingdom, Mineral Kingdom and Mother

Earth with theirs as well! All of it is GOD! If you truly are God, then it is time to start working for GOD and not for the self part of God, if you see my point! GOD is interested in evolving all parts of GOD since GOD is everything! This is why lightworkers need to focus a little more on service and a little less on just achieving initiations! I have seen Spiritual groups and Spiritual people actually competing over initiations! All of these things are corruptions of the negative ego! We have not just come here to achieve initiations and liberation for ourselves, we have come here to be of service! The Divine Mother and Goddess energies bring true compassion and caring for others! If you truly have compassion for others then how can one just focus on one's own ascension and initiation process and not want to be of service to people and this world? An incredible number of people are suffering in this world! If we all are God, then aspects of GOD are in a state of suffering and lack of realization! It is not a sacrifice to serve, that again is the negative ego. If we truly have the unconditional love and compassion of the Divine Mother and Goddess energies then we should want to be of service to help relieve suffering! The help may come on a physical, mental, emotional, energetic or Spiritual level! Too many lightworkers are floundering trying to find their Spiritual mission and puzzle piece instead of getting out there and doing something! Any form of service is better than no service at all! It is not about necessarily making money, or Spiritual vanity, or becoming famous, or having to fulfill some great Spiritual vision. Maybe it will be volunteer work. The vow of the Bodhisattva arises out of the unconditional love and compassion of the Divine Mother and Goddess energies. I am not saying everyone has to make this vow! I am saying that lightworkers need to be of service even if it is not the ideal Spiritual job the negative ego or conscious mind thinks it deserves. It is amazing how the negative ego mind gets its hands in Spiritual matters. Stop waiting for GOD and the Masters to tell you want to do, and get out there and do something until you figure it out! The time for Spiritual floundering is over! It is time for all of us to get our hands dirty a little bit! Look at the example Mother Teresa set! Living a life just focused on Spiritual growth and not on service can be a corruption of the negative ego if one is not careful! It is our responsibility to change this world and society and help the people of the world! All negative ego, competition, comparing, jealousy, envy, false pride, Spiritual vanity, greed, selfishness, self-centeredness and negative ego motivations need to be 100% cleansed and removed from our being, and true unconditional love, caring, compassion and genuine desire to be of service to people, animals, plants, the Mineral Kingdom, Mother Earth, nature, and the civilization and society of the Earth needs to be our goal, purpose and main focus. Focus on your Spiritual growth while you are doing this! Forget about the glamour and negative ego of doing fancy Spiritual projects! If they come, so be it! What is most important is to be doing something of service to people and the planet! I cannot tell you how many lightworkers I meet who have all the glamorous Spiritual ideas and never do anything but talk about them! To be honest, it is a corruption and glamour of the negative ego! If they cannot get it to the earthly plane and manifest it on the earthly plane it really means nothing! It would be better to do volunteer work where you are really touching peoples lives and/or helping the world than making one's ego feel good by talking about a Spiritual project that never happens! Lightworkers have remained, to a great extent, stuck on the Spiritual, mental and emotional plane! Maybe we should change their name from lightworkers to Earthworkers, and they might get more done on the physical plane! I am being humorous here, however, there is a seed of truth in that which I say! Lightworkers are overidentified with the Light and are not recognizing the Light within Matter and the Earth!

Another aspect of the return of the Divine Mother and the Goddess energies is the Mahatma energy, which is a group consciousness Being that embodies all 352 levels of GOD! Lightworkers think of the Mahatma energy as just carrying the 352nd level of GOD energy! The truth is, the Mahatma embodies the energy of the Divine Mother and Goddess energies as well, for it is just as interested in the Material Face of GOD as it is the 352nd level of GOD! I know this for an absolute fact, for the Mahatma has told me this! The Mahatma has greatly helped me in understanding the absolute Divine profundity of the Earth and Earth energies! You will not truly Realize God, my Beloved Readers, until you learn to embody God on Earth and ground your Spiritual mission and purpose on Earth! Stop trying to glamorize Spiritual projects that feed the ego but never manifest on Earth! If you cannot manifest that project quickly and efficiently on Earth then let it go and do something you can! The time for ungrounded Spirituality is over! As Sai Baba has said, "Hands that help are holier than lips that pray"! It is the Divine Mother and Goddess energies that bring to us the incredible importance of the Material Face of GOD and properly mastering but also integrating our feelings, emotions, and Heart energy! My Beloved Readers, do not stay stuck on a masculine path to GOD that never makes it to the Earth! Do not also remain on a feminine path to GOD that has no masculine energy for that will never make it to the Earth as well! It is only when God/Goddess are equally honored and sanctified and all seven Rays are mastered and equally balanced that the true balance of feminine and masculine and Heaven and Earth can be found, realized, integrated, demonstrated and fully embodied on the Earth! Don't just embody God on the Spiritual plane, for if you do, you will have missed out on three quarters of what GOD truly is! Don't just embody GOD on the masculine and Spiritual plane, for you will have missed out on a full half of what GOD truly is. Don't just embody GOD on the feminine and Spiritual plane for you will have missed half of what GOD truly is! Embody GOD as a true God/Goddess fully in your physical body and on the Earth! Make God happen in the Material Universe not just in Heaven! If you never make it to the earthly plane, in truth, with no judgement intended, you will have been somewhat deluded by the negative ego. You will have not integrated fully the Divine Mother and Goddess energies within you! You will have rejected unconsciously one of the Faces of GOD! Do not live a life of only sanctifying a half of GOD or three-quarters of GOD! If you do this you will have blocked yourself from realizing what true God Realization really is! Do not let the negative ego delude you on this point! It will tell you that you are an exception to the rule and you do not need to be part of the Earth or ground your Spiritual mission and purpose. I ask you to consider who is reading this chapter, you or the negative ego! This is a very key existential moment in your life right now! Will you chose to embody God on Earth, or will you only embody God in Heaven! If you choose to only embody God in Heaven, with no judgement intended, you will lose it! For you will have let the faulty thinking of the negative ego confuse your thinking! You will not achieve full God Realization, this is a fact, for you will have not realized the Material Face of GOD and you will have not fully realized the Divine Mother and Goddess energies on the Earth! You will also not have fully completed your Spiritual mission, purpose and puzzle piece to help Mother Earth and her Kingdom, and taken responsibility for the society and civilization of the Earth as you contracted to do before you came into incarnation!

Very few Spiritual teachers take a stand for the Material Universe, the Divine Mother and Goddess energies! It is time we, as the collective stewards for this planet, right this wrong that was set into motion 18.5 million years ago and set it right once and for all! Spirit, the Masters, the Elohim Councils, the Archangels and Angels of the Light of GOD, the Divine Mother, the Lady Masters and the Goddess energies, Mother Earth, Pan, and the Nature Kingdom, put forth now the "Clarion Call" to Spiritual leaders, Spiritual teachers, channels, scientists, healers, counselors, and people in all professions on Earth, to hereby make a Spiritual vow in this moment "to return the Divine Mother, the Goddess energies, The Holy Spirit, The Mahatma, Pan, Mother Earth, the Nature Spirits and Plant Devas and Tree Spirits, to their proper place and perspective to correct this wrong that started in our ancient past! The Clarion Call is now sounded forth by the entire Cosmic and Planetary Hierarchy for lightworkers to make a Spiritual vow in their own lives right now to fully embody the God/Goddess energies on Earth in their own lives and to try to make a difference in this earthly world and civilization to the best of their abilities in a balanced and integrated way! It is time the Divine Mother and the

Goddess energies took their rightful place in the consciousness of the people on Earth as they already are in the consciousness of GOD, Spirit and the Masters in Heaven!

So let it be Written! So let it be Done!

CHAPTER 6

The Incredible Importance of Balancing and Integrating Your Three Minds, Four Bodies, Feminine/Masculine, Heaven/Earth, Three-Fold Flame, Seven Rays, The Seven Chakras, and God/Goddess

My Beloved Readers, I have spent a great deal of time in this book speaking about the importance of releasing negative ego/fear-based/separative thinking and feeling! The importance of this obviously cannot be overestimated. However, to have a balanced understanding it is also extremely important to understand that it is of equal importance to at all times keep the following Spiritual ideals and balances in proper balance and integration. They are: the three minds, four bodies, feminine/masculine, heaven/earth, Three-Fold Flame, seven rays, the seven chakras, and God/Goddess!

Even though I have named this book *How To Release Fear-Based Thinking and Feeling: An In-depth Study of Spiritual Psychology*, it is of equal importance to not only learn to transcend negative ego thinking and feeling and change it to Spiritual/Christ/Buddha thinking and feeling, but to also maintain these Spiritual ideal and proper balances! There are other balances and integrations I could have listed; however, I have purposely chosen this set of Spiritual ideals and balances because they are the most important! So, my Beloved Readers, the two main Spiritual principles that are most important on your Spiritual path are to remain balanced and integrated within these ideals and balances, and to at all times transcend and release negative ego thinking and feeling and change it to Spiritual/Christ/Buddha thinking and feeling! I have written over one hundred chapters in this book to explore every nook and cranny of the Spiritual path and Spiritual psychology. The purpose of this chapter is to synthesize and consolidate your thinking so as to focus on that which is most important.

Now a great many of the Spiritual ideals and balances I have mentioned in this chapter I have already written about in this book, so I am not going to do an in-depth review of all of them again. What I am going to do is just give you a quick overview of these main Spiritual ideals and balances so they remain indelibly imprinted in your conscious and subconscious mind.

I will go through them in the order I have listed them. We have three minds: Superconscious, (Higher Self, and Mighty I Am Presence or Monad), Conscious, and Subconscious. The conscious mind is the more rational mind, subconscious the nonreasoning computer with lots of abilities, and the superconscious our Spiritual mind. We basically need to remain in absolute control of our subconscious mind and reprogram it and use its abilities for a Spiritual purpose. The superconscious, Higher Self and/or Mighty I Am Presence, is our own individualized Presence of God within us. We, as the conscious mind, receive guidance from it just as we give guidance to our subconscious mind. We serve the superconscious, and we make the subconscious serve us through owning our 100% personal power, self-mastery, causal consciousness, unconditional love, and psychological and Spiritual wisdom! This is the proper relationship of the three minds when functioning properly. This way they get linked up like rings on a chain and eventually merge and integrate together, with the conscious mind taking on the consciousness of the superconscious and the subconscious taking on the consciousness of the superconscious and conscious minds. Even though they are three minds through the process of ascension and the 12 levels of "Integrated Ascension" they become one integrated mind even thought, in truth, they are three minds, but they function as one. Is not the same thing true of the Trinity of GOD, my Beloved Reader? Is not the Trinity, GOD, Christ and the Holy Spirit? They are three minds, in truth, however they function as one! "As within, So without! As above, So below"!

Now the next step is balancing your four bodies. These are the Spiritual, mental, emotional and physical. The Spiritual ideal and Spiritual balance here is simple. We all must be balanced in these four bodies. The mind must be balanced with the feelings. Each person must see and practice how our thoughts create our reality. Each person must see and practice how our thoughts create our feelings and emotions. All people must see there are two ways of thinking and only two. You either think with your negative ego/fear-based/separative mind, or you think with your Spiritual/Christ/Buddha mind. The mind is either programmed by one, the other, or a strange mixture of both, which is usually what the case is. The ideal is to think only with your Spiritual/Christ/Buddha mind.

On the other side of the coin we must also properly integrate our feelings and emotions. We must be masters and not victims in life, and cause our feelings and emotions but simultaneously integrate them. This manifests as unconditional love, joy, happiness, bliss, compassion, Spiritual passion, enthusiasm, communication of feelings, sharing of feelings, passion for life, sharing of feelings in relationships of all kinds.

We also need to integrate our Spiritual body. This is the Spiritual body of our own Higher Self and Mighty I Am Presence and/or Monad! The whole process of ascension is to first anchor your Higher Self and merge, integrate and become one with it at the Third Initiation, and then at the Sixth and Seventh Initiation merge with your Mighty I Am Presence and Monad! The other key of course is to also integrate the consciousness of your Spiritual body into your mental, emotional, etheric and physical bodies as well. Many just anchor it Spiritually and not psychologically or physically! For it is absolutely essential that each person achieve Spiritual mastery, psychological mastery, and physical/earthly mastery and then integrate and balance these aspects of self. This is an essential principle of balancing the four bodies!

Lastly, each person must balance and integrate the physical body. They must take good care of it. Eat right, exercise, get proper sleep and rest, fresh air, a little sunshine and so on. Many lightworkers whole program falls apart by not taking proper care of the physical body, which manifests as chronic illness. I am not saying you cannot achieve ascension or fully complete your Spiritual path and mission if this happens, however I am saying it is a lot harder if the physical body is not properly loved and cared for! It is a part of the Four Faces of GOD as well!

So, my Beloved Readers be sure to fully balance and take care of your four bodies and do not ever think one is better than another. This would be a serious mistake. Mystics or emotional types often put down the mind as unimportant or even negative. Nothing could be farther from the truth. Occultists or mental types often put down the feelings and emotions. I say again, nothing could be farther from the truth. No one will ever Realize God unless they integrate and balance both. The same applies to your Spiritual body and physical body! God is as much in your physical body as he is in your Spiritual body! It is the purpose of life that you fully become the Mighty I Am Presence on Earth "Living in and being fully grounded in the physical body!" How can you perform your Spiritual mission and walk the Earth as a fully integrated Mighty I

Am Presence and integrated Ascended Master if your don't fully honor, respect and take care of your physical body? All four bodies are of equal importance! They also reflect the integration that Carl Jung spoke of in terms the four types of people. He was speaking here of properly integrating and balancing the intuitive, thinking, feeling, and sensation functions. The intuitive is, of course, the Spiritual body, thinking, the mental body, feeling, the emotional body, and the sensation function being the five outer senses of the physical body!

Now it is also of the highest importance to balance and integrate the feminine and masculine aspects of self. I wrote a wonderful chapter on this in this book showing all the different balances of the Yin and the Yang, the right brain and left brain. I also showed how when these become out of balance that they could become quite negative in character! As we all know, the Spiritual ideal is to become psychologically androgenous. Learning to achieve this is absolutely essential to achieving God Realization! God Realization cannot be achieved if this is not done!

God Realization also cannot be achieved if the Heaven and Earth sides of self are not balanced. Some lightworkers get way too heavenly and celestially focused and ungrounded. Other people on Earth get way too materialistic and third dimensionally focused. Spiritual people and lightworkers must come to love and appreciate the Material Universe and the Earth and see it as one of GOD's Heavens. They must recognize it as one of the "Four Faces of GOD"! The Four Faces of GOD are the Spiritual, Mental, Emotional and Material Faces! Lightworkers often forget about the Material Face of GOD and think it is less than or not equal to the other faces! My Beloved Readers, listen to me very carefully in this moment! You will not achieve true full God Realization if you do not integrate the Material and Earthly Face of God! Your Spiritual mission is to create Heaven on Earth! Your Spiritual mission is to become the Mighty I Am Presence on the Earth! Your Spiritual mission is to manifest your Spiritual mission and Spiritual puzzle piece on the Earth!

Many people who have achieved some Realization of God on a Spiritual level live in a blissed-out state. Listen very closely to me now, my Beloved Readers, for I have a great Spiritual Truth to share with you. The God Realization and or bliss that those feel on a Realizing the Spiritual level is absolutely nothing compared to the integrated God Realization you will experience doing and demonstrating this Spiritually, psychologically, and on the physical/earthly plane! Then when you also learn to integrate these three levels in your daily life the love, the joy, the bliss, the inner peace, the Spiritual ecstasy is "off the charts." There is still "donkey work" to do, however even that becomes Spiritual love, joy and bliss when everything is integrated and balanced! My Beloved Readers, heed my words of guidance, you will not fully Realize God if you also do not master, integrate, and love the Material/Earthly Plane! GOD is as much in the physical as He is in the Spiritual! You will literally miss out on a quarter of GOD if you do not fully understand and demonstrate what I am now saying. If this is a weak spot for you, read the books I have recommended that focus on this area of how to achieve God Realization through the Physical/Earthly level. It is the most amazing feeling in the world to have your cup runneth over with GOD on the Spiritual level, to have it runneth over on the Psychological level, and to have it runneth over on the Physical/Earthly level as well! Then when you integrate all three properly together in your daily life your integrated cup will runneth over even more! For always remember as well the purpose of life is to "Demonstrate God and Integrated Ascension" on the Physical/Earthly Plane, not just in your mind, or your feelings, or on the Spiritual plane! Your are meant to demonstrate God in all your bodies and on the Material/Earthly plane! We are here to create a fifth dimensional society on Earth!

I have spent a lot of time talking about the Three-Fold Flame in this book, so it is not necessary to go into very much depth here. However, just as a quick overview and summary we each have a Three-Fold Flame in our own heart of "Love, Wisdom and Power!" In this book I have gone into infinite detail showing what can and will happen if you don't keep these three Spiritual/Christ/Buddha qualities balanced and integrated in your daily life! Do not for a second, my Beloved Readers, think that any one of these qualities is better than another. This would be like saying one Ray of GOD is better than another. It is only when they work together in perfect balance and working at their 100% level and capacity that true God Realization will take place. Each person must own their 100% personal power in life to Realize God and be successful in every aspect of life. Each person must own their 100% unconditional love at all times towards self, others, all kingdoms of God and the Earth, to fully Realize God! Each person must own their 100% psychological and Spiritual wisdom at all times to fully Realize God! It is when all three of these flames are operating at 100%, being perfectly integrated and balanced, that this aspect of God Realization can be achieved!

Then adding to this understanding the Seven Great Rays of GOD must be balanced and integrated! These Seven Great Rays make up the true personality of GOD! It is not possible to achieve God Realization without perfectly balancing and integrating these seven rays inside of us. So regardless of what your own personal ray structure is that you came into this life with, all seven rays must be integrated and balanced! These Seven Great Rays and Qualities of GOD are Power, Love/Wisdom, Active Intelligence, Harmony and Artistic Integration, New Age Science, Devotion, Freedom/Ceremonial Order and Magic/Transmutation/Divine Structure/Spiritual Alchemy/Spiritual Grounding!

Since I have talked about these Seven Great Rays in previous chapters, it is not the purpose of this chapter to explore them in-depth again. However, what I do want to say just in terms of a summary is that again we see the overlapping of the Three-Fold Flame and the first three Great Rays of GOD! First Ray is Power, Second Ray is Love/Wisdom! The Second Ray wisdom is a little more the wisdom of Heart, and Psychological and Spiritual wisdom. The Third Ray is Active

Intelligence and is another quality of wisdom that allows one to intelligently manifest one's Spiritual mission onto the Physical/Earthly plane. Many lightworkers have the Second Ray wisdom, but have not yet developed the Third Ray wisdom to manifest their Spiritual mission onto the Earthly plane. This is why the Third Ray is also connected to business. Wisdom of the Heart and Spirit is different than wisdom that allows one to be successful on all levels on the Earthly plane! The Third Ray also involves in its title, "activity" so it is not just the feeling of love and wisdom of the mind, but also activity of the physical body to take action on the Material/Earthly plane of existence! We see here the incredible Divine Intelligence of GOD to structure the Rays in this manner. Then it gets even better, for there are four more Great Rays. The Fourth Ray deals with the need to create harmony on all levels and also deals with the importance of integrating the artistic and aesthetic aspect of life! Then the Fifth Ray, which deals with New Age science! Every aspect of life, in truth, is a Spiritual science of itself. There is New Age Spiritual Science of God Realization on the Spiritual, Psychological and Physical Earthly levels. There is New Age science in medicine, psychology, social work, law, gardening, healing, architecture, astronomy, astrology, Kabbalah, politics, and in creating a whole new Fifth dimensional society on Earth. So New Age Science really integrates into all aspects of life, as in truth, all the Rays do.

Then the Sixth Ray of devotion. Did not Master Jesus say the whole law could be summed up as "Love the Lord thy GOD with all your heart and soul and mind and might, and love your neighbor as you love yourself"! What would life be without devotion to GOD? Devotion also relates to all relationships of love and all aspects of life! Then there is the Seventh Ray, which is a little harder to define in one word, for it reaches into a lot of different areas. It deals with Spiritual freedom on all levels. It deals with ceremonial order and magic! It deals with transmutation, Spiritual alchemy, Divine structure and Spiritually grounding, the Spiritual mission of all souls on Earth into the Earth and onto the

Earth! If you want to understand the true personality of GOD, then these Seven Great Rays are one of the real keys!

Now we come to the importance of balancing and integrating your seven chakras. I have written a wonderful chapter on this subject, so there is no need to go over this in any great depth, however what I do want to say in summary is that the chakras are another great key to understanding the nature of GOD! Just as He has built into our Divine structure the Seven Great Rays and all the other Spiritual ideals and balances I have spoken about so far in this chapter, He has also built into us Seven Great Chakras each representing another Divine Quality and aspect of the Divine! The Seven Great Rays also focus, in an outer professional sense, on the balance and integration in the Divine Plan, of politics, Spiritual education, business, the arts, the sciences, religion, and the creation of a Spiritual civilization on Earth as well as economics! Is not GOD incredibly brilliant and profound how He as has organized and structured ourselves, Creation, and life? This is why it is so important to develop yourself in all the Ray qualities, and try to as well develop yourself and your understanding in all these Seven Ray professions as well. This way you can more fully integrate and demonstrate the consciousness of God on Earth from a "Full Spectrum Prism consciousness" and not from one or a small number of lenses! One cannot achieve true God Realization without integrating and balancing these Seven Great Rays!

The First Chakra deals with the importance of grounding, survival and taking care of one's earthly responsibilities as well as ones physical body! The Second Chakra deals with sexuality, procreation, creativity, and relationships with other people and one's emotional body! The Third Chakra deals with the mental body and emotional body! The mental and emotional body being intimately connected, since it is our thoughts that create our feelings and emotions! The Third Chakra is also connected to our personal power and will! It is connected to the proper use of our mind and to the proper integration of our feelings and emotions! The Fourth Chakra being the importance of opening one's heart, and unconditional love! The Fifth Chakra is focused on the importance of communication, which we have not talked about in this chapter! Again we see the incredible profundity of GOD who misses nothing in his infinite Divine wisdom! Then we have the Sixth Chakra, which is fully opening your Spiritual vision. This means your occult vision, your mystic vision and your psychological vision! Many think the Third Eye is connected to clairvoyance. This is only an extremely small sliver of what the true full opening of the Third Eye is about! Never forget that you don't just see with your physical eyes, you see with your mind. This is one big lesson you have learned from reading this book! Part of opening the Third Eye is the Spiritual wisdom of esoteric knowledge and understanding. Part of the opening of the Third Eye is the study on the psychological level an incredibly profound book, like the one you are reading, and my book *Soul Psychology*. This is why the subtitle of this book is *An In-depth Study of Spiritual Psychology*! This is why there are many clairvoyants who are extremely unclear Spiritually and psychologically, even though they can see into the inner plane. There are even psychics and clairvoyants who do not believe in GOD! Clairvoyance is actually a subconscious ability and/or inner sense. This is why it is possible to have clairvoyance and not believe in GOD! This is why many lightworkers get trapped in the fascination of the psychic world, not realizing that this is a subconscious and/or astral/mental world and is not the true Spiritual world. This is why when you go to "psychic stores" they have all this weird black magic stuff. The owners, who are oftentimes psychically identified, have not made this discernment between the Spiritual realm and the Psychic realm. Lightworkers often give their personal power to psychics and you see now from what I am saying how inappropriate this is. This not only has very little to do with true Third Eye opening, but it is also often a Psychic realm that has no connection to the Spiritual. The psychic may be totally undeveloped Spiritually and psychologically, and yet lightworkers are going to them for advice because of a faulty inappropriate fascination with the psychic realm. My advice is to stay away from it!

Now I will say that it is possible to use psychic gifts for a Spiritual purpose, however please understand that this is not the true understanding of what the opening of the Third Eye is. There are schizophrenics and people in mental institutions who have clairvoyance, and can channel and hear voices. Lightworkers must wake-up and "smell the coffee" on this issue! Clairvoyance and the ability to channel or hear voices are not a sign of any level of Spiritual or psychological growth in the slightest! This is why you see on store fronts in every city of the United States ads for psychic readers, tarot readers, and so on! As I have repeated over and over again in this book and in my other books, all clairvoyance and channeling is filtered through the subconscious mind, belief systems, level of consciousness, philosophy, psychology, psychological clairity, Spiritual initiation and development, character development, trancendence of negative ego thoughts and feelings or lack thereof, ray integration, chakra development, and all the things I have talked about in this book. Given this information, be very Spiritually discerning as to who you give your personal power to in the future, who you choose to seek guidance and advice from, and what you choose to believe in channeled Spiritual books. Some of the most bizarre, unclear, glamour-filled information I have ever found in any books I have read, comes in books that are channeled, and some of them are supposedly channeled by Ascended Masters or Spirit, which of course means nothing for all channeling has to go through all the above mentioned filters I just mentioned. So even if it did once start there, by the time it gets on paper and reinterpreted by the channel, who in many cases is extremely unclear psychologically and not that developed Spiritually even though they do channel, it is so filled with contamination, corruption, and glamour you can barely call it a channeled book, though they do. The undiscerning, impressionable public of course believes it and buys all the information "hook, line and sinker!" So it is my sincere hope and prayer that this little discussion of what the true opening of the Third Eye really is has put things in their proper perspective for you! The opening of the Third Eye also deals with the development and integration of the 22 Supersenses of GOD which I wrote about in this chapter! An enormous number of lightworkers don't truly understand what the full opening of the Third Eye really means! In my humble opinion, after reading this book, and if you will read some of my books on the Spiritual and physical/earthly aspects of God Realization you will be well on your way to almost fully opening your Third Eye in a balanced, integrated and appropriate manner!

The seventh chakra is of course the Crown Chakra. This is our relationship to GOD, Christ, the Holy Spirit, our Mighty I Am Presence, our Higher Self, to the inner plane Ascended Masters, the Archangels and Angels, Elohim Councils, Christed Extraterrestrials, All Knowledge, Universal Mind, the Divine Mind, Intuition, Perfection, and God Realization!

It is only when we fully integrate and balance all seven chakras that true God Realization can be achieved! There are some on the Spiritual path that favor the higher chakras and think the first three are lower or unimportant! This is no different than the rays, all chakras are equally important! The same people who teach such a philosophy are the same ones who reject Spiritual psychology as important and only focus on the Spiritual level. I do not need to tell you after reading this book what a disastrous, corrupted, negative ego result that will lead to! If you do not integrate and balance your lower chakras properly you will not Realize God and this is a fact! The only way you will fully Realize God is if all seven chakras are equally balanced! Those who do not fully balance and integrate their lower chakras will not be right with self, which will corrupt their relationship to GOD, the Masters, all channeling, and a great deal of their Spiritual teaching! You cannot have a right relationship to GOD and the Masters without having a right relationship to self first! This is because your thoughts create your reality and you see with your mind, not just your physical eyes. You can feel the profound

Spiritual and psychological transformation you have gone through just reading this book. This is because you see through your conscious-ness! So if you want to fully Realize God then fully balance and integrate your chakras. Neglect of the lower chakras would also greatly decrease you energy level and could also lead to glandular, hormonal and organ imbalances as well as the potential of other physical health problems. Learn by grace instead of karma, and heed the wisdom of that which I share with you now! The only way to fully Realize God is through balance and integration and "full spectrum prism consciousness" of all lenses of GOD!

The final Spiritual ideal and balance is the importance of integrating the God/Goddess within! This is a new Spiritual deal and balance for lightworkers to focus on! The Divine Mother, the Lady Masters, the Earth Mother and the Goddess Energies have taken a beating in Earth's history. The patriarchal nature of our society has caused them to recede into the background! My Beloved Readers, I am very happy to say that we have finally reached a point of time in Earth's history where the return of the Goddess has finally come! Praise GOD! We each have a part to play by integrating the God/Goddess within ourselves whether we are female or male! Women must integrate both and men must integrate both! No one will achieve full God Realization without doing so!

The Goddess energies, although in truth fully balanced and integrated from the "full spectrum prism perspective" of the Divine Mother, classically have to do with the proper integration of unconditional love, compassion, feminine nature, feelings, the Earth Mother, the Nature Spirits and Devic Kingdom, Spiritual joy, Spiritual passion, Spiritual enthusiasm, Spiritual desire, and the proper integration of the Inner Child! It is the understanding that on the right and left sides of GOD are the Divine Mother and the Divine Father! They are on the two sides of the Cosmic Tree of Life as well! Creation cannot be understood or Realized without fully integrating the God/Goddess within!

My Beloved Readers, in final conclusion what I wish to say is that the Spiritual path is really quite simple. If you want to be with GOD in Heaven then act like God on Earth! There are a great may Spiritual ideals and Spiritual principles I have spoken about in this book. However, in my humble opinion, the importance of practicing and demonstrating transcending and releasing of negative ego/fear-based thinking and feeling and changing it to Spiritual/Christ/Buddha thinking and feeling and the practice and demonstration as well of these main Spiritual ideal and balances I have listed in this chapter, are the two most important things to remember in regard to keeping in one's mind this in-depth study of Spiritual psychology!

CHAPTER 7

The Seven Keys To Releasing Fear and Worry

The first key to releasing fear and worry is to always own your Personal Power and Self-Mastery.

The second you lose your Personal Power and Self-Mastery, fear-based thinking and feeling will begin to creep back into your consciousness. This is the first key! Personal Power and Self-Mastery are nothing more than an attitude that you hold in your mind, which you start your day with and keep affirming to yourself all day long whenever you feel the need to. You will immediately feel better every time when you do a Personal Power and Self-Mastery affirmation. You must be in control of your thoughts, feelings, emotions, energy and physical body to not have fear!

The second key to releasing fear and worry is to place around yourself, every morning to start your day, a semi-permeable Golden Bubble of Protection that keeps out negativity from self and others and allows in only Spiritual and positive thoughts, feelings and energies. This will give you the appropriate sense of invulnerability, and the sense that you cause your reality and are not a victim of your own thoughts, feelings, emotions and energies and those of other people. Others people's negative energies will also then slide off your Golden Bubble of Protection like "water off a duck's back"! This is the second key principle to release fear and worry!

The third key principle to releasing fear and worry is unconditional love towards self and others. It is impossible to release fear unless you adopt an attitude of unconditional love at all times. This is because the opposite of Love is attack and fear! If you don't approach self, people and life with unconditional love then you will approach it with attack and judgement. By the law of karma within your own mind you will live in fear!

The fourth key principle to releasing fear and worry is Prayer! As the Universal Mind said through Edgar Cayce, "Why worry when you can pray?" Every time you worry you should pray! You will find that this instantly causes worry to go away, for what is more powerful than GOD, the Angels and the Masters to help you with whatever you need?

The fifth key principle to releasing fear is doing affirmations! Every time a fear-based thought or feeling enters your mind immediately do a Spiritual/Christ/Buddha affirmation of some kind. There are only two ways of thinking in the world. You either think with your negative ego/fear-based/separative mind, or you think with your Spiritual/Christ/Buddha mind. All fear will be released if every time a fear-based thought or feeling arises you push it out of your mind, and replace it with a Spiritual/Love-based/Christed/Buddha type thought, feeling and/or affirmation. This is the fifth key principle to removing all fear and worry from yourself and your life!

The sixth key principle to release all fear and worry is Faith! Throughout your day at different times, affirm your faith in yourself and your own abilities to Master, Cause, and Create your life and your total faith in GOD, the Ascended Masters, and the Angels! Your thoughts create your reality! If you affirm this it will be so!

The seventh and last principle to releasing fear is to maintain Spiritual Attunement with GOD, your Mighty I Am Presence, the inner plane Ascended Masters, and the Archangels and Angels. What manifests in life is where you put your attention and consciousness. If you keep your consciousness and mind steady in the Light, what is to fear? The idle mind is the devil's workshop! If you allow yourself to lose your attunement to GOD and the Masters then it will drift to the lower-self instead of your Higher Self, and this will cause fear! The fear is only caused by allowing yourself to be too much on automatic pilot and your mind too idle. Keep your consciousness, mind, and activities always in GOD attunement, GOD thoughts, GOD feelings, and GOD activities, and fear will never surface unless you allow it to!

You, my Beloved Readers, are co-creators with GOD, and are Sons and Daughters of GOD made in His image, and you cause and create your own reality!

CHAPTER 8

The Seven Step Process for Releasing Anger

"Aggression, fear, anger...the dark side are they."

Yoda

This is an extremely important chapter, for two of the most common negative feelings and emotions that occur in people's lives are fear and anger. I have already addressed how to release fear from your life in another chapter. Now I will show you how to release anger! This is possible because it is our thoughts that create our reality! It is our thoughts that cause our feelings and emotions! To release anger from our lives, it is just a matter of understanding what attitudes, thoughts and beliefs create anger. By examining these simple attitudes every time any anger arises you can simply release it, for you will always find the cause in one of these attitudes and/or faulty beliefs! This may be one of the simplest but most profound and useful chapters in this book!

The first attitude that causes anger is not owning your personal power! The definition of anger is "a loss of control and an attempt to regain it"! If you always remain in your 100% personal power then you never have to lose control! The idea is to stay in your 100% personal power even when something in your life goes wrong!

The second key attitude to releasing anger is not maintaining or keeping up your "Golden Bubble of Light Protection" 100% of the time! This "Golden Bubble of Light Protection," which you place around yourself religiously every morning when you get up, allows other people's negativity to slide off your bubble like "water off a duck's back"! Or, it bounces off like a rubber pillow! Without this golden bubble, other people's attacks, criticism and negative energy can lodge in your subconscious mind and solar plexus and cause a defense and anger reaction. The ideal is to respond to life and not react. The ideal in life is to be a cause not an effect! The ideal is to be a master not a victim! Keeping your golden bubble of protection up allows you to do this! This golden bubble of protection ideally also protects you from your own negative thoughts, feelings, and content of consciousness. In others words, all thoughts, feelings and content of your own consciousness also must stop at the gate of the golden bubble; so that you are consciously monitoring and being vigilant over your consciousness to make sure that no thoughts, feelings, emotions, desires, impulses, or anything else enters your consciousness that is not of GOD! The ideal is to deny any thought, feeling, impulse, desire, motive, or piece of energy that is not of GOD to enter your consciousness or mind! This is the key to maintaining inner peace. It is as simple as keeping a good mental and emotional diet! The ideal is to push negative ego/fear-based/separative thoughts, feelings and impulses out of your consciousness and/or mind and to constantly affirm Spiritual/Christ/Buddha thoughts, feelings, impulses and motives! The continual process of doing this reprograms the conscious and subconscious thinking over time and you develop the Spiritual habit of only interpreting and perceiving life from your

Spiritual/Christ/Buddha mind! This is why the golden bubble is so important and such a key to releasing any and all anger!

The third key to releasing anger is letting go of attachments. As Buddha said in his Four Noble Truths, all suffering comes from attachments. Whenever you are angry you are attached, and this is a fact! The Spiritual ideal is to change all attachment attitudes to preferences! A preference attitude is one where you still go after what you want with all your heart and soul and mind and might, but if you don't get it you still are happy! Where with attachments you lose your happiness if you don't get what you want. So take some time to introspect, meditate and/or journal write and change every single thing in life you are attached to into a preference! This way, if it is taken away you still have inner peace and happiness! Happiness then becomes a state of mind, rather than something that is controlled by something outside of self!

The fourth step to releasing anger is the necessity to look at everything that happens in life as a "Spiritual test and lesson," not as some kind of bummer and problem! Every time you get angry you are forgetting to look at life as a Spiritual test and lesson! Remember that everything that happens in life is happening for a reason! Everything that happens is GOD and/or life teaching you something! Even most lightworkers who know this forget it and fall back into getting overinvolved with Earth life. They forget that the real purpose of Earth life is nothing more than to see if you can respond to everything that happens in life in a centered, Spiritual/Christ/Buddha consciousness, unconditionally loving, forgiving, and nonjudgmental manner! In every situation of life we either respond from our negative ego/fear-based/separative mind or the Spiritual/Christ/Buddha mind! We either Realize God in that mind or lose God in terms of our realization by how we respond!

The fifth key attitude to releasing anger is to always remember that you cause your own reality! You are a Master, not a victim! You are a cause, not an effect! You cause your own feelings and emotions by how you think! Feelings and emotions are not caused by outside situations and they are not caused by other people! No one has ever in the history of time ever caused you to feel anything! They may have attacked you or criticized you unfairly, but that did not cause you to feel anything! That is what is called the "catalyst"! The cause is your own choices, beliefs and thoughts! If you would have maintained your personal power, let it slide off your bubble, remained centered, not been attached, responded rather than reacted, and not given your power to control your feelings and emotions you would have been fine. It would have slid off your bubble and you would just respond back in a centered, powerful, calm, rational, unconditionally loving manner, setting a better example! The truth is, you are invulnerable psychologically, mentally and emotionally! No one can make you think anything you don't want to! No one can make you feel anything you don't want to. You cause your own reality by how you think! You cause how you feel by how you think! It is just a matter of understanding what thoughts cause what feelings and emotions. This is what I am teaching you in this chapter and this is what I am teaching you to do in this book! The Spiritual path is about becoming a Spiritual master and achieving self-mastery! Even children can do this! Does not a child say "Sticks and stones can break my bones but names can never hurt me"! A child is affirming their psychological and/or mental and emotional invulnerability at that moment! I think this point is clearly made now I think!

The sixth key to releasing anger is to always seek to maintain love within self and from GOD first before seeking it from others. In other words unconditionally love yourself and your inner child! Also fully allow yourself to receive GOD's and the Masters' love for you! This way, before you enter the world you are totally complete and whole within yourself. You go into life knowing you unconditionally love yourself, and you know fully that GOD, the Masters and Angels totally unconditionally love you! This way you go into life feeling filled with love! If you don't do this you are not feeling loved, and hence you will seek love from others instead of finding it first within your relationship to self and relationship to GOD! This will throw your psychological balance off-kilter and throw you back into a type of victim consciousness again! This is the sixth key to releasing anger!

The seventh key to releasing anger is to remember that anger is a form of attack! One of the premiere principles of the Christ consciousness, Buddha consciousness and/or Spiritual consciousness of any Spiritual path or religion is to give up and release all "attack thoughts"! Attack is antithetical to unconditional love! It is the opposite of love! Always remember that anytime a person attacks, they are feeling fear! There are only two emotions in life: love and fear! So always remember, if someone attacks you and negatively criticizes you, they are feeling fearful! So the essence of what is happening here is that, in truth, from GOD's perspective, an "attack is a call for love"! My Beloved Readers, remember if you ever get angry or are beginning to attack, what you really want is unconditional love! Anger is the negative ego thought system's misguided and faulty thinking way of trying to get love! The truth is, however, anger will have only the opposite affect. It will cause the other to become defensive, hurt, and judged, and if they are a victim, which most are, then they will react and not respond, and attack and judge back! Does this serve you and does this serve them? They purpose of life is to be "egoless"! Sai Baba has said the definition of GOD is "GOD equals man minus ego!" You are here to set a better example! Anger will not get you what you want! It will create the opposite. It will create separation and this is not what you want to feel and it is not what you want to teach! Anger is just the negative ego's fearful reactive response! The key is to transcend both fear and anger, which are the two sides of the negative ego philosophy and thought system, and to instead think with your Spiritual/Christ/Buddha mind, which only thinks from the heart and from unconditional love! It transcends this negative ego faulty way of thinking! As Master Yoda of *Star Wars* said, "Do not give into your anger and fear and become seduced by the dark side of the force!" We are here to live in the light! We are here to live in unconditional love, forgiveness, nonjudgmentalness, defenselessness, harmlessness, humility, humbleness, gentleness, patience, tolerance, turning of the other cheek, love your enemies and setting of a better example! You are in your personal power, your golden bubble, and are the cause of your reality, feelings and emotions, so what other people do has no effect on you. You are invulnerable, so what does it matter if other people are into their negative ego or they attack or criticize? That is their lesson between themselves and GOD! All that matters is you wanting to learn your Spiritual lesson and pass your Spiritual test! If you don't, my friends, you will have to reincarnate and do it in the next lifetime! So take the loving advice of your Spiritual brother and learn this lesson now! If you learn the lesson and the other person doesn't, you are freed from the karma! They will have to reincarnate and you won't! This last statement is the ultimate specific motivator for learning this lesson!

In conclusion, the final thing I wish to say on this subject is that it is totally appropriate and necessary in life to own your personal power and be very tough in life! It is necessary in life to sometimes manifest what I call tough love! It is also necessary on this planet, especially in early stages of the Spiritual path until self-mastery is fully gained, to manifest what I would call being a Spiritual warrior in life! This is a very difficult Spiritual school and it takes great courage to live on this Earth and make it through all the lessons at this stage in Earth's history! So at times it may be necessary to muster up Spiritual warrior energy to make it through the difficult times and metaphysical or psychological storms, hurricanes and tornadoes of life! However, a great many people on Earth use anger as a replacement for true personal power and this is not good! Anger is not personal power and self-mastery, it is a demonstration of being out of control! It is a false sense of power that stems from the negative ego! To truly become a Spiritual Master you must replace anger with true personal power! If you always own your personal power then you will never have a need to be angry! If you ever do start to get angry, channel that energy immediately into a creative usage of personal power! Just redirect it with the power of your mind, so it becomes true personal power and Spiritual warrior energy instead of anger. In time as you master these lessons you will find that you have developed a Spiritual habit of being in your personal power all the time and it will be easy. Life will no longer be a struggle, for you will have fundamentally mastered your thoughts, feelings, emotions, subconscious mind, negative ego thought system, and lower-self desire, and are properly parenting your inner child! Then you will have a habit of always interpreting yourself and your life from the Spiritual/Christ/Buddha mind, which will make life no longer a struggle and you will no longer even need to even call on the Spiritual warrior quality within.

These, my Beloved Readers, are the seven great steps to releasing anger and are the process you will go through and are going through right now as we speak to achieve this! Your consciousness has already, by reading this chapter, been completely reprogrammed from the negative ego mind's faulty thinking! Now all you have to do from this moment forward is to be joyously vigilant of all that has been said, so it can become a Spiritual habit! It only takes 21 days to cement a new habit into the subconscious mind! You have it now, just maintain and hold it so it can become a habit! If anger arises just examine these seven steps and you will immediately find the cause of the anger in one of these steps! As you do, do a quick attitudinal adjustment in your mind and you will see the anger instantly disappear! This is an indisputable fact for we are dealing with psychological laws here! Since these are psychological laws and principles they will work every time! If you make a mistake, just stop, gain the golden nugget of wisdom, learn the lesson, make the attitudinal adjustment, and become joyously vigilant once again! My Beloved Readers, I promise you that in the shortest amount of time, if you follow this simple guidance, this will become a Spiritual habit and you will not only transcend all anger, you will transcend the entire negative ego thought system and all negative ego feelings and emotions!

So let it be Written! So let it be Done! The Force is with you my friends!

"Judge me by my size, do you? As well you should not, for my ally is the Force. And a powerful ally it is. Life creates it. Makes it grow."

Yoda

CHAPTER 9

Daily Spiritual Affirmations to Work With

One of the most important and effective tools to maintain self-mastery, reprogram the subconscious mind, and keep one's consciousness in Spiritual/Christ/Buddha consciousness at all times is affirmations! These affirmations I have provided here are specifically created and designed by Spirit, the Masters and myself to do the trick like no others!

The absolute keys to Psychospiritual health are:

- Learning to own your personal power.
- Developing unconditional self-love and self-worth.
- Developing Spiritual attunement and Faith!
- Keeping up your Golden Bubble of Protection.
- Maintaining good physical health.

The following Affirmations are the best I have ever found to help you achieve and maintain these qualities! I recommend doing them three times a day for a minimum of 21, days and to pick out your favorite ones and to keep them with you, and use them any time you need a little pumping up, so to speak, in your mental and emotional body! I know you will enjoy working with them!

Affirmations

Personal Power and Becoming a Creative Cause

- I am the power, the master, and the cause of my attitudes, feelings, emotions, and behavior.
- I am 100% powerful, loving, and balanced at all times.
- I am powerful, whole, and complete within myself. I have preferences but not attachments.
- I am 100% powerful and decisive in everything I do.
- I have perfect mastery and control over all my energies in service of a loving spiritual purpose.
- I am the master and director of my life, and my subconscious mind is my friend and servant.
- I am a center of pure self-consciousness and will, with the ability to direct my energies wherever I would have them go.
- I am powerful, centered, and loving at all times.
- I am powerful and centered at all times, and I will allow nothing in this external universe to knock me off-balance or center.
- I have 100% personal power and I vow never to give it to my subconscious mind or other people ever again.
- I have perfect self-control and self-mastery in everything I do.

Self-Love Affirmations

The following are self-love affirmations for reprogramming your conscious and subconscious thinking:

- I love and forgive myself totally for all my mistakes, for I now recognize that mistakes are positive, not negative.

- I now fully recognize that I have worth because God created me, and I do not have to do anything to earn it.

- I now recognize that I am a diamond, not the mud on the diamond.

- My worth is unchangingly positive because it is a spiritual inheritance. It is not increased by my success nor decreased by my mistakes.

- I realize now that I have total worth and value as a person, whether I learn my lessons in life or not.

- I now recognize that everything that has ever happened in my life has been positive, because it all contained lessons I needed to learn.

- I choose to live in the "now" and not hold the past against myself.

- I hereby choose to approve of myself, so I do not have to go around seeking approval from others.

- I deserve love because God created me, and my mistakes are not held against me.

- I realize that everything that happens in life is a teaching, a lesson, a challenge, and an opportunity to grow.

- I now realize that I am the "I" person, chooser, consciousness, and spiritual being, and that this part of me deserves unconditional love at all times.

- I am the light and not the lampshade over the light.

- I deserve love because my true identity is not what I do in life. I am the "chooser" of what I do.

- I now understand that I am here to learn lessons and grow in life, but if I make mistakes I am still totally lovable and unchangable worthy.
- I hereby choose the attitude of being very firm with myself and unconditionally loving.
- I am the master of my life and I choose to be my own best friend instead of my own worst enemy.
- I choose to love me as God loves me unconditionally.
- I now choose to truly understand that I want to be perfect, with the understanding that mistakes are positive, and part and parcel of the growing process.
- I now realize on the level of my true identity that I am the "I," the chooser, the person, the spiritual being, the soul. I am a perfect equal with every other person in the world.
- I now choose to awaken and recognize that it was only the faulty thinking of my ego that has caused me not to love myself.
- I now choose to undo all the faulty thinking that society has programmed into me and replace it with self-love.
- I choose to recognize that I deserve love and so do other people.
- I choose to recognize that I am guiltless and sinless, because all mistakes are just lessons and opportunities to grow. Mistakes, in reality, are golden nuggets of wisdom and are positive.
- I now realize that God does not hold my misuse of free choice against me, so why should I?
- I love me. I forgive me. I approve of me, and I commit myself from this moment onward to treating myself in a spiritual manner rather than in an egotistical manner. I now fully realize that the way in which I think is the reality in which I live. I have been living in my own self-created hell of faulty thinking. I now choose

to and will live in my self-created heavenly state of consciousness. It is really that simple.

- I unconditionally love me because I am a son/daughter of God, and my misuse of free choice or faulty thinking is not held against me.
- Could what God created not be lovable and worthy?
- I love me because I am innocent and not guilty.
- The only thing in this infinite universe that says I do not deserve love is my "ego." I hereby reject my ego and its false attitude and get back in tune with my true spiritual attitude and self.
- I now, once and for all, release the ego's game of "having to do" in order to deserve love and worth. I now fully recognize that I have always been lovable and worthy and will always be so.

My Favorite Affirmations: Guaranteed to Make you Feel Better if said with Regularity and Enthusiasm!!!

- Mental strength, physical strength, spiritual strength!!!
- Personal power, positive anger, mental strength!!!
- I am the power, I am the master, I am the cause.
- I'm mad as hell and I'm not going to take it anymore.
- Get thee behind me, Satan!!!
- I have perfect faith and trust in God!!!
- Personal power, positive anger, eye of the tiger, and faith, trust and patience in God!!!
- Personal power, causality, steel-like mastery!!!
- The power of my three minds makes me the omnipotent force in this universe!
- God, my personal power and the power of my subconscious mind are an unbeatable team!!!

- My mind power and spirit power are an unbeatable team!!!
- Be still and know that I am God.
- Father, I thank you for the miraculous healing of my...
- "Water off a duck's back," "water off a window pane," invulnerability, invincibility, rubber pillow, filter...
- God, God, God, Christ, Christ, Christ, Jesus Christ, Jesus Christ, Jesus Christ!!!
- Absolute total supreme mastery...
- Tough love, tough love, tough love!!!
- Mental power, physical power, spiritual power!!!
- Faith, trust, patience in God!!!
- Fake it 'til I make it, fake it 'til I make it...
- Every day in every way I am getting stronger and healthier!!!
- God is my co-pilot!!!
- With my power and God's Power and the power of my subconscious I cannot and will not be stopped!!!
- All out war against Satan, for God and love and positivity!!!
- I will be more powerful from this moment forward than I have ever been in my entire life!!!
- As God is my witness, I will not be stopped!!!
- The Force is with me and I am with the Force!!!
- The Source is with me and I am with the Source!!!
- I am sustained by the Love of God!!!
- I can do all things with God, Christ, and my higher-self who strengthens me!!!
- As God is my witness, I will never give away my power to anyone or anything ever again!!!

- God, my personal power, and the power of my subconscious mind!!!
- Not my will, but Thine, thank you for the lesson!!!
- I may lose a few battles, but I am going to win the war!!!
- I declare all-out joyous vigilance to get my life together!!!
- I am going to be the absolute master of my life from this day and moment forward!!!
- God goes with me wherever I go!!!

Read the affirmations again and this time say them with enthusiasm!!!

- I love God with all my heart and soul and mind and might, and I love my neighbor as myself.

Read each affirmation three to seven times!

Emotional Invulnerability

- I am 100% invulnerable to other people's negative energy. Other people's negative energy slides off me like "water off a duck's back."
- I am the cause of my feelings and emotions, not other people. I will not give them this power over me ever again.
- Other people's negative energy bounces off me like a rubber pillow.
- I hear what other people have to say to me. However, I internalize only that which "I choose" to internalize.
- The only effect other people's negative energy has is the effect I let it have. I choose not to be affected ever again.

Trust, and Patience Affirmations

- I have perfect faith, trust, and patience in my Higher Self.

- I have perfect faith and trust that God is now providing for my every need.
- I hereby surrender all problems and challenges into God's hands.
- Why worry when I can pray?
- With God helping me I will succeed for sure.
- I have perfect faith in my own power as well as perfect faith and trust in God's power.
- I have invited God's help, and I know his invisible hands are now working in my life to answer my prayers.
- I have invited God's help and I have perfect faith, trust, and patience He will provide me with what I want, or something better.
- I have asked and I know I shall receive.
- I know God will answer my prayer, in His time not mine, and I will have perfect faith, trust, and patience until that time comes.
- If my prayer isn't answered in exactly the way I want, I know that this is a lesson He would have me learn.
- I have perfect faith, trust, and patience that God will answer my every prayer.
- Prayer, personal power, and affirmations and visualizations are an unbeatable team.
- I have perfect faith, trust, and patience in my self, my superconscious mind, and the power of my subconscious mind to attract and magnetize to me everything I need.

Physical Health Affirmations

- My physical body is in perfect radiant health.
- My physical body now manifests the health and perfection of Christ.
- Every day in every way I am getting better and better.

- I am physically fit with an abundance of energy.
- I sleep soundly and deeply every night and wake up fully rested and refreshed early every morning.
- Father, I thank You for my long and healthy life in your service.
- Father, I thank You for my unlimited increase in the power and energy of my physical battery.
- God, my personal power, and the power of my subconscious mind are now healing, energizing, and strengthening my physical body.
- My physical body is now healing with Godspeed.
- God, my personal power, and the power of my subconscious mind are now returning my body to perfect radiant health.
- Be still, and know that I am God, and my physical body now manifests the health and perfection of Christ.
- Father, I thank You for the unlimited increase in the functioning of my glandular system.
- My glandular system is now operating at its full Christ potential.
- My thymus gland and immune system are now operating at their full Christ potential.
- I am a son or daughter of God, so I cannot possibly be sick.
- God, my personal power, and the power of my subconscious mind are now revitalizing, recharging, and awakening my physical body.
- I am in love with physical exercise, and I am now being filled with an abundance of physical energy.

CHAPTER 10

Developing an Efficient Perception of Reality

In my opinion, one of the most important lessons of life is developing an efficient perception of reality. As we all know, our thoughts create our reality. The mind, in truth, is an amazing process. Whatever we think seems totally real. When a person feels depressed, which of course is created by their thinking, it seems totally real. When a person feels anger, which of course is created by their mind, it seems totally real. The nature of the mind is that however you interpret yourself and life will be the dream you live in. Some people live in a self-created hell, and some live in a self-created heaven. Most people create a combination of both. The purpose of life is, of course, to live in a self-created heaven.

Islamic Fundamentalist Muslims who attack a U.S. Embassy through terrorism really feel that what they are doing is right. People who are involved with cults really believe that what they are doing is the highest form of Spiritual truth. Almost everyone who is involved with a form of psychology or particular workshop or seminar thinks theirs is the best. The same is true of religion and the same is true of different Spiritual paths. Now part of this is the negative ego's need to be the best. Part of this is that we get locked into lenses and we do not realize that we are not seeing from a full-spectrum prism perspective.

The importance of learning to think properly about self and to see life with an efficient perception of reality cannot be underestimated. Every faulty thought about self and GOD will cause you to see the rest of life from an imbalanced perspective. Every imbalanced, negative ego, or faulty thought or belief will cause you to have a blind spot within self and in how you see your world. There are infinite numbers of faulty thoughts, for every Christ/Buddha thought has an opposite negative ego and/or fear-based separative thought. When people see life through the negative ego's eyes, everything they experience seems totally real and all their thoughts, emotions, and actions seem justified, even though they are living out complete illusion.

Have you ever noticed that when you dream at night while you are in the dream everything seems real? You may be having a nightmare and it seems totally real. You may be obsessing about some crazy thought the entire night that seemed totally real all night, yet when you wake up in the morning you say to yourself, "That is the most ridiculous thing I have ever heard of. What was I doing all night?"

This is very much like how life is. The only difference is that most people have not awakened to the fact that they are still in negative hypnosis and are still dreaming. This is because everything we think causes us to feel the way we do, and it seems and feels right. This is true from the negative ego's perspective, but is completely illusionary when seen from a Christ/Buddha perspective.

A person who feels righteously angry really feels justified in this response. However, in truth they are just indulging their negative ego. Anti-abortion activists who kill doctors to save babies really think that what they are doing is right, and they think they are doing this for GOD.

In truth, however, they are completely delusionary in their thinking and behavior. Self-righteous opinionated politicians tainted by misguided fundamentalist values really think that what they are doing is right. They really think that they have GOD on their side. Well, at times they might. However, a great deal of the time they don't, because their beliefs are not coming from GOD, they are coming from a misguided negative ego that has misinterpreted Spirit's true message. AIDS activists who act out at group meetings in a very rude and disrespectful manner really feel that what they are doing is right. They feel this way because they have no understanding of what negative ego is. From the negative ego and personality level perspective it is right, but it is not right from the Soul's perspective and Spirit's perspective.

I have seen Mafia members interviewed on television who have killed hundreds of people, and they are now in jail and they feel what they did was justified and they feel no remorse. An animal activist throws paint on someone wearing a fur coat. Is this right? The animal activist thinks so. I would suggest it is not, from the perspective of the Soul.

My Beloved Readers, people determine truth for themselves depending on their belief system. If you believe in Humanistic psychology then it is alright to express your emotions whenever and wherever you want, even if you attack and hurt people. If one has that philosophy then that person feels quite self-righteous in doing what they are doing. If one is a Fundamentalist Christian, then one feels justified in calling everyone who doesn't believe what they believe being run by the devil. A fundamentalist would also believe that there is only one path to God, and all other paths, including the New Age Movement, are of the devil.

If you are a follower of Carl Jung you must own your shadow. If you are a Behaviorist then we have no free choice, and we are all rats in a maze receiving positive and/or negative reinforcement. My Beloved Readers, is not the mind a funny thing? People get stuck in philosophies and psychologies of all kinds and think they are truth. Each group thinks theirs is the best, until fifteen years later when they find out they have been involved in a cult. This world is filled with so much illusion, glamour, and maya. It is amazing. People also get stuck in a certain lens and think that is truth.

Even a Planetary Ascended Master will have to release many concepts as they evolve to a Solar, Galactic, Universal, Multi-Universal and Cosmic level. Many people hold onto past Spiritual teachings that were true fifty years ago or true 100 years ago but are not as true now. Even Djwhal Khul said that some of what was said in the Alice Bailey books forty years ago would not be applicable in this present time. It was not that what he said was wrong. It was 100% true when he wrote it, but things evolve. That is why Djwhal is constantly bringing through new revelations. There are an enormous number of people who are stuck on past time lines and are not allowing themselves to evolve and receive new revelations.

This is why, my Beloved Readers, it is a good idea to be one hundred percent confident in one's truth but not self-righteous in one's truth. This also brings us to a very key question and that is, "What is truth?" Some would say that truth is relative to each person. I would say this is another negative ego-run belief system. In my opinion there certainly is truth and there certainly is illusion whether people want to believe it or not. What is true is that which comes from GOD or the Holy Spirit or the Mighty I Am Presence perspective. What is illusion is that which comes from the negative ego/fear-based/separative/lower-self thought system. This is why Sai Baba says, "GOD equals man minus ego." The negative ego is illusion, for it is based on a belief in separation from GOD and overidentification with matter that does not really exist in truth. It is a separative self that we created with our free choice that does not really exist. The law of the mind, however, is that your thoughts create your reality, and you will live in the thought creation of your own making.

What is true is the Christ/Buddha/Spiritual thought system. What is illusion is the negative ego thought system. What is true is Love, and what is untrue is fear. What is true is oneness, and what is untrue is separation.

What is *true* is forgiveness, and what is *untrue* is holding grudges and what is untrue is negativity. What is *true* is positivity, and what is untrue is judgement. What is true is nonjudgementalness.

Now it is true in my opinion that there are some aspects of life where truth is relative. An example of this might be in looking at a painting. One person might like the painting and another person may find it completely unappealing. Who is right? In matters of taste there is no dispute. Beauty is in the eye of the beholder. There is a great deal of truth that is relative to each person. Not everyone should live in the same place or wear the same type of clothes, or even follow the same Spiritual path. This is something that each person must seek within oneself. There are, however, "Transcendent Truths which everyone falls under." Any given individual may believe that they do not have to try and transcend their negative ego and lower-self consciousness. They have free choice and can do this if they wish. However, they will not achieve liberation from the wheel of rebirth on all levels. They will not have inner peace, and they will not realize GOD, and this is a fact. They will also not be allowed to pass all their initiations. I like what *A Course In Miracles* says about this in its introduction. It says it is a required course. By this it is saying not that one must read that particular book, but rather that learning to transcend negative ego consciousness is a required course. If you want to learn this through a Christian orientation, Buddhist orientation, Eastern religion orientation, or Ascension orientation that is up to you, but it is a required course. Now, if someone with their free choice does not want to learn these lessons, that is up to them. They can spend eternity on the astral plane if they want to, and they have one hundred percent free choice to do this if they want. They will not be learning their lessons from GOD's perspective. However, they do have the free choice right to do this if they want.

What is amazing is that even Archangels can be taken over by delusion. Did not Lucifer fall from grace? I have personally seen a great many high level initiates and Masters fall, who were anywhere from the seventh initiation to almost the twelfth initiation. Always remember that initiations have to do with light quotient, not with psychospiritual development. Also, just because one has mastery over this process in one phase of one's life doesn't mean they will have mastery over it their entire life. There are a great many Spiritual tests on the Spiritual path, and passing them in one phase doesn't guarantee you will pass them in another. The truth is, most do not. The higher one goes the narrower the path becomes. Even as a twelfth degree initiate and a world famous Spiritual leader, it is a slippery slope. One can fall off the mountain at any moment, and slide down or take a tumble down the mountain at any moment. The negative ego's thirst for power, fame, money, and sex is amazing. The negative ego's thought system, although completely insane, is incredibly tricky and seductive. Out of every one million high level initiates who fall from grace, every single one of that million thinks they have not. Let this be a warning to us all. Very few souls are able to truly keep their GOD purity throughout an entire lifetime especially when power, fame, and fortune come. Most of this stems from overdevelopment in the Spiritual body and underdevelopment in the psychological self. This ultimately leads to corruption and massive negative ego contamination. Even John in the Bible, the apostle of Christ, denied Jesus three times after his death. This is not a judgement, just a reemphasis of how incredibly tricky the negative ego is. To learn to master it, one must become a master psychologist, even if one does not have or ever wants a degree in this field. The negative ego is absolutely brilliant in its ability to deceive. If there is the slightest opening you give it on any level, it will grab it. A great many of my books have been written to help lightworkers to close these doors.

So indeed, my Beloved Readers, there is a Transcendent Truth we each must strive for to Realize GOD. Any person, disciple, initiate, Master, or Archangel can fall at any time. It is hard to believe, but there is a whole hierarchy of beings who have chosen the left hand or dark path and have banded together for purposes of an anti-Christ nature.

These are Sons and Daughters of GOD who have been taken over by the negative ego, and might be called confused souls. They do everything in their power to stop the plan of GOD and to sabotage lightworkers. This is nothing to be concerned about for you cause your own reality, and they have no effect on you as long as you stay in the Light. The best approach is to never think about them and give them any energy, for thinking about them tends to attract them. I bring up this subject to point out only that the possibly billions of souls who have taken this path actually think what they are doing is right. They honestly believe this. I bring this up to emphasize to you over and over again the delusionary nature of the negative ego.

I ask you, how do so many souls get caught up in cults and with false prophets and Spiritual teachers who are totally fragmented and run by their negative egos? This is because they are not psychologically centered and the negative ego is running them. When the negative ego runs a person it blinds them to seeing the negative ego outside of themselves as well. My Beloved Readers, 99% of the world is run by the negative ego to one degree or another. Again this stems from lack of proper education and training. People have not been trained how to master their mind, feelings, emotions, body, inner child, desire body, and negative ego thought system and to replace it with the Christ/Buddha thought system. I share this with you to emphasize again how incredibly tricky and slippery the negative thought system is. All it takes is a single moment of automatic pilot to fall back into it again even if you have been out of it for some time. The most amazing thing is that 99% of the time when this happens, all over the world, people do not know this has happened, and if you asked them they will tell you they are totally centered and clear. I have seen some of the most severe manifestations of disturbed behavior, self-aggrandizement, and ego trips you could possibly imagine. Not only do the people caught up in this not see it, even their followers and most lightworkers in the New Age movement can't see it. It absolutely blows my mind. This occurs because we do not just see with our physical eyes, we see with our mind. We can only see according to the development of our psychological and spiritual consciousness. Most lightworkers have not been trained enough on the psychological level and so they have massive, massive blind spots in their spiritual discernment. A great many lightworkers are ascending or achieving their sixth or seventh initiation. Unfortunately, however, most of them are still in the category of what I would call "fragmented ascension." That is when ascension and initiations that have been achieved in the Spiritual body, but have not been integrated properly into the mental, emotional, etheric and physical bodies.

So, my Beloved Readers, developing an efficient perception of reality is a lifelong process. As soon as you think you have it mastered is just when you are about to fall. "After pride cometh the fall." This is why every thought you think and every feeling you allow yourself to create must be examined. Deny any thought not of GOD to enter your mind. Be joyously vigilant at all times! Try most importantly to retain your GOD purity at all times. Be devastatingly honest with self, and examine your motivations for everything you do. This chapter has been written as a wake-up call to you, my Beloved Readers, as to how easy it is to be deceived and taken over by the negative ego. It is also a wake-up call to emphasize the importance of developing an efficient perception of reality. It is also a wake-up call to emphasize the importance of doing your psychological homework, not just your spiritual homework. If so many people, lightworkers, disciples, devotees, high-level initiates, masters, and even archangels have been taken over and don't even know it, don't think for a minute that it cannot happen to you. The second you think this, you have already fallen! I leave you with the words, "Be ever vigilant for GOD and his Kingdom!"

CHAPTER 11

The Development of One's Conscience

The development of one's conscience is an extremely important aspect of becoming a God Realized being. Our conscience is the aspect of self that tells us right from wrong. It is our "moral compass," so to speak. It is quite interesting to me that a great many people, even in the Spiritual movement, do not have a very developed conscience. I know for myself, as an example, that I have a very highly developed conscience. If I do something wrong, my conscience lets me know and I do everything in my power to correct myself and the situation anytime this happens. I am not a victim of my conscience, for it is important to be the master of all one's energies, however my conscience is highly developed and this is something I feel good about.

I see a great many people who do not have a very developed conscience and this amazes me. As a Spiritual psychologist, I am writing this chapter to help explore why and how this happens, and how one can have a highly developed conscience.

The first aspect of understanding why some people do not have a very developed conscience is that they are not connected to their Spiritual life. Without a Spiritual life their "Moral Code" is basically to do what they feel. Without a Spiritual life, one's feelings will be greatly run by the negative ego and the lower-self. They will also be disconnected from their Higher Self, Oversoul, and Mighty I Am Presence. This may be hard to believe for some. However, the truth is, these Spiritual aspects of self do not pay much attention to the incarnated Soul until the incarnated Soul begins to pay attention to Spirit. The Higher Self and/or Holy Spirit will also let you know when you are doing something wrong. The problem is most people in this world including a great number of lightworkers are extremely ego-defended. Now, it is understandable how someone could not have a developed conscience if they are not open to their Spiritual life. It is not, however, as easy to understand how this happens with lightworkers.

I personally know lightworkers who are absolute sociopaths and pathological liars. A sociopath could be defined as a person with no conscience. They are so self-centered and run by the negative ego that they will say and do anything, and lie to your face over and over again and not even be bothered by it. This amazes me because in my reality, being in integrity goes along with having a highly developed conscience. I am amazed that people like this can even sleep at night. If I acted that way I certainly wouldn't be able to. What is amazing is the people I am thinking of are into channeling and all kinds of Spiritual stuff. Yet they have almost zero integrity and clearly no conscience. How can this be? How can one be on a Spiritual path and into channeling and practicing channeling, and communicating with the Masters, and yet be a total sociopath and pathological liar? This just goes to show the potentiality for fragmentation and disintegration in lightworkers. This, of course, is an extreme case. However, I could give you tens of thousands of examples of lightworkers who are in the gray area and maybe not so black and white as this. I have known tenth and eleventh degree initiates who are extraordinarily lacking in integrity and whom I would call borderline pathological liars. How can this take place? Again it shows the potential for fragmentation and disintegration of high level initiates and even Spiritual leaders. So the key question is what causes this? It is caused by two things: lack of proper psychological training and, hence, the individual being run by the negative ego. The most amazing thing about this process in the examples I have given is the people I have mentioned, and all the people I am speaking about in the gray area, do not have a clue this is going on. This is the degree to which people can of course be deluded by the mind, the negative ego and their feelings and emotions. If you would ask these people if they have a conscience, or are in integrity, and are being honest with themselves and others, every single one will say "yes" and think they are being in complete integrity. When the truth is, from the vision of Spirit, they are being run by their self-centered emotions, negative ego, thirst for power, money, and fame, and do not have a clue that their motives are selfish to the core. This is, again, the incredible potential delusionary nature of the negative ego mind.

So in examining this issue from a Spiritually scientific perspective, we begin to see the development of conscience comes from two places. It comes directly from Spirit and it also comes directly from within one's psychological self. Most people in this world are run by the negative ego. This is why they have a hard time admitting mistakes, apologizing for mistakes, and seeing the infinite number of ways the negative ego causes one to be run by fear and self-centered motives. Most people in this world have not been trained to know that there are only two ways of thinking. One either thinks from the negative ego's perspective or they think from a Spiritual perspective. The amazing thing about the negative ego is that it will convince Spiritual people that they are being Spiritual, when in truth, they are being run by the negative ego.

So, my beloved readers, the development of conscience is blocked first off when one allows oneself to be run by one's feelings and emotions. To allow oneself to be run by one's feelings and emotions is a prescription to be run by the negative ego. Most people on Earth are run by their feelings and emotions. They believe this is the proper way to live and they do not understand that their thoughts are creating their feelings and emotions. They believe that all their negative feelings and emotions are real and come from outside of themselves. This irresponsible philosophy causes them to do what they feel instead of being in integrity and listening to their conscience. Their conscience is, in a sense, drowned out by their overindulgence in their emotional body.

Other people's conscience is drowned out by their letting their mind run them, and they are so run by all the thoughts in their mind that this, like the feelings and emotions, drowns out the voice of the Higher Self and the Holy Spirit, as well as the psychological voice of the conscience. Most people in this world are enormously run by the negative ego and do not realize it. Most people do not even know what the negative ego is. Most people and even lightworkers are very ego-defended subconsciously, and do not realize it. This is not a judgement, just a very clear statement of Spiritual observation as a Spiritual teacher and Spiritual psychologist.

One of the ways that conscience is blocked is by having a faulty psychological philosophy. I know lightworkers who are channels for the Masters who believe that letting out their feelings, even if attacking, selfish and angry in nature, is the right way to live. If one adopts such a philosophy then one's belief system just about completely blocks out one's conscience on both levels. If one adopts a philosophy that one needs to balance everything including negative ego thinking versus Christ/Buddha thinking then a similar blockage of true conscience can take place. I say "true conscience" here because a great many people adopt faulty psychologies, philosophies and belief systems which, unbeknownst to them, are imbalanced, and corrupted to various degrees by the negative ego. They believe they are practicing a true conscience and indeed they are trying, but they are trying from a corrupted philosophy that is controlled by the negative ego. That is denying a great deal of "true conscience" that is clear of negative ego distortions and contaminations.

So we have established that being run by your feelings and emotions, thoughts, and a faulty psychology or philosophy can block a healthy conscience on both levels. Now the fourth way conscience can be blocked is if you are just being run by the negative ego thought system, as opposed to the Christ/Buddha thought system. Each thought system has infinite numbers of thoughts and beliefs. The negative ego thought system is incredibly seductive, even though its philosophy is insane when compared to a Christ/Buddha philosophy. There is so little training in this world on the difference between the two, and how to control one's mind, emotions, and negative ego thought system, that people are being incredibly run by the negative ego and don't realize it. I know people who have written books about it and are still totally run by it. It is almost comical. It has incredibly infiltrated every aspect of life including religion and the New Age movement. Some of the most disturbed people I know, who are the most run by the negative ego, are Spiritual leaders and Spiritual teachers. They may do incredible channelings at times, be great public speakers, be great healers, Spiritual scientists, Spiritual artists, ministers, or lightworkers, yet no matter what initiation level they are, and no matter how gifted they are in one area, they can be absolute egomaniacs and totally corrupted by power, greed, fame, sex, self-aggrandizement, and the like.

One of the areas of the greatest unconsciousness among these individuals is their inability to see what their true motives are. Many are wolves in sheep's clothing. Again I remind you, the antichrist will most probably be a Spiritual teacher. Just because one can give a great channeling or lecture means absolutely nothing as to how controlled that person is by the negative ego. Again, all these people think they are one hundred percent clear. They are also not inherently bad people. They may even mean well. They are just developed Spiritually, but not developed psychologically, which is the fifth reason why conscience becomes blocked.

So in conclusion, my Beloved Readers, by all means listen to and develop your conscience to the highest level you can. The more you refine and purify your consciousness on all levels the more subtle and refined your conscience becomes. For example, as you become a full-fledged Spiritual Master your conscience will immediately speak to you if you start thinking the slightest negative thought, or if you indulge in the slightest negative feeling. It will notify you of even the subtlest forms of dishonesty within self or with others. Your conscience will not allow you to hurt a flea. Your conscience will not allow you to run away from mistakes. Your conscience will not allow you to rationalize away your mistakes or blame them on others. What I am saying to you here is to cultivate the development of your conscience on every level of your being, so it is as refined as possible, and so you are truly taking responsibility for the manifestation of your energies on the subtlest level of what you are causing and creating. Do not be victimized by your conscience, but do be in one hundred percent integrity behind it. An example of this might be, do not let your conscience bother you to the point of not being able to sleep at night or function effectively in your daily life. Do be in one hundred percent integrity and responsibility behind what you have caused and created, even on the subtlest levels. Make an appropriate and balanced choice as to how to remain in integrity at all times. To do this we all must be joyously vigilant at all times over the ongoing process of our co-creating with GOD.

There is also the phenomenon of some Spiritual leaders and/or teachers having a certain degree of conscience and integrity in the formative years of their Spiritual path. However, once they moved into Spiritual leadership and became a little drunk with power, money, and fame, these negative ego qualities, and other ones, squashed and wiped out the voice of conscience and integrity.

Do not be bothered by your conscience, and be able to put this voice on a shelf and quiet it until you have time to deal with it properly. So one should not be a victim of one's conscience, for one has to always be the master of all of one's energies. Yet one should never deny one's conscience and suppress it, whether the lesson is some adjustment or correction that needs to be made within self or outside of self. So one should not be overly sensitive, but not underly sensitive either. Appropriateness is also a key principle. There is always an appropriate way of dealing with every situation. Let's say one is traveling and accidentally forgets to leave a tip at a restaurant two hundred fifty miles back on the highway. We do not want to be fanatical and maybe have to drive two hundred fifty miles back to give the tip. This would not be an appropriate, balanced use of energy. Again, the negative ego can corrupt one's conscience. A more appropriate response might be to call the restaurant upon your return home and send the tip. If that is impossible, apologizing to the person on the inner plane and giving all future waiters and waitresses a slightly larger tip and committing to never allow this to happen again, might be the appropriate response. Sometimes an inner plane acknowledgment that you made a mistake, statement of self-forgiveness, and unconditional love are all that are needed. Other times some action will be needed. It is extremely important to be balanced and levelheaded in determining the appropriate response. The main thing is to not overreact but not to under-react either. Also, do not give this principle to allow the negative ego room to shirk appropriate responsibility.

The demonstration of a high level Spiritual conscience can be very Spiritually inspiring to others. This is not the reason one does it. One does it because one has to, for as we have seen from this discussion, Spiritual conscience stems also from having a very high level of Spiritual and psychological ideals. At times I have been at a store, for example, and they undercharged me. I went through the decision in my mind whether I should say something. Now, I am not saying here that one always has to say something in every situation of life. I think each situation must be examined in the full context of all the ramifications involved. What I will say is that many times when this has happened to me, I made the conscious choice to say something. Now, many times I found that I was mistaken, and there was a twenty percent discount that I did not know about, in one example that I can think of. I felt good, however, because I honored my conscience, and in that particular situation I felt it was appropriate to say something. If everyone is God, then to cheat another is the same as cheating GOD, or myself, which in truth is all one identity and being. Now there have been other times when this occurred and a mistake was made, and I had to pay more money because of it. I must say, however, that my wallet may have been a little smaller, but my Spirit was a little fuller. There have also been times, when I felt compelled to speak up, that the clerk or person who received my money was deeply touched by my honesty. I humbly say, my example left a Spiritual mark on that person, and it inspired their honesty and conscience as well. I do want to say here, however, that I do not want to lay a trip on my readers, or say that all business interactions are the same or require the exact same Spiritual response. A company may have consciously or unconsciously cheated you out of money, and then made a mistake themselves in reverse. The Spiritual lesson and appropriate response may be to not say any-thing for, in truth, this balances the karmic imbalance and is really the universe doing this to achieve balance on a higher level. The key here, however, is to not let the negative ego, delude you or create rationalizations that are not true. Any opening you give the negative ego it will take it. So this again gets back to the importance of being devastatingly honest with self and striving for the highest level of Spiritual purity in all things.

One other very important point is that sometimes conscience is blocked not because people are not trying on a conscious level, but because they are not in complete control of their subconscious mind. So their conscious mind is honestly trying, but their subconscious mind is running a different agenda. This is extremely common in this world, because people are not taught how to master the subconscious mind and how to make it subservient to the conscious and superconscious minds. This is why the development of "true conscience" and integrity depends upon enormous Spiritual and psychological work that is done upon self so true Spiritual and psychological mastery can be achieved. So, what happens in this process is that the individual is trying to stay out of their negative ego on a conscious level, but because of a certain lack of self-mastery the subconscious mind is still run by the negative ego. The subconscious mind hence is very ego-defended and the individual does not realize it.

I would like to explain now what I mean by "ego defended." This means that the negative ego with its infinite number of voices, subpersonalities, belief systems, selfish motivations, narcissism, self-centeredness, separative thinking, fear-based thinking, attack thoughts, negative feelings and emotions, thirst for power, fame, and money, and negative ego ambition has too much of a strangle hold on the personality. It is like the individual cannot see "the forest through the trees." Again, the bizarre thing about the nature of the mind and the nature of delusion is that if you ask the person if they are run by their negative ego, they will say they are complete masters of it. This is so common that it is almost comical, if it weren't such a serious lesson. It reminds me of the common joke among prison inmates. If you ask all the prison inmates in a prison courtyard if they committed the crimes they are in jail for, every single one says "no." The only difference in the case of the negative ego is that people really believe it. This again speaks to the delusionary nature of the negative ego thought system, negative ego feelings and emotions, and glamour, maya, illusion, on the mental, astral, and etheric planes of existence.

Another important point is that it is not only important to develop and refine your Spiritual and psychological ideals, it is also important to demonstrate them. Many people feel it is okay not to demonstrate them. The negative ego rationalizes and says, "I'm only a person," or they might say, "Everyone does it." This may be true, but we still need to take responsibility for our actions and demonstrations. An extremely important principle in life is that mistakes are positive and okay, and ideally should not affect our self-love or self-worth. So I am not saying we should be negative perfectionists. However, I am saying that we should pursue excellence to the best of our ability. If we fall short, that is fine and we should admit that to self and to others. We do not need to advertise our mistakes to the world, however we should not run from admitting them either. The act of being devastatingly honest with self and not deluding oneself to defend one's negative ego can help to develop a healthy humbleness and humility. It can also help to develop a healthy compassion for other people's mistakes.

So in final conclusion, be joyously vigilant against the negative ego and some of the principles I have mentioned in this chapter that can cause one to block and deny their true conscience and integrity. I think you can see from this chapter that the perspective I have provided here is a balanced one, and one that allows you to want to develop the highest level possible of conscience Spiritually and psychologically, while still being the complete master of it and not allowing one's self to be victimized by it, overly sensitive to it, overly bothered by it, or driven to do inappropriate or imbalanced things to appease it. This balanced perspective allows one to live like a God Realized Spiritual Master on Earth in a most refined and purified manner, where you can set the example on Earth of truly taking causative responsibility for your thoughts, feelings, emotions, words, and deeds!

CHAPTER 12

Dealing with Negative Ego Neighbors and People

One of the most difficult lessons of the Spiritual path is the challenge that people face in dealing with relationships. It is in relationships that people often build the most amount of negative energy. The focus of this chapter is how to effectively deal with people and neighbors who are extremely run by the negative ego.

To begin this discussion, it must be understood that when life is looked at from the perspective of the Soul, everything is seen as a Spiritual lesson, challenge and Spiritual test. Every interaction is seen as an opportunity to respond from the Christ consciousness attitude rather than the negative ego attitude. Every interaction is seen as an opportunity to respond from unconditional love rather than fear and attack. Every interaction is seen as an opportunity to choose oneness with GOD rather than separation from GOD. Every interaction is seen as an opportunity to choose forgiveness instead of holding grudges.

It must be understood that every person is one with GOD already, for in truth the negative ego thought system doesn't exist. It is illusion. Although every person is one with GOD, not everyone is one with GOD in terms of his or her realization of this Spiritual ideal. It is our thoughts that create our reality. Most people, not being trained in the difference between Spiritual thinking and negative ego thinking, live in a bad dream filled with negative feelings and emotions, thinking the cause is outside of themselves when, in truth, the cause of all negative thoughts, emotions and negative interaction is an unconscious choice to interpret the situation from the negative ego mind rather than the Christ mind. Does not the Bible say, "Let this mind be in you that was in Christ Jesus"? Said another way, you can interpret every situation from your lower-self or your Higher Self.

When you interpret your interactions with people from your Christ/Buddha and/or Higher Self mind, each of our jobs Spiritually is to set a better example. Did not the Master Jesus say, "Love your enemies"?

So when you approach a person, neighbor, family member, stranger, or fellow worker on the job who is run by the negative ego, the first thing that GOD is teaching you is how not to be. You are also being taught to maintain and remain in your personal power. You are being taught by GOD to remain centered, and remain in your bubble of protection so other people's negativity slides off like "water off a duck's back." You are also being taught forgiveness, and unconditional love. You are being taught to respond instead of react. You are being taught to cause your own reality and to not let other people cause your emotions. You are being taught patience and tolerance. You are being taught to look at all things as teachings and lessons instead of bummers and problems. You are being taught evenmindedness and to maintain inner peace in all situations. You are being taught to maintain your self-love and love from GOD within self, and not to seek it outside of self. You are being taught to remain right with self and right with GOD even though someone around you is not. You are being taught to remain whole in your self and not seek wholeness outside of yourself. You are being taught to have preferences and not attachments. You are being taught to set a better example. You are being taught to let go of all attack thoughts and to be kind instead. In some cases, you are being taught humility and to turn the other cheek. In some cases, you are being taught to remain silent and unaffected. You are being taught to transcend duality. By this, I mean that when truly centered in your God Self you remain the same when criticized or praised, in victory or defeat, in sickness or in health. In some cases you are being taught to speak up in a calm, rational, objective, loving manner rather than a reactive, overly emotional, angry, attacking manner. In the ideal you are being taught to love your enemy and to see the diamond underneath the mud, or the light behind the lampshade. You are being taught to see the Christ within the other person, even though they do not see it in themselves and are not seeing it in you. It must be understood that what you see in others is a mirror of your own consciousness, since outer life is nothing more than a projection screen for your own thoughts. How you see your Brother and Sister is literally determining your oneness or lack of oneness with GOD. Your Brother and Sister are a Son and Daughter of GOD even if they are not acting like it. If you do not see this, it is you who have a lesson to learn in GOD's eyes. Be more concerned about learning your lessons than about whether your neighbor or friend learns theirs.

You are also being taught to remain in the Christ consciousness at all times even when under attack. You are also being taught to stay out of your negative ego at all times. In truth, you are being taught to be a Spiritual Master. From GOD's perspective, you should bless your negative Brother and Sister for giving you the opportunity to learn such wonderful lessons! Quite a different perspective then the negative ego's, wouldn't you say?

So, my friends, your negative ego, neighbor or friend is teaching you God Realization. The proper attitude to all situations in life is to say,

"Not my will, but Thine, Oh Lord. Thank you for the lesson." As Sai Baba says, "Welcome adversity." Everything that happens in life happens for a reason, and the reason is to teach you a Spiritual lesson you need to learn. There are no accidents. Some interactions are actually set up by your Higher Self to test you to see if you are ready for higher levels of initiation and Spiritual responsibility.

Anyone can be Spiritual when things are going well. The true test of your Spiritual Realization is if you can remain in your Christ consciousness when you are attacked. "So what that you gain the whole world but lose your own soul," as the Bible says.

My friends, every single moment of your life your are choosing GOD or your negative ego. What do you really want? Do you want power, fame and money at the expense of GOD? Do you want the permanent or the impermanent? Do you want liberation or endless rounds of rebirth? Do you want Heaven and true God Realization or the glamours of matter and worldly attachments?

If you find yourself choosing wrongly in a given moment, stop yourself, forgive yourself, and choose once again. Perfection is *not*: never making mistakes. Perfection is: not making *conscious* mistakes. When you become conscious that you have chosen negative ego, forgive yourself, forgive the other person, and attitudinally heal yourself by rechoosing the Christed attitude. It only takes 21 days to cement a new habit into the subconscious mind. In conclusion: Bless your negative ego neighbor, family member, co-worker or friend who is run by the negative ego, for you need the blessing if you are to remain one with GOD. Let your mantra hence be "I choose GOD and not negative ego in every interaction with a Brother and Sister." In final conclusion, as the Master Jesus said in *A Course In Miracles*, "Be vigilant for GOD and His Kingdom."

CHAPTER 13

The Importance of Focusing on Your Own Lessons Rather Than Being Concerned About Teaching Other People Their Lessons

One of the most common pitfalls and traps of negative ego/fear-based/separative thinking, is to be focused on teaching other people their lessons rather than learning your own. This is incredibly wide-spread in the New Age movement and the people who are doing it do not have a clue that they are doing something inappropriate! The negative ego is self-righteously thinking it is being quite Spiritual. "Oh, you didn't know that the negative ego could get behind being Spiritual?" The negative ego will use anything to make it be better than another. The negative ego fundamentally feels worse than everyone else. This is the endless mental and emotional loop it is running. Feeling like the "top dog" or the "underdog"! Feeling better than others and/or worse than others! Now, in truth, of course both are illusion and this is an endless game that can be transcended by learning to think with one's Spiritual/Christ/Buddha mind and feelings! However, by definition the negative ego thought system is the exact opposite of the Spiritual/Christ/Buddha thought system, so to do this it would have to die and that is the last thing the negative ego will let happen. That is why you, my Beloved Readers, need to make this happen by laughing the negative ego off the stage. For in truth, the negative ego does not even exist! There is no such thing as separation! You have always been one with GOD, you are one with GOD right now, and you always will be one with GOD! The negative ego is like a bad dream that you are waking up from right now, and now that you are awake you are realizing that it was just a dream you thought was real! By the grace of GOD you see now that you have awakened, was nothing more than a bad dream, no different than waking from a negative dream you had last night. When you wake up from a negative dream when you sleep you are just relieved it was just a dream and not real. This is the same way it is with the negative ego! The negative ego is illusion, maya, glamour, faulty thinking, and does not really exist. It is really just an "imaginary fabrication of your own mind"! It is an aspect of your mind that is making divisions and separations that are not there. In truth, a good example of this is the countries on the Earth. There are no lines that divide countries. This is something that has been created by people, not GOD! Now this may not be the best example for there may actually be some value in having countries, in terms of organization of a society and bringing different aspects of GOD to the forefront. However lines between countries do not exist. They are arbitrary relative boundaries that we are projecting onto this world for the purpose of power, greed and sometimes organization. Most of these boundaries came about through wars with the stronger countries taking over the weaker ones. Even the United States used to belong to the American Indians, and we came in and decimated them! Something often forgotten in the telling of American history. So the example may have some merit after all in showing how the negative ego through wars between countries has decided where these boundaries lie. If the negative ego could change these boundaries it would as Hitler, Napoleon, and other Sons and Daughters of GOD who were run by their negative ego's tried to take over the world! So it is not wrong that we have countries, however it is all an arbitrary earthly warring and legal game of where these boundaries lie!

Now between people in a way it is similar, it is important to have healthy boundaries One needs to know when to say no and when to say yes. One needs to respect one's physical boundaries. I am reminded of an episode of the "Seinfield" television show regarding the "close talker" who would come right up to your face and talk, not respecting your physical boundaries! So appropriate boundaries are healthy, like with countries, however, in truth, there is no such thing as separation between people, and in truth, this is one globe and one planet! That is the purpose of the United Nations concept! We are all one people in the Confederation of Planets! This is not something the consciousness of the leaders of the Earth have come to yet!

There is no such thing as separation. So do you see, my Beloved Readers it is all an arbitrary. To avoid feeling worse than others, the negative ego plays endless mind games to put others down to make it feel good about itself. If the negative ego just recognized that you are God and so are your Brothers and Sisters it would not have to do this, however the negative ego does not believe in God. Remember it thinks you are a physical body! The negative ego sees no way of transcending this endless nightmare of being better or worse than others and constantly comparing and competing, except to attack, anger, judgment, criticism, blame, and lastly focus on other people's lessons rather than one's own! The last one is much more tricky for this one is harder to see. For the negative ego tells you that you are doing a Spiritual thing to point out the mistakes of others. I have seen many Spiritual leaders and teachers do this! They publicly attack other

Spiritual leaders and in their own mind they think they are doing some noble thing to protect lightworkers. Not only are they wrong in what they are doing, if but you examine their true motives, it goes back to selfish negative ego motives and agendas. It may be the want to be better than everyone else, or it may be the glamour of being the archetype of the "Spiritual Protector"! What is even worse about this is half the time what they are attacking or criticizing is not even accurate. Secondly, it is judgement, attack and criticalness which is wrong, however they couch it in sweet Spiritual language so they can convince themselves they are being Spiritual when in truth it is nothing more than the worst kind of poison!

One of the keys to understanding how this process works is to understand that part of the negative ego's backward thinking is to stay focused "outside of self" rather than to "look within one's self!" The negative ego is "other directed" rather than "inner directed." This is another part of the negative ego illusionary game they are caught in. The person sees himself or herself as doing Spiritual service work helping others to see their lessons and pointing out all the lessons other people have. This of course keeps them "pointing the finger" at others and not looking at their own lessons! Now the most bizarre thing is that most of the time this is done, it is done with judgement, criticalness, attack, blame, contempt, self-righteousness, and superiority. This of course does not detour the negative ego, for it sees itself as raising consciousness and calling a spade a spade, not seeing it is doing so from its own negative ego! This is not even taking into consideration that one half of the time the things that it is saying are not even true! Whether it is true or not, however, is not the point, for in either case it is Spiritually wrong what they are doing!

My Beloved Readers, I must stop here for a moment and now give you the third key on this lesson which was brought forth by the Master Jesus. This sums up the whole lesson in a nutshell. This is one of the classic statements of the entire Bible! The Master Jesus said, "Do not try and take the speck out of the eye of your brother when you have a beam or log in your own eye!" My Beloved Readers, it has never been said better!

The people who are doing this do not have a clue that they have a "beam or log" in their own eye! The beam or log is their own negative ego and negative ego thought system! The most amazing thing to watch, my Beloved Readers, is to see this happen with lightworkers! It is almost comical to watch! There are so many examples I do not even know where to begin. First off, the lightworker will point out faults in others coming from a place of total judgment, attack, criticism and even anger, not even realizing what they are doing is far worse than the faults they are pointing out about the other person. Secondly, an even more sophisticated move of the negative ego is to say "I am not angry or being judgemental," yet they go into the most vicious, angry, poisonous tirade you can possibly imagine; "however, they were not being angry or judgmental"! The hypocrisy defies description. Then the real classic is the lightworker who is totally run by their negative ego and dark forces telling another person they are run by their negative ego. The negative ego capacity for delusion and self-deception has no end! Then there is the Spiritual leader or lightworker who presents all their attacks, criticisms, judgements and poison in a "very loving way, telling you they are doing this to help you and raise consciousness. They say they are giving you this information for your consideration, and please tune into your guidance." They continue to say, " I have no opinion on this, I am just presenting this for your consideration!" This is the most vicious poisonous game of the negative ego. For you see how sophisticated it has become in its lies and deceit! It uses all the Spiritual/Christ/Buddha consciousness and language, and presses all the right "Spiritual buttons!" Lightworkers are deceived by it almost 100% of the time! This is usually the work of a Spiritual leader or very advanced lightworker! As the Masters told me, the antichrist will first be a Spiritual leaders and teacher!

My Beloved Readers, be not fooled by these things. The negative ego has infiltrated Religion and has fully infiltrated the New Age movement. The negative ego has learned all the information and language and uses it like a negative ego run lawyer, to persuade its case. Did not the Bible prophesied there would be many false prophets and false teachers at this time! My Beloved Readers, there are some incredibly devious Spiritual leaders, channels, Spiritual teachers, Spiritual scientists, healers, psychics, and practitioners, be forewarned! I have shared with you over and over again in this book how most lightworkers are not trained in Spiritual psychology! They often have great Spiritual development and great earthly knowledge of healing and other things! They have fantastic Spiritual knowledge or Spiritual scientific knowledge. However, Spirit and the Masters are giving you a very stern warning now. Be aware of "wolves wearing sheep's clothing!" It has never been better said than this! What Spiritual leaders do on stage or in a book or in a session and what they do behind the scenes are two different things. Lightworkers need to stop giving their personal power away and putting Spiritual leaders, channels and teachers on fantasy pedestals. This is just more of the negative ego's delusionary work! Keep your eyes wide open, for if you knew what was really going behind the scenes and on the inner scenes of the most well know Spiritual leaders, teachers, scientists, channels, healers, psychics, authors and practitioners, very often you would be absolutely appalled! I do not say this as a judgment, I say it as Spiritual discernment and discrimination. I have seen these things given the position I am in and it has blown my mind to see the amount of negative ego corruption in Spiritual leaders, Spiritual channels, Spiritual scientists, and Spiritual teachers who I have respected and never dreamed in a million years they could be capable of such unconscious negative ego motivations, agendas and behavior. I say to you my Beloved Readers, with total unconditional love in my heart, "to wake up and smell the coffee!" What I am telling you is totally true and is rampant! Most Spiritual leaders and lightworkers are very untrained in Spiritual psychology, are nonintegrated, and in a great many cases do not even know what negative ego thinking and feeling really is. It is concern enough to see this taking place in so many Spiritual leaders, channels, teachers, and Spiritual scientists, however what is even worse is to see how lightworkers get seduced by these people and their negative ego con games and manipulation! The lack of Spiritual discernment in the New Age Movement among lightworkers is staggering! They cannot see any of this. This is because they have not been properly trained in Spiritual psychology and all this stuff I have been speaking of in this book and my book *The Golden Book of Melchizedek: How To Become An Integrated Christ/Buddha In This Lifetime*! We don't see with our eyes, we see through our Spiritual and psychological Training! Unfortunately this world does not train us properly in the field of Spirituality and Spiritual psychology! This creates massive blind spots and limited lens seeing! If you have not been trained to see every aspect of how the negative ego is operating within yourself, my Beloved Readers, you are not going to be able to see it in others! My Beloved Readers, if you do not develop a Full Spectrum Prism Consciousness within self, you are not going to be able to see one half to three quarters of what is going on outside of self. If you are run by your own negative ego and emotional body you will not be able to see it in others, even though your negative ego is telling you that you can! You can't my Beloved Readers, for these are not whimsical things I speak of here. They are laws of the mind and heart! This is why it is so important to receive this training, do this Spiritual and psychological studying, and practice and demonstrate all the information and tools I am giving you! You are the hope of the world! This training is not being given in the world. It is not being given in traditional religion! It is not being given in the New Age movement to a great degree! It is incumbent upon you to integrate this training into your consciousness, and not just read about it but become it! Demonstrate it in your every thought, word and deed! Then go out and teach it! It is up to those Spiritual leaders and lightworkers who are truly "pure of heart," who truly want only God Realization and God Purity with no negative ego deception or delusion, to go out into this world and raise consciousness! It is for this reason that I have written these particular books! For these books can give the Spiritual and psychological training that should have been given to us in school! Can you imagine if reading books like this were part of your training or your schooling beginning in first grade? This is the fundamental flaw of our society! We actually have an educational system that is devoid of Spirituality, psychology, morals, ethics, values, and the purpose of life! Only the negative ego could come up with such a backward idea. You know why this was done. It was done to separate Church and State. Do you know why? Because the negative ego infiltrated religion, and religious zealots and fanatics were trying to shove their egotistical form of religion down people's throats! So innocent children had to be protected from this form of negative ego as well. However, in doing so, we have "thrown the baby out with the bathwater"! The negative ego is protecting the negative ego from the negative ego! Now isn't that an interesting process. Hence what is left is negative ego! We have a school system that is totally outwardly focused and has no inner training whatsoever. Is it any wonder that so many Spiritual leaders and lightworkers are fouled up? It is not really their fault, it is really the responsibility of our society to train them properly. People are forced to go to school and receive outer training but do not receive any psychological or universal Spiritual training! I said the key word here, "Universal *Training.*" This is what will occur in the future to solve this dilemma of protecting the negative ego from the negative ego! A type of "Universal Spiritual and Psychological" training will be given much like that which is in this book and my other books! It will be a training that honors and respects all religions and all Spiritual paths and shows that they are all one and all teach the same thing! In a similar vein Spiritual psychology and all forms of psychology will be taught in schools showing how they all support Spiritual psychology. Who knows, maybe one day my Spiritual Encyclopedia might be used in a manner that gives a synthesis type of training, so no religious group would be offended, for they all would be honored and included. The basic teaching would be to show the fundamental similarities of all teachings, which is the truth. They all teach the Fatherhood/Motherhood of GOD and the Brotherhood/Sisterhood of the people of the Earth! Please note how I have taken this out of the patriarchal model and placed it within the God/Goddess model! All are included! How can there be any lack of inclusion in GOD?

So my Beloved Readers, in putting together an "Educational Training Program" such as this, there would be no need to "throw the baby out with the bathwater"! For this program would not be offensive to anyone! So you see my Beloved Readers, this "Understanding and Model of Synthesis" is really the key to revamping our society on every level! For if we really want to change our society on a massive mass consciousness scale we must revamp our educational system! This stuff should be taught in school! This stuff should be taught to our children! Can you imagine how many children would love school if this kind of thing were taught? It would be the answer to all the problems of our society! For all the problems of our society stem from one and only one thing! This is negative ego/fear-based/separative and imbalanced thinking and feeling!

So this is what has happened to lightworkers. From no real fault of their own, they have not received this training so they become channels, Spiritual teachers, Spiritual scientists, ministers, religious leaders, healers, psychics, Spiritual scientists, with out this training in Spiritual psychology! Their Spiritual level training may be great and their earthly level training may be great! However I guarantee you their training in Spiritual psychology was not great! Please listen very carefully to what I have to say here for I know what I speak of here. Besides being a Spiritual leader, teacher, channel, I am also Spiritual psychologist, and licensed Marriage Family and Child Counselor! I grew up in a family of psychologists! I have studied psychology through undergraduate, graduate, and postgraduate Ph.D. programs schooling! I humbly suggest I am a Master of Spiritual Psychology, and I tell you Spiritual psychology is not being taught as it needs to be almost anywhere on this planet. It is not happening in our educational system. It is for sure not happening through parents, for they certainly have not been trained in it. It is not for sure happening in traditional religion! It is not being taught in the field of psychology and this I know for a fact! Through all my training as a psychologist and a licensed Marriage, Family, and Child Counselor, I never once encountered any of the information or material I am teaching you in this book! This is all self-taught and taught to me by Spirit, the Masters and some books that have given me small slivers and slices. I took it upon myself to develop a new system of understanding, to bring all these slivers, slices, tools, and understanding to a new form of Spiritual psychology which I shall call a "Synthesis of all that I have learned in life"! I have taken the best of all schools of thought and created and brought through new cutting-edge revolutionary understandings in the field! What you are studying in this book is the Spiritual psychology of the future, and it is time to integrate and ground it into mass consciousness now! This is part of the Divine Plan for this world. Spirit and the Masters are putting forth the Clarion Call to lightworkers and people around the world to help do this! This information is what the world needs more than anything else. For it is one's right relationship to self and Spiritual psychology which forms the foundation and first floor for all Spiritual work and earthly work! All three floors are equally important. However, Spiritual psychology is the foundation of all Spiritual work for it is our thoughts that create our reality, and it is our consciousness that determines what we see! It is also the development of consciousness, which all Spiritual work is channeled through! If our basic psychological consciousness is not 100% clear, it will contaminate all Spiritual work and all earthly service work as well! One's "second floor and basement" is going to be greatly determined by what is going on within a person's Spiritual psychology! This point cannot be emphasized enough! One's right relationship to self is the most important relationship in a person's life for if this relationship is wrong, all other relationships will be wrong as well! You cannot be wrong with self and right with GOD and the Masters and right with other people! It is impossible! To whatever degree you have not cleared or have any remnants of negative ego/fear-based/sep-arative consciousness, imbalanced thinking and limited lens seeing from mass consciousness earthly programming, it will contaminate your Spiritual channeling, teaching, healing, psychic work, scientific teachings, and earthly service work. This is an indisputable fact for it is a law of the mind and a law of the heart and soul! Spirit and the Masters are asking you, my Beloved Brothers and Sisters, to take this work into the world and to the masses. Do this in any way you see fit. It may be by raising con-sciousness. Turning people on to this book, *Soul Psychology*, and if they are ready *The Golden Book of Melchizedek* as well! Helping friends, family, and students may do this! Teaching classes may do it! Getting this information onto the television, radio, magazines, bookstores, books, and other forms of media may do it! If any of you have inroads into the educational system this would be tremendous! This work will spread like wild fire. It just needs Spiritual leaders and lightworkers like you to light the match!

This work is not being taught in our schools, by our parents, grandparents, extended family, and peers or in our churches or tem-ples. It is also not being taught, I can tell you for an absolute fact, by psychologists, marriage counselors, family counselors, child coun-selors, social workers, and psychiatrists! I am not saying what they are doing is not of value, for it is of great value. However it is much more on a personality level of self-actualization, not on a soul or Spiritual level of self-actualization, which is totally different! So peo-ple and lightworkers have not been able to get it from the counselors, psychologists, social workers, or marriage and family counselors! Most Spiritual leaders, Spiritual teachers, Spiritual channels, and Spiritual scientists have not been fully trained. Many have parts or certain slivers and lenses; however, they do not have the whole train-ing of what negative ego thinking and feeling really is, nor do they have a complete understanding of the vast number of balances and integrations that must be kept, nor do they have an understanding of the vast science of limited lens seeing and blind spots! This is not a judgment, just a Spiritual observation of fact that this is not the strongest part of their training. They usually are much more advanced Spiritually and in an earthly sense, which I honor them for! However, this weakness in the area of Spiritual psychology as I have been talking about in this book has incredibly serious consequences in regard to their Spiritual work and earthly service work! If this training is not received, the work can become enormously contaminated with nonintegration, fragmentation, negative ego corruption and contamination, limited lens seeing, blind spots, personal agendas, wrong motives, imbalances, imbalanced teachings, selfishness, misinterpretation, misperception, faulty thinking, and lack of synthesis and integration, to just name a few!

Spiritual psychology is a specific type of training that is needed! Lightworkers have not recognized this fully! They have received kind of a hit and miss training! I have had the unique training of being born into a family of psychologists, being trained as a psychologist and licensed Marriage and Family Counselor, doing this work for a living for 25 years, besides being a Spiritual teacher, channel and minister. So I have a very keep eye for not only Spiritual vision but also psychological vision and physical earthly vision! I have focused my life on developing all three! It is incredibly clear to me and I have discussed this extensively with the inner plane Ascended Masters as well, that this is one of the biggest challenges that confronts our world at this time! This is why Spirit and the Masters have guided me and asked me to write these books! It is the single greatest blind spot in religion and the New Age Movement at this time! It is also a great concern for Spirit and the Masters! I have spent hours and hours and hours discussing these issues with them! This is why they have told me that they are not really into ascension! They are into "Integrated Ascension"! For what is ascension worth if it is done only in the Spiritual body and is not properly integrated into one's mental body, emotional body, etheric body, physical body, and earthly world! It has become a type of nonintegrated and fragmented ascension! This, my Beloved Readers, is the current plight of the New Age Movement! The New Age Movement is the hope of the world; however, like traditional religion it is filled with negative ego misunderstanding, imbalanced thinking, limited lens seeing, blind spots, glamour, illusion, maya, self-deception, faulty thinking, separative consciousness, psychological unclarity, disintegration, fragmentation, corruption, personal agendas, wrong motives, selfish interest, jealousy, competition, improper alignment, lack of consistency on all levels, improper understanding, lack of proper training, lack of God Purity, lack of honesty with self, unconsciousness, improper education on all levels, mass consciousness contamination, lack of an integrated Spiritual/psychological/and physical/earthly ideal and lack of an integrated Spiritual ideal. The world desperately needs more people that can teach this work in all fields of Spiritual, psychological and physical/earthly work! There are actually three levels of vision in life! Spiritual vision, psychological vision and physical/earthly vision! This is one of the great revolutionary insights of this New Age. This book, *Soul Psychology* and *The Golden Book of Melchizedek* have been written to fully open your psychological vision and a great deal of your Spiritual vision as well! My books *The Complete Ascension Manual, Beyond Ascension, Cosmic Ascension,* and *Revelations of a Melchizedek Initiate* have been written to fully open your Spiritual vision. My books *Manual For Planetary Leadership, Your Ascension Mission: Embracing Your Puzzle Piece, Hidden Mysteries, The Golden Keys To Ascension and Healing, The Souls Perspective On How To Achieve Perfect Radiant Health,* and *Empowerment and Integration of The Goddess,* have been written to fully open your physical/earthly vision!

My Beloved Readers, when these three levels of vision are fully opened, that is when you more fully see and know God in every aspect of your life! This is what you must strive for! These levels of vision are greatly open in a great many of you! My job and service is to polish the diamond on all three levels. My job and service is to help remove any last impurities or toxins on all three levels that are causing you to see unclearly Spiritually, mentally, emotionally, etherically, energetically, physically or on the earthly plane! My job and Spiritual assignment is to make sure we all do not have a "beam or log in our own eye"!

My Beloved Readers, it is for this reason this chapter has been written! Be less concerned about teaching other people their lessons and be more concerned about learning your own lessons! Leave teaching other people their lessons up to GOD! That is his job, not yours! So what that other people are not learning their lessons? That is their karma! How come you are so concerned about it! Are you attached to them learning their lessons, or is it a strong preference? What are your true motives? What are your true intentions for doing so? Are you being too outer focused and not inner focused? Are you being judgemental? Did they ask for your help in teaching them their lessons? Are you sure you are not coming from anger? Are you sure you are not attacking? Are you sure this is not serving the negative ego to make you better than they are? What does it matter if they don't learn their lessons, why is it such a concern of yours? Have you been appointed their Spiritual teacher? Have they asked for that? Did they ask for your advice or suggestions? Did you ask them if they wanted to hear it? Are you in truth invading their boundaries and space by giving something that has not been asked for?

My Beloved Readers, these are but a few questions you might ask yourself on this most important issue! It is always Spiritually safer and better to focus on your own lessons first! One of the first clues that you are caught in negative ego thinking on this issue is if you have any attachment or lack of inner peace if you don't say anything! The negative ego can be quite tricky and will change forms every time you catch it trying to convince you to do something with selfish motives. It is always safer to just focus on your own lessons. I am not saying you should not help people however make sure it is appropriate. We all know how offensive it is for religious fundamentalists to push their teachings down your throat. My Beloved Readers, the negative ego is like a fundamentalist in everything it does! It is not necessary that people do things the way you do them, even if you think it is right! Everyone must watch out for trying to be people's mother or father psychologically. I have news for you, they already have one! It is a better policy to take the philosophy that if you don't have anything nice to say, don't say anything at all! Certainly never judge! Do not publicly criticize other Spiritual leaders! For, "He that hath no sin, cast the first stone!" "Judge not that ye not be judged!" Be sure to give suggestions and advice only when asked or when it is appropriate! It is often okay for people to do things their own way even if it is not the most efficient way! Be careful not to invade people's Spiritual, psychological, mental, emotional, and physical boundaries in this regard! I see lightworkers all the time giving advice that was not asked for. I see psychics giving psychic readings when it was not asked for. I see channels giving Spiritual channelings when they have not been asked for! I see Spiritual teachers giving Spiritual teaching when it has not been asked for! I have seen healers give healings when it has not been asked for! I see people give advice and suggestions when it is not appropriate or asked for. These people are 100% totally invading people's space thinking they are doing Spiritual work and in truth they are "demonstrating egotism!" They are falling into the trap of being do-gooders and being of service while trampling over people's Spiritual, psychological, and physical/earthly boundaries! My Beloved Readers, do you see how easy it is to get caught in focusing on other people's lessons and not learning your own! It comes in many forms and many negative ego guises! In truth it does not matter that other people do not learn their lessons! So what! If you get into a conflict with someone, what does it matter if they learn their lessons or not? This is one of the biggest traps I see lightworkers fall into. It doesn't matter! Lightworkers get so into teaching other people their lessons they miss their own. You are not here to teach anyone anything! You are here to demonstrate Godliness! Most often the best example is through actions and by words! If you are right with self and right with

GOD it should not matter in the slightest if other people learn their lessons or not! That is between them and GOD!

There was a book I saw 20 years ago called *What Other People Think of Me Is None of My Business*. I thought this was a cute title! The reason that this is important is that we must seek our love from our self and from GOD and the Masters first! This way we go into life with self-love and self-worth and filled with the Love of GOD and the Masters. This way we do not care what other people think for we know fully what we think and feel and how GOD and the Masters think and feel about us, which is all 100% unconditionally loving! If one doesn't do this they will not be whole and complete within themselves in entering life. One will feel total unconditional love by giving firmness and unconditional love to the inner child and self, and receiving it from GOD and the Masters! This way they will not need to seek love, approval, or worth outside of self! This is why this title of the book is a cute title because "What Other People Think is None of Your Business"!

In the same regard, my Beloved Readers, I have a second subtitle for this chapter that I will share with you now, and you know what is coming! "Whether Other People Learn Their Lessons Or Not, Is None Of Your Business"!

My Beloved Readers, it is only when you are totally interested in learning your own lessons in life, and are not attached in the slightest whether other people learn theirs, can true God Realization be achieved! The true test of this will come when you are in conflict with someone. The negative ego will want to teach that person a lesson! The negative ego cannot imagine not striking back and giving that person a piece of your mind! The negative ego cannot imagine being attacked and remaining silent! The negative ego cannot imagine turning the other cheek and just giving unconditional love! Well my Beloved Readers, I have news for you. You are not negative ego, you are God! Choose who ye shall serve! You cannot serve two masters! Every moment of your life you must ask yourself, "Do I want GOD or do I want my negative ego? Do you want Truth or illusion?

Do you want that which is permanent or impermanent? To choose negative ego is to choose nothing, for it does not even exist, except in the machinations of your own mind! As Sai Baba says, "GOD equals man minus ego!" If you want to realize GOD you must get rid of all negative ego/fear-based/separative thinking and feeling from your reality! Choose once again!

My Beloved Readers, the supreme test of this will come when you get into an ego battle conflict with someone and you realize it and because you have God Purity, and because you put GOD first and have no false gods before Him, you admit your mistakes and apologize to this person who is also caught in their negative ego and probably much, much worse than you were. By taking the action you have done, you have learned your lessons even if the balance of responsibility was only 10% yours and 90% theirs. By taking responsibility for your 10% you have remained in God Purity and remained one with GOD in terms of your realization of God in that moment! That is all that is important my friends, and nothing else. Now it would be nice if the other person learned their lesson and you will give them a chance to do so. However more likely than not they won't, for they do not have the same love for GOD and God Purity that you have! So you may end up apologizing or saying nothing and the responsibility may be 100% the other person's who attacked and judged you! It happens all the time! That is what people run by the negative ego do! It is rampant all over the world and it is rampant in the New Age movement. So all that is important is that you stay in God Purity and learn your lesson. The other person may or may not learn their lessons. Whether they do or not is none of your business! It is their business and GOD's business, not your business! All that matters is that you learn your Christed lesson! Now I am not saying here the lesson is always to say nothing or just turn the other cheek and practice humility. Sometimes it will be! It depends on the situation. If there is no way the other person is going to learn their lesson and it is just going to continue being an ego battle, then what's the point? Let it go! The lesson is to do whatever you have to do to practice God Realization and Spiritual/Christ/Buddha consciousness and be silent! On other occasions if there is a possibility for real calm, rational, unconditionally loving communication do so! If you come to an impasse, then unconditionally lovingly agree to disagree and end the conversation in a win/win manner not a win/lose manner! Also, frame the conversation by saying we have different perceptions of the situation and are seeing it through different lenses which is fine! End it by saying we can disagree but this does not have to create separation or lack of unconditional love between us my friend!

The only purpose for communicating is if the other person is open to sharing and mutual learning and taking responsibility for their lessons. If they are not, what is the point? Learn your Spiritual and psychological lessons and cut loose! Let it go! Whether they learn their lessons or not has absolutely no effect on you! You have your 100% personal power, your 100% unconditional self-love, your 100% unconditional love from GOD and the Masters! You have your Golden Bubble of Protection up! You have your Spiritual/Christ/Buddha consciousness up! You have strong preferences and not attachments! You are looking at this as a Spiritual test, lesson, challenge and opportunity to grow Spiritually! You are the cause of your own reality and you are a Master and not a victim! They cannot program or affect your feelings and emotions for you create these with your own mind, so you are emotionally invulnerable! Even children can do this. They say "sticks and stones can break my bones but names can never hurt me!" They are affirming their emotional invulnerability! You cause your own reality my Beloved Readers, so why would it possibly matter whether they learn their lesson or not! Plus if you learn your lesson you will not have to reincarnate to learn the lesson next lifetime. You will be free but your friend will have to reincarnate, but you won't for you will have learned your lesson even if they don't! So my Beloved Readers, as you can see it really does not matter in the slightest if other people learn their lessons or not. It is only when you are fully right with self and right with GOD in this manner that you then can truly be prepared to go out and teach in the proper manner! For you are hence going out to teach from a clear psychological and Spiritual manner, and can truly be a clear mirror and reflection to your friends and students! None of your psychological material, buttons, negative ego programming, and negative ego agendas in regard to this issue will be getting in the way! Only then as well, will you be able to make the appropriate decision as to when to talk and when it is really best to be silent! It will also save you unbelievable amounts of time and dealings with sometimes very negative and disturbed people by learning to have humility, turn the other cheek, and just be silent. Their attacks, criticisms, and negativity have no effect on you for you have your Golden Bubble of Light and all their negativity slides off your Golden Bubble like water off a duck's back! My Beloved Readers, approaching life in this manner will give you a "peace that passeth understanding"! It will also create only unconditional love and harmony in your life. It will also insure that you learn your lessons and that you graduate and achieve liberation and not have to reincarnate on this plane or the mental and emotional plane. It will insure that you are not going around in life thinking you are demonstrating God, but really demonstrating negative ego. Lastly it will insure that when you do give advice or suggestions that you do it without a "beam or log in your own eye"!

CHAPTER 14

How The Negative Ego Sabotages Your Ability To Manifest

This, my Beloved Readers, is another very interesting study of how the negative ego/fear-based/separative thought system can sabotage your ability to manifest success in every aspect of your life, both inwardly and outwardly! I will go through this process step by step, trying to focus on the most important principles first! You have become quite sophisticated in understanding the intricacies of how the negative ego/fear-based thought system operates, so I am not going to take a lot of time to go into great depth on each point since this has been done previously. The reading of this book and my book *Soul Psychology* will give you all the insight, training, and tools you will ever need to under-stand, undo and reprogram any thought or emotional pattern covered in this chapter or any other chapter. This is why I have written these two books, to give lightworkers the Spiritual and psychological training they should have received in school. Eventually these things will be taught in school from a very early age! Spiritual psychology, Spirituality, physical/earthly mastery will be as equally important in the future as reading, writing and arithmetic! Earthly school, as practiced in our world, has become an outer endeavor and focus that is devoid of any Spiritual, psychological or physical/earthly training to become God Realized. It is a training of the personality, not of the Soul or Spirit! These two books have been written to give you, in the comfort of your own home, that training course you missed! It is all quite simple once you understand it. However, it is essential to at least take the course once! I am not the only person teaching this course, however, this version of the course is, I humbly suggest, one of the most comprehensive, easy to understand, most practical and cutting-edge! What is nice about this particular course is that you don't have to go to school or an outer classroom. This is designed as a home self-study course in Spiritual psychology! On this note we will begin your next phase of training on how to avoid the pitfalls and traps of the negative ego in relationship to the laws of manifestation!

The first way the negative ego/fear-based/separative thought system sabotages your ability to manifest is that it has you not own your 100% personal power! My Beloved Readers, be clear about this. You will never be able to manifest anything in your life inwardly or outwardly if you do not own your full personal power! Your personal power puts the force behind everything you do! Awareness without personal power is total victim consciousness. This is why some people lacking in personal power say, "Ignorance is bliss." No one who has personal power would ever say this! Your personal power is what allows you to be assertive in life but not aggressive! Personal power is what allows you to maintain self mastery over your thoughts, feelings, emotions, subconscious mind, negative ego, inner child, desire body, physical body and Earth life! All manifestation begins with the need to own your personal power!

The second way the negative ego thought system sabotages your ability to manifest is it will have you not unconditionally love yourself and not unconditionally love others! Law number two is you will never be able to manifest unless you do both. Power must be tied to love to manifest. If you are not loving, you will be fearful and attacking. That will only create negative karma. Negative karma is not good for manifesting anything but negative things. If you do not love yourself, you will feel undeserving and or unworthy and this will sabotage your ability to manifest!

The third way the negative ego thought system sabotages your ability to manifest is by making you passive, indolent, and procrastinating. As Carl Jung the famous Swiss psychologist said, "Man's greatest sin is his indolence"! Don't put off later what you can do now. He who hesitates is lost! Part of manifestation is owning your power and taking physical action! This is called "Active Intelligence"! It is not enough to just own your personal power and love your-self and others to manifest. You also must take physical action. Many get the opportunities they seek, however they don't take action when the opportunity arises!

The fourth way the negative ego sabotages this process is it has you act without wisdom. It does this often among lightworkers. They are too impulsive, too scattered, and too emotional. They make a phone call but have not thought out what they wanted to say or got their thoughts organized in their mind. They make a process that should take one step into one that takes five steps! They allow the subconscious mind to make them psychologically and mentally not prepared and clear!

The fifth way the negative ego sabotages the manifestation process is it keeps you disorganized. If you are disorganized you are never going to be able to manifest effectively. The hermetic law states, "As within, so without. As above, so below"! If you are disorganized then what you will manifest in your life is disorganization and chaos! Part of wisdom is having the smarts to start your day by getting organized first. Many people run around like chickens with their heads cut off! They are like a mouse on a wheel, putting out a lot of energy but not going anyplace. Get organized first! A clear mind and heart will help to create a clear manifestation.

The sixth way the negative ego mind sabotages manifestation is to cause you to worry! This, my Beloved Readers, is negative affirmation and negative meditation! Your thoughts create your reality. If you think fearful thoughts long enough you might create that which you are thinking! The Universal Mind through Edgar Cayce said, "Why worry when you can pray?" The negative ego sabotages you by making you forget to pray. My Beloved Readers, why make your life hard for yourself, you have the Power of GOD, Christ, the Holy Spirit, your Mighty I Am Presence, your Higher Self, the inner plane Ascended Masters, the Archangels and Angels, the Elohim Councils, and the Christed Extraterrestrials all there to help you with your every need! There is only one problem! They are not allowed to help unless you ask! Ask and you shall receive, knock and the door shall be opened! Life is a co-creation, not a one man or one woman show!

The next way the negative ego sabotages the manifestation process is that it "carries its cross itself, instead of letting GOD and the inner plane Masters help! This is called surrender! After you pray, give your cross to GOD and the Masters. Yes, you will do your part, however, let GOD and the Masters do their part. Let them carry your responsibilities with you! It is a team effort!

The next way the negative ego sabotages the manifestation process is that it makes you attached to what you want instead of making what you want a "prayer preference"! A basic law of the universe is, that which you are attached to you repel! Have only super strong preferences, not attachments, and you will remain happy all the time whether you get what you want or not. Happiness becomes a state of mind, not something outside of self!

The next way the negative ego blocks manifestation is that it makes you forget to use the power of your subconscious mind. The subconscious mind is the real attracting and magnetizing aspect of your being! It is the real powerhouse of your energy! It is the seat of your feelings and emotions! It is the storehouse of your energies and all your programming! This is why it is essential to do affirmations and visualizations, and give your subconscious mind self-suggestions to program it to manifest what you what! It will attract to you that which you affirm and visualize into it. It will amaze you with its abilities. The negative ego sabotages you by having you to forget to do your affirmations and visualizations. Use the ones I have outlined in this book. Use the ones in my book *Soul Psychology*. Make up your own! Remember that an idle mind is the devil's workshop! Keep your mind affirming and visualizing what you want. Use all five senses! Make it incredibly real! If you keep it up the subconscious mind will amaze you with its ability to manifest. You must just remember one thing, however. The subconscious mind has no reasoning, and is always manifesting every moment of your life. So if you are not affirming positive thoughts and images into it then negative ones are getting in. That is why some negative things are being attracted and magnetized into your life. Do not let the negative ego make you forget to continuing practicing your affirmations, visualization and continual positive self-suggestion!

The next absolutely critical key to manifestation which the negative ego thought system tries to sabotage is the necessity of maintaining your Spiritual/Christ/Buddha thinking and feeling at all times and to never ever think or feel with your negative ego/fear-based/separative mind. This is also called maintaining a positive mental attitude and feeling at all times. This is absolutely crucial, for remember your thoughts create your reality! As within so without, as above so below! If you only think and feel with your God/Christ/Buddha mind and feelings then that is the only thing you will manifest. You will manifest things only of GOD! If you think with your negative ego/fear-based/separative mind, then that is what you will manifest! My Beloved Readers, it is essential to remember that every thought and feeling you allow into your mind is an affirmation and visualization! Please realize the profundity of this last statement. Every thought and feeling you allow yourself to think or feel is not only an affirmation and visualization, but once accepted into the conscious mind it imprints itself on the subconscious mind like a tape recorder or computer! It will then attract and magnetize that! As I said, the subconscious is always attracting and magnetizing. It is just a matter of what you allow it to magnetize and attract. So the moment-by-moment thoughts and feelings you allow in your mind and heart are actually the process of doing affirmations and visualizations every moment! You need to own your 100% personal power at all times so you can use it to keep negative thoughts and feelings out of your mind and only allow in and affirm Spiritual/God/Christ/Buddha thoughts and feelings! Deny any thought or feeling not of GOD to enter your mind!

I have given many key ideas here so far in this chapter. However, the four keys to manifestation lie in this statement. GOD and the Masters, my personal power, the power of my subconscious mind and my physical body are an unbeatable team! There is much profundity in this affirmation and you should say it often! It is one of my favorite affirmations I ever created! This is how the Integrated Ascended Master manifests. He or she works the laws on all four levels. They use personal power and Spiritual/Christ/Buddha thinking and feeling on the conscious level, prayer on the Spiritual level, affirmations, visualizations and self-suggestion on the subconscious level, and right physical action on the physical level. The negative ego will try to make you forget one of these levels. If you do, it will sabotage the process. All four levels must be maintained and continued in a structured, self-disciplined and continual manner and if you do this, success will be assured!

The next way the negative ego sabotages manifestation is by having you work your program for a little while and then get distracted by side roads, temptations, Spiritual weariness, lack of self-discipline, lack of Spiritual structure, or giving up. Beloved Readers the only way to manifest is to work your program! This is not a hundred-yard dash and then it is over and you are back to your regular life. This is a lifelong program! Being a Spiritual Master and a master manifestor with the "Midas Touch" is a full time job! Life is a marathon, not a sprint! You need to set up a Spiritual regime and structure. It is just like going to the gym three times a week and working out. You don't exercise for three weeks and then stop. You must stay in shape! Well, my Beloved Readers, as the *Rocky* movie stated, it is time to get back "the eye of the tiger"! It is time to get back to the "old gym"! It is time to get back to the Spiritual gym, the mental gym, the emotional gym and the physical/earthly gym! It is time to pay your rent to GOD on all levels! It is time to get physically fit, mentally fit, emotionally fit and Spiritually fit! You will never become a master manifestor with the "Midas Touch" without having this attitude and demonstration! The negative ego will try and sabotage this. It will say, "I can't, I am too busy with the romantic relationship I am involved in. I am too tired! I have other things to do that are more important. I will do it tomorrow! I will give in this one time! I give up!" Do not listen to the feeble negative ego excuses. You must ask yourself, do you want God Realization and God manifestation in every aspect of your life? If the answer is yes, then work your Spiritual program and do not stop your Spiritual practices! Do them with your partner!

The next way the negative ego sabotages is that it creates doubt, fear, and impatience. I say to you, my Beloved Brothers and Sisters, that one of the keys to manifestion is faith, trust, and patience! You must have faith in GOD, the Masters, and GOD's Laws that I am sharing with you! How could you own your full personal power and positive thinking and feeling, with GOD's and the Master's full love, wisdom and power, with the power of your subconscious mind, and with right action and applying all the insights and suggestions given in this chapter not be successful? We are not dealing here with a whimsical thing. We are dealing with Cosmic and Universal laws. If you apply them they work every time! For this reason have faith, trust and patience in GOD and GOD's Laws! Things work a little slower on this plane than they do on the higher planes when you are not in a physical body!

Another way the negative ego sabotages your manifestation is that it makes you go on automatic pilot, and fall asleep while living your life. The negative ego makes you go unconscious and fall back into self-hypnosis. You must be conscious and aware at all times if you want to be a Spiritual master and master manifestor! The key lesson here is do not lose your "Joyous Spiritual Vigilance" against the negative ego and all its negative thoughts, images, feelings and wrong actions it would try to have you make!

Another way the negative ego blocks manifestation is that it doesn't have you engage the emotional body in the process. Remember what I said about the subconscious mind being the powerhouse of attraction within your relationship to self. This is because it stores all the feelings and emotions. So to engage the subconscious mind you must manifest and do your Spiritual practices with Spiritual passion, enthusiasm, love, joy, happiness, and Spirit! If you are going to take the negative ego's view that this is drudgery and just go through the motions, it is not going to work. As *A Course In Miracles* says, "True pleasure is serving GOD"! What else are you going to do with your time, indulge your lower-self? The negative ego has this backwards as it has everything backwards. This is not drudgery, this is living life in Praise of GOD! It is making your life a Song of GOD! It is making your life a creation like Michelangelo's Sistine Chapel! I humbly submit to you that I work 100 times harder than the average person, and get about 100 times more done than the average person, however I never ever consider myself working. I can't wait to get up in the morning! I can't wait to get out of bed! The more I do my Spiritual practices and work the more energy I have! If GOD gave me a billion dollars I would be doing the exact same thing! Serving GOD is pleasure! Serving the negative ego is work! That is what is draining beyond belief! I love doing GOD's Spiritual practices and work! I look at it, experience it and feel it as bliss, for what was once self-discipline when the negative ego, subconscious mind and emotional body were in control becomes total joy, bliss and "my cup runneth over" once one develops a habit of living as a Spiritual master and master manifestor! Practicing being a Spiritual master and master manifestor on all levels will not take away energy, it will give you infinite amounts of love, energy, joy and bliss! It will give you a "peace that passeth understanding"! It will bring you success beyond your wildest dreams and expectations in every aspect of your life! So engage your feelings and emotions in this process, for by engaging the feeling and emotional body this engages the subconscious mind and Spiritually electrifies your whole being, which makes the manifestation infinitely stronger and faster! Look how you feel reading this chapter and entire book. This book does not put you to sleep, for it is integrated and engages Spiritual passion and enthusiasm. There is nothing worse than going to hear a speaker with no Spiritual passion! There is nothing worse than reading a dry boring booking except if you want to use it as a sleeping pill before bed! You also do not want to be a boring person. Master your feelings and emotions in service of GOD. Do not let negative ego feelings and emotions manifest within you! However, fully integrate your feeling and emotions and unconditional love, Spiritual passion, and enthusiasm, for this is a key ingredient to God Realization and a key ingredient to being a master Spiritual magnetizer and attractor!

Another way the negative ego sabotages manifestation is by not having you take care of earthly business. To manifest effectively you must get your Spiritual house in order, your psychological house in order, and your earthly house in order. This means taking care of errands, taxes, phone calls, correspondence, e-mail, faxes, and other earthly things that need doing! If you have to hire someone to help you, so be it. However, stay on top of this thing. The pursuit of excellence must be maintained on all three levels: Spiritual, psychological and earthly at all times at a 100% level to the best of your ability. Do not settle for anything less in everything you do!

The next way the negative ego sabotages this process is by not being in integrity and honesty! Remember, everything in the infinite universe is a part of GOD! So if you are not in integrity, or are dishonest or negatively selfish in your business, you are stealing from God, which is yourself! Even if you have no money, maintain your integrity, honesty, egolessness, and selflessness. "What does it profit a man that he gains the whole world but loses his own Soul"!

Another way the negative ego sabotages the manifestation process is that it tells you that you are working for self instead of GOD! This of course is the great illusion of the negative ego, as if a separate self actually existed from GOD! How can this be when all that exists was created by GOD! We all live and move and have our being within GOD; and we all are Gods! So the concept of the word "work" is an illusion. This is a word that was created by the personality and negative ego thought system. I never go to work; I go to "Service"! It does not matter what you do. You could clean toilets, or collect garbage! This is a most holy and sanctified service of GOD! The "Material Universe" is a Face of GOD as well! All cleanliness and purification on every level is a Spiritual practice! It does not matter what type of work you do, it is the attitude and perspective you take towards it! See each customer as God, which is who and what they are, and treat them as such! See yourself as God! See the process as Son and Daughter of GOD serving Son and Daughter of GOD in service of GOD! Once we become Spiritual masters the main reason for being here is to serve! Taking this attitude makes work not work, but makes work a Spiritual practice which is the joy of serving GOD and the joy of serving your Brothers and Sisters in GOD!

Another way the negative ego sabotages the manifestation process is that it makes you forget to chant the names of GOD inwardly or outwardly in your life! If your mind is always filled with GOD, then your feelings will always be filled with GOD! Then your subconscious mind will only be filled with GOD! Then your actions will only be filled with GOD! Then you will manifest only things of GOD! Let life be a joyous song of love and praise to GOD! In your free time, or if a negative thought, image or feeling tries to get in, push it out, and immediately start chanting the names of GOD! You will find these listed in my books *The Golden Book of Melchizedek: How To Become An Integrated Christ/Buddha* in this lifetime, and in my book *The Complete Ascension Manual*. There is a larger list in the first book I mentioned! This is a most wonderful practice that many Westerners don't think about. The names of GOD can also be put to music in the forms of devotional songs or bhajans! One of the total keys to manifestation I am sharing here is the importance of keeping the mind and attention steady in the Light! What manifests in life is where you put your attention! Keep your attention only on GOD, only on Love, only on the Light! When temptation or negativity arise, one of the many tools I am presenting here is to inwardly or outwardly chant one of the many names or mantras of GOD, which will keep the mind where it needs to be! For as I said before, an idle mind is the devil's workshop! This bears repeating! Chanting the names of GOD can be an invaluable and joyous Spiritual tool!

The next way the negative ego sabotages the manifestation process is by having you forget who you really are and who your Brothers and Sisters really are. In the business of third dimensional life the negative ego has you slip back into third dimensional or personality level seeing instead of Soul seeing and Spiritual seeing. Spiritual consciousness has you see yourself and others as incarnations of God, Christs, and Buddhas who are one with you, in truth. The negative ego has you see self and others as just physical bodies and personalities who are separate from you! The negative ego viewpoint and perspective is, of course illusion! One of the keys to manifestation is to own the fact that you are God and you are serving

God, and that you are one with that which you are trying to manifest! Being an incarnation of God, in truth you are and have everything already! You are God! All Creation is, in truth, contained within you! One of the blocks to manifestation is when the negative ego and personality try to manifest and they do so from the consciousness of being separate from Creation instead of being a part of creation! You are one with that which you are manifesting! Your manifestation will be infinitely more powerful if you remember that you are God, your Brothers and Sisters are God, you are one with all Creation, and your Brothers and Sisters who you are serving are one with all Creation! So God is manifesting an aspect of self, to serve God, and GOD!

Another way the negative ego sabotages the manifestation process is, it has many false gods or idols that it puts before GOD! It puts money, material things, success, power, fame, sex, food, sleep, comfort, and relationships before GOD. There is nothing wrong with money, success and material things. However, you must ask yourself what comes first, GOD or these things. What are your true motivations, not just consciously but also subconsciously? Are you really being honest with self? Is GOD really the most important thing in your life? Do you seek GOD above all else! Do you have these things in proper perspective or do you want those things more than GOD! Does not the Bible say, "Seek ye the Kingdom of GOD and all things shall be added unto thee"! One of the keys to manifestation, my Beloved Readers, is to seek only GOD and GOD will be the only thing that manifests back! This is not to say you can't own your personal power, pray, affirm, or visualize to try to make money and increase your business. However, the key question you always must ask yourself is, does GOD come first? Have you passed the "Abrahamic Initiation"? Abraham had to place his son on the altar and be willing to kill him upon the Archangel's request! This was because Abraham put his son before GOD! Once he was willing to kill his son and put GOD first, the Archangel said you don't have to do that! It is not that GOD will kill that which you put before Him, you will! Your own negative ego attachment and thinking will repel that which you want! So I ask you, my Beloved Readers, have you placed everything and I mean everything on the "Altar of GOD" and do you truly put GOD first? Have you passed your own "Abrahamic Initiation"? If you wish to achieve God Realization and become a master manifestor, I humbly suggest you do so! It is just a matter of adjusting, your attitudes and perspectives. Do a Spiritual inventory in your mind's eye or talking to GOD or both, and place everything on "GOD's Altar" and put GOD first! Then you shall "Love the Lord thy GOD with all your heart and soul and mind and might and you shall love your neigh-bor as you love your self!" You shall then also "Seek ye the Kingdom of GOD and all things shall be added unto thee"!

The last way the negative ego sabotages the manifestation process is that it has you read all these things that I have written about in this chapter and book and have gotten excited about, but does not have you "Demonstrate the Presence of God in your moment by moment daily life"! The final ingredient is to not just Spiritually attune, think, feel, and act; but also to fully Demonstrate God and "Integrated Ascension" in your daily moment-by-moment life! This final ingredient completes the puzzle so to speak! This final ingredient now gives you, my Beloved Readers, a "Full Spectrum Prism Consciousness and Understanding" of GOD's Laws of Manifestation and how to prevent the negative ego from sabotaging this process! My Beloved Readers, put into practice and demonstration these Spiritual understandings and tools that have been given forth in this chapter and you will achieve Spiritual and earthly success beyond your wildest dreams and expectations. You will do so effortlessly and easily, for it will be GOD who is guiding the process! You now have all the understanding and tools you need to become the master of the Spiritual and earthly processes! Go in peace, create inward and outward abundance, be of service, thank GOD for your success, and be Spiritually vigilant for GOD and His Kingdom!

Chapter 15

The Three Levels of Spiritual Vision

This is a most interesting chapter I have very much been looking forward to writing. It deals with the three levels of vision. Most people have not thought about there being actually three levels of Spiritual vision. When most people think of Spiritual vision they think of someone being clairvoyant. Someone being able to see auras, Spiritual beings, and into the inner Spiritual worlds. This is certainly one type of vision, which a relatively small number of people have in this world. Spiritual vision is not necessarily a sign of advanced Spiritual growth This may surprise some of my readers that I say this. Spiritual vision on this level is connected with the development of one's subconscious inner senses, not any superconscious level necessarily. There are people who are schizophrenic who are clairvoyant and see into the astral world. It must be understood that there are a thousand different degrees of Spiritual vision at this level. Everyone's clairvoyance is not the same. Some people can see into the astral plane, some into the mental plane, some into the buddhic or causal plane, some into the soul plane, some into the Spiritual plane. Some people can see one layer of the aura, another person two, another person three, and so on into infinitum. Some people can see into chakras and other people can't. Some people can see Spirits and other people can't. Some people see lots of light and color, other people can see clearly the inner plane worlds.

There is one thing that must be understood, and that is one cannot separate the development of consciousness from one's clairvoyance. How developed or undeveloped one is will totally affect one's clairvoyant abilities. This is because ones thoughts create one's reality, and this will act as a lens and filter for one's clairvoyance. It will attract and magnetize certain types of sight and repel other types. This type of Spiritual vision is one of the many Spiritual gifts of GOD, however it is not necessarily needed to become a full-fledged Ascended Master on Earth.

The second type of vision I am going to speak of here is Physical vision. Now some people might not think of this as a type of Spiritual vision, however I assure you that it is, for GOD is as much in the physical body and material universe as he is in the Heavenly universe. There are four faces of GOD, and the material face is one of them. Just as Spiritual clairvoyance can give important information about what is going on in and around ones reality, physical vision gives equally important information. The ideal of course is to develop an efficient perception of reality. One cannot do this without being balanced and integrated, Spiritually, psychologically, and physically. There are all kinds of things going on in one's physical reality that gives all kinds of important Spiritual information. The appearance of any given person, their body language, the way they talk, the way they sound, the clothes they wear, their demeanor, their posture, their eyes, their stride, how they decorate their home, their desk, just to name a few. To have an efficient perception of reality it is also important to physically perceive well. Life is full of misperceptions and some of these can come from improper physical sight as well. This is why it is always a very good idea to take good care of your physical body and if you need glasses to get them. If you are reading a book and cannot see physically you are going to misread the words. This is going to cause an inefficient perception of reality. Certain lessons may occur which require physical vision as well to understand the whole story, and if your physical vision isn't good it will be that much less information to see the situation from a Full Spectrum Prism Perspective. I could go on, however I think you, my Beloved Readers, get my point here.

The third type of Spiritual vision is the most important level and profoundly affects the other two types of vision and very few people on Earth realize the extent to which this takes place. All three levels of Spiritual vision are important, however the psychological Level is the most important. As I have said many times, we just don't see with our physical eyes we see with our minds. We also see with the images in our minds and through our feelings and emotions. We also see through not only our conscious minds, but we see through our subconscious minds. The last one is the kicker. For the subconscious mind is the storehouse of all our programming from all of this life and even past lives. So most people do not see in the Holy Instant, most people see through their past programming. This is a very profound statement and I suggest pondering very deeply upon this.

This third type of Spiritual vision profoundly affects the other two types of vision. This is because a persons channeling and clairvoyance are filtered through the consciousness and/or subconscious programming of the person who has these abilities. This is why very psychologically disturbed individuals with these abilities are usually tuning into the astral plane and channeling astral entities even though they have these gifts. Their consciousness attunes them to and attracts its level of understanding and development. This is something a great many lightworkers do not understand.

This whole understanding of this third level of psychological vision is a fascinating one and also one that most of the world does not realize is going on and that includes lightworkers. The world, in truth, is actually a neutral screen and we each project our thoughts and programming onto this world, and we see, experience and feel what we are projecting, but it all happens so fast we think it is coming from outside of ourselves. We give the meaning the world has for us. All the feelings and emotions we feel in relationship to the world and all people are coming from ourselves, not from anything outside of ourselves. This again is because there are two ways of interpreting reality and only two. Every person on Earth interprets life from his or her Spiritual/Christ/Buddha consciousness or from his or her negative ego/fear-based/separate/lower-self mind. This, not what is coming from outside of self, governs what you experience and how you feel in life. All meaning of the outside world comes from your interpretations, perception and belief system.

There is a way of interpreting life that will bring you unconditional love, joy, happiness, inner peace, and evenmindedness at all times. There is another way of interpreting life that will bring you an emotional roller coaster of ups and downs. It is not in the world, it is in your psychological vision, perception, interpretation, programming and belief systems.

To see how greatly our Spiritual vision is affected by our psychology, philosophy, programming, interpretations and belief systems is actually fascinating to watch. My Beloved Readers, let me give you some examples to shed some greater light on this subject. Have you ever noticed when a person reads a book or article out loud that, they skip certain words, and add other words that aren't there? This is called "subconscious interference", and this is, in truth, an entire new study in the field of psychology and vision that needs to be studied much more closely. Did you ever have someone edit something for you they wrote, and they cannot see the easiest mistakes even though on a logistical level they perfectly understand these simple grammatical or spelling lessons. This is subconscious interference. We are all aware of the process of "Freudian Slips," where words come out that a person doesn't mean to say, but slip out anyway to show one's true thinking and meaning. Subconscious interference is so prevalent in our society and even among lightworkers that it is mind blowing. A person parks their car in the mall and on their return from shopping is looking for it, but they have a fixed idea in their mind where the car is and so they walk right by it even though it is right in front of their physical eyes. In the field of hypnosis which we have all seen demonstrated in stage shows, by a mere suggestion to the subconscious mind a person can be made to hallucinate any of the five senses and any thought or image that is planted in their mind. My beloved readers, they actually see these things and they are not there. They can be made to see, hear, taste, touch and smell things that are not there. They can be made to think or see any image that is planted into their subconscious mind even though it is not there. A glass of water can actually taste like a martini. A flower can be made to smell like a garbage can. A person can be told everyone in the audience is nude and they will actually see this. A person can be told that they are nude and they will believe that. I could go on for hours explaining infinite numbers of possible hallucinations that a person can be hypnotized to experience and what ever thought or image is given to them that is exactly what they will experience.

My beloved readers, the implications of this are mind-boggling. The reason being is that most people on Earth live in hypnosis 99% of the time, even though their eyes are open. Most people on Earth, including lightworkers, are run by their subconscious minds an enormous amount of the time. If a person is not the absolute master of every thought and feeling and are choosing and causing them every moment they are under a subtle form of hypnosis. Hypnosis basically means a person is under the influence of the subconscious mind and not the conscious mind. The vast majority of the world is run by the subconscious mind. Their emotional body and subconscious mind run the vast majority of lightworkers. When you feelings and emotions run you, you are being run by your subconscious mind. My beloved readers are you beginning to intuit and sense the implications of this for distortion of Spiritual vision in a person's life? You do not need a trained hypnotist to create hallucination and distorted vision, it has already been done by parents, teachers, ministers, rabbis, friends, television, radio, magazines, newspapers, past life programming. Most of what the people on Earth are seeing, including lightworkers, is a massive hallucination of their subconscious mind. People see all kinds of negative feelings and emotions that are not really there. Negative feelings and emotions are hallucinations of negative ego programming. Hallucinations may be slightly too strong a word, and maybe distortions of true Spiritual vision would be more accurate, however there is some truth to describing things in this manner.

I remember a friend who wears glasses told me a story of how they had been at a party and thought they had left their glasses there. They went back to pick them up and the host of the party said to my friend when they came to the door that they were wearing the glasses. This is a true story. Another friend was at the dinner table and said where is my fork? Everyone started laughing because it was in their hand. There is no hypnotist; they are doing this, for we are living in a state of hypnosis when the subconscious mind is running us. Any beliefs and images we have in our mind will be made manifest in our Spiritual vision. Our programming will distort even what a person hears. You can listen to a phone message that clearly says Richard Smith. Another person will hear something completely different. How can someone distort something that is so obvious? The answer is subconscious interference.

When one is run by the subconscious mind it is like being drunk. What happens when a person gets really drunk? They do things they would not normally do. A lot of the times they black out for long periods of time and have no memory of doing all the bizarre things they did. A person who is run by their feelings, emotions and subconscious mind will say and do things and have no memory of doing them, and they did not have a touch of alcohol. Alcohol throws one even more into the subconscious mind, however most people in the world are there anyway. This is why alcohol is absolute poison for a great many people.

When a person is run by the subconscious mind they are also automatically run by the negative ego interpretation of life. This is because the subconscious mind was never created to be the director of your life. When you let your feelings and emotions control you, the negative ego will run your life. The entire negative ego thought system, philosophy, and interpretation of life, which occurs every moment of our lives, is one massive hallucination. Fear, separative thinking, materialism, negative feelings and emotions, lower-self indulgence, being run by lower-self desires, are all massive hallucinations. I do not use the word hallucination in a disturbed way as in a schizophrenic, but just in the sense of creating illusion, glamour, and maya, as the Eastern world calls it.

People are constantly projecting their thoughts and images onto the world and creating a reality that does not exist. My beloved Readers, how can twelve people not convict the police officers who beat up Rodney King when they had a half our of video tape showing the police officers beating him mercilessly. Some might ask the same thing about the O.J. Simpson trial. It is not our judicial system; it is that every juror brings with them their conscious and subconscious programming. This is why lawyers have a science to picking jurors, for there is no such thing as an impartial juror. I would not want my life in the hands of a jury. I do not mean this as a judgement, but people have such strange programming and they make all their decisions according to this programming. I remember another case where that famous female tennis player Monica Seles was stabbed on live television with a knife and couldn't play tennis for two years because of it, and they jury never even gave the deranged individual jail time. My beloved readers, are you beginning to see the profundity of that which I am speaking about here in terms of this third level of Spiritual vision?

People are constantly seeing, tasting, touching, smelling and hearing things that are not there because of subconscious interference. People are constantly hallucinating things from thoughts and images that are being programmed into their minds, from the past, by themselves, and from other people in the present, that are not really there. This is called self-hypnosis used to create self-induced hallucinations. It is also called hypnosis used by other people who are not trained hypnotists or even know anything about hypnosis, yet they are doing it quite effectively. We have all heard of victim consciousness. How many people in their world are victims in one degree or another? How many people are victims of other people and outside situations? How many people are victims of their own thoughts, images, feelings, emotions, subconscious mind, physical body, inner child, fear based thinking, lower-self desire? One is either a master in life or a victim. When a person is a victim, they are also run by the subconscious mind, and they are living in a state of "hypersuggestability." Most people do not have to go to a hypnotist to get hypnotized; they are already in hypnosis. I am actually licensed by the State of California in the practice of hypnosis but most of my work is not hypnotizing people, it is "dehypnotizing" people. Almost everyone is in hypnosis and I am trying to get them out of it. The majority of this world spends most of their time hallucinating.

One of the most comical things is to see this manifesting in the New Age movement. People want to see the inner plane Ascended Masters manifest on Earth and if they won't this does not matter because people think they see them anyway. If they don't see them outside of self, they will hallucinate that they are them. They create elaborate stories about how certain Masters are incarnated on Earth, and this is a massive hallucination of their own subconscious mind. They make up massive stories about Earth changes, and make maps of what is going to happen and most of it is a massive hallucination of their own minds that no longer has any basis in truth. They tell you they are at the 32 level of initiation when nothing can be farther from the truth. They tell you that they are total Cosmic Masters, yet they haven't even completed their own Planetary Ascension process. The give pat answers and pat interpretations about peoples' problems and lessons because they read it in some pat answer book, and they think they know what they are talking about. They get channeled readings from unclear channels who are running their own personal agendas and who are filled with glamour themselves, and believe all that they say, even though fifty percent of everything the channels are saying is illusion. People get past life readings and three quarters of the planet was Cleopatra or one of Christ's Apostles. It is even comical. I could go on for hours.

We all know the game of telephone where a message is passed along to someone to give to someone else, and when it finally goes around the circle the message is nothing like the original message. This is subconscious interference. You ask someone to do something for you and you even give them explicit notes as to what to say, yet when they give the message it is nothing like what you asked them to do. It is because they do not listen and follow instructions they and let the subconscious mind interfere with the process.

My Beloved Readers, why when an accident occurs and twenty people see it but everyone has a different interpretation of what happened? Is it the physical eyes? Well maybe a couple of people had poor physical vision, but this could not be the case with all twenty people. No, it usually is one's psychological consciousness that is distorting a true efficient perception of reality.

People who channel the Masters think they are getting a true perception of reality when 99% of all channeling is astral and mental in nature and is not even coming from the Spiritual plane. From the one or two percent that is coming from the Spiritual plane at least half or more of that is a total hallucination and distortion as well. This is because the person doing the channeling has tons of belief systems, personal agendas, subconscious programming, past life programming, and negative ego programming that is coloring the channelings. Yet lightworkers believe every word that is said. The channel has become the hypnotist, and this leads to even more hallucinations. There is so much hallucination, glamour, illusion, maya, negative ego, faulty thinking, personal agendas, and subconscious interference in the New Age Movement it is mind boggling. The lack of spiritual discernment is mind-boggling as well.

Lightworkers, believing they are Spiritual, create Spiritual meaning out of things often that have none. A bird may die and they may interpret this as a sign there is going to be some death in their life of some kind. Well maybe the bird died just because the cat killed it. Sometimes an overly Spiritual meaning can be put onto things. The list of potential spiritual misinterpretations, glamours, and distortions is infinite.

Another fascinating way that Spiritual vision is limited is looking at the four types of people relating to their four-body system. There is the more Spiritual, mental, emotional or physical type. Because of a person's programming, people tend to focualize their consciousness through certain lens, and not through the Full Spectrum Prism that GOD would have us see life from. Some people see life through their feelings and emotions. In any given situation that is all they tune into and they are not interested in anything else. Other people are more intuitive and see life through that lens mainly. Other people still are more mental and see life through their mental body and are not interested in intuition or feeling or their physical bodies. Other people see life through their five senses and are called sensation types. Others stills are combinations like intuitive/feeling or intuitive/thinking or any combination you can think of. The ideal of course is to be integrated and to see through all four perceptual lenses in an integrated and balanced manner. I know you, my Beloved Readers, can totally understand how this greatly limits one's Spiritual vision in any situation and this is just the tip of the iceberg.

Spiritual vision is then greatly restricted and seen through just a lens rather than a full spectrum prism by our Ray structure. A First Ray person sees life through power and politics. A Second Ray person sees life through love/wisdom and how to Spiritually educate people. A Third Ray person sees life through wisdom and how to put that wisdom in action into the world. A Fourth Ray person sees life through harmony, aesthetics and beauty. A Fifth Ray person sees life through the lens of science. A Sixth Ray person sees life through a devotional lens. A Seventh Ray person sees life through the lens of ceremonial order and magic, freedom, liberty, alchemy, transmutation and developing structures to create freedom. When any given person is not integrated in these seven rays their Spiritual vision of any given situation will be cut into as much as 1/7th of what a Full Spectrum Prism Consciousness could be as a full-fledged integrated Ascended Master. I could go on for another two hours listing other lens that limit our Spiritual vision, however this is a not the time or place and I have written other chapters on this subject. For our purposes, however, other lenses are our religion, race, socioeconomic level, country and city we live in, schooling, parents, spiritual psychology, philosophy, past life programming, subconscious programming, gender, profession, friends, political affiliation, education, astrological horoscope, numerological configuration, archetypal identification of the twelve major archetypes, to name just a few. My Beloved Readers, when we add all of these restricting factors of Spiritual vision I think we can see that most people on Earth see life through one one-millionth of the lens that GOD is looking at life from. Even the profession one is in makes one focus through that lens. A doctor looks through that lens, an artist through another, a lawyer through another still, a gardener through another. My Beloved Readers, this is why it is so important to become fully integrated in life and it is why I stress so much in my books of not just becoming an Ascended Master, but becoming an Integrated Ascended Master, otherwise you will pass your seven levels of initiation but you will continue to see life through an extremely limited lens instead of the Full Spectrum Prism Consciousness.

My Beloved Readers, I think you are beginning to gain now a little greater understanding of what Spiritual vision really is and how most people's Spiritual vision is extremely limited even though they may be lightworkers. I hope you can also see now the extraordinary affect our psychological and consciousness development has on Spiritual vision. I also want you to see now how most people doing channeling are not that developed in their psychological vision. People think that because they are channeling or are clairvoyant that this makes them a direct and clear channel for Spirit and the Ascended Masters. I am here to help you wake-up and have much more Spiritual discernment in this regard. Their clairvoyance and channeling is brought through their consciousness and psychological development and level of Spiritual vision they have developed. "One cannot separate one's consciousness and psychological development from one's channeling or clairvoyant abilities. Lightworkers naively think that if a person channels this is the direct voice of the Ascended Masters and Spirit. This is incredibly naïve and undiscerning. All channeling has to come through the lens, filters, consciousness, programming, and psychological vision of the person doing the channeling or clairvoyant work. I hope this little discussion will help you to be a little more spiritually discerning about the channeled material you read or any external channelings you may receive from others. If you really knew how many filters, programming, lenses, subconscious interference, and personal agendas that the information is brought through, you would think twice before accepting all the information just because it is supposedly channeled. In truth, there is no such thing as channeling. There are only people at different levels of psychological and Spiritual development bringing through guidance that is being reinterpreted by all their filters, lenses, belief systems, subconscious programming, and level of psychological vision. This whole area is an incredible blind spot and lack of understanding of how the process of channeling actually works by most people in the Spiritual movement. This is why there is so much distorted information, ego, glamour, maya, and illusion in the New Age Movement.

My Beloved Readers, I hope you can also see now very clearly how much our psychological vision affects our physical vision as well. Does not the Bible speak of this when it says, "If people have the eyes to see and the ears to hear"? Everyone has eyes and ears, but most people cannot see or hear. This is because this Biblical verse is speaking of your Spiritual and psychological eyes and ears, not just your physical ones. The truth is, my Beloved Readers, if Christ was to return to Earth he would not be known or recognized and would be completely rejected by the majority of the world and this is why he does not come. Most people in this world and most lightworkers think they have excellent Spiritual vision and think they are seeing exactly what is going on. The truth is they do not have the slightest idea how their negative ego is controlling them, or how much their belief systems, philosophy, psychoepistemology, subconscious programming, subpersonalities, ray structure, archetypes, four-body system identification, horoscope, lens background, education, just to name a few of the things we have talked about in this chapter, are restricting their vision. Everyone thinks they are seeing life perfectly clear, even if they are completely run by their emotional body, subconscious mind and negative ego. People cannot see their own blind spots and limitations so they do not think they are there.

This chapter has been written to help you, my Beloved Readers, see more clearly about the true nature of Spiritual vision, and to inspire you to develop yourself psychologically and in your consciousness to the highest degree possible. This way your channeling, clairvoyant, and Spiritual work can come through as clear a channel as possible and you will be one that sees life from an Integrated Full Spectrum Prism Consciousness and not through such a limited perspective as most people and lightworkers see life from. This chapter has been clearly written to help you see the unbelievably profound effect your psychology and consciousness has upon your vision and the effect it has on all channeling, clairvoyant and Spiritual work, as well as the extraordinary affect it even has upon your physical vision of reality. It is your Spiritual job and mission to not only integrate this ideal within self, but to also share it with others. The completion of your initiations and the building of your light quotient and light body is not enough. I think you can see from this chapter that you can develop these things I have just mentioned and still have incredibly shortsighted Spiritual vision. This is what the Masters have called "Fragmented Ascension." It could also be called "Non-Integrated Ascension". A great many lightworkers are achieving their ascension, however they are still run by the negative ego, emotional body, are still victims, are run by the inner child, are not developed psychologically, have improper psychoepistemologies and/or philosophies, are fragmented, disintegrated, are overidentified with their mind or emotions, are overidentified in certain rays, archetypes, astrological signs, bodies, chakras, programming, belief systems, subpersonalities, and perceptual lenses. If you truly want to realize GOD and have true Spiritual vision then you must do this at the highest possible level psychologically and in your consciousness on the Spiritual level and on a physical/earthly level as well. It is only then you can become a fully Realized "Integrated Melchizedek/Christ/Buddha" on Earth.

Lightworkers are also constantly giving Spiritual meaning to things that are total illusion as well. They interpret their dreams which is noble, but they do so from an imbalanced psychology and Spiritual philosophy, so they think they have gotten a confirmation on their belief system when in truth the negative ego is interpreting their dream and reinforcing its own philosophy. The same thing happens when reading certain Spiritual books. They are reading a book about the negative ego and they think they are reading the book, but in truth the negative ego is reading the book through their eyes and body, so the negative ego tells them that they have learned all these lessons and integrated all this material when nothing could be farther from the truth. They receive guidance from the Masters concerning a possible correction and they reinterpret the guidance as a compliment. They get feedback from others who share a similar lens and psychological imbalance, and think they are getting accurate feedback, when in truth they have just found a small group of friends who share the same hallucination.

People meet others and the other person tells them they don't look well physically. They felt fine before they met that person on the street or at the party. Later they feel sick because that person has hypnotized them without necessarily meaning to. It occurs because the individual is a victim and too hypersuggestible. The person is now sick and it is a massive hallucination. Not that they aren't sick now, but the sickness came from allowing that negative thought to be implanted into the person's subconscious mind and now the subconscious mind has made the person's physical body sick. This is why doctors in Japan often do not tell the patient of a serious illness so they do not create a self-fulfilling prophecy. If a person believes they have to die from AIDS and or Cancer they probably will, when in truth this is not the case.

My Beloved Readers, people are constantly projecting their thoughts and images on a conscious and subconscious level onto the world and something that is not there. They are also constantly allowing other people to plant thoughts and images into their minds and seeing things that are not theirs. A person goes to see a violent or scary movie, and then all night after the movie they think they are seeing and hearing possible scary or violent things. My Beloved Readers, are you all fully getting the point her? People are constantly hallucinating and seeing, hearing, tasting, touching and smelling things that are not there, which is being caused by "subconscious interference."

This is why it is so important, my Beloved Readers, to become the absolute masters of every thought, feeling, emotion, piece of energy, physical body, inner child, subconscious mind, negative ego, subpersonality, and to become the absolute cause of your reality at all times and not a victim. This is why it is absolutely essential to own your personal power at all times and to remain in unconditional love with your Golden Bubble of Protection up at all times, and to not allow yourself to go on automatic pilot or hypersuggestability. This is why it is essential not to live your life in a state of hypnosis, but to be joyously vigilant for GOD and His Kingdom at all times. This is why it is so important to completely clear your conscious and subconscious thinking of all negative ego/fear-based programming and replace it with Spiritual/Christ/ Buddha consciousness programming. This is why it is so important to do your psychological homework as well as your Spiritual and physical/earthly homework and not become imbalanced on my level. If you want to see life with "True and Clear Spiritual Vision", you must pay the utmost focused attention to keeping yourself clear psychologically at all times. This chapter has been a "pep talk", to help you my Beloved Readers, to see the utmost importance for doing this. Do not let the negative ego tell you that you have mastered all these lessons in the Spring of '72, for all it takes is a single moment of slipping into automatic pilot, no matter what your level of initiation or self-mastery, and the whole process can start up again. "After pride cometh the fall," as the Bible says. I do not mean this as criticism but some of the worst offenders of these things are Spiritual leaders, channels, Spiritual teachers, Spiritual scientists, and lightworkers. It is when one thinks they are the master of these things that they are most in danger. Even if one has mastered it for periods of time or even long periods of time, this does not change the potential to fall into it "hook, line and sinker" again. It is my sincere hope and prayer that this brief discussion of the three types of Spiritual vision has given you, my Beloved Readers, a little more in-depth Full Spectrum Prism Perspective how you are the absolute cause and master of your life in service of GOD and unconditional love!

CHAPTER 16

Paying Your Rent to GOD on All Levels

My Beloved Readers, this next chapter is a most interesting subject to consider that many lightworkers have possibly not considered fully. It has to do with the potential imbalances that can occur if Spiritual growth is not approached from an integrated perspective.

To begin this discussion, most often new seekers to the path open up Spiritually with an incredible opening of some kind. This could be a Spiritual experience, a good book, a class, or even a discussion with a friend. Their Spiritual body starts opening in leaps and bounds. Over time however, if the person's psychology and consciousness isn't addressed, in some people problems can take place. Especially those who begin opening to talking with their Spirit guides. If their psychology is still very much personality centered and run by the negative ego and victimized by the emotions, it will attract more astral and mental plane entities rather than the Ascended Masters. In the beginning they may be Spiritual, but over time this psychology of the person will draw and attract its frequency and attunement. This is easy to fix if people would study my books, *Soul Psychology, Integrated Ascension*, and *How To Clear The Negative Ego*. The problem is, however, Soul and Spiritual psychology is not very understood in this world even by the professionals and lightworkers. From this above mentioned example one can see the importance of developing one's self psychologically and Spiritually.

Another example of this is, that even the most advanced Spiritual initiate and Master who is even way beyond the seventh initiation, if focusing much more on the Spiritual level, channeling, Spiritual teaching, Spiritual science, or healing to name a few, will become completely corrupted by the negative ego, and its thirst for power, greed, fame, glamour, self-aggrandizement. I cannot tell you how often I have seen this happen with high level Spiritual leaders and teachers. It al stems from having tremendous development spiritually and in many other areas, however not being fully trained in Spiritual psychology. It creates corruption, personal agendas, self-centered motives, and corruption every time. It happens so often that I'm actually surprised now when it doesn't happen. The negative ego is incredibly seductive and manipulative and it takes tremendous training, dedication, joyous vigilance and commitment to purity to not let it come in over the long haul.

Now the reverse of this process is where a lightworker develops themselves psychologically but not Spiritually. I see this occur very often as well. Some approach the Spiritual path through the Spiritual door and some through the psychological door. It is interesting, half the people I talk to tell me their favorite book of mine is *Soul Psychology*, the other half tell me their favorite book is *The Complete Ascension Manual*. This symbolizes these two doorways. My personal feeling is I love them both equally, for I have a deep appreciation of the profundity and importance of levels. Now what happens to people who come through the psychological door is very fascinating. Because Spiritual psychology and/or Soul psychology is so poorly understood in our world people get involved in what I would call traditional psychology and/or fragmented understandings of Spiritual psychology. Traditional psychological theories will actually cut oneself off from their own Higher Self and Mighty I Am Presence. These fragmented Spiritual psychology understandings will do the same but not as completely as traditional psychological theories. I have seen many extremely high level Spiritual teachers, who because of the lack of understanding of Soul and Spiritual psychology, really go off the deep end and really cut off their Spiritual connection because of this unconscious, imbalanced understanding. The best way to explain this is to give an example. There are a certain number of Spiritual teachers who believe in their psychology that they have to balance everything. Now at first glance one might say, "What is Joshua talking about?" This sounds perfectly normal and proper. My Beloved Readers, balance is a wonderful thing, however there is one thing we do not want to balance in life and that is negative ego consciousness versus Christ/Buddha Consciousness. This is why His Holiness the Lord Sai Baba has said that the definition of GOD is "GOD equals man minus ego." Sai Baba said "minus" ego, *not* balance your negative ego. They are opposite philosophies of life. If you try to balance Christ consciousness and negative ego consciousness this would be like trying to balance forgiveness and holding grudges, unconditional love and conditional love, patience, and impatience, judgementalness and nonjudgmentalness.

My Beloved Readers, I think you can see how imbalanced and inappropriate this is. Yet some of the most well known Spiritual leaders in the Spiritual movement and their followers hold such fragmented Spiritual philosophies. They may be doing wonderful work on a Spiritual level. But their psychology is completely corrupting their work and ultimately it contaminates every aspect of the work because their foundation is totally off-kilter. The lack of understanding of the negative ego and the need to transcend it allows the negative ego to run rampant in their personal, professional and Spiritual lives. This ultimately leads to enormous problems in their organization, with relationships and corruption in the teachings, channeling, and any kind of scientific endeavor.

It is very strange that someone can be so advanced spiritually yet hold very odd and strange psychological philosophies. In my personal experience, without meaning to be judgemental in the slightest and just trying to bring light to an area of unconsciousness, this is the case 98% of the time to varying degrees. The world does not need more channels, more Spiritual teachers, or Spiritual scientists; it needs more trained Spiritual counselors, Spiritual psychologists, and Spiritual teachers who are fully trained in Spiritual psychology. If this is not the case, the negative ego will contaminate and corrupt the guidance and information coming through these other vehicles without the people ever being aware of it. If one is not right with self, or is off-kilter in self and one's psychology, it is impossible for this imbalance and off-kilteredness not to exist in their channeling, clairvoyance, healing, spiritual teaching, spiritual science work and in relationships.

The danger of a person coming through the psychological door is that they get stuck in a particular psychological theory, and this creates a certain lens they get stuck in for seeing life, which serves also as a type of blinder, like a horse who has blinders on while running a race. Having blinders on at times can be good if one's psychology is fully integrated in a soul and Spiritual perspective but not in the previous case.

What happens is this type of person attracts and magnetizes people and lightworkers of a similar imbalanced philosophy yet still Spiritual. They think they are getting healthy feedback from others but really what they are doing is just attracting a small group of people who keep collectively reinforcing their psychological neurosis.

Again, I say this with no judgement just with the loving light of Spiritual discernment to see this phenomena in your own life or in others so as not to doubt self just because a small group of people hold a similar imbalanced psychology or philosophy. In truth, almost the entire world is involved with this. There are the Freudians, Jungians, Adlerians, Cognitive Therapy followers, Behaviorists, Family Therapists, Humanistic followers, Gestalt followers, and Transactional Analysis followers. Then there are all the different Spiritual groups, gurus, Spiritual teachers, religions, mystery schools, and channels. Each one can be seen as a lens or group of lenses in the full spectrum prism seeing of GOD. The path of Synthesis teaches one to appreciate all of them and to not get caught up in just one, where one's vision of life is seen through a single lens or small numbers of lenses in a prism that contains, in truth, thousands if not millions of lenses. This, my Beloved Readers, is the danger of coming through the psychological door and being caught in a certain form of psychology that has a type of myopic vision that does not see the whole picture and often even cuts off one's Spiritual connection. I have seen this happen so often to absolutely brilliant Spiritual and psychological leaders, teachers, scientists, and friends.

My Beloved Readers, think about it if one's thoughts create one's reality, how could this not be so! It cannot be emphasized more emphatically that we do not just see with our physical eyes, we see through our mind and belief systems. It is only when we see life through the full spectrum prism of Soul and Spiritual psychology, and are able to demonstrate this self-mastery in our daily lives, can full integrated Self Realization and God Realization take place.

Now the third aspect to this discussion, which has not been addressed, is the physical/earthly level. I have seen an enormous number of lightworkers become highly enamoured with the Spiritual or Heavenly level and become too ungrounded and create physical health problems. They may be highly spiritual and even be channels or brilliant Spiritual teachers, however they may not eat right or exercise. They may drink too much coffee or smoke cigarettes, which eventually takes a toll on their physical health. They may eat too much sugar or not get enough sleep. All their energy is in their higher chakras and very little energies in their lower chakras and this will take a toll on the physical organs and glands in the physical body.

Another way this problem manifests is that the person is raising their vibration and frequency Spiritually at an astronomical rate and they may even have achieved their ascension, which is a certain percentage of light quotients. If the physical body isn't evolved at a similar rate of growth in terms of raising the frequency, one can and often will get sick a lot. This is a type of cleansing crisis to raise the vibration and frequency of the physical vehicle to catch up with the spiritual vehicle.

So the question is how does one raise the frequency of the physical vehicle? This is done by eating a good diet, physical exercise, sleep, grounding one's spiritual energy, holding and demonstrating a proper Spiritual psychology, drinking the Water of Life, connecting with nature, practicing the Presence of GOD on Earth and creating Heaven on Earth in your daily life. I would also add to this enjoying Earth life instead of trying to escape Earth life as the ultimate goal.

Another reason balanced Spiritual growth is important is that those on an accelerated ascension and initiation process will experience Christ/Buddha mutations in their physical vehicle which is the result of the high level infusions of light quotient, love quotient, power quotient, higher bodies, higher chakras, and DNA transformation.

If one does not take care of the physical body and pay one's rent so to speak, one can develop chronic physical health lessons which greatly impede one's Spiritual and psychological progress. Life becomes much harder when the physical body is not supporting the Spiritual and psychological work. It still can be done, however, it is much harder and takes more personal power, self-mastery and self-discipline to do it. So my Beloved Readers, evolve and take care of your physical body as well, for as you know it is the Temple of the God you are.

Imbalance can also occur in the physical body if the psychological level is not addressed properly. The subconscious mind runs the physical body; this can be clearly proven by the practice of hypnosis. Most people do not have mastery over their subconscious mind, emotions, and negative ego. This causes too many negative thoughts, negative emotions, and too many negative orders given to the subconscious mind which will cause it to manifest all kinds of physical health problems, pain, and illnesses. Every thought you think manifests in the physical body. Every emotion you feel manifests in your physical body organs and glands. Most people who suffer exhaustion and excessive fatigue feel this as a result of an imbalanced psychology. Your psychology totally affects your physical immune system. If you do not have a healthy psychological immune system over time you are going to have a weakened physical immune system.

So my Beloved Readers, can you see why so many people are sick, fatigued, exhausted and not in good physical health? This stems often from overidentification with the Spiritual, improper psychology, improper care for the physical body and then living in a world filled with physical pollutants such as smog, petrol chemicals, chemical pollutants, drugs, pesticides, imbalanced ozone layer, polluted water, polluted air and polluted Earth, caused by imbalanced psychospiritual relationships to the Earth in the mass consciousness of the world. It is amazing that our bodies function as well as they do, given all the abuse they take.

The final place in this puzzle is paying one's rent to the Earth itself not just the physical body. A great many lightworkers are so busy meditating, channeling, and focusing on Celestial realms that the Earth and Material Universe is forgotten about. This again is a type of ungrounding. Meditating, channeling, and focusing on the Celestial realms are fine as long as it is done in proper relationship to the Earth. The purpose of life is to create Heaven on Earth. The purpose of life is to become your Mighty I Am Presence on Earth in a balanced and integrated manner.

A great many lightworkers do wonderful Spiritual things and sometimes even psychological things, however it often stops there. They cannot seem to take the final step of fully grounding their mission and purpose on Earth. Making money is part of this. Taking care of all the responsibilities of Earth life. Taking proper care of the Earth. Physically manifesting your mission on Earth in a fully functioning manner. I always love the quote of Sai Baba who says, "Hands that help are holier than lips that pray."

Most lightworkers avoid politics and a great many of the social causes of Earth. This needs to change for it is our collective responsibility to create a utopian society. We each must pay our rent Spiritually, psychologically, in our physical bodies and to the beloved Earth Mother who sustains us with physical food and provides us with the material foundation to manifest GOD's plan on Earth. It is only when one's rent is paid on all four levels that full, Self Realization and God Realization can be achieved. My Beloved Readers, it must be remembered that GOD lives as much in the physical and material universe as He does in the emotional dimension, mental dimension, and Spiritual dimension. These are aptly called, esoterically, the Four Faces of GOD. It is absolutely essential that we pay our rent to all four faces or all four levels in a balanced manner! This includes working to revamp our earthly civilization as well as taking care of the Earth Mother and nature. As we enter the New Millennium and the Seventh Golden Age it is now time for lightworkers to fully ground their Spiritual paths on Earth and dedicate their lives to transforming our civilization and society into a fifth dimensional, fully functioning society on Earth. For as we have seen in this chapter if we don't approach our Spiritual path in this integrated and balanced manner on a daily basis, over time it can create major imbalances in your own four-body system, and create some major impediments and blocks to achieving the full Self-Realization and God Realization you seek. I end this chapter with the words of His Holiness Lord Buddha, who from his own personal life experience came to the truth, "Maintain balance and moderation in all things!" It is only when this approach is taken that full God Realization will be achieved in ourselves hence then our earthly world and civilization can realize God in the way we all live and function on Earth in all facets of our daily lives. This can only happen if we dedicate our lives to not only loving the Earth Mother and nature, but also fully loving our earthly civilization, and doing everything we can to help all the institutions and laws of the Earth function with Spiritual principles, instead of negative ego and personality level principles. It is time for all of us to each embody GOD in the puzzle piece and purpose we each have been given to transform our earthly society in this manner. It is then we will experience GOD not only fully in ourselves but we will experience GOD also in a fully functioning God Realized society on Earth. For too long lightworkers have waited to ascend and escape Earth. This New Millennium, Aquarian Age, and Seventh Golden Age now teaches us just the opposite. Love the Earth, love nature, and love our society and civilization and make it reflect GOD in a similar manner that His other three faces reflect on a Spiritual, mental and emotional level. It is now time to manifest GOD on Earth and in our society and civilization. This will only happen when we as the lightworkers and lightbearers of this New Age dedicate our lives to doing this. It is not GOD's job and it is not the inner plane Ascended Masters' job. It is our Spiritual assignment and mission for we are the ones inhabiting physical bodies. One cannot achieve true Self-Realization and GOD Realization without fully loving the Earth and our earthly civilization in this manner. By doing so we will each integrate the Four Faces of GOD on all levels and fully integrate the Divine plan on Earth as GOD and the Masters would have it be. By taking this approach in this balanced manner you will fully experience the full totality of GOD on every level and you will have the opportunity of fully being and demonstrating God on Earth and sharing this wondrous experience with other lightworkers embodying GOD on Earth in a similar manner. Transforming our earthly civilization into one that functions fully on Spiritual principles in all its countries and institutions is not an easy task. It is, however, what we have collectively come here to do. Let us now take hold of the sword of Lord Michael in a balanced manner and courageously and joyously realize our destiny and fully realize the "Great Souls" that we collectively all are. We cannot fail, for GOD, the inner plane Ascended Masters, the Elohim Masters, the Archangels and Angels, the Christed Extraterrestrials and the strength of our own personal power and unconditional love for GOD in all His four faces is an unbeatable team!

CHAPTER 17

Spiritual Alchemy:
How To Turn Negative Experiences
Into Positive Ones!

It is extremely important to understand that everything in life happens for a reason and there are no accidents! Everything in GOD's infinite universe is governed by laws! If something happens in life, be it positive or negative as you interpret it, it has happened to teach a Spiritual lesson. In truth, everything that happens is good. To even look at something as negative or bad is an interpretation of the mind. Everything is good in the sense of everything being a Spiritual lesson and Spiritual test! It is certainly okay to have preferences for certain things to happen and this is as it should be, and you should go after your preferences with all your heart and soul and mind and might. However, the lesson is to be happy whether you get it or not! Happiness then becomes a state of mind, not anything outside of self!

Now, it is a fact that very often in life no matter how dedicated, good, pure, Spiritual or even Christed we are, things in life will not go according to our preferences. This can be caused by personal factors that we set in motion in this life or past lives! There are also many things that happen that do not meet our preferences that are caused by other people, for we are not alone in this world. There are 6 billion other souls in this Planetary Mystery School called Earth. Certain things happen because of personal karma and certain things happen because of group karma. There are other things that happen because of Planetary karma or Historical karma. Why something happens, in truth, does not matter, for if it happened, the fact is you needed that lesson! The cause of why it happened is unimportant. One cannot cry over spilled milk! It is spilled and nothing is going to change that! Many times things will not go according to our preferences because we have made mistakes. Sometimes we make very big mistakes and there is great karma to pay! This is not a judgement and is not bad, just a statement that certain mistakes have greater implications than others. Everything is, of course, forgiven and everything is a lesson, so in truth, forgiveness is the healing balm that heals all!

Now the question is, how does one turn something negative that has happened into a positive? Certainly the first way is gaining the "Golden Nugget of Wisdom" from what happened! Also, one can make a specific Spiritual vow to oneself and God to never let this happen again!

So let me review. The first thing that turns every situation of life that is not your preference into something positive is looking at it as a Spiritual lesson and Spiritual test. The second thing that causes this Spiritual alchemical process is forgiveness and unconditional love towards self and others. The third thing that turns any negative into a positive is the "Golden Nugget of Wisdom" learned from your mistake or the mistake of others and/or the Spiritual tests you get to practice! The forth thing that turns it into a positive is just recognizing that everything works for the good in GOD's infinite universe and that GOD always makes good out of everything! We have all used the expression this was a "Blessing in Disguise"! Very often, if not most often, those things that we thought turned out to be the worst turned out to be the best!

A person gets cancer and they think this is the worst thing that could happen. The cancer turns out to be the Spiritual teacher that sets the person on a Spiritual journey they would have never gone on if it weren't for the cancer!

When I write books, it is my life experience that I use very often for the chapters I write. It is the insights I have about myself and what I observe in my students, friends, and colleagues that serve to be the grist for the mill for ideas for my chapters. Whole books and book after book have been written in this manner. So what at first seems terrible turns out to be the idea for a chapter. This very chapter I now write is an example of this. Something occurred in my life that was not according to my preferences. However, I was very taken by how I turned this experience into a positive. That insight was the inspiration for writing this chapter! That which could have been interpreted as a negative has become an inspiration chapter to help others!

My Beloved Readers, what I am trying to show you is that everything works that way, if you will just see it as such! Job had everything taken away and it turned out to be the best thing that ever happened to him! He got to take the supreme test of faith and righteousness in GOD, and passed.

A person may have a relationship end, which seems like the worst thing in the world. Twenty years later it is seen as the best thing that ever happened! A person may get a terrible health crisis, which seems like the worst thing in the world. They may not be able to work, change professions, take years off work, and GOD only knows what else. If the person has the "proper" attitude, which is the key to what I am talking about, they can look at it as a Spiritual test and focus on what they can do instead of what they can't do. This situation may force them to become more Spiritual. It may force them to meditate more. It may force them to become more inner-directed. It may force them to develop in other areas that they never would have ever developed!

So Spiritual alchemy will take place in every aspect of your life if you have the philosophy that GOD would have you think with, which is how can I make good out of this! So it is this set of attitudes and this last one I just spoke about that is the key to turning any negative situation into a positive one! Whatever the catastrophe, maybe you are supposed to learn about that and be the crusader on Earth to prevent this from happening to others!

This book, and my book *The Golden Book of Melchizedek*, I consider to be the two best books I have ever written out of the 27 I have written so far. Both came out of watching all the negative ego corruption, contamination, glamour, illusion and maya going on in the New Age Movement among a great many Spiritual leaders, students, and even friends I was working with! I could not believe all the "negative ego corruption" I was seeing in channelings, Spiritual teachers, Spiritual scientists, psychics, and so on. I would sit for hours and hours on end talking with the inner plane Ascended Masters about all the disintegration and fragmentation going on in religion and the New Age Movement, even among some of the most well known Spiritual leaders, channels and teachers on this planet who I have been privy to know! I was seeing things that were blowing my mind! Instead of allowing myself to be brought down by it, I looked at it in unconditional love and with Spiritual discernment, and decided to write a series of masterpiece books that would explore every aspect of the corruption going on that I was seeing as a Spiritual teacher, Spiritual channel and Spiritual psychologist! I turned something that I could have let deflate me or lessen my enthusiasm into what I now consider to be some of the best books I have ever written.

My Beloved Readers, no matter what your situation is, it can be turned into a positive if you will look at it that way and pray to GOD, Christ, the Holy Spirit, the Masters, the Angels, the Christed

Extraterrestrials, and the Elohim Councils to help you! The negative ego is very conniving and manipulative. However, the negative ego is not as smart as GOD! If you pray to GOD and the Masters and use your own GOD-given creative mind, there is always, and I mean always, a "silver lining"!

I tell you, as GOD is my witness, a person who practices such a philosophy could go to jail and would look at it as a Spiritual retreat! They would say my meals are taken care of. I don't have to work! What a great opportunity to practice forgiveness and unconditional love. They would say I will spend my days physically exercising, reading, studying the Bible or some other book, and bilocating to the ascension seats of GOD! Calling in light showers and love showers from the Masters! Doing inner plane service work! Looking at everything that happens as a Spiritual test! Seeing how Christ-like they could be under the worst circumstances!

Many things happen in life we don't understand. Many things happen because of past life karma. Many things happen because of group karma! Many things happen because of this lifetime's programming. Many things happen because of mistakes by self or others. It all doesn't matter! No matter how catastrophic the situation, it can be turned into a positive!

The AIDS patient ends up totally changing their priorities. Living in the moment. Appreciating life a million times more. Becoming a speaker traveling around the world speaking for people with AIDS!

Again, there is the inspirational example of Christopher Reeve who broke his spine while riding his horse. Who has not been inspired by his example?

Another excellent example is that of Nelson Mandela, who was imprisoned for over 25 years, and comes out of prison with total unconditional love, and becomes the president of South Africa, and gives total amnesty to everyone! He could have been destroyed in prison and/or become completely embittered, but instead he comes out as a Christ!

Christ was crucified and killed, and used it as an opportunity to practice forgiveness! "Forgive them Father for they know not what they do"!

A person loses their leg and becomes a Special Olympics athlete! If you have chronic health problems, "join the club." So did Mother Teresa who had a failing heart. So did Saint Francis! You look at it as your Spiritual test and "cross to bear," and you bear it every day blessing GOD and saying to GOD, "Not my will but thine; thank you for the lesson!" It is fine to pray for a miracle healing every day as well, but since you have given up your attachment attitudes for preference attitudes, you are happy whether you get it or not!

My Beloved Readers, there is no such thing as death, no one can really die for you are not your physical body, you are the soul incarnating into it. Your body cannot be deformed! Maybe your physical body can, but the second you die you get a new one! We are eternal and immortal beings whether we like it or not. It is not up to us to decide such things because we didn't create ourselves, GOD created us! So all these so-called challenges, or crosses, or negative things are temporary! Life in truth goes by in a twinkling of an eye. GOD deals in expanses of time such as "100 billion years of Brahma." You don't want to know how long that is! One lifetime is like a grain of sand in relationship to the infinite universe! The way it works is very simple, and Earth is a Spiritual school and place to serve. To achieve Spiritual liberation and graduation we must maintain a Spiritual/Christ/Buddha attitude and perspective regardless of what comes down the pike! If it is meant to be that we go early then so be it! This may not be our preference but there is no such thing as death and you will see all your family and friends soon on the inner plane anyway! So let's be serious here. Isn't death the worst case scenario? Some would actually look at it as a blessing, for we are visiting here and this is not our true home. Our true home is in Heaven!

The story of Job is of course the best example, for everything is stripped away. He loses his health, money, and family, everything all at once! He had a bad attitude for a little while but GOD helped him to see the truth. In having everything go wrong all at once he got rid of all his attachments. Isn't that wonderful! Did not Buddha say in the Four

Noble Truths that all suffering comes from attachments and all suffering comes from wrong points of view? Does this not sum it all up right there. Your suffering, my Beloved Readers, is your attitude and your attachment, not what is going on in your life! Everything that is happening in your life and in everyone else's life, in truth, is a "blessing"! This is the way GOD sees it and this is the way it is! It is just a matter of time until you will let go of the negative ego's interpretation of what is going on and accept GOD's, Christ's, and the Holy Spirit's and the Spiritual/Christ/Buddha consciousness interpretation of what is going on! Sai Baba says to "Welcome adversity"! If someone attacks you and criticizes you, "bless them and thank them" for giving you the Spiritual opportunity for practicing personal power, keeping your Golden Bubble up, turning the other cheek, getting to practice forgiveness and unconditional love, loving your enemies, recognizing that an "attack is a call for love," practicing innocent perception and seeing that person as the Christ even tough he or she does not see themselves that way!

My Beloved Readers, this world we live in has everything completely backwards from the way it really is! This is because the personality and negative ego interprets the reality for mass consciousness instead of the Soul, the Higher Self, The Mighty I Am Presence, the Holy Spirit, and the Spiritual/Melchizedek/Christ/Buddha consciousness!

Thank GOD for everything that is happening in your life! Thank Him for the opportunity to learn all these wonderful lessons! Focus on what you can do, not on what you can't do. Focus on what you have gained, not what you have lost! Is the glass of water half empty or half full? Do you look at the donut or the hole? In 1929 the stock market crashes and one person jumps out the window of a building and commits suicide and the other person says, "Easy come easy go!"

One person goes through the Job Initiation and commits suicide! Job says, 'Naked I come from my mother's womb and naked shall I leave. The Lord giveth and the Lord taketh away, Blessed be the Name of the Lord"!

As you can see, my Beloved Readers, I love this quote! Anyone who goes through the Job Initiation is actually more blessed than the richest man or woman in the world. For in going through the Job Initiation one has "found GOD"! Do not try and make the Joe Initiation happen, for that is not the purpose of life. However, if it does happen and that is your fate even though it was not your preference, then use it for the Glory of GOD!

If you have an incurable illness then use it "For the Glory of GOD"! Then GOD will come to you at death and say to you "This is a Soul I am well pleased with, for they bore this cross to my Glory!" Remember the words of Master Jesus who said, "Be ye faithful unto Death and I will give thee a Crown of Life"!

My Beloved Readers, you are now being Spiritually challenged by Spirit and the inner plane Masters to Spiritually, mentally and emotionally perform Spiritual alchemy on whatever is going on in your life in the past, present and in the future and to turn any perceived past, present or future negative situation into a positive! Use your own GOD-given Christed mind to do this and ask for help from Spirit and the Masters to do this! GOD and the Masters will not forsake you! They will turn lemons into lemonade if you let them, and if you will co-create this with them! The most profound thing of all is that this is truly how GOD perceives the situation! All you are doing, in truth, is getting your consciousness in harmony with your God consciousness! There is not any situation that has ever occurred in the past, is occurring now, or will occur for anyone in the future, where this cannot be done! I am not saying life cannot be very tough at times. This, however, is the reason you have come! You are made of a substance stronger than anything life can throw at you and test you with. You are made of GOD! Does not the Bible say, "Ye are Gods and know it not"! Does not the Bible say, "Let this mind be in you that was in Christ Jesus"! You are fully capable of passing any test, for if you weren't, GOD would not have sent you! Whatever is going on within you or without you, there is a Spiritual way of interpreting the situation that will bring you inner peace, that will help you to pass the Spiritual test you are going through, and will help you to find a way to use what has happened as a means for Spiritual service! If you do take this attitude and perspective as I am suggesting, towards whatever has happened to you, GOD will use it like "fire in a steel factory forges steel," to fully transform you into a "fully Realized Christ and Realized Buddha" of the strongest and most profound nature! This is the true purpose of all that has happened to you, is happening now, or will ever happen to you! Spirit and the Masters now ask you to fully accept and take on this "Full Mantle of the Christ" and to let GOD now forge you like steel with His Spiritual tests and lessons, so you can develop the Spiritual/Christ/Buddha consciousness to such a degree of self-mastery and dedication that you will live in this world "fully God Realized" for you will have used it for this sole purpose and you will have chosen wisely! In this Spiritually poignant moment you are being asked by Spirit and the Masters to dedicate your life to this noble purpose and cause, no matter what the Spiritual tests and obstacles! If you do this you will achieve God Realization in this lifetime, you will achieve liberation from the wheel of rebirth, you will have Spiritually graduated, you will achieve the Crown of Life, You will have passed the Job Initiation, you will have fully achieved the Spiritual/Christ/Buddha consciousness, you will have transcended your negative ego/fear-based separative consciousness, and you will, my Beloved Readers, have achieved "a peace that passeth understanding"!

CHAPTER 18

The Negative Ego's Effect on the Seven Chakras

The subject of this chapter is a most interesting study! In this book and my other books on psychology I have studied the effects of the negative ego/fear-based/separative mind on the mind, feelings, the physical body, the Seven Rays, archetypes, tree of life, feminine and masculine energies, lenses, the initiation process, the laws of manifestation, astrology, channeling, psychic work, Spiritual teaching, Spiritual scientists, healers, relationships, the inner child, real children and all aspects of Spiritual life. One area I have not done this in yet is how the negative ego/fear-based/separative thinking and feeling affects our seven main chakras.

I always love to find a new area of exploration to decipher and uncover. It is like a "Holy Manuscript" that needs to be deciphered, or a magnificent Spiritual puzzle to be put together in an easy to understand

and practical form! I share this with you to share my personal excitement and enjoyment in writing this chapter!

Let us begin this discussion with the first chakra. I should say before I begin that this discussion and these dynamics apply to all lightworkers regardless of how many chakras they have anchored or what level of initiation they have taken! The negative ego mind can enter at any time and Spiritually test a Master or initiate!

The first chakra deals with survival and grounding issues. When the negative ego mind or the mind of imbalance enters in, this chakra becomes overly focused on issues of survival, not having enough money to pay your bills and eat, and possibly homeless issues. There is a possible focus on finding a job! Health crisis or chronic debilitating health lessons would be another example. Another example might be manifesting your business! Instead of being able to focus on one's Spiritual life and service, just making it through Earth life and surviving becomes the focus. This is not a judgement of course for just about all people on Earth at one time or another have been in this place. The ideal is to get this earthly aspect of life together so one can focus on higher Spiritual pursuits! This is why it is so important to take care of the physical body and develop mastery of prosperity consciousness. It is also why it is important to master Earth energies and earthly life.

This now brings up another issue, which is that the first chakra can become out of balance by negative ego thinking. This deals with the Heavenly/Earthly Balance. Many lightworkers become very ungrounded on the Spiritual path. They do not live in their physical bodies. They may focus too much on celestial things or esoteric things and not feel earthly things are important! They may not get involved in Earth life. They may not ground their Spiritual mission on Earth. They may not be connected enough to the Earth mother, nature, the nature kingdoms, animals, plants, minerals, nature spirits, or the Devic kingdom. I have dedicated a whole chapter in this book to help lightworkers ground their Spirituality more! To become God on Earth! Being too vertical and not horizontal enough in life! Too isolated and not involved with people enough. Not loving the Earth and earthly life! Not loving their physical bodies! Not mastering Earth energies to the same degree they master psychological energies or Spiritual energies! Not loving, honoring and sanctifying the Material Face of GOD! All of these issues can create a little imbalance in the first chakra. This would be termed underactivity in the first chakra.

On the other side of the coin is the issue of being too materialistic, which many lightworkers are, even though they are on a Spiritual path! Being too materialistic, too focused on money, too focused on business, having an improper diet! Becoming too focused on earthly life. Becoming too horizontal! Too caught up in the enjoyments and pleasures of Earth life! Too grounded to the point of being disconnected from Spirit, or the psychological focus of life! Too focused on food, vanity, gaining things, relationships, and putting people and material things before GOD. All of these issues can manifest as imbalances in the first chakra.

So we are seeing here that imbalances come in the form of causing over or underidentification in each of our chakras. This is important for Spiritual reasons of God Realization. People who are too materialistic in an extreme can even get disconnected from their Higher Self and Mighty I Am Presence within their own consciousness. It is important in terms of your psychological balance and inner peace. I mention the psychological level, for an imbalance in the first chakra could throw someone into fear or worry over earthly matters which of course is a psychological issue. In reverse, someone who is too materialistic or earthly focused is going to be, by definition, run by the negative ego mind, which will cause other negative ego feelings and emotions. It is also important in terms of your physical health, for each chakra is connected to one of the seven major glands. Over- or underactivity in the glands affects your hormones! This is often why people are over or underactive in the function of their gonads, lydig gland, adrenal glands, thymus gland (immune system), thyroid gland, pineal gland and pituitary (master) gland. So, as we see this study of the chakras and the effect that the negative ego mind has in causing imbalance in each chakra, is quite an interesting study and Spiritual science in and of itself!

Let us now move to the second chakra. The second chakra deals first off with sexuality. So the negative ego mind will have one either be overindulgent in sexuality or underindulgent. Overindulgence causes a weakening of the lydig gland, and will put a strain on the kidneys and other organs as well. It must be remembered that everything is connected in our physical body and psychological system and Spiritual system. When one area gets weakened it affects other areas as well! The other side of the coin is non-sexuality, and this can manifest as no energy being in this chakra! The same thing can happen in the first chakra as well. Many lightworkers have no energy in this chakra! This affects one's energy level, and the energetic feeding of those glands and organs connected there. Now, some people choose to be celibate and this of course is a valid life choice for some. Then other adjustments need to be made to bring energy into these chakras. To be God Realized all chakras need to be balanced! God Realization does not mean having energy in your higher chakras and none in your lower chakras. This is called lack of "Integrated Ascension"! Physical exercise, doing Hatha Yoga, stretching, certain Polarity exercises and most of all just being "Integrated" Spiritually, psychologically and in a physical/earthly sense will do this!

Having friendships and relationships will help fill the energy in this chakra. This chakra is also connected to creativity! It is also connected very much to "integrating your feelings and emotions"! Those who are too closed to their feelings and emotions will have less energy in this chakra! On the other side of the coin, those who are too run by their emotional body, too focused on friendships and relationships, and too horizontal to the neglect of the vertical will have too much energy in this chakra. Always remember, integration and balance are the key. Too much or too little is not good! We must live in the "Tao" in each chakra and within the balance and integration of all the chakras! Too much or too little will overactivate or underactivate the lydig gland and all the organs energetically connected with this chakra. Over- or underactivity in this chakra could affect intestines!

We now move to the third chakra in our Spiritual, psychological, and physical/earthly scientific study of the effect of negative ego/fear-based/separative thinking and feeling on the chakra system! The third chakra is our solar plexus and deals with the mind and emotions, as well and with the will, will power or personal power! This chakra is connected to the adrenal glands. So overactivity in this gland will cause what is commonly known as too much adrenaline in our system. This is not good, for adrenaline is meant to be used for emergency energy only. Too much in the system will have a weakening effect. Too much tapping of the adrenal gland an also cause what a great many lightworkers have, which is "adrenal exhaustion"! This is why they are tired so much of the time. This causes the body's energy systems to have to pull on other glands for energy, which over time can weaken them as well! Underactivity in this chakra can be caused by a person not owning their 100% personal power, not utilizing the full power of the mind, or not causing their reality with the use of their mind. Also not causing their emotional life by seeing and demonstrating that their feelings are caused by their thoughts! On the reverse side, some overuse their will, will power, personal power, Spiritual Warrior energy, and deplete themselves this way. They may rely too much on their personal power for example, and not pray enough and call on GOD and the Masters for help. They may also not rely enough on the incredible powers of the subconscious mind to help in manifestation or whatever else they need! They may be lacking in faith, hence use too much personal power or effort! Others in reverse don't use enough of it! In the ideal state, life is a balance between personal power, prayer, and the power of the subconscious mind! So you do not want to overuse the mind or underuse the mind. The mind must be in perfect integration with one's intuition and/or Spiritual senses, feelings and psychic senses, instincts and sensation/function or five outer senses! No aspect of self is more important or better than another. GOD gave us them all to use in perfect balance and integration. Often lightworkers think one is more important than another, which is the direct negative ego key to create imbalance on all levels, which will be reflected in your chakra system!

The third chakra is still also very connected with one's feelings and emotions. Feelings and emotions, in truth, cannot be separated or disconnected from the mind, for it is our mind, thinking, interpretations, perspectives, belief systems, perceptions, and lenses that cause us to feel the way we do! When we allow the negative ego/fear-based/separative mind to interpret our life instead of the Spiritual/Christ/Buddha mind, we create all kinds of negative thoughts and negative feelings and emotions. This will all be reflected in the third chakra. It will be more and more in chaos, the more we allow the negative ego mind to interpret our reality! This again can cause stomachaches, ulcers, intestinal problems, and digestive problems, although these are not the only reasons these can occur. Sometimes there are physical reasons, electrical reasons, etheric reasons or Spiritual reasons. This kind of negative ego activity will also weaken the adrenal glands. It will also affect all the organs—liver, pancreas, spleen, gall bladder, kidneys, and so on. Overuse of will or personal power will cause a weakening of the pancreas. Underuse of personal power will do the same! Too much anger and too much thinking and planning will weaken the liver! Too little thinking and planning will do the same! All our thoughts and feelings totally affect our aura, chakras, glands and organs. This again is why "Integrated Ascension" is so important! The third chakra is often one of the hardest chakras for lightworkers to balance! It is for this reason and many others that this book has been written!

So we see that overuse or underuse of personal power, the mind, feelings and emotions will all cause imbalance in the third chakra. Only living in the "Tao" and achieving "Integrated Ascension" will bring each chakra and your entire chakra system into balance! The most important thing is to keep the negative ego/fear-based/separative mind and thought system out of your consciousness and to only think with your Spiritual/Christ/Buddha mind and feelings, for this is what will perceive balance and integration in all things and only create positive and Spiritual thoughts and feelings!

The fourth chakra is of course our heart chakra! It remains in balance and focused on unconditional love when we think from our Spiritual/Christ/Buddha mind! When we think from our negative ego/fear-based/separative mind the heart chakra becomes imbalanced, for conditional love, addictive love, anger, lack of forgiveness, guilt, impatience, irritation, judgment, intolerance and separative feelings and emotions have been allowed to enter your consciousness and are hence reflected in your fourth chakra. The heart chakra is interestingly enough your immune system, for it is connected to the thymus gland. When you learn to see life only from the eyes of the Spiritual/Christ/Buddha mind, your physical immune system will function much more perfectly. Isn't that interesting! Unconditional love is the key to perfect health! Conditional love of the negative ego mind will have a weakening effect on the thymus gland and heart chakra!

The fifth chakra deals with communication! Virginia Satir, the well-known marriage counselor, said something to the effect that "Communication is to a relationship what breathing is to living"! I thought that was well stated. We are here to communicate, to talk to GOD and the Masters, to share, to have fellowship with our Brothers and Sisters, to have romantic relationships, to have personal relationships, friendships, and to serve and help others. We do this through various forms of communication. When this chakra is in balance we communicate from our Spiritual/Christ/Buddha consciousness, not our negative ego/fear-based/separative consciousness. We hence share that which GOD, our own Mighty I Am Presence, our Higher Self, our Soul, the Masters, and the Angels would have us share. We share things of Unconditional Love, Oneness, and Godly matters and issues! The fifth chakra becomes imbalanced when it is used by the negative ego mind! This chakra will also become imbalanced when overused or underused! Some people or lightworkers spend too much time communicating. They can overuse this chakra, which drains the thyroid gland and can create thyroid problems. This type of person may process too much, or be too overidentified with service. They may have fear so they look too much to try to overcome the fear they have not mastered. They may communicate too much to try to increase their business they are worried about. They may talk too much for they do not have enough faith, trust, and patience in GOD. They may communicate too much, for they do not know how to quiet their mind, feelings, and emotions. They may communicate too much because they have too many negative feelings and emotions that are too stirred up from negative ego thinking! They may talk too much because they are not whole within themselves and do not love themselves! They may communicate too much because they do not know how to meditate and appreciate just "Being and/or being in the Silence"! They may communicate or overuse this chakra because they are so busy doing and achieving they do not know how to just "be"! They also may communicate too much because they do not know how to set boundaries with self or others!

On the other side of the coin, there are many people and lightworkers who undercommunicate. As the Universal Mind said through Edgar Cayce, "There are sins of omission or commission"! There are many that undercommunicate. This is commonly seen, of course, in men in romantic relationships. We don't want to stereotype, for of course this can happen to anyone. Women on the whole, however, as a fair generalization, tend to communicate more freely, especially about their feelings! There can be a danger here if there is too much of a preoccupation with the emotional body, which hence then will create an imbalance as well in the fifth chakra. Balance, once again, is the key! The lesson here is to know when to talk and when to be silent. Don't talk when it is time to be silent and don't be silent when it is time to talk. Part of coming into one's Spiritual service work is the proper opening of this fifth chakra! In relationships, when a person is afraid to express their thoughts, feelings and emotions, this can create an imbalance in the heart chakra and throat chakra. The inability to express love or even to say the words "I love you!" would be an imbalance of the heart chakra and throat chakra. Any place in a person's life where they need to be communicating and are not as GOD would have it be shows an imbalance in this chakra. All imbalances in the chakras, and all imbalances and problems in life, are caused by only one thing, which is negative ego/fear-based/separative thinking! It is the negative ego that causes us to make imbalanced choices. This book is dedicated to showing you all the different ways the negative ego does this, so we can be more conscious, aware and joyously vigilant to always think only with our Spiritual/Christ/Buddha mind!

Other examples of imbalance and the negative ego mind creating problems in the fifth chakra are: gossip, speaking judgmentally about others, bad-mouthing others behind their back, breaking confidentiality, backstabbing and speaking negatively about others! As the saying goes, if you don't have anything nice to say, don't say anything at all!

The sixth chakra is our Third Eye and Spiritual vision center. The Third Eye is properly opened by the study of many of the things you are studying in this book! Spiritual vision occurs really on four levels. There is awareness of Spiritual things and esoteric knowledge and wisdom, which opens the third eye in a positive balanced manner! There is psychological wisdom, the likes of which you are also studying in this book, which greatly opens the Third Eye. For this is the Spiritual science of how to think with your Spiritual/Christ/Buddha mind and not your negative ego/fear-based/separative mind! The thinking with your negative ego mind is what closes the Third Eye and causes blocks and imbalances in it. It is what creates blind spots, and limited lens seeing! Every person either has negative ego vision or Spiritual vision. We don't just see with our physical eyes, we see through our mind and belief systems! Our thoughts create our reality! Our thoughts create our feelings and emotions. Our thoughts create our behavior! Our thoughts create what we attract and magnetize into our lives! You have been learning in this book the Spiritual science of proper psychospiritual vision, which is hardly discussed in Religion and the New Age Movement, and is, in truth the foundation of your Spiritual life!

Then there is your physical/earthly vision, which is connected to how you integrate and ground your Spiritual life into your physical body and into Earth life! Are you a fully integrated Ascended Master living in your physical body? Have you fully manifested your Spiritual mission on Earth? Are you fully integrating your Spiritual life into your earthly life? Have you found a way of being of service on Earth? Are you mastering and fully integrating Earth energies? Are you balancing and integrating the God/Goddess within? These are all issues of Spiritual sight on an earthly level.

Many do not realize that your Spiritual/Psychological/Earthly mastery and integration will affect your physical sight. "As within, So without! As above, So below"!

A great many lightworkers think that Spiritual sight is being clairvoyant and being able to see into the Spiritual world! This is a type of opening of the Third Eye. However, you do not need this to achieve God Realization or Integrated Ascension! A great, great, great many of those who have clairvoyance of this kind do not have the type of Spiritual vision and Third Eye opening of esoteric knowledge and wisdom, psychological wisdom and clarity, physical/earthly psychospiritual vision! They have what I call "Mystic vision" but not occult, psychological, and physical/earthly psychospiritual vision! So, we see that this type of vision is only one quarter of what the true opening of the Third Eye is about. A person can have mystic clairvoyance, they can be a Spiritual, psychological, and physical/earthly mess, and often are! This lack of clear third eye vision on these other levels also greatly contaminates and distorts their mystic vision. It is impossible to separate a person's consciousness from their mystic vision or channeling abilities. This is why it is to your best interest to be much more Spiritually discerning before you give your power to an external channel or clairvoyant!

The opening of the third eye is also connected to the opening of all your Spiritual senses such as: intuition, knowingness, comprehension, knowledge, wisdom, Spiritual idealism, all knowledge, beautitude, active service, divine vision, revelation, healing, Spiritual telepathy, response to group vibration, Spiritual discernment, discrimination, emotional idealism, and imagination, to just name a few! A person could have their mystic clairvoyance opened and not be very developed in the rest of these inner senses that open the Third Eye! This is not even counting all the Spiritual and esoteric knowledge and wisdom, psychological vision, and physical/earthly psychospiritual vision, and for that matter just plain physical/earthly vision, which is a type of Spiritual vision in truth! Some people have better physical third dimensional vision than others. The ideal is to have good Spiritual vision in all these levels, and it is all of them that open the Third Eye and sixth chakra. Mystic vision is less than ten percent of what fully opening the Third Eye is about! Let this be a lesson to all of those lightworkers that think mystic clairvoyance or channeling is the be-all or end-all and will give them all they want. I know channels, who are clairaudient channels, but very weak in all these other senses and in the three basic levels of Spiritual knowledge, psychological vision and physical/earthly psychospiritual vision. My Beloved Readers, this is more often the norm and that is why you must be extremely careful about not giving away your personal power, Spiritual discernment, and not giving too much credence to what comes through external channels and psychics!

Not only is it very likely they are not developed in a lot of these other areas, they also do not know you from Adam! Their channeling and psychic work is not only based on all that I have stated so far, but is also based on the knowledge and attunement they have of you. Their channelings are coming through all their filters, subconscious mind, belief systems, personality, psychological clarity and development, Spiritual knowledge or lack thereof, earthly mastery or lack thereof, Ray structure, archetypes, astrological configuration, perceptions, negative ego agendas, chakra balance or lack thereof, information banks from this life or past lives, fatigue level, personal opinions, overall integration and balance, philosophy, psychology, Spiritual path they are on, lenses they are stuck in, blind spots, and on and on. All of these things are acting as filters to what an external channel is telling you or what their mystic vision is telling you. I am not saying that it is not of value. I am just saying, "Be discerning!" If any channel says they are not affected by any of these considerations "run for the hills!" It is when a mystic clairvoyant or channel can admit to themselves and to you that all these things can affect clairvoyance and channeling that they might be able to be trusted a little more! Any channel or mystic who thinks that these things do not affect their channeling or clairvoyance, with no judgment intended, is living in faulty thinking! Every channel on planet Earth, including myself, is affected by these aspects of consciousness! When channeling comes through it has to be interpreted by the subconscious and conscious mind of the person doing the work. It is not like some open telephone call, and if anyone thinks so, they are deluding themselves. Even Edgar Cayce had filters. Why did the channelings come through in a "stilted" English? This was Cayce's past life programming. The Universal Mind through Cayce said that Cayce's abilities were stemming from a past life and lives in Egypt. Sai Baba in India is a Universal Avatar and his channelings are totally affected and colored by his Indian upbringing and background! He does not speak of the Ascended Masters or Ascended Master teachings as we do in the West. His work is colored by the lens of Indian teachings. This is not a judgement, for Sai Baba is incredible! Lightworkers must understand how channeling, clairvoyance and psychic abilities really work. There is this incredibly naïve and undiscerning belief that these abilities are separate and not influenced by a person's consciousness, mind, emotions, psychology, subconscious, negative ego, philosophy, Spiritual development, psychological development, physical/earthly development, and so on. This is ludicrous, my friends! Lightworkers are way too naïve and impressionable. They give away their personal power too easily. They believe anything they read! They think if it is channeled it is true. Nothing could be farther from the truth!

The reason all this takes place is that their Third Eye and sixth chakra is not fully open on all these levels I am speaking about here! They are so enamored with channeling, clairvoyance, or psychic abilities they are blinded to the truth. The are not seeing from a "Full Spectrum Prism Vision"! They are overidentitified with the Spiritual level and do not see the astronomical effect that the consciousness, psychology, and physical/earthly psychospiritual aspect, as well as all these other filters I have mentioned, are affecting the process. They are not recognizing the 90% of other inner senses they have forgotten about! My Beloved Readers, please take these other factors into consideration. I am attempting to more fully open your Third Eye in reading this chapter! I am attempting to help you develop your Full Spectrum Prism Vision from all levels, not just one fragmented lens or type of vision! The third eye will never ever be fully open until all these factors are taken into consideration!

Now, it is possible to open the Third Eye too much or too little. I have been talking about what causes the Third Eye or sixth chakra too open to little! There is also a need for protection in life, which a lot of lightworkers say is unimportant. This of course is not true. The Third Eye is like the physical eye in some ways. The pupil of the eye opens and closes in terms of how much light is coming into the room. There are times to close the Third Eye a little. If you go to the movies and there are some violent scenes you might want to close it a little. Too many stimuli can be coming in at times. This needs to be monitored.

There is also the aspect as well of overusing the third eye. Lightworkers may spend too much time working with this chakra to the neglect of others! This may cause headaches, eyestrain, or depletion of the pituitary gland! This is very important to not let happen, for this is the Master Gland of our body and affects all the other glands and organs. It is interesting that the Third Eye or sixth chakra is connected to the Master Gland or pituitary, is it not! In this discussion we see the incredible importance of having a clear Spiritual, psychological and physical/earthly vision in our lives. We see from this discussion the enormous effect our Spiritual/Psychological/Physical/Earthly vision has on our lives! It is our thoughts and images in our mind that creates our reality! Would it not make sense, given that the Third Eye and sixth chakra are connected with the vision for our whole life, that it would be connected to the Master Gland of the body, the pituitary? Is not GOD ingenious!

So the key here is to not underuse or overuse your Third Eye and sixth chakra, but to fully open it and keep it in balance with all the rest of the chakras! For we don't want to overactivate or underactivate the pituitary gland, among other things!

The seventh chakra is, of course our crown chakra and connection to GOD, Christ, the Holy Spirit, our Mighty I Am Presence, our Higher Self, our Soul, the Oversoul, the inner plane Ascended Masters, the Archangels and Angels, Elohim Councils, Christed Extraterrestrials, the Universal Mind, Universal Knowledge, Spiritual knowledge and wisdom, anchoring of Higher Light Bodies, anchoring of Higher Chakras, Divine Plan, Monadic Conscious-ness, Ascension, The Godhead, Esoteric knowledge, Revelation, Inspiration, Intuition, Meditation, Prayer, Chanting the Names of GOD, reciting Mantras of GOD, using the Power Names of GOD, Highest form of Spiritual Healing, All Knowledge, Higher God Senses, the Highest form of Channeling, Perfection, Realization, Active Service, Beatitude, Highest form of

Egolessness, Spiritual idealism, Divine vision, Highest Form of Spiritual telepathy, and overlighting by Masters!

It is, of course, the ideal to open one's crown chakra! However, one does not want to be overidentified with it to the point of overactivating and stimulating it to the improper integration and balance of the other chakras. If one does this, for example, improper grounding can take place. All the energy in the etheric body will be in the upper chakras and not in the lower chakras. This could cause headaches! Not being in the physical body! Not embodying the physical body! Not grounding your Spiritual mission on Earth! Being too preoccupied with esoteric knowledge and not doing service work. As Sai Baba says, "Hands that help are Holier than lips that pray"! Living in the Heavenly world, but not properly integrating the psychological level, or physical/earthly level! Having Spiritual wisdom but not psychological or physical earthly wisdom! Being overidentified with the guru or Spiritual teacher role! Being too vertical and not integrating the horizontal aspect of life! Not living in the marketplace! Not being involved enough in relationships and with people! Spending too much time channeling and not living! Spending too much time meditating and not fulfilling your Spiritual mission on Earth. Thinking the Spiritual worlds are more Spiritual than the psychological world and physical/earthly world. Being Spiritual but not mentally and emotionally balanced. Having an open crown but a closed heart! Not dealing well with relationships or people, but being a Spiritual teacher. Being so Spiritual you don't communicate with others effectively. Being highly developed Spiritually, but totally fragmented and not integrated on other levels. Being so Spiritual you can't take care of yourself in a physical/earthly sense! I have seen many of these types in the Spiritual movement! This is not the ideal and not what we are meant to embody!

All these things I have mentioned are examples of how someone can become overidentified with the crown or seventh chakra and hence overactivate it and create massive imbalance in other areas of your life which are equally important! If the crown chakra is not opened enough, the pineal gland will be understimulated or nourished. If the crown chakra is overactivated, the pineal gland will become overstimulated and eventually exhausted! It is integration and balance we seek my friends! Any chakra that is over or under identified will create "blind spots" Spiritually, psychologically and in a physical/earthly sense, which is, in truth, antithetical to God Realization! God Realization in terms of our chakra system is the proper integration and balance in our daily lives of all seven chakras, so that no chakra is overactivated or underactivated in a long-term sense. There are times, of course, where it is quite appropriate to focus on one chakra more than another for a certain Spiritual purpose or project. However, in the greater scope of one's life and in the big picture of one's life the seven major chakras need to be basically balanced! This, my Beloved Readers, is another one of the real golden keys to achieving God Realization! It is my sincere hope and prayer that this Spiritual study of this most important subject has been enlightening and helpful in helping you to make some subtle Spiritual, attitudinal, emotional, energetic, and physical/earthly adjustments to make this Spiritual ideal of "Integrated Ascension" even more of a reality in your life!

CHAPTER 19

Transcending Negative Ego Archetypal Dualities and Spiritual Psychology Charts

In my work as a spiritual psychotherapist and spiritual teacher, I have developed certain models and paradigms for understanding spiritual and soul psychology. One revolutionary model that has come to me from Spirit for understanding the difference between negative ego thinking and Christ thinking that I feel is one of the clearest ways of understanding how the negative ego works, has to do with the understanding that the negative ego has an upper and lower side to it. They are like two sides of a coin. If you get caught on one side of the coin, you will also unavoidably get caught on the other side of the coin. The only way to achieve true Christ consciousness and inner peace is to transcend the whole system. In esoteric and Eastern thought this might be aptly called transcending duality. Let me begin here by listing some of the archetypal negative ego dualities that every lightworker must learn to ultimately transcend. Again, remember the first quality listed will be the upper side of the negative ego. Under it will be the lower side of the negative ego and horizontally across from both of them will be the Christ Consciousness attitude, antidote and cure. So on this note, let us begin with the first negative ego archetypal duality and its Christ Consciousness antidote.

Negative Ego Archetypal Dualities and their Christ Consciousness Counterpoint

Negative Ego Duality or *Christ Consciousness Attitude*
Attack/Fear *or* Unconditional Love
Anger/Depression *or* Bubble of Protection, Preferences, Looking at things as lessons, Never giving up
Win/Lose *or* Win-Win
Rejecter/Rejected *or* Not meant to be, Not GOD's Will, "I'm O.K., you're O.K."
False Pride/Low Self-esteem *or* Self-confidence, Unconditional Self-love and Self-worth
Manipulator/Victim *or* Own personal power through Love and Non-attachment
Attachment/Non-attachment *or* Preference attitudes
Self-righteous/Self-doubt *or* Knowingness while still allowing others to have beliefs
Needing no one/Loneliness *or* Ability to be alone but still interrelate with others
Aggressive/Passive *or* Assertive
Worry/Uncaring *or* Concern
Too Self-centered/Too Other-directed *or* Proper Selfish-Selfless balance
Sociopathic tendencies/Guilt-ridden *or* Properly balanced conscience and Self-forgiveness
Pollyannaish/Pessimistic *or* Optimistic

Arrogant/Insecure *or* Self-confident tempered with Unconditional Love
Holding a grudge/Being a doormat *or* Forgiveness
Overindulgence/Underindulgence *or* The Middle Path, Moderation in all things
Fear of failure/Fear of success *or* Pursuit of excellence, Mistakes are O.K.
Judgmental/Embarrassment *or* Nonjudgmentalness
Impatient/Too laissez faire *or* Patient
Blame/Shame *or* Self-responsibility, Bubble of protection
Hate/Possessive conditional love *or* Unconditional Love & Forgiveness
Too controlling/Out of control *or* Self-control, Not controlling over others
Betrayer/Betrayed *or* Utterly secure within self & not attached to situation
Abandoner/Abandoned *or* Complete, full, whole within self & bonding in relationship from that place
Jealousy/Open relationships *or* Commitment without co-dependence
Too independent/Dependent *or* Independent, interdependent and group consciousness
Sadistic/Masochistic *or* Doesn't believe in giving or experiencing suffering
Overly responsible/Irresponsible *or* Responsible
Too closed/Too open *or* Proper boundaries
Mean/Hurt *or* Invulnerable, Bubble of protection, Cause own reality
Too selfish/Too selfless *or* Selfish/Selfless balance
Overly confident/Insecure *or* Quiet confidence
Attack/Defense *or* Defenselessness, Harmlessness
Accepts no feedback/Approval seeking *or* Seeks feedback from appropriate people
Too Impulsive/Indecisive *or* Appropriately decisive
Dictator/Herd consciousness *or* Uses & owns personal power in loving manner only
Insensitive/Overly sensitive *or* Sensitive, Divine detachment
Workaholic/Hedonist *or* Work/Play balance
Obsessive-Compulsive/Disorderly *or* Organized without being overly perfectionistic

Driven/Lazy *or* Hard worker within reason

The Pusher/Procrastinator *or* Strives for completion without being obsessive

Immobilized/Reactive *or* Respond

False sense of security/Vulnerable *or* Faith, Invulnerability, Confidence, yet practical & realistic

Too affectatious/Too repressed *or* Integrated and balanced expression

Emotionless/Moodiness *or* Mastery of emotions in service of Oversoul and Monad, Joy

Overly giving/Overly taking *or* Giving/Receiving balance

Intimidate/Too shy *or* Own power in a Christed manner

Too future focused/Too past focused *or* Live in the "now," with appropriate past/future thinking only

Overly deserving/Undeserving *or* Deserving because GOD created us

Greed consciousness/Poverty consciousness *or* Prosperity consciousness

Too serious/Too lighthearted *or* Serious/Lighthearted balance

Fault-finder/Undiscerning *or* Love-finder, Spiritually discerning

Rebel/Conformist *or* "Above all else, to thine own self be true."

Overly organized/Disorganized *or* Organized

Felix Unger(Obsessively clean)/Oscar Madison(Slob) *or* Clean, but not neurotically clean

Overly jubilant/Sad *or* Evenminded, Unceasing joy from positive thinking

Can't admit mistakes/Everything's my fault *or* Admit mistakes when they happen

Too trusting/Too distrustful *or* Trusting with spiritual discernment

Too focused/Too scattered *or* Ability to see through full prism & single lens as moment requires

Too brazen/Too cautious *or* Assertive with spiritual discernment

Too critical inner parent/Too permissive inner parent *or* Firm and loving parent

Too goal-oriented/Too process-oriented *or* Goal & Process balance

Too loquacious/Too silent *or* Appropriate talking/silence balance

Too rigid/Too flexible *or* Firm/Flexible balance

Too disciplined/Out of control *or* Discipline/Flowing balance

Too structured/Too flowing *or* Structure/Fluidity balance

Too willful/Too allowing *or* Willful/Allowing balance

Too impersonal/Too personal *or* Impersonal/Personal balance

Good luck/Bad luck *or* No such thing as "luck," cause own reality, past life karma

Too vertical(spiritually inward)/Too horizontal(relationship focus) *or* Vertical/Horizontal balance

Too expansive/Too contracted *or* Appropriate Expansion/Contraction balance

Uptight/Too laid back *or* Own personal power & surrender to GOD simultaneously

Too tough/Too coddling *or* Strong but respectful of laws of nature

Sins of commission/Sins of omission *or* Responding appropriately as GOD would have it be

Summation

In summary what I would like to say to you, my Beloved Readers, is that what I would recommend is that you get out a piece of paper and pen and very carefully go through each one of these negative ego dualities and the Christ Consciousness attitudinal antidote. Intuitively determine for yourself if there is any upper or lower negative ego aspects influencing your personality and/or character development. Do this from a totally unconditionally loving, non-judgmental attitude towards self. Remember mistakes are O.K., and the true lesson here for highest integrated ascension potential is to be devastatingly honest with self. Make a list on your paper where attitudinal adjustments need to be made. I would then suggest making a log for yourself and listing those qualities and their antidote; and every day, maybe twice each day, giving yourself a percentage score in how you are doing controlling the negative ego attributes and demonstrating the Christ attitudes and qualities. You might also consider writing up some affirmations for those negative ego dualities that need the most work in clearing. Also, pray to GOD, the Ascended Masters, your Angels, and your own Higher Self and Monad for help in attitudinally changing those qualities. Also, write out on a piece of paper a spiritual vow to GOD and yourself about your commitment to create a flawless character. Also, ask the Ascended Masters of your choice to perform the core fear matrix removal program on those specific negative ego dualities that you intuitively feel are still present. The Ascended Masters will actually pull these dark weeds out of your four-body system. This work, in combination with your logging, affirmations, prayer work, spiritual vows and overall conscious commitment to Christ thinking at all times, will do the trick. Also, call to the Holy Spirit for help in undoing all past programming. The Holy Spirit has a specialty in this area of undoing negative ego programming and mistakes.

This multifaceted program I am suggesting is worth its weight in gold. No time spent working on self is more valuable than proper character development. It may not be as glamorous as communing with celestial realms or other esoteric studies, however, I am here to tell you, my beloved readers, that this is the real key to making integrated ascension work. Without proper character development, all other aspects of your spiritual life will become poisoned by the contagion of negative ego. In truth, it is just illusion or faulty thinking and is nothing to be feared, however since our thoughts create our reality on every level, it is essential that you make your number one spiritual goal to remove negative ego thinking from your consciousness. For added information and support read my books *Soul Psychology, How to Clear the Negative Ego, Ascension Psychology, Your Ascension Mission: Embracing Your Puzzle Piece,* and *Ascension and Romantic Relationships.* The first two books listed being the most important in this regard.

It is well worth your time and energies to meditate upon the upper and lower sides of the negative ego to get as clear a sense as possible as to how the negative ego operates. To transcend negative ego thinking you transcend both sides of the negative ego, both upper and lower. As the Bible says, "After pride cometh the fall." You must learn to laugh both sides off the stage. This is called transcendence. Most people on planet Earth remain stuck in the washing machine cycle of negative ego thinking. The only reason they are not able to get out of it is that no one ever taught them how the negative ego thinks and how the Christ mind thinks. It is really that simple. If it were taught in school and church, everyone would be doing it. It really is not that hard to do. It is just a matter of changing your thinking. Your emotions come from how you think, as does your behavior and what you attract and magnetize into your life. Change your thinking and you change your life. As the Bible says, "Be ye transformed by the renewal of your mind."

The process is very simple. Every time a negative ego thought or emotion comes up in your consciousness push it out of your mind and replace it with the Christ consciousness attitude and antidote. By not giving energy or water, so to speak, to that weed it will die within three weeks time. That is how long it takes to cement in a new habit into the subconscious mind. By not giving water to negative ego thinking and emotions and watering Christ consciousness attitudes and feelings they expand and grow. Soon, you have a habit of Christed thinking and feeling and a habit of being in inner peace and joyous all the time. The happiness you seek is an attitude and perspective that is attached to nothing outside of self, and nothing having to do with another person. "Let this mind be in you that was in Christ Jesus," the Bible tells us. So my recommendation, my beloved readers, is to do the program I have suggested for at least 21 days. I give you my solemn oath it will be the best energetic time investment you have ever made. When your mental and emotional body are properly integrated, your spiritual growth will accelerate a thousand-fold. You will develop the Midas Touch. Your channeling will become a thousand times better in whatever form you do it. Every aspect of your life will become a thousand times better. Your relationship to yourself is the foundation of your life. Take the time to build a Christed foundation and only Godliness will then be built upon this spiritually integrated structure.

I have purposely made this chapter as easy to understand as possible. I have strived here to bring the whole process down to its very bare, quintessential essence. If more support and/or understanding is needed read the first two books I have listed, with *Ascension Psychology* being the third I would recommend. With the understanding and the tools I have provided, this work can be easily done as long as you are willing to take the time to commit your-self to the process and as long as you are pure in your intent to achieve true integrated ascension and GOD Realization.

My Beloved Readers, "the Force is with you," so be about the Father's business and take advantage of the profundity, clarity, and simple practicality of this information. This new wave of the psychology of the future is being made available to you now. As the Bible says, "The truth will set you free." It is time to wake up from the nightmarish illusory dream of the negative ego and to realize that the negative ego and all its hallucinations don't really exist, we just think it does. The law of the mind, is what you think is the reality you live in. It is time, my beloved readers, to wake up from this negative dream and to instead think and live in GOD's dream of total unconditional love, forgiveness, inner peace, equanimity, joy and bliss!

CHAPTER 20

The Art of Loving from a Spiritual Perspective

There have been many books written about "The Art of Loving," but very few written from the perspective of Spirit, the Soul, and the Ascended Masters'. Most books written on "The Art of Loving" are written from the perspective of the personality, rather than from the perspective of the Soul and Mighty I Am Presence. I have been inwardly guided this day to write a chapter on "The Art of Loving" from a Spiritual and/or Higher Consciousness perspective.

Love from the perspective of the personality deals very much with feelings and the importance of expressing one's feelings. This is fine. However, this is, in truth, only one quarter of what love really is. Feelings are by their very nature very amorphous. They are here one moment and then gone the next. Anyone who bases their relationship just on how they feel at any given moment is going to have a relationship that has enormous ups and downs, and is very rocky to say the least. In truth, "The Art of Loving" is so much more than this.

The true "Art of Loving" deals not only with how one feels, which is connected with the subconscious mind, it also deals very much with the conscious mind and superconscious mind. The true "Art of Loving" involves not just the feeling of love and romantic and sexual feelings, but also what I would call a mental attitude of love. This means first off a commitment to be unconditionally loving at all times with your partner even if you don't feel like it. You may feel angry and feel like emotionally attacking your partner. However, in the true "Art of Loving" this is not something you give into, for from a Spiritual perspective this would be a total indulgence in your negative ego. My Beloved Readers, we begin to see now for the first time some of the initial differences between personality level love and true Soul and Spiritual love.

"The Art of Loving" from a Spiritual perspective is always unconditionally loving and never conditionally loving. It is never attacking or judgmental. It only shares loving observations, Spiritual discernments and preferences. The Spiritual "Art of Loving" always forgives even if your own negative ego doesn't feel like it. Spiritual love always communicates in a calm, rational, unconditionally loving manner and does not argue or engage in ego battles. Spiritual love is tolerant, patient, and always a love finder, not a faultfinder. One of the keys to "The Art of Loving" is having an attitude of love, not just feelings of love. Over the long haul of a long term relationship, it is very unlikely that any relationship would last without both partners developing "The Art of Loving" in their mental bodies as well as their emotional bodies and sexual bodies. People who have developed "The Art of Loving" in their mental body understand that to be right in a relationship one must first be right with self and right with GOD. If one is not right with self and right with GOD they will also be off-kilter and disconnected from their partner. This is because our thoughts create our reality. In truth, fifty to seventy-five percent of the problems that people are having in their relationships stem from not being right with self and right with GOD. They think it is the other person, but from the Soul and Spirit's perspective it is not. In truth, everything your partner does is a Spiritual test to teach you to practice unconditional love and transcendence of your own negative ego thought system and emotions. Most people, not having been trained in how to master their own negative ego and emotional body, are letting some of this spill over into their relationship. This is not a judgment, just a very important Spiritual insight. When I used to do a lot of relationship counseling, being a Spiritual psychologist and Marriage, Family and Child Counselor, I found that seventy-five percent of the relationship problems cleared up after doing two or three sessions to help each individual in the relationship get right with self and right with GOD. This means helping each person get fully back into their 100% personal power, unconditional love and self-worth, Golden Bubble of Protection, attunement to their own Mighty I Am Presence, preference instead of attachment attitudes, looking at everything as Spiritual lessons and tests, and transcending the negative ego thought system and practicing the Christ/Buddha thought system. The individual counseling served as a complete polar axis shift of their own consciousness, which made them see their relationship in a whole new light and understanding. It broke all the co-dependence and seeking wholeness and love outside of self, and established this empowerment, love, and wholeness within self and relationship to GOD first. This also breaks all victim consciousness and seeking happiness outside of self, instead of inside of self first and foremost.

The superconscious mind is involved in "The Art of Loving." It is the name I am giving to represent the Soul, Higher Self and Mighty I Am Presence within each person. When the superconscious or Spiritual level is integrated into the equation of "The Art of Loving" besides what has already been mentioned, there is an extremely high level of Christ/Buddha consciousness that is infused into the process. This manifests as a tremendous desire within each person in the relationship to be of the highest Spiritual purity and integrity. It manifests as a desire to give rather than take or receive. It manifests in a Saintly quality that is always desiring to be the first to forgive, apologize and admit mistakes. It manifests as a willingness to be devastatingly honest with self in the highest Spiritual sense, and to not defend one's own negative ego. It manifests in an unbelievably high degree of individual self-mastery, self-discipline and Spiritual vigilance to not allow negative ego thoughts and feelings or emotions to take over one's consciousness and to never take them out on their partner. It manifests as a desire to give pleasure to one's partner on all levels as a priority, rather than just seeking one's own self-pleasure and satisfaction. It manifests as an extreme desire to be positive and optimistic in all aspects of self, life, and the relationship. It manifests as a willingness to always walk the extra mile for your partner even when psychologically and/or physically tired or fatigued. It manifests as an ability to remain unconditionally loving, positive and upbeat even when your partner is not. It manifests as a willingness to compromise and to sacrifice one's own preferences to make your partner happy. This is done with total Spiritual love and sincerity, not with the attitude of being a martyr. The superconscious mind or Spiritual level also manifests as a desire to be selfless rather than selfish. It manifests as a spirit of unconditional love and goodness that always gives their partner the benefit of the doubt. It manifests as a commitment to never hold on to negativity, and if something is bothering them they either communicate it in an unconditional loving, uncritical, rational and non-self-righteous way or they forgive and let go of this process within self. They do not give in to moodiness, and they maintain their Christ/Buddha consciousness and ideals even when physically tired. They practice detachment, defenselessness, harmlessness, and humility, at all times, even when attacked or criticized. They look at every negative interaction as another opportunity to practice greater Christ/Buddha consciousness and unconditional love. The superconscious and Spiritual mind infuses the desire for unconditional love rather than needing to be right or win as one's ideal. The superconscious and Spiritual mind have the individual do all these things even if the other person is not always doing them. This is done for the purpose of achieving God Realization within self and for the purpose of setting a better example in their relationship, which most often inspires the other to do the same. Lastly, the superconscious and Spiritual mind inspire the individual to lovingly recognize the psychological and/or Spiritual weaknesses in their partner and to not only not hold this or use this against them, but to instead make adjustments and compensations in one's own consciousness to allow these character weaknesses to be developed over time. This is not done from a "holier-than-thou" attitude, for your partner is doing the same and/or will do the same for any weaknesses, bad habits, or mistakes you shall experience as well. So in the highest level of "The Art of Loving" from a Spiritual perspective, the main "fight" two Masters of this practice will have is who will give and serve the other more!

My Beloved Readers, "The Art of Loving" from a Spiritual and Higher Consciousness perspective not only includes the feeling, thought, and Spiritual level, also described here as the subconscious, conscious, and superconscious level. It also includes the physical/earthly level. It manifests this superconscious and Spiritual love, giving, and selflessness in the way one approaches sexuality. It manifests in one's generosity in dealings with money. It manifests this Spiritual quality in being willing to take earthly responsibility and chores. It manifests as a willingness to take on the other's responsibilities and chores during times of physical sickness, psychological exhaustion and/or undue stress. It manifests in remembering birthdays, anniversaries, and holidays. It manifests as buying flowers, sweet gifts, and leaving sweet notes or messages for no special reason. It manifests as telling your partner you love them as often as possible and constantly giving them kisses, love and affection. It means being willing to make large physical sacrifices at times, regarding such things as where one lives, jobs, and certain material expenditures to please your partner that you would not necessarily make on your own.

When mistakes are made, they are quickly forgiven by both people in the relationship. If negative feelings and emotions do manifest, they are communicated in an unconditionally loving manner, while still taking responsibility for the fact that we each cause our own reality by how we think. In this vein, no one is blamed for how the other feels, for victim consciousness is not practiced even if negative feelings do arise at times. If they do arise they are made part of the communication process, for as Virginia Satir stated, "Communication is to a relationship what breathing is to living."

So, my Beloved Readers, in conclusion, we can see very clearly that the true "Art of Loving" is a four-fold process involving the Spiritual, Mental, Emotional, and Physical/Earthly levels. It is when "The Art of Loving" is practiced from this integrated Spiritual and Higher Consciousness perspective, that you will have the greatest possible fulfillment and success within self and within your romantic Spiritual relationship!

CHAPTER 21

Balancing the Feminine and Masculine and the Transcendence of the Negative Ego

Another way of approaching the clearing of the negative ego is through the need to balance feminine and masculine energies. Whenever these two complimentary aspects of Self get out of balance, negative ego qualities develop. As with the archetypes, rays, astrological signs, houses, and planets, they each have a negative and positive expression. Before we can understand the negative expression we first must understand the positive expression of the yin and the yang.

The balance of the yin and yang is the basis of Taoism. When yin and yang are in balance we live in the "Tao." Imbalance and negative ego could be looked at from this frame of reference as the same thing. The following list shows the positive yin and positive yang.

Feminine/Masculine
Loving/Powerful

Open/Closed
Sensitive/Organized
Nurturing/Willful
Unfocused/Focused
Process Oriented/Goal Oriented
Listening/Talking
Warm/Concentrating
Flowing/Strong
Feeling/Thinking
Fluid/Rational
Flexible/Disciplined
Play/Work
Right Brain/Left Brain

Every man and every woman needs a balance of both of these energies within themselves. This is called androgyny. When this balance is lacking with-in ourselves, we usually seek it outside of ourselves in another. Hence we have the father-daughter relationships and mother-son relationships, or variables on this theme.

One of my favorite examples of living in the Tao is the idea of surfing a wave. If you go too fast when you are body surfing you will get dumped by the wave. If you go too slow you will miss the wave. The idea is to stay in the Tao. This applies to every aspect of life. There is a time to talk and a time to be silent. There is a time to be assertive and a time to be receptive. There is a time to think and a time to feel. There is a time to be right-brain and a time to be left-brain.

If you choose to be yin when it is time to be yang, you are out of balance. If you choose to be yang when it is time to be yin, you are out of balance. The key word here is "appropriateness." In every situation and moment of life there is an appropriate response, as guided by your own soul and Mighty I Am Presence. If you stay attuned to your Higher Self you will always be guided properly in every situation. When guided by the voice of the negative ego you will be guided inappropriately. Most people don't realize that the yin and yang or masculine and feminine have a negative expression. This manifests when one is "too yin" or "too yang."

Negative Yin
Inferiority complex/Low self-esteem
Hurt too easily/Weak
Prone to rejection/Sadness
Depression/Fearful
Victim/Needy
Dependent/Clinging vine
Too sentimental/Too open
Hypersensitivity/Hedonism
Meditating too much/Too flexible
Too right-brain/Lack of self-love

Negative Yang
Anger/Violence
Rigidity/Too intellectual
Workaholic/Too organized
Too much First Ray energy/Talks too much
Too closed and shut down/Too left-brain
Superiority complex/Critical
Impatient/Attacking
Controlling/Manipulative
Argumentative/Intolerant
Intimidation/Aggressive
Hatred/Demanding
Too harsh

Yin energies without the proper balance of yang energies turn sour. Yang energies without the proper balance of yin energies turn sour.

Imbalance of your feminine and masculine energies manifests as negative ego emotions and feelings rather than Christ emotions and feelings. Imbalance equals negative ego, which equals lack of Godliness in that moment. One can, in truth, never lose their Godliness for that is beyond what can be lost. One can, however, lose one's realization of their Godliness in any given moment, which is us falling into glamour, maya, and illusion like in a bad dream.

This issue of balancing the feminine and masculine obviously relates very much to balancing one's four bodies (physical, emotional, mental and spiritual) and the need to balance one's three minds (conscious, subconscious and superconscious).

This need for balancing the feminine and masculine could be seen in Carl Jung's "Theory of Types" in which he said there were four types of people.

Intuitive
Feeling
Thinking
Sensation/Function Type

People tended to lean towards one or two types within themselves. This is not a judgment. However, the ultimate ideal is forever balance.

In astrology and Chinese medicine they speak of the need to balance the four elements.

Fire
Water
Air
Earth

In nature we see this balance again in the four seasons: winter, spring, summer, and fall.

We see this same need for balance in the left- and right-brain.

Left-Brain/Right-Brain
Logical/Imagination
Deductive reasoning/Dreaming
Rational/Intuitive
Verbal/Psychic
Physically observable/Creative, Inductive thinking, Asking and listening

One side of the brain is not better than another. One needs both sides to fully Realize God, and to clear away negative ego. The keys here are striving for balance, integration and moderation in all things at all times. Another key is to listen to the voice of the Holy Spirit and your own Higher Self at all times, and not the voice of the negative ego and lower-self. To achieve this you must maintain mastery over your energies, and secondly be able to listen to the "still, small voice within."

The masculine side provides the power to master your energies. The feminine side will provide the ability to listen to the intuitive guidance that is always forthcoming in every situation. This will also allow for the blending of the First Ray and the Second Ray. This is the blending of the power and the love with the wisdom. Power without love is like Nazi Germany. Love without power is to become emotionally dysfunctional.

A woman likes a man who is strong, but sensitive and loving. A centered man wants a woman who is loving and sensitive, but who can be strong and powerful. More and more, these two sides of ourselves, which might be considered the ultimate archetypes, are coming together. The key to our society changing is for this merger and integration to first occur within oneself. The ultimate example of this in our universe is the Lord Melchizedek, our Universal Logos!

Masculine and Feminine Balance List

Masculine or Feminine:
Courage or Caution

Sun or Moon
Self-Confidence or Humility
Assertive or Receptive
Left brain or Right brain
Scientific or Musical
Logical or Intuitive
Fire or Water
Heal or Earth
Able to accept everything or To be able to differentiate
Thinking or Feeling
Occultist or Mystic
Psychological or Psychic
Focused or Flowing
Closed or Open
Firm or Loving
Detached or Sensitive
Goal oriented or Process oriented
Work or Play
Talking or Listening
Fixed or Flexible
Air or Water
Fire or Earth
Disciplined or Spontaneous
Organized or Fluid
Prayer or Meditation
Willful or Allowing
Deductive or Inductive
Asking or Listening
Mathematical or Artistic
Active or Passive
Yang or Yin
Inner parent or Inner child

Impersonal or Personal
Apollian or Dionysian
Structure or Free-flow
Acetic or Hedonistic
Patriarch or Matriarch
Heavenly Father or Earth Mother
Divine Mother or Divine father
Linear thought or Imagination
Waking or Dreaming
Horizontal reality or Vertical reality
Form or Formless
Doing or Being
Control or Surrender
Selfish or Selfless
Yogi or Aphrodite
Intuition or Sensation function
Contained or Expressive
Tough or Nurturing
Serious or Humorous
Priest or Priestess
Adventurer or Homebody
Teacher or Student
Ruling or Obeying
Lightning-like speed or Circumspection
Caution or Courage
To command everything or To possess nothing
To have no ties or Loyalty
Contempt for death or Regard for life

Duality of Cerebral Functions:
Left side of body/Right side of body
Non-dominant/Dominant

Unconscious/Conscious
Spatial Relations/Verbally aware
Pictures/Language
Images/Words
Symbolic: right/Literal: left
Metaphorical brain/Definitive brain
Intuitive/Logical
Synthesize/Analyze
Accepting/Discriminating
Abstract/Concrete
Musical/Mathematical
Artistic/Scientific
Simultaneous/Sequential
Wholistic/Linear

Methods of Obtaining Information

Left Brain: Yang/Right Brain: Yin
Logical/Imagination, Dreaming, Inner Senses
Deductive Thinking/Intuitive, Psychic
Physically Observable/Creative
Rational/Inductive Thinking
Verbal/Asking & Listening

Yin and Yang

Positive Yin/Positive Yang:
Loving/Personal Power
Compassion/Discipline
Forgiving/Assertive
Joyous/Discernment

Cooperation/Focused
Self-Love/Self-Mastery
Self-Worth/Responsible
Acceptance/Non-attachment
Humility/Patience
Humble/Faith
Gentle/Decisiveness
Peaceful/Organized
Flexible/Perseverance
Sensitive/Giving
Receptive/Logical
Open/Confident
Intuitive/Co-creator
Feeling/Non-judgmental

Negative Yin/Negative Yang
Rejected/Neurotic
Moody/Uptight
Defensive/Intolerant
Insecure/Critical
Worry/Superiority
Lazy/Prideful
Guilt/Revenge
Self-Pity/Resentful
Loneliness/Jealousy
Shyness/Selfish
Procrastination/Workaholic

CHAPTER 22

The Importance of Equally Developing Your Subconscious, Conscious and Superconscious Minds

The conscious mind as you all know is the reasoning mind and its job is to own its' personal power and direct all the energies from within and without and reprogram the subconscious mind. It is of the highest importance in life to balance one's development in each of the three minds: conscious, subconscious and superconscious. If a person is developed in the conscious mind they will have a great deal of personal power, self-mastery and will be very much the cause of their reality.

If one is developed in the subconscious mind, the person will have often a great deal of creative ability, access to their feelings and emotions, psychic abilities and artistic abilities. The psychic abilities may include clairvoyance, clairaudience, and clairsentience, to name a few. Many past life gifts resurface through the subconscious mind of abilities developed in ancient times. This is why a young girl could be a master painter without ever being trained. This is why a ten-year-old boy could have already graduated from college and has an IQ that is off the charts. Other abilities could be dowsing, working with a pendulum, healing abilities, and musical abilities. The list is endless. Most people do not realize that psychic abilities and clairvoyance, clairaudience, and inner taste stem from the subconscious mind and not the superconscious mind. Channeling is a subconscious ability not a superconscious ability. This is why so many people are channeling astral entities and why even people who are schizophrenic can hear voices. People who are artistic often have latent channeling abilities because of the development of their outer and inner senses.

Very often what happens is people tend to be either highly developed in their subconscious mind or conscious mind. The development of the conscious mind usually also goes along with high mental development. This is why sometimes psychics or artists have extraordinary psychic gifts or artistic gifts but do not necessarily have great mastery over their emotions, desire body, inner child, physical self and sometimes their negative ego as well. So, in other words, they are psychically gifted and creatively gifted but are not in full psychological mastery. None of this, of course, is a judgement; it is rather just an insight into how the three minds work and the importance of developing all three functions. If a person is developed in the conscious mind but not the superconscious mind, their consciousness and abilities might be very scientific, rational, and concrete in nature, but will not be attuned to the higher mind or abstract mind of the Spiritual seeker.

If a person is developed on a subconscious level and not a superconscious level, the person will be very developed artistically but the art will not have any Spiritual flavor. They may be highly developed psychically but they may not even believe in GOD. This may seem hard to believe that a person could be extremely psychic, clairvoyant, clairaudient, and clairsentient but not believe in GOD. My Beloved Readers, I have met many people like this; it is why many "psychic type" stores have all kinds of black magic stuff in them. They are more tuned in to the psychic level than the Spiritual level. Many people are fascinated by the psychic hot lines we see advertised on television. I would guide you to avoid them because they are appealing to this psychic fascination. If the person has not learned to be attuned to GOD and transcend negative ego consciousness, the reader's personal agendas and belief systems will color the psychic interpretations. The ideal psychic, or artist for that matter, would be advised to develop all three minds in proper balance. There are many that are, and those seeking help should be discerning to the factors I have mentioned.

The superconscious mind development deals with what I call the higher senses and abilities that transcend the senses of the conscious and subconscious mind. Some of them are most certainly intuition, knowingness, higher comprehension, attunement to the higher mind and abstract mind, attunement to one's Higher Self and the Mighty I Am Presence, the gifts of the Holy Spirit, "Higher" telepathy, attunement to the inner plane Ascended Masters, Angels, Elohim Masters, and Christed Extraterrestrials such as the Arcturians and the Ashtar Command, to name a few. Other higher senses of the superconscious level are response to group vibration, Divine vision, idealism, beatitude, active service, Realization, perfection, and all-knowledge. In our earthly world these higher senses are not even recognized by most people, psychologists and even lightworkers.

It is only when these three minds are equally balanced that full GOD Realization can take place and full integrated ascension can take place. It is very easy to follow the line of least resistance and develop oneself in the mind that you are most accustomed to having expertise. The real trick of the Spiritual path is to develop yourself in the mind or minds that you currently have the least development in. It is then that you can more fully comprehend GOD in all His manifestations from a full spectrum consciousness vision that includes conscious, subconscious and superconscious Realization!

CHAPTER 23

The Importance of Developing a Flawless Character, Integrity, and Clarity

All aspects of the Spiritual path are important, however in my humble opinion, one of the most important is developing a flawless character, integrity and clarity in everything one does. Because of the nature of my work and the large scale global focus of what I am trying to do, I am in contact with a lot of people and I am continually amazed at a great many of the lightworkers I have contact with who do not focus on this level. It could seem to me to be the meat and potatoes or should I say vegetables and potatoes of the Spiritual path. Please excuse my vain attempt at humor here, but in all seriousness, I have done business and professional work with a great many lightworkers who are highly developed spiritually, who are into channeling and all kinds of metaphysical things, yet their level of integrity and lack of character development is astounding. If one makes an agreement then one should keep that agreement. If one sets a deadline and makes a promise to complete something then one should meet that deadline or at least have the courtesy to call and apologize for not being able to keep it. If one says they are going to return a phone call they should do so or they should not say they are going to do it. If one makes an appointment, they should not break it at the last second unless it is an emergency. If one makes a promise then they should keep that promise or not make it in the first place. If one says they are going to be at a certain place at a certain time then they should be there at that time or not make the commitment in the first place. If one makes a mistake they should admit their mistake and apologize.

In truth, every word you speak is GOD speaking. Spacing out on what you have done, or the passage of time does not let one off the hook. If one borrows money they should pay back that money, and if they can't then they owe an explanation to that person and not run away like a frightened child and deny that it ever happened. I am absolutely astounded by the behavior of many lightworkers I run into, some of which are at extremely high level of initiation. I personally consider one's integrity one of the most important things of all. Many lightworkers are so focused on channeling, initiations, celestial activities, extraterrestrials and/or esoteric information that they are missing one of the most important aspects of the spiritual path. Again I ask, what does it matter if you've passed seven levels of initiation but you are completely lacking in integrity and character development? One of the main purposes of life and the Spiritual path is to develop the Melchizedek/Christ/Buddha qualities and attributes. This can be hard work and it takes joyous vigilance every moment of one's life to ensure that one doesn't fall off the wagon, so to speak. My Beloved Readers, I ask you what does it matter if you've passed your seven levels of initiation and one is still filled with negative ego selfishness, self-centeredness, narcissism, self-indulgence, selfish motivations, anger, upset, grudges, judgement, jealousy, competition? I ask you, is this GOD Realization? How can this be? What is the cause? The cause is lack of proper psychological education and training. The cause is a complete lack of understanding of the difference between negative ego thinking and Melchizedek/Christ/Buddha thinking. So what that you can channel the Ascended Masters and you allow the emotional body and negative ego to run your life. So what if one is a library of Spiritual information if lack of integrity and proper character development is not being demonstrated. Another word for character development is developing Christ and Buddha consciousness in one's mental and emotional body. I do not mean to be harsh in stating these facts, but rather I am pointing out a Spiritual observation I see taking place far too often. Lightworkers are often enamoured with the Celestial Realms and are not doing their psychological homework. Channeling, achieving initiations, spiritual information, becoming successful writing books, making tapes, being psychic is all fine and wonderful and is an important part of one's Spiritual path, however it must be done in a balanced manner where Godliness is also made manifest in your every thought word and deed and also made manifest in your every interaction with other people. All the lessons of life are constantly testing us in this regard. Once one has achieved higher levels of initiation, Spiritual leadership, and public recognition, this becomes even more important because even if you have learned these lessons once, you will be tested again because the negative ego will have tasted power, success, fame and money and this often causes lightworkers to throw everything they have developed out the window. The true test is can you keep your Godly purity when Spiritual and worldly success has been achieved. How do you treat other people who are "not quite yet at your level of spiritual, financial, social, psychological and worldly success." Do you treat them exactly as you did before you achieved these things. How do you treat the gardener, the maid, the gas station attendant, the farm worker, the homeless person on the street, the person who asks you for money, the people who call you on the phone or who write you now that you are successful? Do you have time for them now? Do you treat them as GOD?

My Beloved Readers, strive to always maintain the highest integrity! Strive to be honest in everything you do. Strive to maintain your Melchizedek/Christ/Buddha Consciousness in your every thought, even when alone. Strive to keep it in the feelings and emotions you choose to create. Certainly keep it in every verbal interaction. Keep it in every action you take and every behavior you demonstrate. Keep it in relationship to your interaction with the Animal Kingdom, Plant Kingdom, Mineral Kingdom and all sentient beings. Do not allow yourself to be lazy and procrastinate, to be hedonistic, to give into fatigue or to use your physical body and its elements as an excuse to break your integrity and striving for a flawless character!

The last quality I wish to speak of is the importance of clarity in everything you do. Pay attention to detail and be precise in your every thought, word and deed. Do not give into being sloppy or fudging when you are working on a project. Do it properly or do not do it at all. Pursue excellence in every moment and aspect of your life. Look at mistakes as positive and forgive yourself and unconditionally love yourself when you make them. Part of integrity however, is also learning from your mistakes.

Carl Jung, the famous Swiss psychologist, said "Man's greatest sin is his indolence." This is laziness; this is giving too much into the emotional body and the line of least resistance in the subconscious mind.

My Beloved Readers, these three qualities of integrity, character development and clarity in everything you do is of the highest importance in truly becoming a full-fledged integrated Ascended Master on a Spiritual, psychological, and physical/earthly level. Do not fall into the trap of developing your Spiritual body to the neglect of your psychological body and physical/earthly body. All three of these levels must be mastered on their own plane. A great many lightworkers fall into the trap of trying to use Spiritual practices to develop psychologically thinking that just doing Spiritual work will automatically develop all aspects of self. Being a master psychologist myself, I am here to tell you that that is not true. You must master the lesson at the level of the problem. For example, if you are having a problem controlling your negative ego or controlling you anger or getting upset too much in a particular relationship, chanting all day is not going to help, neither is meditating all day. This may sound odd to some; however, I know thousands of people who follow Eastern paths who do this and they can't figure out why their lives are not working. Channeling all day will also not help in the slightest. I know people who channel the Ascended Masters who are some of the biggest emotional victims and are more run by the negative ego than anyone I ever met. Yet they channel all day for a living. I know others who do ascension work all day and the exact same thing is true. You can also focus all your time building your light body and light quotient and this will not help you control your negative emotions or solve your relationship problems. You can read books on ascension and fill your information banks with wonderful esoteric knowledge and this will not solve your psychological lessons.

One last important point in regard to this issue of the importance of developing your integrity, flawless character and clarity is that this is not only of the highest importance in becoming a full-fledged integrated Ascended Master, it is also unbelievably important once you attain Master status and Spiritual leadership. What you will find is that once you have a lot of students and a lot of people coming to your workshops, lectures and so on, you will be under a microscope of the highest order. Your every word, deed, action and written word will be microscopically examined. If there is the slightest bit of lack of integrity, inconsistency, character flaws, lack of clarity on any level, your students and the general public will see it and throw it back at you. Many Spiritual teachers and leaders are not prepared for this and go through many hard lessons because of it. Some of the feedback will be appropriate and some of it will be other people's negative ego looking for faults and criticizing to make themselves feel better because of their lack of self-worth and being caught in the negative ego. Not only will the public be an incredible mirror of your thoughts, words and deeds on every level, but even if you remain in integrity and demonstrate a flawless character and clarity you will still be attacked and criticized by people in the public who are very run by their negative ego. A great many people do not feel good about themselves and are totally run by the negative ego. This being the case, they are run by jealousy, competition, judgementalness, faultfinding, comparing, and the only way they can feel good about themselves is to attack others. So, even if you are perfect in all the qualities I have mentioned in this chapter, you must be very firm in this within yourself. So when you have to deal with all these strange and eccentric people, you have developed a thick skin, so to speak, and you are so solid and clear in the integrity and clarity by which you do everything that you are not knocked off balance or even affected by the strange feedback that will most definitely come from a certain small segment of the population that is very disturbed psychologically and spiritually. This comes with the territory of being an integrated Ascended Master, having Spiritual leadership, and being in the public eye!

The Master Jesus certainly had to deal with it. All he did was love and heal people yet everyone wanted to kill and crucify him. This stems from the ego over sensitivity and lack of understanding of other people and nothing that the Master Jesus demonstrated. This is what I am trying to explain to you and this is why it is so important to become as solid and clear as you can within self on every level, so you don't question or doubt self when irrational and erroneous criticisms and attacks come from people who are trying to build up their egos that are caught in the negative ego.

His Holiness, the Lord Sai Baba, has had to deal with it. It is hard to believe anyone would attack or criticize him, and on one occasion someone tried to poison him! This is amazing given that he is a Universal Avatar and the most advanced incarnated Spiritual Master in the history of the Earth. Yet even he is attacked and criticized. Sai Baba being of the highest order of integrity, character development and clarity of course does not let this phase him in the slightest. For as he has said, "Nothing can or will stop his mission." He is at a Spiritual level where he can drink the poison, and did just that to teach the people a Spiritual lesson even though he knew it was poison in advance.

I could share many other examples of Spiritual leaders and teachers who have had to deal with this. In truth there is not one Spiritual leader, teacher or prophet who hasn't. So I share these things to again emphasize the importance of doing your homework now on every level so you can be as clear as possible now and in the future when you will be even under a greater microscope!

This is why, my Beloved Readers, I have actually written three sets of books in my easy to read Encyclopedia of the Spiritual Path. If you want to develop the spiritual aspect then read *The Beginners Guide to Ascension, The Complete Ascension Manual, Beyond Ascension* and *Cosmic Ascension*. If you want to develop the psychological or psychospiritual level then read my books *Soul Psychology, How To Clear The Negative Ego, Integrated Ascension, The Golden Book of Melchizedek*, and *Ascension and Romantic Relationships*. If you want to develop the physical/earthly aspect of self, read *Manual for Planetary Leadership, The Golden Keys to Ascension and Healing*, and *Empowerment and Integration of the Goddess*. I have purposely written these easy to read and practical books to help lightworkers master and integrate these three most essential aspects of true GOD Realization. My Beloved Readers, if you feel a little weak in one of these areas or if you feel good in these areas but just want to refine and build even more, then focus on the books in the area that you feel most guided to expand. I humbly suggest they will help you to master and integrate your given focus in a very easy, practical and accelerated manner. My Beloved Readers, it is my sincere hope and prayer that this brief discussion of the importance of integrity, character development and clarity in all aspects of life has been beneficial and clarifying in terms of bringing proper balance and integration to your approach to your Spiritual path!

CHAPTER 24

An Overview of the Incredible Importance of a Healthy Psychology, Philosophy and Integrated Spiritual Understanding

My Beloved Readers, this is a most interesting chapter. The inspiration for this chapter stems out of seeing how a great number of Spiritual leaders, Spiritual teachers, channels and even friends get detoured and even have their work become quite dark in many ways. What is amazing is that a great many are quite evolved and sharp in many ways. Many have done some great work or have many followers. Many have written books or have been excellent channels. Many have clairvoyant abilities. Yet all the ones I am considering here have taken a severe tumble down the "Spiritual Mountain" and the cause is always the same. The cause is that even though they are extremely evolved Spiritually, and many have absolutely brilliant minds and sincere and good intentions, even good hearts, their psychology, philosophy, and integrated Spiritual understanding was skewed or off-kilter, which caused a fragmentation, disintegration, and contamination of the work by their negative ego and sometimes dark forces as well.

I have been inwardly guided by Spirit and the Masters in this chapter to do a type of overview of some of the common ways this corruption often takes place. This is, in truth, quite a serious issue, for a great many of the people I have seen this happen to have a great many students and followers. So as the Spiritual teacher, channel, or scientist goes, so do all their followers. What is also of concern is how many Spiritual leaders, teachers, channels, and Spiritual authors this is happening to. This whole study is actually quite a fascinating process to examine and I am greatly looking forward to examining this with you.

The first example of this that comes to mind, which is unbelievably common in the New Age Movement, is an imbalanced theory a great many lightworkers hold because of imbalanced Spiritual teachers who are not clear themselves. This is the Spiritual theory of trying to balance everything. Now, at first glance this sounds right, and this is part of its seduction. Now, you all being familiar with my writings, you know how no one pushes the importance of balance and integration more than I. However, you will also notice that the only other thing I preach more than that is Sai Baba's famous saying that the definition of GOD is, "GOD equals Man minus ego"! It is true that everything needs to be balanced and integrated except for one thing! This one thing is negative ego/fear-based/separative thinking versus Spiritual/Christ/Buddha thinking. These are opposites and the only way to realize GOD is to transcend negative ego thinking. This is the greatest blind spot in lightworkers' understanding on planet Earth, and this includes most Spiritual leaders, Spiritual teachers, and Spiritual channels, and psychics. So the philosophy they have taken on is to try to balance everything. I have seen certain major teachers try to balance the Light and the dark. They may show horror films to try and integrate the dark side like this is something that is good! I am here to tell you it is not good! Your thoughts create your reality and what you think about manifests. What you think about and put your attention on you attract! Deluded Spiritual teachers have come up with a deluded theory and are poisoning their students unwittingly.

I have seen other extremely well-intentioned and even brilliant world famous Spiritual teachers and leaders try to balance Spiritual positive feelings and emotions with all the negative feelings and emotions. This, of course, is absurd. Negative ego thinking is the cause of all negative feelings and emotions. We are not here to experience jealousy, hate, anger, impatience, conditional love, envy, depression, sadness, or upset. Negative ego thinking causes all these. You will not Realize God by indulging in negative feelings and emotions and trying to balance them with positive Spiritual feelings and emotions. Yet, I cannot tell you how many lightworkers on Earth have gotten seduced into such nonsense by well-intentioned, wonderful Spiritual and psychological leaders who are just confused. Such a theory will just block and contaminate your channel and cut you off from Spirit and the Masters to a great extent. It will also corrupt all channeling, and fill it full of negative ego agenda.

Another similar, totally corrupted teaching by a great many quite well-known Spiritual leaders and teachers is that you are supposed to balance your lower-self and your higher-self. They think that this is what the balance of Heaven and Earth really means. This will, of course, lead to only the height of corruption and contamination of the negative ego. It is a theory that says negative ego thinking needs to be balanced with Spiritual thinking. I would go as far as to say that half the lightworkers on Earth and most of the people involved with traditional psychology are caught up either consciously or unconsciously in such corrupted psychological, philosophical and Spiritual nonsense. These are theories that will lead you to becoming totally run by your negative ego and could lead you to becoming a twilight master. A twilight master is someone either consciously or unconsciously who is serving both the light and the dark sides.

Now, my Beloved Readers, be clear on this point. There is a Spiritual Hierarchy of Ascended Masters that governs this planet. However there is also another hierarchy called the Black Lodge who are also referred to as the dark forces. When you follow such fragmented, negative ego-run theories, you are opening yourself unconsciously to getting taken over by dark forces. I am not saying this always takes place. However, it often can take place. This can especially take place if any kind of substance abuse is going on. This can be alcohol, pot, cocaine, or other types of substance abuse.

The aforementioned theories will also cause you to be victimized by your emotional body, desire body and subconscious mind. It is negative ego thinking that causes dark forces to begin to be attracted to you. It is only when you stop negative ego thinking and feeling and think only with your Spiritual/Christ/Buddha mind that you live totally in unconditional love, forgiveness, inner peace, joy, happiness, bliss, patience, faith, nonjudgmentalness, humility, humbleness, tolerance, evenmindedness, equanimity, positivity and the Light! Does not the Bible say, "Let this mind be in you that was in Christ Jesus"? It is the same thing Buddhism Teaches. It is what Edgar Cayce taught, what *A Course In Miracles* teaches, what Yogananda teaches, what the Vedas teach, what the Ascended Masters teach, and what all true religions and Spiritual paths and mystery schools teach. Do not try to balance the Light and the dark, lower-self and higher-self, negative ego and Christ/Buddha consciousness, Love and fear. It sounds absurd to even think that anyone would even consider doing such a thing; however, I am telling you half the world's population is doing just this. Not because they are bad people, for they are not. They just have not been trained, as they should have been at home, in school, in churches, in temples and by clear New Age Spiritual teachers, in proper Spiritual psychology, Spiritual philosophy, and integrated Spiritual theory.

If you have found yourself caught up in such improper theory, no big deal, just immediately change it and you will feel instantly better! Your thoughts create your reality. You are here to live in the Light! Your are here to live in Love! You are here to live in positivity all day! Study this book and my other books: *Soul Psychology, Integrated Ascension, How To Clear The Negative Ego, The Complete Ascension Manual*; and I can easily teach you in the comfort of your own home to just make this slight adjustment in your thinking, theory, and perspective to give you this unchanging Love and Peace you seek. It is really quite simple once you understand it. Do not be seduced by these corrupted theories for they will not bring you the God Realization, Love, or Peace you seek!

Now, other confused Spiritual teachers are caught up in this theory of trying to integrate everything. So they want to integrate their negative ego and love their negative ego. Well, as Sai Baba has said, "GOD equals man minus ego"! This is just a spin off of the aforementioned theories. You do not integrate the negative ego thinking for its philosophy is the exact opposite of the Spiritual/Christ/ Buddha thinking! You either choose GOD or negative ego! You either choose Love or fear! You either choose separation or oneness! You don't try to integrate fear, separation, negative ego, and lower-self, and then love it. This is like eating poisonous food physically and trying to love the poisonous food while doing it, thinking that following such a philosophy will turn it into Light. This is delusion and will lead the person to illusion, glamour and maya and make them sick. When someone offers you poisonous food physically, mentally, emotionally, energetically, or Spiritually, you refuse to eat it! You refuse to put it in your body, in your mind and in your heart. This is what "GOD equals man minus ego means"! As *A Course In Miracles* says, "Deny any thought not of GOD to enter your mind"! It is only when you deny negative ego thinking and affirm God consciousness, Christ consciousness, and Buddha consciousness that true God Realization will take place. Did not Jesus say to one of his disciples who started complaining, "Get thee behind me, Satan"! Jesus did not say, "Come integrate with me Satan!" Jesus did not say, "Come integrate with me and let me love you and take thee into myself and into my bodies so I can turn you into Light!" The Master Jesus said, "Get thee behind me, Satan"!

The only way to achieve God Realization and inner peace is to not let poisonous food, negative ego thoughts, negative ego emotions, and negative ego dark energy into your consciousness, mind, emotional body, etheric body and physical body. Otherwise you are literally eating "poison" to support some deluded theory.

My Beloved Readers, do not underestimate the things lightworkers will do of a deluded destructive nature to try to support a deluded theory of life they want to believe is true but is not! If you follow such theories you will take a fall down the "Spiritual Mountain," your life will reflect your imbalanced theory, and you will attract dark forces, energies, and experiences to yourself. As the saying goes, "As within, So without! As above so below"! The thoughts, theories and beliefs you hold in your consciousness will manifest in your physical body and outer life. If you want a Spiritual/positive life, you had better hold only Spiritual and positive balanced thoughts in your mind. You are to become the Light, not balance Light and darkness. You are here to become Love, not balance unconditional Love and fear and attack. You are here to become God, not balance God and negative ego! Negative ego is the opposite of God! You are here to become and fully embody your Higher Self and Mighty I Am Presence, not indulge in your lower-self! You are not here to balance positivity and negativity! This sounds completely irrational when it is described here, yet this is what an enormous number of lightworkers believe. They do this not because they are not good and fine people, but because no one has trained them, for even the Spiritual leaders and teachers are to a great extent confused in their psychology, philosophy and Spiritual theory! This is not meant as a judgement, just a loving Spiritual observation and fact! I am in contact with an enormous number of Spiritual leaders, Spiritual teachers, Spiritual channels and lightworkers and am very well studied, and I read and see and they tell me what they believe. Being a Spiritual teacher, channel and psychologist I am trained to see these things. It is actually quite fascinating to me to see all the different variations of fragmented and disintegrated theories that people believe in. This is why I wanted to write this chapter. As a case study it is quite fascinating. It is my hope that this chapter clears up a lot of these misconceptions!

Other deluded theories lightworkers get caught up in are Jung's theory of the shadow! I happen to like Jung! My parents were originally Jungian psychologists. He was a brilliant man and probably the best of all the traditional psychologists. His theory of the shadow is incorrect. This is another slant on what I have been talking about this entire chapter. You don't try and integrate your shadow! This is just another way of saying you are trying to integrate the negative ego, lower-self, fear, or darkness. It is amazing how tricky and seductive the negative ego is. It will try and trick lightworkers any way it can into embracing it instead of God and Christ as their leader. You must recognize that there is a negative ego philosophy of life and way of thinking, and there is a Spiritual/Christ/Buddha consciousness way of thinking. It is essential in life to know and understand this. It is also essential to know and understand how the negative ego thinks as well as how the Spiritual/Christ/ Buddha consciousness mind thinks, so you can be vigilant against the negative ego way of thinking and can hence continually affirm and think with your Spiritual mind. This is what I am doing in this chapter. I am showing you the various delusionary philosophies of the negative ego and how it tries to trick and seduce lightworkers into following them. Now, if this is what you want to call integrating your shadow, that is fine. However, the idea that we have to integrate our shadow or darkness of any kind into our self is absolute delusion and negative ego contamination. As the Bible says, "Ye are Gods and know it not"! "You are made in the image of God"! "Be still, and know that I am God"! We are each Sons and Daughters of GOD! We are made in GOD's image, which is totally perfect, and positive, and made only of Love and Light! There is no shadow or darkness in GOD, and there is none in you or I! The negative ego in truth does not really even exist! In Eastern religions they call it illusion and maya! The mind is a brilliant instrument! Be aware, however, it can be used by the negative ego self or by the God Self! These theories I am sharing with you have been created by the negative ego-self to try and retain power and not die! For if the negative ego dies, only GOD exists. Now, the truth is, GOD exists even if you indulge your negative ego mind. However, the law of the mind is that you will have to live in the nightmare, negative hypnosis, and bad dream of your own negative ego thinking, for your thoughts create your reality! Is the glass of water half empty or half full? It is all how you look at it. You can see life from GOD's perspective or the negative ego's perspective. One will bring you positivity and one will bring you negativity! One will bring you Love and one will bring you attack and fear! One will bring you Truth and one will bring you illusion! One will bring you a peace that passeth understanding and one will bring you conflict, imbalance, chaos and war! One will bring you Light and one will bring you darkness! One will bring you nothing but joy and happiness, and the other will bring you suffering, sadness and negative feelings and emotions! The choice is yours! You must choose one or the other! The aforementioned theories will throw you into the "twilight zone," serving half one and half the other. Do you really want only half GOD and half negative ego? Do you really want half Love, and half fear and attack? Do you really want half positivity and half negativity? It is absurd when I point it out in this way and manner, and that is why I have been guided by Spirit and the Masters to write this chapter. They want you to see with a magnifying glass and a clear rational mind how absurd and ridiculous these negative ego philosophies really are. Banish them this instant and choose GOD's Integrated Spiritual Understanding and Theory! This is the only path to finding true Love, peace and success in this world.

Most definitely balance your feminine and masculine side. Most definitely balance Heaven and Earth! Most definitely balance your four-body system (Spirit, mind, feelings, and physical body)! Most definitely balance your superconscious, conscious, and subconscious minds! Do not, however, I repeat, do not try and balance negative ego/fear-based/separative thinking and Spiritual/Melchizedek/ Christ/Buddha thinking! As Sai Baba says, "GOD equal man minus ego"!

Another common theory the people in the consciousness movement get caught up in is traditional psychology! These are all theories, psychological theories based on the personality. There are three levels of Self-Actualization. First there is Self-Actualization of the personality, then the Soul and then the Monad or Mighty I Am Presence. I am not saying here that traditional psychology is of no value, for it is of great value. I am a psychologist myself and have gained much from my extensive study of this field. However, my Beloved Readers, to follow such theories will never take you beyond personality level Self-Actualization. You will never ever realize the Soul and the Mighty I Am Presence until you change theories! This is a fact! Jung was one of the few famous traditional psychologists that began to explore the Soul and Spirit levels and should be greatly commended for this. However, he did not go far enough and did not come to a complete understanding. He began the process and created a transition but did not come to a full understanding. Have the courage, for those that are focused on this, to take the next step! Honor what you have learned, for it has served you greatly, and take the next step! I still use a great deal of what I learned from traditional psychology. However, I do so from the perspective of the Mighty I Am Presence and I cast out those things that are overidentified with the personality to the rejection of the Soul and Monad. The problem with traditional psychology in all its various theories is that it does not fully understand how our thoughts create our reality. It does not understand the difference between negative ego/fear-based/separative thinking and Spiritual/Christ/Buddha thinking! It does not integrate enough of Spirit and the Masters into the picture. It has not integrated the superconscious mind, Higher Self, Oversoul, Monad and/or Mighty I Am Presence into the picture. It does not hence understand unconditional Love, or how to maintain unchanging inner peace and evenmindedness! It definitely helps, but it will only take you from "A to G," and will not take you from "A to Z"! Have the courage to now take the next step and build upon that which you have learned!

The next common theory I have noticed in the world is the basic "emotionally-run theory"! This is the one that most people in the world are run by although I have seen a great many lightworkers as well! This one is an overidentification with feelings. They feel their feelings are GOD's gift to mankind. It is like the Humanistic Movement and Encounter groups, where feelings were everything. It doesn't matter that all the feelings are being programmed by the negative ego. They have no understanding that their thoughts are creating their feelings and emotions. So, this faulty theory is the unconscious type that just follows their feelings, for this is the line of least resistance. This, of course, is just a prescription to let the non-reasoning subconscious mind run you!

You can only trust your feelings if you have mastery of yourself and you are fundamentally trying to stay in control of your negative ego mind. Otherwise you will take your anger, impatience, irritation, intolerance, and all your other negative emotions out on others.

The next faulty theory I see a lot of is people's overidentification with the Spiritual and Heavenly realms, and the belief that they mastered the Psychological Level in the "Spring of '72." This theory is rampant. They give lesser importance to the Psychological Level and all their focus is on the Spiritual! This can also manifest as putting all their focus on Spiritual science since they are a Spiritual scientist. They have never really been trained in Spiritual psychology or focused on that level, for they feel they mastered it. In the meantime the subconscious mind and negative ego are creating havoc right and left and they don't have a clue.

There are also, of course, the Mental types who are more intellectually focused, focused on Esoteric knowledge, and also do not focus on the Psychological Level.

This overidentification with the Spiritual Level is extremely common in the Eastern philosophies. A great many of them are not balanced. The entire focus is on meditation, chanting, and on the Spiritual level, and the people in these groups are a psychological mess. They try to heal psychological problems with Spiritual practices, which will never work. All lessons or problems must be mastered at the level of the problem. Contrary to popular opinion, Spirit and the Masters will not control your mind for you!

Interestingly, this is why a great many lightworkers are under psychic attack! They pray their hearts out and can't understand why Spirit and the Masters won't help them. This, of course, is a projection, for Spirit and the Masters are helping them. However, the problem is not a Spiritual one, it is a psychological one. That is what is allowing the psychic attacks to continue! Even Spirit and the Masters cannot fully stop psychic attack if one's psychology is not mastered! Most people in this world do not have a clue about what negative ego thinking is, and the need to stop it and replace it with Spiritual/Christ/Buddha thinking! Even 98% of all lightworkers really do not have a full handle on it! This is why there is so much glamour and illusion in the New Age Movement!

The next faulty theory I see quite often is the overidentification with channeling. This theory sees channeling as the answer to everything. They do not recognize how much channeling on the planet is filtered through people's subconscious mind, personality, filters, belief systems, past life programming, information banks, ray structure, psychology, philosophy, level of clarity, Spiritual evolution, psychological evolution, negative ego control or the lack thereof, to name a few. This group tends to believe that if it is channeled, it is true. Nothing could be farther from the truth! So, with every channeled book that comes out, no matter how contaminated, no Spiritual discernment is shown and they believe it! It is almost comical. "The world is coming to an end, I better not sign up for this workshop!" I tell you, I have seen it all and I am sure you have as well! They don't recognize how much of life is a "co-creation"!

The next faulty theory I would like to explore that is incredibly prevalent in the New Age Movement is what I call the Master Teacher/inner child syndrome. This is so common it blows my mind! These are Spiritual teachers, channels, psychics, Spiritual scientists, and Spiritual authors, who give masterful presentations on stage or with their clients, and can be quite brilliant and do some good work. Then, as soon as the session is over or the workshop presentation is over, they are back to being run by their inner child. They have no idea how to parent the inner child. They are not in control of their lives the inner child is. It runs them ragged! It is mind boggling to watch how someone who can be so masterful on stage and such a skilled Spiritual teacher or channel can be so run by the inner child in their personal life! This type of faulty theory is rampant in the Spiritual Movement!

Another faulty theory that is similar and that causes a lot of problems for Spiritual leaders and teachers is that they are sometimes amazing Spiritual channels or teachers, but, on a personality level they are very undeveloped. So, when it comes to dealing with people, Spiritual leadership on a daily basis, dealing with employees, other people's negative egos, and so on, they are not equipped to deal with the lessons that come!

Then there are those who have a faulty theory of being too Heavenly and Celestially oriented and are not grounded! They are too ethereal and not really even in their bodies. There is very little energy in their first and second chakras! This can also manifest as being very Spiritual, but never being able to manifest their Spiritual mission on the Earth. They are not able to manifest their business or make money! They are not good at dealing with all types of earthly matters and earthly energies. They do not fully recognize or appreciate that there are Four Faces of GOD, and one of these is the Material Face of GOD! One will never fully Realize GOD until the earthly level is integrated as well! Much can be learned about GOD by fully embracing the physical. One will never fully learn to Realize God until they come to fully love and appreciate Earth life and earthly civilization!

Then, of course, the most common type on Earth are those people who are overidentified with material life in the type form of being too materialistic! Amazingly enough, a great many Spiritual people are that way as well. They think they put GOD first but they really don't! They do all kinds of service work, but the bottom line is money! If they don't get paid or if their material concerns are not met they will not serve. I am not saying that money is not important, I am saying that GOD needs to be put first, and an enormous number of people think they are putting GOD first but are not. The selfish negative ego has tricked them with improper motives! This is incredibly common!

Then, once in a while I have come across the Hedonists, who believe that there is nothing they have to do in life to Realize God! They either think they are God and nothing else has to be achieved, or that they have completed their mission and purpose in past lives or this life so all they are here to do is enjoy themselves. This of course is total illusion, for although we each are God and Christ, in truth this does not mean you have fully realized this truth! There are 352 initiations to fully Realize GOD and no one on Earth has ever achieved this. This also does not take into consideration that we are here to serve!

Another common type is the Spiritual channel who can channel the Masters, but who is a psychological and emotional mess! Contrary to popular belief, channeling is not a sign of great Spiritual or psychological development! This is a lesson a great many lightworkers need to understand and learn! The psychological and emotional unclarity of the person doing the channeling creates havoc in the actual channeling, creating all kinds of power issues, personal agendas, judgmentalness, inaccurate information and total contamination of the channeling, even though they may be channeling the Ascended Masters. Undiscerning lightworkers think that the information is still coming from the Masters. However, the whole process is so filled with contamination that, in truth, only the smallest fragment is really the Masters but the channel has learned how to put on a good show and act! Undiscerning lightworkers most often believe this act and show!

Now the next faulty theory is very similar to the last one, but it is not with a channel for the Ascended Masters or Angels per se, but with a Spiritual teacher. The Spiritual teacher has all kinds of brilliant New Age, Esoteric, or Biblical information, which is very attractive. However, the Spiritual teacher on a psychological level is totally fragmented and unclear. This is unbelievably common! So all the person's power issues, fame issues, greed issues, vanity issues, manipulation issues, and possibly sexual issues are at play! This is where we get the cults, false prophets, false teachers, unintegrated teachers, and fragmented teachers! This is probably one of the most common of all the faulty theories! It is absolutely rampant in the New Age movement and in religion!

The next faulty theory is what I call the Twilight Master! Here the person is parading around as a major consciousness teacher or even Spiritual teacher, but in truth they are corrupt to the core. They do not really call on GOD or work with the Masters or Angels. They are really operating out of a psychological theory that is not really Spiritual. Even some psychics fit into this category, but most are more like Spiritual teachers, psychologists, and counselors who are often extremely gifted. They are similar to psychologically focused magicians or metaphysicians. They are capable of doing some good psychological work and having some amazing results. They are often very attractive physically, and can dazzle people with their charisma and psychological and metaphysical magic. However, the only problem is they are selfish to the core. All they are really concerned with is making money, selfish motives, power, fame, vanity and having sex with their followers. This is much more common then many of you would actually like or want to believe! It blows my mind to see how lightworkers and people are seduced by these types.

The thing you must understand is that if you do not do your 100% Spiritual and psychological homework, in fully grasping all the intricacies of Spiritual psychology and all the corruptions, contaminations, glamours, pitfalls and traps of the negative ego mind within yourself, you will also not be able to see it in others. Hence, twilight masters are serving the dark and the Light! It is unbelievably important for lightworkers to be Spiritually discerning of this potentiality within self, and to certainly be on the lookout for this in others. The key is to look for where the true motives lie. Do not be seduced by glamour, appearances, magic, "smooth operating", and "razzle-dazzle"! Examine where the true motives are stemming from!

I am not supporting here a theory of thinking negatively of others, for this is another trap and glamour or the negative ego. I am saying see with true Spiritual discernment and have an efficient and truthful perception of reality within self and in regard to others! Be on guard and vigilant against those that serve two masters, the dark and the Light!

Another faulty philosophy and psychology among lightworkers is the skipping of levels. Because of the negative ego's need for self-inflation and self-aggrandizement, certain Spiritual leaders and teachers skip levels and think they are too big to deal with the Planetary Ascended Masters, Solar Masters, and even Galactic Masters, they will only deal with Melchizedek or the Cosmic Masters. The Planetary, Solar, or Galactic Masters are too low for them. Hard to believe, but true!

Next we have the group that are claiming to be God Realized beings, Avatars, Ascended Masters, and/or to have achieved their Cosmic Ascension, or completed all 352 levels of initiation! We have quite a collection. Unfortunately there are an enormous number of Spiritual leaders, Spiritual teachers, channels, and Spiritual scientists caught up in this one. It is almost comical to see some of the things that come out. I think I have met over 200 that are married to Jesus or Lord Buddha. Then you have the ones who think they are Jesus, Lord Maitreya, Archangel Michael or various other Ascended Masters or Angels. Then you have the ones declaring their Omnipotence, Omnipresence and Omniscience. Then we have the Avatars! The word "Avatar" means "God Realized at birth"! There is only one true Avatar on this planet and that is Sai Baba. He was God Realized at birth and at the age of five he could materialize things right out of thin air. He never had any form of Spiritual training. He was God Realized at birth. This only occurs in the descent of an Avatar. Everyone else claiming to be is not!

Then we have those claiming to be God Realized! I am here to tell you that there are 352 levels of initiation to become truly God Realized. Those claiming God Realization are usually between the fifth and seventh initiation. So in truth, they are about 345 levels and initiations away from achieving their claim. The only thing they have realized is the negative ego, in most cases. Would a true God Realized being or Saint claim to be one? As soon as you hear this, run for the hills! The negative ego's need for self-inflation and self-aggrandizement is unbelievable. I am not saying that one can never say anything positive about their mission or share certain details. One must be very careful that if this is done, that it be done appropriately and for a good reason, and that there not be selfish, negative ego motives for doing so. The only exception I would make in this understanding is Sai Baba, who truly is a Universal Master living on Earth. In the true descent of an Avatar it would be appropriate to share such things. In all other cases, certain things can be shared, but one must be very careful that one is doing it for the right reasons.

Then we have those who think they are Cosmic Ascended Masters and have completed all 352 levels of initiation. This of course is delusion, self-aggrandizement, and megalomania at its highest. This is the negative ego completely out of control! Yet there are people who have claimed and are claiming such things! My advice is to run for the hills! Then we have the people claiming to be Ascended Masters. This, of course, is a tricky one for by definition after you take the beginning of the sixth initiation you can officially call yourself one. However, in truth you are a "kindergarten" Ascended Master. This, of course, is not always advertised! The negative ego has a tendency to leave this out. I wonder why?

One is not really a full-fledged Ascended Master until they complete their seventh to ninth initiation and also fully integrate these initiations into their mental, emotional, etheric, and physical vehicles and earth life. Some of the most disturbed people I know are sixth, seventh, eighth, and ninth degree initiates. These initiations only denote the amount of Light in your aura. I know one person who is a seventh degree initiate who I would honestly call schizophrenic. I know others who are sociopaths, and pathological liars. I know others who are completely run by the negative ego and emotional body in extremely disturbed manners. I know other high level initiates who are drug addicts, heroin addicts, and alcoholics. I know others who are complete and total victims. I know others who are at these levels of initiation who have totally fallen down the "Spiritual Mountain" and have fallen from grace. I know others who are actual semi-criminals. I know others who are total hedonists! So, next time you think that one's initiation level is a good measure of God Realization, think again. Initiation means only the percentage of Light quotient in your field, and has absolutely nothing to do with psychological development. I know people who I would not even consider as unconditionally loving who are high level initiates. I know people who suffer from a split personality, the Dr. Jeckle/Mr. Hyde syndrome, who are high level initiates. So, for any person trying to call themselves an Ascended Master because of their initiation level better think twice. This is why the Masters are not really into ascension, they are into "Integrated Ascension"! A true Ascended Master has not only the initiation level, but also the Spiritual, psychological, and physical/earthly mastery and integration of all levels in a very refined state! So let this be your true goal and purpose!

Then we have the Spiritual con men! These are people who want to make money and who are slightly Spiritual and have lawyer-type minds or scientific-type minds and actually con people into believing they are some God Realized being when they are not! They are really into it for power, money, and fame as their true motives and see a fast way to make a buck. They proclaim to love others or the Earth, but all they really love is themselves. After a while they begin to believe their own delusion! They know how to put on the Spiritual charm, yet behind the scenes they are some of the most conniving, vicious, anger-filled, hateful, selfish, and evil people you would ever want to meet. How much of this is unconscious and how much is conscious is really hard to say! I am praying that this is unconscious, however I am not totally sure. Some of the most well-known Spiritual teachers in the New Age Movement fit into this category! As the Masters told me one time, the antichrist will be a Spiritual teacher!

Another faulty philosophy is to be either too overidentified with the Goddess or God side of the coin! This is extremely common in the New Age Movement and in religion. It is the overidentification with the Patriarchy or the Matriarchy. Most often in this world there is a patriarchal imbalance. The Divine Mother and the Goddess energies are rejected! All books are written in masculine form. Why? Now, part of this is the limitations of language, and I do not want to lay any unfair trip on well-intentioned Spiritual teachers and authors. So, I am not really focusing on this as much as cases where there is a blatant rejection of the Divine Mother and the Goddess, and abuse of the Earth Mother!

The glamour of the Goddess sometimes manifests in feminism, and/or overemotionalism that is glamorous in nature. It can also manifest as glamour in channeling, like some kind of Spiritual show or drama is going on! It can happen in traditional religion, as with the ministers who are crying all the time and their real motivation may be to make money! It happens in the New Age Movement quite often too!

Another classic faulty theory is people who think they are channeling or people who are writing books that claim to be channeling, but really aren't! They are really channeling their own subconscious mind or their beliefs of what Ascended Masters or Angels are like. They are also sometimes channeling old thoughtforms that are outdated, like Earth changes that are no longer true. Because this information is in a lot of books, they are channeling this old, out-dated thoughtform energy. Or they are channeling, but it is an astral entity claiming to be an Ascended Master. Very common! Or a mental being from the inner plane who doesn't even believe in God, but because he is channeled people think he knows what he is talking about even though he doesn't! Lightworkers think that if a being is speaking from the other side, it has more knowledge, which is totally untrue!

Then, of course, we have the classic theory that, "Only my philosophy is true"! The classic example is the Fundamentalist Christians who say Christ is the only way, and if you don't believe what I believe you are run by the devil! We have seen this in many religions, however it is just as prevalent in the New Age Movement. I am not going to say any names. However, if you look at a great many of the old-time mystery schools and organizations based on certain prophets, channels or Spiritual teachers, they can be just as bad as the Fundamentalist Christians. They say things like our channel is the only true channel. There has been no other true channel since then. They say, our prophet is the only true prophet! It is unbelievable!

This brings me to the next theory that is a most interesting one, which correlates with the one above. This faulty theory is one an enormous number of lightworkers fall into it is "getting stuck on the timeline"! This comes from their identification with a certain prophet, old-time channel, or Spiritual teacher. This could be 5000 years ago or 50 years ago. They read the books that were channeled or given forth, and they become identified with those teachings as the supreme truth on the planet. They are indoctrinated by the funda-mentalists in that particular organization to believe that no Spiritual channel, prophet or teacher since this writing has ever channeled accurately, or been as clear as this channel, prophet or teacher. Hence, the person stays stuck on the timeline never advancing beyond 1945 or the 1930s, or even the late 1800s or 2000 years ago, or 5000 or

10,000 years ago. They are literally stuck, and do not evolve past this time period! This is unbelievably common in the New Age Movement and in traditional religions around the world!

Another extremely fragmented and negatively egotistical psychological and philosophical approach that I have seen quite prevalent in the New Age movement is what I call the "Competitive lightworker"! This is quite a contradiction in terms, since everything in truth, is GOD! This means GOD is competing against Himself! Do not underestimate the negative ego in lightworkers, however. It manifests in amazing ways. The "Competitive lightworker" studies teachings, and their need to be better then everyone else is so deluded and so great that the insane mind of the negative ego will go to any and all lengths to achieve its objective. They will tell their students that they will help them anchor ten thousand chakras, 42 million strands of DNA, 98 thousand Light Bodies, and the six millionth initiation. They will take the current set of Masters of the Spiritual Hierarchy and replace them with a new set of their own. My Beloved Readers, you think I am being humorous here but I am not. I am telling you the truth. This is going on! Now, even more disturbing than the idea that any unconscious soul could come up with such nonsense, is that lightworkers often believe it! This person is, of course, the highest being on the planet and their disciples are the second highest beings on the planet. They will of course never be able to catch their teacher, but at least their teacher has made them the second highest group of beings on the planet. My Beloved Readers, never underestimate the corruption of the negative ego in lightworkers. Also, never underestimate the lack of Spiritual discernment and the low self-esteem of lightworkers to buy into this stuff.

Another variation on this theme but not as extreme, is the Spiritual teacher constantly pumping up their students how great they are and how they are the highest beings on the planet to receive and be a part of these teachings. Their egos are being constantly fed, and the lightworkers eat it up hook, line and sinker. The main motivation of the leader of course, is to pump themselves up, have power, and make money! Lightworkers will not come back if their egos are not fed. This occurs in channeling and Spiritual teaching. In channeling, the students are fed with all this glamour-filled information that they were these famous past life figures, or are the daughter of Buddha, or some other crazy thing, and lightworkers lacking Spiritual discernment would tend to believe it. The channel's negative egos are feeding their client's egos just as they feed their own, under the guise of an Ascended Master channeling that is totally contaminated by the personality, for the purpose again of getting clients to come back, to make money, and to have power and influence.

Usually the way it works is, the higher the initiation level this type of lightworker has attained and the more fame and students they have, the more this power goes to their head! Again I do not mean to be judgmental, but this is going on in the New Age Movement and it is rampant, and pure, sincere, truly dedicated lightworkers need to be aware of these seductions within self and to be aware that this is going on all around them. When the Bible prophesied that there would be many false prophets and false teachers it was telling the truth! When I see so many good and sincere lightworkers being caught up in this kind of stuff, both as a teacher and student, all I can do is shake my head! I have written this chapter as a way of trying to stop this insidious corruption and fragmentation going on in the New Age Movement and the Ascension Movement!

Another example of this is Spiritual teachers going around giving ascension, like they really have the power to do this! They only beings with the power to give ascension are Lord Maitreya, Lord Buddha, Sanat Kumara, and Melchizedek, and no one else. They are the High Priests, and, in truth, Hierophants, for this process. If any person says they can do this for you, run for the hills. It is illusion and negative ego! No one can give true initiations except these Masters. Other people say they are giving initiations, but they are not real initiations.

Then we have groups giving ascension by telling you the only thing you have to do is change your attitude. Now it is quite noble and good to suggest to people to keep a good attitude. I would certainly not ever disagree with such a point, and proper attitude and perspective is one of the absolute keys to the true Integrated Ascension process. However, calling ascension just the holding of certain attitudes is illusion. These groups have completely left out the Spiritual level, the Ascension Masters and Angels, all ascension activation work, all grace of Spirit and the Masters, all Light quotient and love quotient anchoring work. It will never work and will never actually facilitate you achieving your ascension. Again, this is just another example of a fragmented teaching that is a sliver of truth, and which the teachers and students of such, think is the whole picture. Plus, they charge unbelievable fees of money to receive this information that to be perfectly honest with no ego intended, you could receive in a much clearer form for $15 in one of my books. In this other form of teaching you must pay $15,000 or something like that. Lightworkers tend to often believe the more it costs the more Spiritual value it has. I am here to tell you it is usually the opposite.

Then we have another fascinating process. This is the reverse corruption that often takes place of what lightworkers want. A great many lightworkers feel insecure if they are not able to channel or are not clairvoyant. What most lightworkers don't recognize is that even though there are many lightworkers with some of these gifts, they don't realize how unclear they are on other levels. They are often emotional victims, run by the negative ego, and are not at that high a level of initiation. They are often run by the inner child and desire body. They are often addicted personalities, smoking tons of cigarettes, keeping lots of bad habits or eating terrible diets, and most importantly are not that psychologically or Spiritually clear. Yet lightworkers give them all their personal power, because they are channels and clairvoyants! I call this the "Glamour of Channeling and Psychic Abilities"! Lightworkers don't realize that a great deal of the time those without these abilities are much more advanced Spiritually and psychologically, and actually have much greater Spiritual and psychological vision. They have other Spiritual gifts that are not commonly recognized and glamorized, such as psychological clarity, keen intuition, psychological wisdom, Spiritual wisdom, comprehension, Realization, Divine vision, Spiritual idealism, telepathy, Spiritual discernment, discrimination, active service, beatitude, perfection and knowledge. These equally profound Spiritual gifts are not known about in the Spiritual movement, so there is a glamour placed on channeling, clairvoyance and clairaudience. If lightworkers only realized how much of this work is filtered through people's consciousness, subconscious mind, personality, filters, belief systems, ray structure, past life programming, childhood programming, information banks, psychological clarity, Spiritual development, and Spiritual knowledge, to name a few, they would think twice about getting such readings, and secondly, if they did, they would make sure the person was truly qualified in an "Integrated Ascension" sense.

I still have not gotten, however, to the original point that started this discussion. It has taken me all this time to just give the reverse side of the negative ego on this point, which actually has been quite an interesting discussion. Now, the reverse of this also occurs, which is equally as corrupt and contaminated by the negative ego.

The reverse of this, which is also occurring in the New Age movement, is people who can channel are stopping to do so when they achieve higher levels of initiation, often for the wrong reasons. They are stopping because their negative egos have taken over, and they are in a sense competing with the Masters. The negative ego is telling them they need to do their own thing and that they are equal with the Masters, which is not really true in a Realization sense. Everyone is equal in a Spiritual sense but not in a Realization sense. Melchizedek is a higher level of Realization of God than any of us are now, so to say that you are an equal is true in the Spiritual ideal, but not in the evolutionary process of Realizing God through the initiation process, psychological clarity, Spiritual leadership, world service, and the grounding of God in a physical/earthly sense! The lack of understanding of this point is a whole other corruption in the New Age movement that I will get to in a moment! The point I want to make first, however, is that many light-workers stop channeling because they feel they have to "feel their own oats," so to speak. Now, some of this can be valid and true, and even the Masters and Angels who are being channeled will tell you this. However, many lightworkers "throw the baby out with the bathwater." They make this decision for the wrong reasons, and do so because of unclarity of the negative ego, and for negative ego reasons. It is also possible to go beyond channeling which is to be a co-creator with the Masters. This is what I have always done, and I humbly state here, it is why my books are as good as they are. It is because I don't just channel. I do channel, how-ever, I am also a Master in myself and fully embody the energy myself, so my books are a co-creation with the Masters. This is why they are so packed full of useful, practical, easy to understand, comprehensive, and cutting-edge information. They contain all my knowledge as a Spiritual teacher, Spiritual psychologist, minister, healer and channel. It is this co-creation which makes the books so dynamic. It is this co-creation which creates this sparking of Light and information. You receive the Masters' mastery, my mastery and the sparking of the two! This is why the books are so packed fully of useful information. You have the best of both worlds. Do you see why overidentification with channeling is a glamour? Do you also see why needing to stop channeling can be a glamour as well?

Now, the next faulty theory that I would like to speak of is quite a dangerous one, unfortunately. The negative ego has really "gone to town" on this one. I began to explain this previously. It is the corruption of the negative ego that stems from not understanding the difference between the Spiritual ideal and the process and importance of Realizing God. It is true that each of us is the Christ or the Buddha or a Son and Daughter of God. This is an indisputable fact! It is a fact whether you like it or not. You are not a sinner, you are a Son or Daughter of God. You are the Christ. No matter what you thought you were or how low your self-esteem or opinion of yourself, and no matter what bad deeds you did in past lives or this one, you are the Christ! You cannot change this, for you did not create yourself, GOD created you. This is true and this is a wonderful thing to realize. Many have called this the "Second Birth"! It is the recognition of your true identity! This is why the Bible says: "Ye are Gods and know it not," "You are made in the image and likeness of God," "Be still, and know that I am God"! Many wonderful Spiritual books in the New Age Movement teach this. Now here is where the corruption of the negative ego comes in. Many books in the New Age Movement and in channeled information from great Spiritual Masters are written from the "lens" of this Spiritual ideal. The problem is they are not written from an "Integrated Perspective"! This does not turn these wonderful books into bad books. It just makes them written from one lens. The problem is that lightworkers who are not properly integrated misinterpret this information, and think that they are the Christ and there is nothing they have to do to Realize God! Life is often a paradox! You are the Christ and you are God! You are one with GOD and always have been and always will be and there is no such thing as separation. Yet, it is also a Spiritual truth that GOD has also created an evolutionary process that every being in the infinite universe is involved in, each at varying stages, even though we each are the Christ in the Spiritual Ideal no matter what we have done or will ever do. We also must realize this truth in our Spiritual Body, Mental Body, Emotional Body, Etheric Body, and Physical Body, in Earth life, and in terms of grounding our Spiritual mission on Earth or on whatever level of evolution a being finds themselves. Some are working on a Planetary Level. Some Beings in God's infinite universe are working on a Solar Level. Some Galactic, some Universal, some Multi-Universal and some Cosmic! There are

352 levels of initiation to Realizing God! So you are the Christ in the Spiritual ideal, but you also must go through the process of evolution, pass all your levels of initiation and integrate these levels of initiation into your Mental, Emotional, Etheric, and Physical Bodies! Now, there are some in the Spiritual Movement who read these books that give forth the message of the Spiritual ideal, which is good and wonderful. Some of these books are channeled and are some of the most profound books on the planet. However, lightworkers have misunderstood them and the "Lens" that they were written from, and think they have don't have to do anything on their Spiritual path because they already are the Christ. Now I realize this sounds bizarre to some of you. However, I am here to tell you this is taking place and there are an enormous number of lightworkers who are and have been very confused on this point of the Spiritual ideal versus the process of evolution and Realization!

One more faulty psychology, philosophy and fragmented theory that many lightworkers fall into is what I call "The Glamour of the Psychic Abilities and the Subconscious mind"! This is another fascinating area in which the negative ego deludes many lightworkers. It gets them enamored with psychic abilities. Psychic abilities actually come out of the subconscious mind, not out of the superconscious mind. The subconscious mind, even though it is a non-reasoning mind, has enormous gifts and abilities within it. It contains the inner senses of sight, hearing, inner smell, taste, and touch. It has the ability to dowse for things or work with a pendulum. We have all seen what amazing things people can do when they are under hypnosis. I actually have a license in hypnosis from the State of California, and have a great appreciation for the powers of the subconscious mind both in a psychic and hypnosis sense. Many lightworkers are enamored with the powers of the subconscious mind and actually lose their Spiritual path. They become more interested in the glamour of these powers than in true Spirituality. This may be hard to believe, but there are many psychics who have incredible psychic abilities to see into the future, see past lives, and access the most amazing personal information that is really quite astounding, but they do not even believe in GOD! Now isn't this an interesting dichotomy. In a similar vein I know people who are Master Hypnotists, and can hypnotize people almost instantly and put on stage shows that would absolutely blow your mind, demonstrating the powers of the subconscious mind and hypnotic suggestion, and they may not necessarily believe in GOD either. These people may have extraordinary abilities in these areas. Abilities that are absolutely extraordinary. Truly extrasensory perception! However, this does not say one whit, about their level of Spiritual initiation, Spiritual evolution, psychological development, character development, or psychological clarity, whether they are run by the negative ego or not, whether they are victims, or whether they cause their own reality! Whether or not they have any mastery over their thoughts or emotions! Whether or not they are unconditionally loving, or whether they believe in GOD and the Masters and Angels! I could also say the same thing about healers! Even though a person has the ability to sense and feel energy and even heal people, everything I have said in this paragraph and section applies equally to them!

So the key lesson here, my Beloved Readers, I am trying to make, is that just because you may have some of the abilities I have written about in this chapter, it does not make you necessarily a Spiritual Master! As you can see, Spiritual gifts in one area do not make you a Master, for if "Integrated Ascension" is not achieved then fragmentation in the other areas, be it Spiritual, mental, emotional, physical and/or earthly, can and will cause corruption and contamination of the negative ego and imbalance in the other areas. Undiscerning lightworkers often think if a person has this one gift they must be a great Master. Nothing could be farther from the truth. This chapter has been written to emphasize to sincere lightworkers around the globe the incredible importance of becoming a "Master and becoming Integrated and Balanced on a Spiritual, Psychological, and Physical/Earthly Level!" It has also been written to fully open your "Spiritual and psychological clairvoyance in an occultist sense of the term." I bet you didn't realize that there are two kinds of clairvoyance. There is the clairvoyance of the Mystic and the clairvoyance of an Occultist. The clairvoyance of a Mystic is being able to see auras, and see into the Spiritual and/or inner worlds. What most lightworkers don't realize is that there is another type of clairvoyance that is equally important if not even more important. It is the clairvoyance of Spiritual vision, psychological clarity, Realization, comprehension, Spiritual discernment, Spiritual idealism, efficient perception of reality on Spiritual, psychological and earthly levels, discrimination, response to group vibration, Spiritual telepathy, intuition, knowingness, healing, knowledge, perfection, active service, and beatitude. These are Spiritual senses that are all equally as profound as the inner senses of clairvoyance and clairaudience of the Mystic. What most lightworkers do not understand is that a great many of the Mystics who have these abilities are not developed in the Occult type of clairvoyance I am training you in now. This is why they often have a lot of personal problems and are not fully balanced within themselves or in their relationships. This is also why the Occultist often evolve even quicker than Mystics, yet often feel insecure because they want the abilities of the Mystic, for they think it is the key to God Realization. I am going to tell you a great secret right now my Beloved Readers! This is not true! The inner senses I have listed here in the Occult type of clairvoyance are equally as profound and, in truth, even more profound! I am not trying to create competition between Occultists and Mystics, for the ideal is for Mystics to integrate their Occult side and for Occultists to integrate their Mystic side. In my books I train Mystics to integrate their Occult side and Occultists to open to their Mystic side. I would never teach competition or comparing, for that is totally antithetical to GOD! What I am trying to show you is the corruption of the negative ego and what it does and can do to both sides, for this is another enormous faulty psychological and fragmented Spiritual theory, which enormous numbers of lightworkers are falling into. The Spiritual ideal is ever integration. I am calling on all Mystics to have the openness and courage to integrate this information and fully open their Occult clairvoyance on a psychological and Spiritual vision level. I am calling on all Occultists to have the openness and courage to open to their Mystic natures. I am calling on both types of lightworkers to give up all comparing, competition and judgementalness. For, another trap of the negative ego is for Occultists to be judgmental of the Mystics and for Mystics to be judgmental of the Occultist. This is illusion and delusion, my Beloved Readers. How can God judge God! There is only one being in the infinite Universe and this is GOD, and we all share in this One Identity as Sons and Daughters of GOD! Occultists need to fully recognize their incredible ability to access and sense GOD, even if it is not their fate or Spiritual destiny to channel or have the clairvoyance of the Mystics. Mystics need to fully recognize their ability to access GOD through their unique gifts. Both Occultist and Mystic need to never compare, never compete and never judge. Occultists and Mystics need to both fully appreciate the gifts that GOD has given them and not try to live out a puzzle piece that is not theirs to live out. Yet at the same time, both Occultist and Mystic need to be open to not being too comfortable where they are, and to strive with all their heart and soul and mind and might to become as integrated and balanced as they can in both their Mystic and Occultist parts, for we all have both parts within us. GOD has made each person unique and different. Not everyone is meant to have all abilities or the same abilities. Seek and Realize GOD with the abilities He has given you, for they are more than enough. Do not seek for GOD powers, for that is another trap of the negative ego as well. Seek for GOD purity and unconditional Love and egolessness. Seek the balancing of your Three-Fold Flame of Love, Wisdom and Power! Seek "Integrated Ascension," for these things are the greatest GOD powers of all! The studying of this book and my other books will help all Occultists greatly refine their Occult clairvoyance and develop their Mystic clairvoyance as GOD would have it be. It will also help all Mystics refine their Mystic clairvoyance and help them develop their Occult clairvoyance as GOD would have it be! So all will be a fully "Integrated Ascended Master," exactly the way GOD would have it be. Each Son and Daughter of GOD will be a "100% Integrated Ascended Master," but each of you will have just a very slight tendency or emphasis toward the unique pattern and manner in which GOD has created you. Again, it is like "beautiful flowers in the garden of GOD"!

Another area or trap that lightworkers fall into is focusing on Ascended Master powers, or siddhis, rather than focusing on GOD purity, unconditional Love, the balancing of one's Three-Fold Flame, integrated ascension, and egolessness as GOD's greatest gifts and most important powers. Focus on these things, and if the Spiritual powers come, so be it. At least if they do come, they will be used in the proper way and manner, and not for any corrupt purposes of the negative ego!

Another faulty psychology and philosophy of the negative ego in the Spiritual Movement is not loving Earth life. This is extremely prevalent. Earth is seen as some kind of prison or less evolved place, and one that we are here to escape from as soon as possible. Life becomes a goal to the ego to achieve liberation in the sense of not appreciating or enjoying the process. The Material Universe is not seen as a Heaven of GOD! The Material Face of GOD is not seen! The Earth Mother is not loved! The Nature and Elemental Kingdoms are not appreciated. Earth energies are not mastered or appreciated as a Spiritual practice! Ascension is not grounded! The Mighty I Am Presence is not fully grounded into the physical body! One's Spiritual mission is not fully grounded into the Earth! Earth life is not fully loved, appreciated and enjoyed! I am not saying that Earth life is not difficult! I am not saying this is not a difficult school! I am not saying that part of me does not look forward to being in Higher Realms without the limitations of a physical body and physical laws. Although all this is the case, it is still imperative that all lightworkers, and I mean all lightworkers, become happy on Earth and learn to love Earth life. If you do not do this you have not and will not fully Realize GOD, for GOD has four Faces and one of these Faces is the physical. If you reject or disown the physical, you have rejected and disowned an aspect of GOD and yourself!

One other corrupt psychology and philosophy of the negative ego which is unbelievably common in the New Age Movement, and which I have already begun to touch on, is this issue of trying to live out another person's puzzle piece. Nothing will send you on a path of self-destruction quicker than this. Not everyone has been created the same by GOD! We each have a different Spiritual mission and purpose! We each have a unique puzzle piece in the Divine plan to fulfill! Not everyone has been given the same Spiritual, psychological/physical earthly abilities! Not everyone is destined for the same Spiritual leadership and planetary world service work. Not everyone is destined for the same level of public recognition. Now, the negative ego has infiltrated every aspect of life, including religion and the New Age movement. The negative ego thinks it can outsmart GOD! The negative ego has a plan for your life that is contrary to GOD's plan. Oh, and by the way, I forgot to mention that it will destroy everything and everyone in its path to get there. It will betray, lie, backstab, manipulate, compete, and more, to get what it wants. It is filled with jealousy and envy. It is not happy for other people's success. It is often filled with anger and even hatred! It will judge, discredit others and trample on others to try and get the power, fame, money, and vanity it seeks.

The most common way this plays out is when a lightworker wants to be famous. Or it shows in a lightworker wanting to channel or be a clairvoyant in a Mystic sense, when this is not their puzzle piece. It will manifest as the person wanting to be a Spiritual leader and major player! The things lightworkers will often do to become famous are not always of the highest integrity. They will steal names of Centers, or make false claims about themselves. Basically, they will use any means necessary to get there, and will not necessarily hold to Christed principles. There is nothing wrong with Spiritual ambition if it is manifested from a healthy integrated Christ perspective. I am speaking here of negative ego ambition and trying to force something that is not meant to be and is not one's puzzle piece. Even if one achieves this wrong puzzle piece for a temporary period of time, it will never last, for there will always be this sense of uneasiness within the person that something is not right. For in truth, they are going against their Soul's and Mighty I Am Presence's plans for them. Students will sense it as well. They will not be successful either, for it is not Spiritually or psychologically right and people will feel this! The fastest way to success is to follow GOD's plan for you. Not everyone is meant to be world famous or a clairaudient channel. To be honest, if it is not your puzzle piece it would bring you nothing but aggravation. They key is to find that thing and way of service that brings you excitement, joy, and makes you feel comfortable. Like a duck takes to water. This is also the path that will allow you to evolve in the quickest manner and fashion!

The other big trap of course in the New Age Movement is the guru and the know-it-all. The negative ego type of guru is the one who seeks to always remain in power, instead of fully empowering their students to know that they are God, and not trying to keep their students locked in a position of worshipping them for their own ego gratification and vanity. A true guru must be ego-less, or they are not really a guru. Many think they are true gurus. However, their motivations are coming form the negative ego. The guru mentality is more in the East and not in the West. In the West we have Spiritual teachers. The danger here is to be too much the know-it-all, being too self-righteous or claiming that your teachings are the only true path to GOD. This, of course, is not true, for there are many paths to GOD! It is very important for a Spiritual teacher and/or guru to not keep themselves in some kind of "ivory tower," or use their guruship or Spiritual teacher status as a form of separation, or be stuck in Priest or Priestess mentality that is used by the negative ego to be better than everyone else. It is important to be a real person and interact with people. To be a part of the marketplace, so to speak. To be involved with friendships and possibly romantic relationships. If involved in a romantic relationship, to not be so corrupted by the negative ego that you have to stay in control and make your lover your student or disciple instead of your equal. This, in my opinion, is just the negative ego's corruption and game to defend the negative ego rather than surrender it and truly Realize God in a relationship!

Now another psychological and philosophical breakdown that occurs frequently among lightworkers is what I call the "superconscious, conscious and subconscious mind schism!" This can happen in one of two ways. First off, the conscious mind thinks it is acting Spiritual or like the superconscious mind or Mighty I Am Presence but is not, in truth! There is an inconsistency between what the Higher Self and Monad think and what the conscious mind thinks it is doing! The second way this manifests is that there is another schism between the conscious mind and the subconscious mind. In other words, the conscious mind thinks it is demonstrating and controlling the subconscious mind and manifesting its energies in a certain direction, but the truth is the subconscious mind is a rouge or out of control. An example of this is the conscious mind thinks it is transcending negative ego and has mastery of the emotional body, however, in truth the negative ego is running rampant and negativity is all over the place. The lightworker has such an inefficient perception of reality, they do not realize they don't have mastery over the subconscious and are out of tune with the superconscious. Extremely common! Most people in this world do not have full self-mastery over their subconscious and, hence, over their mind, emotions, inner child, desire body, negative ego, energies, physical body or subpersonalities!

Then we have the Seven Great Rays, which make-up the Personality of God! Here we have lightworkers overidentified or underidentified with all the permutations and combinations of the Rays. Even though we each have a unique Ray configuration, it still is the ideal to integrate and balance all the Rays! Full God Realization and success inwardly and outwardly comes when these Rays are balanced and integrated. All kinds of lessons and problems occur within the inner and outer life when this is not done. Since I have written extensively about this in this book and other books, it is not the time or place to go deeply into this now. However, I am sure all of you, my Beloved Readers, understand the incredible science of the Rays, and the enormous impact that overidentification and underidentification has on the integration and balance of every lightworker!

Another very interesting fragmentation and/or faulty thinking that takes place within lightworkers is an imbalance in the vertical and horizontal axis! The vertical axis is one's relationship to GOD and the Masters. The horizontal axis is one's relationship to people and life. Many lightworkers, because of past life programming or early childhood programming, overemphasize the vertical axis to the point of not socializing or not becoming involved with people and life. It is one thing if it is one's true Spiritual destiny to do this, however, more often than not it is faulty thinking and programming, that is causing it! On the other side of the coin there are also a whole set of other lightworkers who overidentify with the horizontal axis and get so involved with people and life they do not fully and properly integrate the vertical, or their relationship to GOD and the Masters! This again is very common in the Consciousness Movement and among lightworkers!

In the same manner that the Rays need to be balanced, the same is true of the Signs of the Zodiac, Archetypes, Numerology, Sephiroth of the Tree of Life, and Aspects of the Tarot Deck. Lightworkers overidentify and underidentify with these different aspects which is what causes again infinite numbers of permutations and combinations of faulty thinking, blind spots, limited lens seeing, misperceptions, and character weaknesses! I again have written extensively about these sciences in my other books so this is not the time and place to discuss this. However, as part of this overview I did want to mention this!

One other very strange, yet often common psychological, philosophical and Spiritual faulty thought system and fragmentation is that lightworkers who are sometimes very advanced, but we extremely run by their emotional body, personality, and negative ego, think they are demonstrating Christ consciousness in their lives, but in truth, most of the time they are being run by the emotional body, the desire body, the negative ego, personality and subconscious mind. The are filled with negative feelings and emotions. They are filled with competition, jealousy, anger, selfishness, envy, thirst for power, thirst for fame, gossip, backstabbing, ranting and raving always behind people's back, and judgement, and are in total ego battles constantly but are blaming it on others. I think you get the point. They are so filled with negative feelings and emotions and negative ego, that their perception of reality is totally disturbed and distorted. They often have a type of split personality, between the super Spiritual and sweet to your face, and then almost possessed by a demon behind the scenes. They are often clinical pathological liars and are filled with hypocrisy. In their own minds, they think they are in Christ consciousness, when nothing could be farther from the truth! They are actually very disturbed people who even sometimes have serious psychopathologies. There are less extreme examples where this is also not the case as well. However, in both examples or cases, the person totally believes they are in the Christ consciousness all the time. They may channel the Masters or may just be Spiritual teachers or healers. They think they are extremely highly evolved, but, in truth they have some Spiritual gifts, and yet are so psychologically disturbed and such victims of their feelings, emotions and negative ego that their channel has become corrupted and contaminated. However, in their own mind they think they are totally in the Christ consciousness and do not have a clue they are being totally run by negative ego feelings and emotions. Their baseline for what they think Christ consciousness is, is really being run by the negative ego and their feelings and emotions, but they call it Christ consciousness. They are extremely self-righteous and opinionated, usually, and power has gone to their head even though, in truth, they don't have any. They see themselves as major Spiritual players, however, in truth, they are not and never will be. I bring up this type for it is very common, and I wish you to see very clearly that what a person thinks about themselves or claims does not necessarily have anything to do with what true demonstration of Spiritual/Christ/Buddha consciousness really is!

One more example of this glamour and faulty Spiritual, psychological, glamour-based thinking is sometimes people give themselves glamorous Spiritual names, which is not really fitting to who they are and what is Spiritually appropriate. Now I want to be clear here that I am not saying changing or adopting a new Spiritual name is wrong. It is often extremely appropriate. I am just pointing out that some do it for the wrong reasons and do it for glamour and negative ego motivations. They also may choose the wrong name that does not fit their essence but rather fits the power, fame, greed and money the negative ego is really looking for. Undiscerning lightworkers hear these fancy names people give themselves, which I shall not name, and think this person must be highly evolved for he or she has this famous Spiritual name. Be aware that this person with this famous Spiritual name may be, in truth, totally run by the negative ego and corrupt to the core. They may be psychologically disturbed, but be able to put on a good act. They may be able to give a great lecture and charm people with their so-called loving nature, but behind the scenes they are filled with competition, anger, corruption, selfishness, thirst for power, jealousy, backstabbing, betrayal, thirst for fame, vanity, and greed, to name a few. I do not mean this as a judgement, however, if lightworkers realized what was really going on behind the scenes with some of the well-known Spiritual leaders, they would be totally shocked! I am not saying this is true with all the Spiritual leaders, of course; I am just saying it is true for some of them. I do not share any of this as a judgement. I am just asking you, my Beloved Brothers and Sisters, to keep your Spiritual and psychological eyes and ears a little more open and to look a little deeper. Not to judge, but just to lovingly, Spiritually observe and discern. Just because a Spiritual leader has a fancy name or can give a good lecture, or channeling, or write a good book, does not make them a true reflection of what a Self-Realized being really is. One must look at the whole picture. What are these person's true motivations? What is this person like off the stage, not just on the stage? My Beloved Readers, you will see and hear about what I call the "red flags"! They are everywhere. You will hear about it on the Internet. You will see strange reports at times. You will see very bizarre and strange contradictions in their teachings at times. You will see them engaging in ego battles with certain people. What Spiritual leaders, Spiritual channels, Spiritual authors, Spiritual scientists, and Spiritual healers do on stage and what they do off stage behind the scenes is often unbelievably different. Keep your Spiritual eyes and ears open and do not blind yourself to the "red flags" that will appear and are appearing! If you take this chapter to heart and integrate what it has to offer, these things will be totally obvious to you. You will not even have to try. These Spiritual discernments are given so we can all avoid, most importantly, letting these things happen to ourselves, and so we also do not allow ourselves or students to get seduced or taken over by false prophets, cults, false teachers, corrupted teachers, and corrupted channels! The Bible predicted this would be the time when all this would occur! It is upon us now, my Beloved Readers. There are many good, wonderful and pure Spiritual leaders, teachers and channels. There are also many that are not! This chapter has been written to bring forth the "Spiritual Rod of Discernment" so you are able to fully see the difference, as GOD would have you see it!

One more very classic set of faulty psychological, philosophical and Spiritual fragments deals again with the Mind and the Heart. Many lightworkers, usually of a more Occult nature, get very much into theory and models of the universe. The problem is there are thousands of different models and systems that lightworkers use for everything under the sun. What this constantly leads to is a clashing of theory among lightworkers. They key point here is that if one is overidentified with the importance of the mind and theory and the negative ego gets involved, this is going to create separation and arguments. The ideal is to agree to disagree and to never allow a difference in theory or beliefs to create any lack of love or any separation! If there is imbalance and faulty thinking here, this often does take place.

Now, on the other side of the coin, you have the Mystic types who are not really too into the mind, and don't read books, which is fine. However, if they become too overidentified with GOD just being Love and nothing else they can, because of a lack of Power and Wisdom, be wreaking havoc all over the place in the name of Love! If you do not have an equal balance of Power and Wisdom as you do Love, in truth, it is impossible to truly be unconditionally loving. You may think you are but you are not. Love, Wisdom, and Power rely equally on each other. It is only this most sublime balance of this Three-Fold Flame that allows God to truly manifest. Without this balance there will be blind spots, limited lens seeing, mistakes, misperception, faulty beliefs, and an inefficient perception of reality. Mind and Heart must be perfectly balanced. In truth, intuition, Mind, Heart, feelings, and instincts must be balanced to truly Realize God! Many lightworkers falsely believe that Heart is all God is and they don't need Mind, or anything else. This is illusion, for one's thoughts create one's reality. One cannot separate these aspects of GOD and see one is better than another is. These are the four aspects of GOD—intuition, mind, feeling, and sensation/function, which is the physical! These all must be balanced and integrated. It is when the mind and feeling are in perfect feminine and masculine, yin and yang, God/Goddess balance that all one's energies are manifested and demonstrated through the Heart. If you overidentify with any aspect and disown the opposite, there will be imbalance and corruption of the negative ego. Another definition of negative ego could be imbalance and lack of integration. If your feeling and mind and intuition and five earthly senses are in balance, then negative ego cannot enter and you live a life of total unconditional love all the time!

There are lots of different Spiritual practices and they are all important. However, in my opinion the most important or the one at the top of the list is the demonstration and practice of unconditional love! When you live a life of "Integrated Ascension," this means you will live a life of only unconditional love towards Self, GOD, and others at all times! This is the highest siddha, power, and Spiritual practice! If you do nothing else this lifetime, strive to be integrated and balanced in your ascension process, and demonstrate unconditional love at all times and you will be on the right track!

The last thing I want to say here, before I do my official closing, is that I want to apologize if it seems I have been a little hard on lightworkers. This has not been my intention! I humbly say to all of you, my Beloved Readers, that I have been in a unique position of Spiritual leadership to see a great many things and to know a great many people and what they think and believe. I also have the unique background of growing up in a family of psychologists, and besides being a Spiritual teacher and channel, I am a Spiritual psychologist myself. Because of the combination of these aspects and my mission as author of Spiritual and psychological books, and having spent 25 years doing Spiritual and psychological counseling and teaching classes on both the Spiritual and psychological levels, I have an extremely keen eye for negative ego corruption. This is a great weak spot in the New Age movement, which I say with great unconditional love and compassion! This is not the lightworker's fault; for they have not been trained! This is because there are not a lot of people who really have a strong handle on all this stuff! I am really writing this chapter to inspire all of you, my Beloved Readers, to take this work out into the world and help others. Lightworkers are thirsting for it. If given the information they can easily apply it and demonstrate it. I have great confidence and faith in my fellow Brothers and Sisters. The New Age movement is, in truth, the hope for the world! It is here that the purest and most advanced teachings on a Spiritual/psychological/physical/earthly level are being given out all over the world! It is because I love the New Age movement and lightworkers so much and recognize them as the true "lightbearers" for the New Age that I speak so passionately on these issues. The Spiritual leaders in the New Age Movement and the lightworkers around the globe are the externalization of the Spiritual Hierarchy. We all are the Ascended Masters, High Level Initiates and Disciples on Earth! The inner plane Ascended Masters, the Elohim Councils, the Archangels and Angels, and Christed Extraterrestrials on the inner plane are counting on us to represent them on Earth! I totally love my fellow Brothers and Sisters and have enormous faith and trust in them and in you! In my many discussions with the inner plane Ascended Masters on this subject they have told me that they are not pleased with the degree of fragmentation, imbalance, and lack of integration either! It is for this reason they had me write my many books addressing these issues! We as Earthlings are Great Souls and Noble Beings, and we are better than some of the things that are currently going on. It is not happening to all lightworkers, but it is happening to way too many, I think you will all agree. I know for a fact that I am not alone in seeing how much glamour, illusion and maya is being tossed around! It has been my passion this lifetime to not only help lightworkers achieve their ascension and 12 levels of initiation, but to also help them do this in an integrated and balanced way! This is and continues to be my passion! I expect nothing less than God purity and total integrity from my Brothers and Sisters, for they are a noble breed and are Great Beings of Light and Love! I dedicate this chapter to my Spiritual Family of Light and Love to quickly and efficiently make any and all needed adjustments in self, and go forth into the world and serve and help others achieve this same God purity and God integrity! If lightworkers are given the information, they will instantly pull it together! I put forth the Clarion Call to light-workers around the globe to help spread the word of the importance of such principles in one's ascension process! So let it be written! So let it be done! For as the Master Jesus said, "Be ye faithful unto death, and I will give thee a Crown of Life"!

In conclusion, it is my sincere hope and prayer that this Spiritual over-view of faulty psychological, philosophical and fragmented Spiritual philosophies has been helpful to you on your own Spiritual path and as a means to be more Spiritually discerning in regard to your involvement with other Spiritual channels, Spiritual teachers, mystery schools, and even Spiritual books. The purpose is not to judge, but to see what is truly going on from a "full spectrum prism consciousness," that sees with an efficient perception of reality from a clear Spiritual, psychological and physical/earthly framework and is fully integrated and balanced! It is important not to judge and it is important not to be Spiritually undiscerning. Both sides of the coin are the negative ego. It is my sincere hope and prayer that this chapter has opened your eyes a little bit to some of the pitfalls, traps, and glamours of faulty psychologies, philosophies and fragmented spiritual theories that are most common in the New Age Movement, the Consciousness Movement, and in religion in the world today!

CHAPTER 25

The Incredible Importance of Setting Up Spiritual Battleplans

As I have mentioned in other chapters in this book, there is a stage you will reach on your Spiritual path where life no longer becomes a struggle! This occurs when your consciousness is so merged with your personal power, self-mastery, being a cause of your own reality, unconditional Love, Spiritual and psychological wisdom, integration and balance of the Seven Rays, self-love, Golden Bubble of Protection, preferences rather than attachments, looking at things as Spiritual tests and lessons, acceptance, surrender, and Spiritual/Christ/Buddha consciousness and your mind is so steady in the Light that you have reprogrammed your subconscious mind, and balanced your four bodies and three minds! When this fundamental transcendence of negative ego/fear-based/separative thinking and feeling has occurred, life is no longer a struggle. In truth, "it never was a struggle, you just thought it was!" It was your negative ego/fear-based/separative thinking that made it a struggle! Your consciousness was battling life instead of working with life and learning from life! The only true struggle is not really with life; it is with mastering self! When self is mastered, life no longer becomes a struggle either. This is a most wonderful state of consciousness to be in. There may be occasional slight slips or unconscious mistakes. However, they are quickly attitudinally adjusted and there is a fundamental steadiness, even-mindedness, inner peace, unceasing joy and, of course, unconditional Love that one just continually stays in.

What must be understood, however, is that there is a process to get to this point! The process is the movement from child to adult. The movement from victim consciousness to Master consciousness. As children we are run by our mind, emotions, physical body, desire body, inner child, and negative ego. The process of Spiritual evolution to become a Spiritual Master is to reverse this! To do this we must undo all the mass consciousness programming! We must get in complete control of the subconscious mind and not let it run us, and instead we must become the total computer programmer of it! So there is a phase of the Spiritual path, in all disciples, initiates and Masters, of the "Battle of Armageddon" waging within the seeker of God! This is good and appropriate! This is why Krishna said to Arjuna in the Bhagavad-Gita, "Give up this unmanliness and self-pity and get up and fight"! It is why Paramahansa Yogananda said, "Life is a battlefield!" It is why Western esoteric literature refers to the "Battle of Armageddon" so often! There is the Battle of Armageddon in the cosmos and the Battle of Armageddon in each of us! On a personal level, it is the battle between the lower-self and the higher-self. The battle between truth and illusion! The battle between the Sons of Belial and the Law of One! The battle between fear and Love! The battle between positivity and negativity! The battle between separation and oneness. The battle between GOD and ego! The battle between the forces of Light and the forces of darkness! The outer battle that is talked about is just a reflection of this personal battle that every seeker of truth must fight and must win. Each person must master the dweller on the threshold. The dweller on the threshold is the conglomeration of glamour, maya, and illusion within self! In essence as Sai Baba has so eloquently stated, "GOD equals man minus ego"! We each must win the battle over our negative ego/fear-based, separative thinking and feeling! We must become Spiritually victorious in this battle! It does not happen in one day! It is a process! However, there is a psychological law that it only takes 21 days to cement any new habit into the subconscious mind! So in the initial stages of the Spiritual path, there is a battle that is going on whether people want to believe it or not. I am not saying it has to last a long time, for it doesn't! This is up to you! My job in this book and my book *Soul Psychology* has been to give you all the insight, tools, and understanding you need to easily win this battle and win it quickly and decisively! It is not hard to win this battle if you are given the training! This has been the key problem. Most people have been battling and struggling their whole lives, not because they have to, but because not very many people really understand on a very deep level the in-depth laws and tools that govern Spiritual psychology! It is for this humble purpose that this self-help book has been written! It has been designed by Spirit, the Masters and myself in a co-creative collaborative effort to specifically and scientifically help you to easily win this battle and become Spiritually, psychologically and physically/earthly victorious in all aspects of life! If you have the understanding and tools it is really not that hard to do! Without this Spiritual training, you can struggle for a whole life and hundreds of lifetimes and not figure it out yourself. For it is extremely simple when you understand it, but also incredibly complex! This sounds like a paradox and it is! It is really so profoundly simple when you understand it, but, to try and reinvent the wheel and figure this all out on your own is close to impossible! I am happy to say, on behalf of Spirit and the Masters, that it is totally unnecessary to have to reinvent the wheel! I am happy to say I have a spare one in my

Spiritual trunk! Please use it and share it with others! Training in Spiritual psychology is the number one most important thing that lightworkers around the globe need more than anything else! Please share this book and *Soul Psychology*, and my book *The Golden Book of Melchizedek: How to Become an Integrated Christ/Buddha in This Lifetime*! I have truly packed these books with everything you need to know to easily win this battle! Even just after reading this book you will never be the same! You will never ever see self or life in the same way!

Now, everything I have said so far in this chapter has just been preliminary, to lay the foundation for this next most wonderful tool I will share, which will guarantee victory in every aspect of your life! The key to living effectively and successfully is to always be the cause not the effect! It is to always be asserting oneself towards life, not letting life beat up on you! The key is your attitude and perspective! As long as you are always asserting yourself towards life and not letting life attack you, you will feel good! Notice my choice of words here! I did not say be aggressive towards life as in war in a third dimensional sense. I have used the word be "assertive" towards life! This is why I have called this chapter "The Incredible Importance of Setting Up Spiritual Battleplans"!

Now, my Beloved Readers, life is always throwing us a curve, and no matter how Spiritual we are, no matter how hard we try, no matter how pure we are, and not matter how much we change or attachments to preferences, things are not going to always go our way. This is, in truth, only a problem from the negative ego mind, for it is not a problem or issue for the Spiritual/Christ/Buddha mind! The Spiritual/Christ/Buddha mind says, "Not my will, but Thine, Lord. Thank you for the lesson!" As Sai Baba says, "Welcome adversity!" As Buddhism says, "Nonresistance!" As psychology says, "Acceptance and surrender!"

This does not mean, however, we are fatalist! No way! The true Spiritual Master does let go of all attachments, but does fight for their Spiritual preferences and Spiritual desires with all their heart, and soul and mind and might! The true Spiritual Master never gives up! The true

Spiritual Master is unceasing in his or her quest for God Realization and success on every level, and will not be stopped no matter what happens! As Job said when all was taken away:

Naked I come from my mother's womb! Naked shall I leave!

The Lord giveth and the Lord taketh away! Blessed be the Name of the Lord!

When everything is taken away, my friends, and everything goes wrong, that is the true test of a person's Spiritual faith!

Now, there is a most wonderful tool to help you feel wonderful no matter what is going on which I figured out early on in my life! As the saying goes, "Necessity is the mother of invention"! I live to feel good and at inner peace all the time, so I figured this out and it has served me well my entire life, and has helped me achieve success in every aspect of my life! It has also helped me to feel good no matter what goes on in my life!

This Tool is called the "Spiritual Battleplan"!

How it works is this! Every time something goes "wrong" in your life, instead of feeling bad about it, be assertive! Be a Master not a victim! Be a cause, not an effect of life! Set up a "Spiritual Battleplan!" If you are having financial problems, for example, set up a Spiritual Battleplan! Make a list of every single thing you are going to do to win this Spiritual battle, to make the money you need to make and make your business a success! I will make a Spiritual Battleplan right here as an example!

Spiritual Battleplan to Heal Money and Business Challenges

- I will do a Huna Prayer twice a day, every day, for the next two months!
- I will do to prosperity affirmations three times a day, every day for two months!
- I will practice five minutes of creative visualization morning and night, visualizing what I want to happen with my five senses!

- I will own my personal power and not give up until I succeed!
- I will make a list of every single physical action I can take to increase my business!
- I will create new quality advertising!
- I will call all my friends and ask for their help!
- I will call every single past business contact I have ever made!
- I will read Dr. Stone's chapter in *Soul Psychology* called "The Laws of Manifestation!"
- I will read the book *Think and Grow Rich* by Napoleon Hill!
- I will go to that "Prosperity Seminar" I was thinking about going to!
- I will make all those phone calls I have been putting off!
- I will get totally organized in my business every morning as my top priority!
- I will call on the Masters to work the Core Fear Matrix Removal Program to remove any blocks!
- I will read Dr. Stone's book *Soul Psychology: Revised Edition* where he teaches how to ask the Masters to remove all Alien Implants and Negative Elementals!
- I will keep working my program on a Spiritual, Psychological, and Physical Level unceasingly!
- I will take advantage of every possible lead that comes in!
- I will get my taxes done!
- I will hire a personal assistant to help!
- I will get those sleep tapes on prosperity!
- I will do self-hypnosis to program myself for success!
- I will get those tapes on prosperity and work with them every day!

- I will call on the Holy Spirit to undo all blocks on a conscious and unconscious level in my 12-body system as described in this book!
- I will do Dr. Stone's Personal Power, Self-Love, Invulnerability, and Favorite affirmations every day to keep me pumped up!
- I will read Dr. Stone's chapter in *The Golden Book of Melchizedek* called "The Laws of Manifestation and the 14 Levels of Power"!
- I will play those subliminal prosperity tapes as background music!
- I will read Dr. Stone's books every night and become so filled with Spiritual thoughts and feelings I will be an absolute spiritual magnet for prosperity and good karma!
- I will strive to put GOD first and put service first and be in total integrity in my business!
- I will make this Spiritual Battleplan a super strong preference, not an attachment!
- I make a Spiritual Vow to pass this Spiritual Test if it is the last thing I ever do!
- I will fake it until I make it!
- I will visualize myself making deposits in my bank account of a really large nature!
- I will visualize my business being unbelievably successful!
- I make a promise to myself that every time I start to worry I will pray and do even more affirmations!
- I will make a Spiritual Vow to not procrastinate or be lazy anymore!
- I will ask my spouse and friends to help me brainstorm and come up with ideas and suggestions!
- I will write in my journal every day to keep all my thoughts and feelings on the up and up!

- I now make a Personal Vow to keep my Three-Fold Flame of 100% Unconditional Love, 100% Wisdom, and 100% Power in perfect balance and integration at all times!

My Beloved Readers, I could go on and on, but I think you get the idea! You just write down every idea you can possibly think of that you can do on a Spiritual, Psychological and Physical/Earthly level to turn your lesson around! The key is to work your program! Just the act of doing this, even though your wallet and bank account has not changed yet, will make you feel better and that is half the battle! By doing this you are attacking life instead of letting life attack you! I have always noticed how people say, "How is life treating you?" This is victim consciousness! The expression should be changed to, "How are you treating life"! So the key is to have Spiritual battleplans in every aspect of your life that needs development. You could have a physical health battlplan, Spiritual development battleplan, relationship battleplan, psychological battleplan, or earthly mastery battlplan! Basically, the idea is that for anything that ever goes wrong of a larger nature, create a Spiritual battleplan to resolve and heal the situation. List every idea you can possibly imagine. Pray to GOD, Christ, the Holy Spirit, the Masters and Angels for more ideas and for help in doing this! This is the key to winning this Spiritual battle! You must work on four levels, first by Spiritually praying and calling for help. Secondly, on the level of personal power, and taking decisive action. Thirdly, utilizing the power of your subconscious mind through affirmation, visualization, suggestion, self-hypnosis, and sleep tapes! Fourthly, by taking physical action on every level! My Beloved Readers, you must remember that life is co-creation between you, Spirit and the Masters! How can you not be successful? God, your personal power, the power of your subconscious mind and your physical body are an unbeatable team! If GOD be for you, who or what can be against you! Why worry when you can pray! If you pray to GOD, Christ, the Holy Spirit, your own Mighty I Am Presence, your Higher Self, the inner plane Ascended Masters, the Archangels and Angels of the Light of GOD, the Elohim Councils, and the Christed Extraterrestrials, and you fully own your 100% personal power and your full 100% conscious mind power, and you do affirmations and visualizations to program your subconscious mind to attract and magnetize what you want, and you take every physical action that is possible for you to take, how can you fail? It is impossible! GOD and the Son and Daughter of GOD cannot be defeated! Against what, illusion? Against what, fear? There is nothing to fear but fear itself! Everything in GOD's universe works by laws! It is just a matter of working GOD's laws! The reason you have not been successful is that you are not working GOD's laws on all four levels to your highest potential! The key is you have to unceasingly work your program! To be honest, if you work these laws it is actually impossible not to be successful. I am being quite serious! These laws are as exact as mathematics is! Ask yourself, can GOD, all the Masters, all the Angels, all the Elohim Councils, all the Christed Extraterrestrials, all your 100% personal power, the 100% power of your subconscious mind which you are programming, your 100% physical action on the Earth plane, your getting help from all your friends and family, and your use of your full ability as the Son and or Daughter of GOD that you are, as a co-creator with GOD, not be successful? It is literally impossible not to be successful, especially if you read and study this book and keep a Spiritual/Christ/Buddha consciousness at all times! Do you see how you are already starting to feel better just by reading this chapter and generalizing it to your present concern! The attitudinal adjustment of using this Spiritual tool has already worked! Now imagine applying it to every aspect of your life, so you are working these laws and this program in every aspect of your life! It is just a matter of time before you start totally breaking through! Working these laws is your stocks and bonds and financial security!

It is also of the highest importance to always specifically remember to keep your Three-Fold Flame balanced and always to do this battle-plan from 100% unconditional love, 100% wisdom and 100% power, and not overidentify with any one of these qualities to the exclusion of another! This is of the highest importance, otherwise this can throw off your ability to manifest!

Now, my Beloved Readers, I will give one more example of a Spiritual Battleplan so you can be 100% assured to be able to use the examples I have given and translate them to any area of your life!

Spiritual Health Battleplan for Chronic Health Problems

- Do a Huna health prayer as described in this book!
- I will pray constantly to GOD, the Masters, Archangels, Christed Extraterrestrials, and Elohim Masters for help in my healing!
- I will fully own my personal power 100% of the time from now on!
- I will not give my personal power ever again to my physical body!
- I will take incredibly good care of myself!
- I will read Dr. Stone's book on *How to Achieve Perfect Radiant Health*!
- I will consider drinking the Water of Life that Dr. Stone recommends!
- I will not eat too many sweets!
- I will call on my healing angels all the time!
- I will call on Dr. Lorphan and the Galactic Healers as described in Dr. Stone's book *The Golden Book of Melchizedek*!
- I will try and get 20 minutes of fresh air and sunshine every day!
- I will work out three days a week!
- I will drink six big glasses of water a day!
- I will go to a homeopathic and/or naturopathic doctor!
- I will try and find a good Spiritual Healer!

- I will get an Ascension Clearing and/or Negative Implant and Elemental Removal session from Dr. Stone's Academy!
- I will do 100 Physical Health Affirmations a day as described in this book!
- I will call on the Holy Spirit to undo the cause of this health lesson!
- I will unconditionally love my physical body as I do GOD, myself and Brothers and Sisters!
- I now make a personal vow to keep my Three-Fold Flame of 100% Unconditional Love, 100% Wisdom and 100% Power in perfect balance and integration at all times!
- I will call on the Masters for the Core Fear Matrix Removal Program to remove all negative programming that might be causing this lesson!
- I will practice self-hypnosis and give myself suggestions for perfect radiant health!
- I will call on the inner plane etheric surgeons to repair my etheric body!
- I will call on the inner plane acupuncture team to help in my healing!
- I will get a good night's sleep!
- I will not burn the candle at both ends!
- I will be sure to take all my vitamins and minerals every day!
- I will see that Spiritual Psychic I have wanted to see, to see if there is anything else I need to learn!
- I will work on developing a high-functioning immune system on all three levels!
- I will give myself 15 thymus taps a day!
- I will go see a traditional medical doctor as well!

- If necessary, I will go and see a chiropractor!
- I will work with Dr. Stone's meditation in the book *How to Achieve Perfect Radiant Health* "The Fifty Point Cosmic Cleansing Meditation"! I will call on the Platinum Net three times a day to cleanse my fields!
- I will make this Spiritual battleplan a super strong preference and not an attachment
- I will work with color and sound to help heal myself!
- I will work with my crystals to help heal myself!
- I make a Spiritual vow to never give up even for a second until I am 100% healed!
- I will visualize healing for five minutes, three times a day!
- I will keep a really good attitude and keep my inner peace, even though this is going on!
- I make a Spiritual vow to heal myself if it is the last thing I ever do!
- I make a Spiritual vow to be 100% happy until I do heal myself!
- I make a Spiritual vow to adjust my lifestyle to have the proper respect for my physical body!
- I make a Spiritual vow to totally love my physical body at all times!
- I make a Spiritual vow not to coddle or baby myself, on one side of the coin, and to also take extremely good care of myself!
- I make a Spiritual vow to fulfill my Spiritual mission regardless of the health lessons I am suffering!
- I will do faith, trust and patience affirmations!
- I make a Spiritual vow to bear this cross with the proper Spiritual attitude!
- I make a Spiritual vow to turn lemons into lemonade!

My Beloved Readers, I think you get the point! Now, I want you to tell me how much better you feel after setting up such an assertive plan to heal yourself! Now, tell me, is there any way in GOD's infinite universe that in utilizing such a plan that you will not have improvement? Again, you are utilizing your full personal power and mind power, GOD and the Godforce full power, all the different healing teams, and the power of your subconscious mind, are applying all GOD's physical laws to heal you and are, going to qualified health practitioners on a Spiritual, psychological, psychic and physical level of a traditional and nontraditional nature for help! Is there any possible way you would not improve by not doing all these things? Even more, the way you have set things up in your mind is that you will not be attached! By doing this, my Beloved Readers, you have now gotten your mental and emotional bodies in the proper perspective! You are a cause, not an effect! You are treating life instead of letting it treat you! You are working your program on all four levels! You are working GOD's laws on all levels! It is impossible not to be successful! If you are not, which is close to impossible, but on the remote possibility that occurred, that is fine too, for you have a totally Spiritual/Christ/Buddha attitude and you are not going to let your physical body take away your inner peace! Inner peace is an attitude and state of mind and has nothing to do with the physical body or anything outside of self! However, taking such an attitude is that which prepares you for GOD's miracles! Hence, part of your Spiritual battleplan shall also be to pray with all your heart, and soul and mind and might for a miracle of GOD every day! You shall be like Jacob in the Bible who grabbed onto the Angel's foot while pretending to sleep under the tree, and held on to the Angel's foot and said, "I will not let go until you bless me"! This is the proper attitude to take in terms of working this program! You hold on to it like Jacob held on to that Angel, and do not let go even for an instant until GOD and GOD's laws bless you with the results you want! While your are doing this, go for it with all your heart, and soul and mind and might, but make it a super strong preference and not an attachment! This way, until your Miracle Healing comes, you will still be 100% happy!

So now the lesson is, my Beloved Readers, to take what I have done for you here as examples, and set up your own Spiritual battleplans with even more ideas in every area of your life in which you feel challenged or there is a problem! I absolutely 100% guarantee you that if you do this, you will feel instantly better about whatever it is you are dealing with, and if you work this program, in the shortest amount of time it will resolve itself! How can it not when you are utilizing the full Love, Wisdom and Power of GOD, the Godforce, your own 100% personal power and mind power, the full 100% power of your subconscious mind, the full 100% power of your physical body, and the full 100% personal power of friends, family, and Brothers and Sisters in GOD, to help you in their given areas of expertise? My Beloved Brothers and Sisters, I tell you with all my heart, and soul and mind and might that it is literally impossible not to feel good and be successful! The power of GOD and the Godforce and the 100% power of your 100% will and mind power, cannot be stopped! Your willpower and mind power together are literally an unstoppable force, and will be aligned with the laws of GOD as well, which is exactly what you are doing in this chapter and in this book! My Beloved Readers, my final statement I shall make to conclude this chapter is that GOD and the Godforce and the Son and/or Daughter of GOD who owns their 100% Love, Wisdom and Power in service of GOD can literally not be stopped from achieving total and complete success in whatever they put their mind, heart and prayer into! So my Beloved Readers, create those battleplans and be about GOD's business and your business, for you are literally in truth, an incarnation of GOD, the Christ, the Buddha, the Eternal Self, creating these Spiritual battleplans for the Glory of GOD and for yourself which are One, in truth!

So let it be Written! So let it be Done!

CHAPTER 26

GOD is In the Details

One of the insights I have come to understand about GOD and the Spiritual path is that GOD, being as infinite as He is, is not impressed with glamour, and is also as much impressed with the little things as the big things. A great many lightworkers have dreams and aspirations of being famous or doing channelings or giving Spiritual teachings for thousands of people. I have it on good authority that GOD is just as impressed with a small act of kindness or attention to the small things, with as what we perceive as the big things. I make this point "as what we perceive as the big things," because to GOD Earth is just one planet of billions of planets in this universe, and GOD has infinite numbers of universes within his Cosmic Omniversal Body. So GOD looks to the essence and motivation of things, more than numbers. There are many Spiritual leaders and teachers who gather crowds on occasion, yet if you examine their motivations they are truly serving self, not GOD. As the Bible says, "So what that you gain the whole world and lose your own soul"! In truth, it is not about size, or numbers, it is about living each

moment properly in service of GOD, be it communion with a flower, a
rock, an ant, a cat, a dog, the wind, a nature spirit, one person, or five
thousand people. GOD does not care about fame, or money, or so-
called power, or social status, or perceived vanity. All GOD cares about
is that you live each moment in a Godly manner, wherever you happen
to be, with unconditional love and true Spiritual sacredness.

Now to add to this understanding, GOD very much likes his Sons
and Daughters to pay attention to details. Lightworkers sometimes are
so caught up in their glamorous visions of starting major Spiritual
Centers or being an Avatar and having thousands of students, which
may or may not be their true puzzle piece, that they completely miss all
the "details" GOD would have you pay attention to! The truth is, more
often than not, GOD would have you pay more attention to the profundity of the Divine structure of a green leaf or a plant, the glory of a
beautiful sunset, and the plant spirits playing in your garden. GOD is
just as impressed that you remembered to smile at a stranger walking
down the street who passes you, that you remembered a person's name
who you had been introduced to, and that you remembered to call
someone back who you promised to call.

So many people and lightworkers think that it is being famous or having a worldwide impact on the Earth that GOD is only interested in. This
may, in truth, be the mission for some of them to do it with GOD Purity
and egolessness. However it is just as important to GOD that you pay
attention to details. Did you remember to water your plants and feed all
the animals? Did you remember to put the toilet seat down for your wife?
Did you remember to wash the car this week? Did you consider buying
some flowers for your spouse? Did you go out on Sunday morning and get
a cup of Starbucks coffee for a loved one? Did you remember to compliment an employee on how nice they look this day, if that is the case? Did
you set the table and put some flowers on it to make it a little more beautiful, even though it was not a special occasion? Did you kiss and hug your
loved one before they left in the morning and before bed at night and tell

them how much you love and appreciate them? Are you complimenting your employees and thanking them for helping you? Are you being in integrity with everything you do? Are you apologizing for your mistakes no matter how small? Are you not getting so caught up in the celestial world or intoxicating feeling and ideal of unconditional love that your are not paying just as much attention to earthly details? GOD is in the Earth, Earth life and Matter as well. Did you take the time to fix that little statue that broke? Did you take the time to decorate your home and garden? Did you take the time to do your taxes and not wait until the last second? Did you remember to put food in the bird feeder so the birds can eat, and did you remember to feed the fish? Did you remember to open the door for your wife and a friend, and open the car door for them? Did you take the time to get the right card and present for their birthday? Did you remember your anniversary! Did you write that thank you note that was appropriate to write? Did you get back in a timely manner to the people that call and write you? Are you kind and friendly to the bank teller, the grocery clerk, and the gas station attendant? Are your kind and friendly to the gardener, and the person that comes to clean, in the same way and manner that you would be if a famous person came to your house, or does social status, fame, and money determine how you treat people? Did you offer the delivery person a glass of water or soda after lifting that heavy box or piece of furniture in? Did you let that person make a turn in front of you or cut in front of you who was in a hurry or blocked by traffic? Did you take the time to sweep the porch? Did you take the time to write that letter to your congressman? Did you take that time to tell a loved one or a friend how much you love, appreciate, and care about them? Did you give that money to that charity or homeless person you have been meaning to do? Have you taken time to thank GOD for all you have to be grateful for? Have you taken your car in for the car maintenance it needs! Have you gotten your car washed so it is more pleasant for others to drive in? Did you go out of your way to help that person who needed help? Did you write to that person who needed your help although you will not get paid and there is no financial benefit for doing it?

As you can see, I could go on and on. However, I think you get the point! GOD is as much impressed, and maybe even more impressed, with the "Details" as anything else. One of the real Spiritual tests of the Spiritual path is, will the Spiritual leader, Spiritual teacher, Spiritual channel, if they move into a position of power and public recognition, all of a sudden stop doing these things? Will their personality change? If it does, it means negative ego corruption has taken place. This is not a judgement but just an insight that an attitudinal adjustment and correction needs to be made. This is often the case on the Spiritual path. The person feels they are "too big" for that, or that GOD has more important things for them to do. Well, I am here to remind you of another Biblical proverb, "After pride cometh the fall"!

GOD would have you know that the "Details," every moment of your life, "is your Spiritual path"!

This lesson also means controlling your thoughts, and not procrastinating or being lazy. It also means not placing love as the only purpose, for power and wisdom are equally important to balance. This means paying attention to what you are doing, trying to not make mistakes if you can, and using wisdom in everything you do. I have seen many lightworkers who think love is the only thing, and they are so lacking in personal power, self-mastery, and wisdom it is mind blowing. They are constantly making mistake after mistake, never learning their lessons, and, in truth, not being loving; although they think they are. The truth is they are not! Being Spiritual also means having self-mastery, self-control and self-discipline. It means paying attention to what you are doing! It means having self-mastery over every thought, your feelings and emotions, your subconscious, and your negative ego/fear-based/separative thought system. You can go around trying to be unconditionally loving. However, if you don't do the things I just mentioned, you will be creating disaster at every turn in the name of love. This is not love; this is victim consciousness and self-delusion! I have met a great many lightworkers who are on this path! This is why it is so important to balance your Three-Fold Flame of Love, Wisdom, and Power!

When you read a letter, read it carefully so as not to create any misunderstanding. When you listen to a message on the phone service, listen carefully to get it right. When you write down a phone number, do it with all your attention so as not to transpose the numbers. A great many lightworkers get so celestial, right brain, and spacey that they are constantly spaced out and scattered. They do not pay attention to details. They make the same mistakes over and over again after they are reminded not to make them. They live too much out of their subconscious minds, and too much on automatic pilot. Part of the Spiritual path is pursuing excellence in everything you do, as well as being unconditionally loving. This means when you make a mistake, remembering to not do it again! It means being more Zen-like, really living in the moment, and paying attention to what you are doing when you are doing it! This is part of paying attention to the details! When you drive a car, let this be your sole focus, otherwise you may be living yesterday or tomorrow or in your grocery list and get into an accident. Part of being Spiritual means staying focused, concentrating, not being on automatic pilot, and being more conscious and vigilant! A great many lightworkers go around trying to be loving, but they are constantly creating mistakes, accidents, misunderstandings, miscommunication, disorganization, repeating the same mistakes over and over again, and they think because they are focused on being loving they are being Spiritual. They are deluding themselves, for this is not being loving, it is being out of balance with Self and insensitive to others. It is creating a lot of lessons and problems for others, and it is not learning ones own lessons! GOD is the perfect balance of Love, Wisdom and Power, not the fragmentation of and overidentification with one of these

Flames, which creates corruption and contamination of negative ego in all of them when they are not balanced!

GOD wants all his Sons and Daughters to be balanced and "pay attention to Details" in all three qualities and aspects of life! Someone who, in the name of love, is constantly letting their subconscious mind and astral and emotional body run them and sabotage them, and make mistake after mistake in everything they do in the name of unconditional love, does not know what this ideal really means. One cannot be unconditionally loving unless your personal power is 100% owned and Self-Mastery is 100% achieved! To whatever percentage you do not own your personal power, is the extent to which the subconscious mind, astral body, emotional body, inner child, negative ego, lower-self, and glamour, illusion and maya will run you! Ponder on this last statement, and for this is something a great many lightworkers need to hear. Part of paying attention to "Details" is owning you personal power 100% of the time, and controlling your mind so your are not scattered, spacey, too right-brain, too ungrounded, too celestial, too caught in the subconscious, too run by the inner child, too caught up in your emotional body, or too caught up in your desire body! Enormous numbers of lightworkers live in this state I am speaking about right now! This is not a judgment; this is a "Wake-up call"! Part of "Paying attention to Details" is owning your 100% personal power at all times. Being in Self-Mastery 100% of the time! Staying focused and concentrating 100% of the time! Being conscious 100% of the time and never allowing yourself to go on automatic pilot! This is what a Spiritual Master does! If you don't, you will live in a hypnotic state, making tons of mistakes, being scattered, making the same mistakes over and over again, and creating misunderstanding, miscommunication, and confusion in everything you do even while you are focused on being unconditional loving! This is not unconditionally love. I say again, this is victim consciousness and negative ego sabotage! This is so widespread in the Spiritual movement it is amazing! This is a wake-up call to all lightworkers to not forget to fully own their Power Flame and full Wisdom Flame along with their Love Flame! Then you will be able to pay attention to details in a balanced manner that is truly reflective of GOD!

So, in conclusion, never forget that "GOD is in the Details!" If you live each moment in full 100% personal power, in full 100% wisdom, and in full 100% unconditional love; living each moment perfectly as GOD would have you live it in total focus, concentration, dedicated only to GOD and service of GOD, self and your Brothers and Sisters, then the rest of your life will unfold as it is meant to be! Not everyone is supposed to be well-known or famous for their service work! GOD does not care about this in the slightest. All GOD cares about is that each moment of your life is dedicated in perfect Power, Love and Wisdom to Him, and that you pay attention to the details that make up your Spiritual path, for it is in the details that unconditional love can be most perfectly given!

CHAPTER 27

Learning to Integrate Your 12 Major Archetypes

Another factor in becoming clear and free from glamour, illusion, and maya is the understanding of archetypes. If I am not mistaken, this was a term that was coined by the famous Swiss psychologist, Carl Jung. My dear friend Marcia Dale Lopez, a Spiritual teacher living in New York, has defined archetypes in a very clear and concise manner.

"Archetypes are underlying mythic themes that can be found in all races and cultures at all times. The archetypes are ageless roles or key stereotypes that portray different forms of behavior. In other words, the archetypes are universal role models or personifications of perennial themes. They can be identified as the main characters found in legends, fairy tales, Shakespearean dramas, and Bible stories."

The following are twelve of the basic, most well-known archetypal forms. In my personal opinion, the purpose of these archetypes, as of any role, is to play them if it is appropriate to one's life and Spiritual path and, most of all, to play them consciously. The danger comes when these universal roles and archetypes "play the disciple," instead of the disciple playing them.

The second key point is the danger of living out one particular archetype that might make one psychologically imbalanced. This can be a type of glamour, for example, a person may live out the Martyr archetype; however, one of his spiritual lessons might be also to learn to be spiritually selfish.

The Wise One archetype may need to learn to be the Fool in order to find balance. Every subpersonality has an opposite subpersonality. Hence, an archetype, being a type of universal mythic subpersonality, may need to be balanced also, as long as in doing so one is not serving the negative ego and lower-self.

Many people find themselves identifying with a large number of these archetypal roles and patterns, and that is fine too. There is no right or wrong, there is just what is appropriate for one's Spiritual path and mission in this lifetime, and the issue of being whole and balanced in life. Within the framework of the bigger picture, it is essential to master and integrate all twelve of the basic archetypes.

In a similar sense, one has to master all 12 signs of the Zodiac and the 10 Sephiroth on the Tree of Life. This doesn't mean that one has to do this all in a single lifetime. There is also the possibility of another soul extension being stronger in certain archetypes, while one's self is, stronger in others.

It is a good idea to allow oneself to role-play these different archetypes during this life, so as to gain the greatest sense of wholeness one can possibly have. Many of these archetypes have been lived out in past lives and so don't have to be lived out in this life.

The bottom line is to let the guidance of one's soul and monad to lead one to the appropriate application of these universal states of consciousness. Thinking and meditating upon these twelve archetypes can be quite interesting.

The Archetypes

Destroyer
Change-maker
Enemy
Betrayer
Evil-doer
Mischief-maker
Devil
Rascal

Fool
Risk-taker
Clown
Flake
Lunatic
Madman/Madwoman
Philanderer

Innocent
Artist
Child
Youth
Harmless One
Lover
Trusted
Wonderer

Magician
Fairy Godmother
Merlin
Priest/Priestess

Shaman
Sorcerer
Trickster

Martyr
Great Soul
Saint
Savior
Loser
Struggler
Unfortunate Victim

Patriarch
Ancestor
Father/Mother
Old One
The Great Father/The Great Mother

Ruler
Aristocrat
Emperor/Empress
Judge
Prince/Princess
Queen/King

Servant
Assistant
Attendant
Person Friday
Right-hand Person
Slave
Subject

Subordinate
Worker

Seducer
Deceiver
Enchanter
Lover
Philanderer
Tempter/Temptress

Seeker
Adventurer
Explorer
Hermit
Hunter
Monk
Pioneer
Pursuer
Wanderer

Warrior
Fighter
Gladiator
Hunter
Knight
Rival
Soldier
Survivor
Teacher
Thinker

Wise One
Guru
Holy One
Master
Mystic
Oracle
Philosopher
Prophet
Sage

CHAPTER 28

The Incredible Importance
of Demonstrating GOD and
Integrated Ascension

My Beloved Readers, this may be one of the most important chapters in this book! This chapter speaks to the incredible importance of "Demonstrating Integrated Ascension"! What I am saying here is, I am not talking about just thinking about Integrated Ascension! I am not talking about just feeling what Integrated Ascension is! I am not talking just about just channeling Spirit, the Ascended Masters, or Angels! I am not talking about being and having intuition, knowingness, insight and comprehension at any given time! I am not just talking about meditating and praying! I am not just talking about being a library of Spiritual and occult information! I am not just talking about having Spiritual gifts! I am not just talking about being a Master Healer! I am not just talking about reading Spiritual books! I am not just talking about doing service! I am not just talking about giving a fantastic lecture! I am not just talking about being a Master Spiritual scientist! I am not just talking about going to church once a week! I am not just talking about being a Master Spiritual Teacher! I am not just talking about being a Master Psychic! I am not just talking about being a world famous Spiritual leader! I am not just talking about having millions of Spiritual students! I am not just talking about being physically healthy or being an Olympic athlete! I am not just talking about being a world famous author! I am not just talking about being a Master Spiritual Counselor or Minister! I am not just talking about being a Master Mediator! I am not just talking about having revelations of GOD! I am not just talking about having epiphanies and profound insights about GOD! I am not just talking about being extremely successful in a worldly and Spiritual sense! I am not just talking about completing your seven levels of initiation! I am not just talking about being the head of some major Spiritual center! I am not just talking about being world famous for all the world service work you are doing! I am not just talking about having some very Spiritual name! I am not just talking about being the head of some world famous church, temple, or Spiritual organization! I am not just talking about being a world famous public speaker!

I am not talking about doing workshops, seminars or conferences for 100 people or 100,000 people! I am not talking about the ability to perform miracles! I am not talking about considering oneself an Avatar, God Realized Being, and Ascended Master, overlighted by the Masters, or a past incarnation of some famous saint or Spiritual person!

My Beloved Readers, all of these things are wonderful, but they are not "Demonstrating God and Integrated Ascension"! All these things I have listed are wonderful slivers of what God Realization might look light at times for some people. However, none of these things mean you are actually "Demonstrating and practicing the presence of GOD"! Each one of these things might be seen as aspects or parts of God Realization, but I am not talking about Realizing God in one of your bodies or with one or more of your Spiritual senses. I am not saying all these things I have listed are not incredibly important. What I am saying is that there is a difference between doing one or more of these things and actually "Being God in your daily life"! Let me be more specific now and give some examples!

The first classic example is that we all know that going to church or temple means nothing, if you don't practice what you are learning in your daily life. Yet many go to church and temple and they feel they have paid their rent to GOD!

On a mental level there is also a difference between "Demonstrating God in your daily life" and just thinking about God! You can, for example, read Spiritual books or be a Spiritual author all day long, and this is wonderful and essential for your Spiritual growth, but there is a difference between thinking about God and actually "being that which you are thinking about"! Are you "Being" in your daily life the Spiritual principles you are reading or writing about? It is possible to be a library of Spiritual information and not be demonstrating moment by moment that which you have stored in your Spiritual information banks, and/or that which you are reading and writing about!

On a Spiritual level, I know extremely well-known Spiritual leaders who are channels for Spirit, the Ascended Masters, the Angels, and Christed Extraterrestrials, and as bizarre as it may sound, they are not demonstrating Godliness or Spiritual/Christ/Buddha consciousness in their daily lives! They may be wonderful channels for the Masters at times, and bring through profound Spiritual teachings, and the words may flow out of their mouths like Spiritual poetry! I am here to tell you, my Beloved Readers, this has absolutely nothing to do with "Demonstrating Godliness"! I know well-known Spiritual leaders who are channels and who are extremely unloving! I know others who channel the Masters, but are totally run by their negative ego, and are complete emotional victims! I know others who channel the Masters who are so run by the negative ego and so filled with false pride and self-aggrandizement, that it is mind blowing that anyone on planet Earth could be so run by the negative ego, let alone a Spiritual person who channels the Masters. I know other channels for the Masters who are some of the most corrupt, unscrupulous, conniving, manipulative, disturbed people I have ever met in my life! Yet they claim to channel the Masters and Angels, and the public believes it! I know other Spiritual leaders who are channels that I would actually call schizophrenic! I know others who I would call criminal and sociopathic in their behavior. This is not demonstrating God!

I know people who can perform Spiritual miracles where they materialize things right out of the ethers. Yet, they are totally run by the negative ego and emotional body! I have known others who are run by their sexuality! This is not demonstrating God!

I know others who can Soul Travel to the Throne of GOD and bring back the most incredibly profound Spiritual information you can possible imagine! Yet on a psychological level and personality level they are run by the negative ego!

I know people who have had past lives of the most extraordinary nature and even been the disciples and apostles of the most well-known Spiritual masters, prophets and saints that have ever lived on this Earth, even those upon whose teachings the world's religions are based upon, and I tell you my friends, some of these individuals are run by the negative ego to such a degree that it almost defies description. This is not demonstrating God!

I know others who have extraordinary psychic abilities who can read minds, read the future, and read past lives, are clairvoyant to the highest degree, are clairaudient and can heal, and yet in their daily lives they are not demonstrating God! They are often run by the negative ego and emotional body. They smoke too much, eat too much junk food, and more importantly do not practice Spiritual/Christ/Buddha consciousness in their daily lives. This is not demonstrating God!

I know other people who are very Spiritual and loving, are more of a Mystic nature, and are on the Goddess path that focuses more on feeling God! This is wonderful, however this is only one aspect of what it means to be God-Realized. Just focusing on the feeling aspect of God is not demonstrating God and Integrated Ascension! To not properly integrate the mind, intuition, the physical body, or the Earth because of a more primary focus on the feeling nature is not demonstrating God! It is focusing on only an aspect of God! Very often this type of person is unconsciously overidentified with the emotional body, and does not see how their thoughts are causing their reality. They often do not see how they are being victimized by their emotions. If the mind and emotions are not properly balanced, the negative ego will run the personality, and this is an indisputable law of the mind! There is not one side or aspect of GOD that is better than another! If one thinks so, one is already caught by negative ego faulty thinking. This is not a judgement, of course, just a quick adjustment in one's attitude and perspective that one needs to make!

I know other people who are world-famous, incredible Spiritual teachers and counselors who can give incredible lectures and give incredible Spiritual sessions. However, once they get off the stage they can be some of the most corrupt, deceitful, dishonest individuals you would ever want to meet. I realize this may seem hard to believe. However, I tell you I have seen it with my own eyes, over and over and over again, and it blows my mind! How can someone who can be at this level of Spiritual development, have this much Spiritual knowledge, and have this amount of fame and Spiritual students be this incredibly corrupt? The answer is, they never got trained in the difference between negative ego/fear-based/separative thinking and Spiritual/Christ/Buddha thinking!

I do want to say here, however, that this above example is an extreme one. I am also talking about Spiritual Teachers who are pure and mean well, but get so caught up in their Spiritual teaching, service work, channeling, writing and counseling that in their daily lives they are not "demonstrating God"! There is a difference between doing service work and demonstrating God!

Let me explain here even deeper now what I am talking about, as I am laying the foundation for the essence of the teaching of this chapter. What I am talking about here is that the person may be thinking, teaching, reading, studying, meditating, channeling, or feeling all these things about GOD. However, how does this translate into the issue of demonstrating God? In other words, in the person's daily life when they are not teaching, reading, studying, meditating, channeling, doing healing work, doing service work on being blissed-out on love, are they doing some of the following things: Are they staying in self-mastery over their mental body and not being too disorganized, scattered, unfocused, or mistake-prone? Are they controlling their subconscious mind, causing their reality, and causing their feelings and emotions by how they think? Are they staying in self-mastery over their emotional body or are they letting negative feelings and emotions manifest? Are they being emotional victims? Are they causing their feelings and emotions, or are their feelings and emotions "causing them"? Are they overidentified with their feelings and emotions and not integrating the mind? Are they overly identified with the Goddess energies? Has becoming overly feeling and emotional become glamour? Is the negative ego programming the feelings and emotions, or is the Spiritual/Christ/Buddha mind? Is the person integrating and balancing the Earth and Earth energies, or getting too focused on Spiritual, heavenly, and celestial levels? Is the person properly integrating the psychological level? Is the person properly balancing their masculine and feminine energies? Is the person balanced in their God/Goddess energies?! Is the person balanced in their Three-Fold Flame of Love, Wisdom and Power?! Is the person balanced in their Seven Rays, which is the personality of God? Is the person balancing their 12 major archetypes? Is the person balancing Heaven and Earth? Is the person properly integrating and balancing their three minds? Is the person properly integrating and balancing their four-body system on a physical, emotional, mental and Spiritual level? Is the person staying in self-mastery at all times and staying out of their negative ego/fear-based/separative thought and feeling system, only living moment to moment in their daily lives out of the Spiritual/Christ/Buddha thought and feeling system? Is the person remaining in their personal power and Golden Bubble at all times, and letting other people's negative energy slide off like "water off a duck's back"? Do they have preferences or attachments? Are they getting so much into service work that they are not demonstrating true Godliness? Is the person remaining in their self-mastery and not getting overly emotional, and not being prone to outbursts? Do they look at everything that happens as a Spiritual test and Spiritual lesson? Have they let go of all their attachments and replaced them with preferences? Do they truly have self-love and self-worth! Have they let go of false pride? Do they really strive for egolessness? Do they truly put GOD first? Do they remain focused and dedicated at all times? Have they kept their God Purity even though they have become so successful and famous? Are they humble and do they have humility! Are they able to maintain a full spectrum prism consciousness, or do they keep getting caught up in their blinds spots and limited lens seeing? Are they able to get all the Spiritual principles they believe in into proper balance and integration, and most of all demonstrate them, not just believe in them or teach or channel them? Is the person able to admit mistakes and apologize? Is the person able to let go of the role of being the teacher, channel and/or Guru and be a person? Are they involved with people and earthly life, or are they "too good" for that? Can they get involved in an equal romantic relationship, or do they always have to have the upper hand and have power? Have they let go of self-righteousness? Can they learn from others? Can they hear feedback from others? Have they let go of all false gods? Are they in integrity at all times? Are they striving to have a flawless character at all times? Are they balanced and integrated Spiritually, psychologically and on a physical/earthly level? Do they take care of their Earthly responsibilities? Do they meet their family obligations and duties! Are they so caught up in their work they are not truly demonstrating Godliness! Are they clear in their communications with others! Can they turn the other cheek! Can they love their enemies!

Can they truly forgive! Do they stay out of ego battles? Are they constantly working on themselves, trying to improve, make adjustments, purify and refine their character and being on all levels? Are they truly trying to "demonstrate all they know and not just to do service work"? Are they self-disciplined? Are they too run by the inner child or desire body! Is the person fully demonstrating the Mighty I Am Presence throughout every aspect of their being? Is the person fully demonstrating the Mighty I Am Presence and Christ Self in the physical body and in a grounded way? Is the person demonstrating the anchoring of the Mighty I Am Presence and Christ/Buddha Self in the marketplace? Is the person demonstrating the Mighty I Am Presence and Christ Self in their Spiritual mission on Earth? Does the person have a right relationship to self and right relationship to GOD? Does the person have the proper respect and relationship to the inner plane Ascended Masters? Does the person have right relationships with other people? Is the person fulfilling their right Spiritual puzzle piece in the Divine plan? Does the person truly cooperate with others or are they competing? Is the person truly egoless in their example? Do they truly put others first? Are their motivations on the deepest level, truly coming from GOD or are they selfish? Do they pray for GOD's help and the Masters' help? Do they demonstrate consistency on all levels! Is there consistency between the superconscious, conscious, subconscious, physical body, and what is being demonstrated on Earth? Is there consistency in every thought, word and deed? When they say they are going to do something do they do it, or do they always give an excuse the next day, such as I was tired, or I forgot, and then do the exact same thing the next day? Are they lazy or do they procrastinate? Do they balance work and pleasure? Are they giving enough time to their spouse, children and family? Do they practice what they preach! Is there consistency between the beliefs and Spiritual principles they hold dear, and what they demonstrate in their daily lives? Do they demonstrate "Integrated Ascension and Godliness" every single moment of their lives, not just when they are on stage, in front of a TV camera, or when doing a session?

My Beloved Readers, I could go on, but I think my point has been made. However, I am still not complete with describing the essence of what Spirit wishes me to convey. I would like to take this discussion even one step deeper. We are peeling the onion, so to speak! We are now going to the final core of this discussion. All the layers have been absolutely essential to fully understand what it means to truly demonstrate "God and Integrated Ascension!"

On the feeling side there are those that are very love-focused and feeling-focused, which is good and excellent; however, there can be a danger of an overidentification with the Love Flame to the neglect of the Power Flame and Wisdom Flame. An example is someone who is Sixth Ray and/or too devotional. They are all heart and feeling, which is wonderful, but it can be over-devotion, as to a guru, or the tendency to put people on pedestals and become too idealistic and hence have an extremely weak Spiritual discernment. There is also a danger of giving away their personal power in their total focus on feelings and love, and becoming overidentified with the Goddess path, which can become a glamour of being focused too much. There always needs to be the balance of love, wisdom and power! Another example is a person on the feeling side who may be very feeling and loving, but might be also overly Second Ray or overly Rays Two, Four and Six and very weak in Rays One, Three and Five, which have a little more power, mental, and scientific energy. They have the Second Ray of Spiritual love, which is fantastic, but we all know how the First Ray, Second Ray and Third Ray must all be balanced. So the person is loving, which is great, but the lack of personal power causes an overidentification with the subconscious and hence tons of unconscious mistakes are made, they have a lack of self-discipline, they are very unfocused, scattered, and overly impulsive, they say they will do things and they don't.

Another example would be someone who is very developed in feeling and love, but their lack of Third Ray causes an inability to ground their Spiritual mission or get their work done. This person is being way too disorganized, procrastinating too much, and demonstrating an inability to get one's work done in a grounded earthly sense, because of being so focused on love of the Second Ray all the time. They might be too vertical and not horizontal enough, and might never be able to read a book. The lack of Third Ray makes them terrible in business and dealing with money. They are all heart, so they get too caught up in the personal and don't know how to be impersonal. They are all heart, which is great, but they can be too swayed and pushed around by feelings and emotions. They often don't see that it is their thoughts that are causing their feelings and emotions. They may believe they cause their reality, but their overidentification with the feelings and heart, and rejection often of the mind, causes them to not see how their thoughts are causing their emotional reactions. This sometimes manifests as negative feelings and emotions, although the person overall is a very unconditionally loving person, which is good. The preoccupation, however, with just the feelings and the heart can cause a great many blind spots to occur if it is not properly integrated with the mind, the intuition, the instincts, five senses, and the balance and integration of all seven Rays. The person may also be all heart and feelings, but may be hence also a little too overidentified with the desire body and the inner child! Then may not always parent the inner child properly, and be a little too run by the inner child. They may also at times be lacking not only in Spiritual discernment and be taken in by people and semi-Spiritual scams or cons, but also be lacking in logic and common sense at times. So none of this is meant as a judgment, for unconditional love and feelings are wonderful things! I am just most lovingly pointing out the dangers of overidentifying with unconditional love and feelings, and how this is not the full demonstration of GOD and integrated and balanced Integrated Ascension.

Now, just to be Spiritually objective and fair, and to show that I am not taking sides, the same thing can happen on the power flame or mental side of things. Just as some people have overidentification with feelings and/or unconditional love as their total focus, other people often get too overidentified with the power flame and the mind. They may be brilliant Spiritual teachers and be libraries of esoteric knowledge and wisdom. However, if this information is not connected to one's feelings and heart, no matter how profound it is, it is not demonstrating true Godliness and Integrated Ascension. This process can manifest in a great numbers of ways. It can manifest as a person who has incredible Spiritual and esoteric knowledge, but one who is not unconditionally loving in their life and personal relationships. It can manifest in being too intellectual. It can manifest as people who are too scientific and stuck in the concrete mind! It can manifest as Spiritual people who are too stuck in the Universal Mind and not balanced with the Universal Heart! It can manifest as a Spiritual teacher who channels or teaches without passion or enthusiasm. This occurs even in politics, for I have been watching some of the conventions, and the speakers who are most enjoyable to watch are the ones who really speak with total passion and enthusiasm. So, no matter how high the Spiritual knowledge and wisdom is, if it is not connected to the heart and feelings it is going to fall on deaf ears and put everyone to sleep!

This overidentification with the power flame and/or mental body can also manifest as a focus on personal power and Spiritual discernment, which is great and unbelievably needed in this world, because it is so incredibly lacking. However, if this is done at the expense of unconditional love and feelings this is not truly demonstrating God and Integrated Ascension! What is very interesting about this chapter is that in other chapters the negative ego was pointed out; however, in this chapter we are seeing how many people have extremely admirable Spiritual qualities. Examples of some of these qualities are personal power and Spiritual discernment or unconditional love and feelings, passion, joy and enthusiasm. However, if one is overidentified with one part of the Three-Fold Flame over another, imbalance can occur. So, we are not so much talking about negative ego as much as what might be called "limited lens seeing," which is a very profound and cutting-edge new psychological science I am now attempting to bring through in this book. It is so incredibly easy to overidentify with one of the Three-Fold Flames. It is so incredibly easy to become overidentified and underidentified with one of the Seven Great Rays of God! In truth, there are infinite numbers of lenses one can become over- or underidentified with. Because this is such a profound concept, I have actually written a whole chapter on this in this book. However, I did want to initially mention this to you, My Beloved Readers, because it has great application here to seeing how we can all become unconsciously overidentified or underidentified with personal power and the mind and/or the heart and feelings!

Now I want to now get back now to continuing my discussion on the overidentification with the personal power flame and the mind and other ways this can manifest. This can also manifest in one's Spiritual teaching, one's speaking, and one's writing, and in being too critical and/or judgmental rather than coming from a more integrated place of unconditionally loving Spiritual observation, unconditionally loving Spiritual discernment, and unconditionally loving Spiritual discrimination. Do not get me wrong here for Spiritual discernment is one of the most important Spiritual qualities on the Spiritual path and for achieving Christ consciousness, but it must be blended with unconditional love!

Another example of this overidentification with personal power and the mind might manifest as certain Spiritual teaching, speaking or writing coming across as being angry! Personal power and the mind without love will begin to manifest as anger, resentfulness, attack, impatience, irritation, intolerance, over hardness, and over harshness.

This next example you will find very interesting. A person who is overidentified with power and the mind, and not connected enough to the heart and feelings, when channeling will cause the information coming from the Ascended Masters to be very authoritarian, commanding, domineering, and unfriendly! I have seen this happen with channels many times. Unsuspecting lightworkers think that this just must be the way the

Ascended Masters are. I have seen entire Spiritual organizations based around such channelings. This, of course, with no judgement intended, is caused by this limited lens seeing and lack of psychological balance within the channel, which is causing the information coming from Spirit or the inner plane Ascended Masters to be filtered, interpreted and channeled improperly. This, of course, can happen in reverse in the same way. A channel overidentified with love and feelings, will give overly loving, glamorous, super flowery channelings that are totally feeling-based, lacking in any real power, and devoid of any specific detailed information. This is also extremely widespread in the New Age Movement. The imbalance in the Three-Fold Flame here can cause the channelings to be contaminated, as well being negative ego agendas from both sides of the pendulum! Both of these cases, of course, are not true demonstrations of God and Integrated Ascension!

Other examples of being overly identified with personal power and the mind are to come across as acting superior to everyone else, lacking in humble-ness and humility! To be overly prideful, competitive, rigid, lacking in compassion, possibly lacking in forgiveness, lacking in harmlessness or gentleness, too firm, too tough, too much the warrior, too inflexible, too left-brain, too aggressive, too willful, too serious, overidentified with the teacher role, giving unwanted advice, too goal oriented, argumentative, intimidating, too structured, too work focused, not playful enough, not friendly enough, and too susceptible to falling under the veil of illusion!

The person overidentified with love and feelings is more prone to being oversensitive, ego sensitive, unable to take constructive criticism, overreacting emotionally, prone to feeling hurt, rejected, or abandoned, too empathic, overly mothering, too child-like, overly sentimental, moody, not assertive enough, occasionally self-doubting or insecure, shy, spacey, too open, a little too free-flowing, unable to concentrate or be focused for too long, too process-oriented, too focused on play and having fun to the point of not getting Spiritual work done, lacking in boundaries, lacking in firmness or Spiritual toughness at times, lacking in proper structure, too right brain, too selfless, overly affectatious, and too susceptible to falling under the veil of glamour!

My Beloved Readers, I bring up these examples of being overly identified with the power flame and the mind and being overly identified with the love flame and one's feelings as more excellent examples of how, even though both of these qualities when developed are outstanding, wonderful qualities, that if not seen from a "Full Spectrum Prism Perspective" as GOD would have you see it, those qualities will not be the full demonstration of God and Integrated Ascension one is looking for! The other examples I have given have been people with more pronounced Spiritual gifts in the various areas of a their entire self. This example is very interesting, for it is about someone giving psychological gifts rather than Spiritual gifts, but the result is the same. Even though these areas of self are highly developed, which is very good, it still is not the full demonstration of God and God Realization! Just as all the specific Spiritual gifts in certain aspects of self are not an indication of demonstration of God or full God Realization, the psychological areas of self that lightworkers are very developed in are not necessarily an indicator of demonstration of God and Integrated Ascension either! I bring up these psychological examples, for they are very common in the Spiritual movement, as are the various gifts. The profundity and teaching of this chapter is that all Spiritual or psychological gifts are not necessarily an indicator that one is truly demonstrating God and Integrated Ascension as they think they might be! This chapter is given as a Spiritual gift to clear any veils of illusion, glamour and maya so true demonstration of God and God Realization may be achieved, for this I know, my Beloved Readers, we all want! We all want to have an efficient perception of reality and not be ridden unconscious by "limited lens seeing" or by the "negative ego"! We are all striving for the highest level of God Realization, God purity, and God honesty we can achieve! This chapter, I humbly submit, can be helpful in recentering you back into your own "Full Spectrum Prism Integrated

Consciousness" and demonstrating this more fully, as well as helping you to develop your Spiritual discernment of these same Spiritual and psychological principles in others. This can be of great help to yourself in having the proper Spiritual discernment and efficient perception of reality in dealing with all the Spiritual leaders, Spiritual channels, Spiritual teachers, Spiritual scientists, Spiritual psychics, Spiritual healers, psychologists, counselors, lightworkers, and people you have dealings with the rest of your life. Being able to have this Spiritual discernment within self will allow you to have this Spiritual discernment outside of self and with others as well. My Beloved Readers, is it not a most wonderful, unconditionally loving, and balanced and integrated thing to be able to see self and see others from a more "Full Spectrum Prism Integrated Consciousness"! Is it not even a more wonderful to thing to understand that these insights and understandings will help you to more fully demonstrate God and Integrated Ascension? It will help you to see and deal with all in the aforementioned list of Spiritual leaders, channels, teachers, lightworkers and people more clearly. It will finally also allow you to be of much greater Spiritual service to all your Spiritual brothers and sisters, Spiritual friends, and family by helping them to see life from a much greater "Full Spectrum Prism Integrated Consciousness," and hence most importantly be able to "Demonstrate God and Integrated Ascension" in their daily lives as well!

The final layer in this discussion of what it means to truly demonstrate Godliness and Integrated Ascension now goes not only into how one is thinking, and feeling, the state of their consciousness and how all of this is being demonstrated, but also now how the consciousness of each person is being demonstrated physically, with people, and outwardly, on a moment-to-moment basis! Let me explain what I mean here in the deepest and most profound way I can!

Is the person truly demonstrating Godliness, and all they Spiritually believe, with other people they are working with while doing their service work? Do they use their personal power properly? Is their personal power always channeled through unconditional love? Do they keep their Three-Fold Flame truly balanced in the way they demonstrate their life on a moment-to-moment basis? How do they treat their employees? Do they get angry? Do they misuse their power? Are they truly psychologically and Spiritually wise in the way they conduct their life? How do they treat others of lesser socioeconomic status or Spiritual status? How do they treat their maid? How do they treat the gardener? How do they treat the bank teller, and grocery clerk? Do they treat them with the same love and respect as a famous Spiritual leader and teacher! Do they put GOD or money first? Do they judge others behind their backs? Do they gossip? Are they ego sensitive?! Do they ever give in to attack thoughts towards others? Do they know when to talk and when to be silent? Are they Spiritually politically savvy? Do they know how to be appropriate? Do they have common sense? How do they treat animals, pets and plants? Do they have the proper respect and love for nature? What is their relationship to the Divine Mother, the Earth Mother and the Goddess energies? Do they truly put the Earth first, or power, fame and money first? Do they control their sexuality properly? Do they demonstrate the Spiritual principles that they believe in even when under stress? Do they maintain their unconditional love even when major Spiritual events are going on? How do they respond when attacked and criticized? Do they respond or react? Do they respond with evenmindedness, forgiveness and unconditional love? Do they see attack as a call for love? Do they maintain joyous vigilance at all times? Do they change identities or do they stay the same Spiritual self at all times in all situations? Has the power and fame gone to their head? Do they pursue Spiritual excellence and immaculateness in all that they do? How do they deal with the public once they have gotten successful and climbed to the top of the Spiritual mountain? Do they still serve with the same Spiritual selflessness, sincerity, and God purity as they once did? Do they really take time to help others even if people don't know about it? Do they help others even if they don't get paid? Are they really selfless servants and instruments of God and the Masters? Are they truly seeking to glorify GOD in everything they do or are they seeking to glorify self? Do they keep the highest ethical and moral standards at all times? Do they ever take their power out and/or abuse their students? When faced with losing that which they have built up in one form or another, do they throw Spiritual principles out the window? How do they deal with total Spiritual or worldly crisis and emergency? Do they remain the same Spiritual person even then? Do they demonstrate the Spiritual/Christ/Buddha consciousness at all times no matter what example or we could come up with? The true test of a Spiritual person is how they deal with work, stress, crisis, emergency and catastrophes. How do they deal with other people's mistakes and incompetence? Do they remain in forgiveness and unconditional love and deal with it in a Christed manner? How do they deal with their own mistakes? How do they deal when badmouthed, backstabbed or betrayed by another? Do they still maintain their Spiritual/Christ/Buddha consciousness? How do they deal with situations when they are stolen from and lose incredibly large sums of money? Do they still remain in a Spiritual/Christ/Buddha consciousness? How do they treat strangers on the street? Do they practice the Holy Encounter and treat each person as God and the Christ? How do they treat their neighbor, now that they are so successful Spiritually and in a worldly sense? Do they still have time to visit with their neighbor? Do they still have the consciousness to speak kindly and be friendly to the bank teller, grocery clerk, and gas station attendant? Do they smile at the stranger on the street as a Spiritual brother or sister, or just ignore them? Do they go around acting better then everyone else? Do they have an efficient perception of reality, or do they tend to try to create things to build their egos? Do they truly love GOD with all their heart and soul and mind and might and love their neighbor as they love themselves? Do they see everything on Earth in all kingdoms as an incarnation of GOD? Does the person pay attention to details in the same way they did before, now that they are so Spiritually successful and successful in a worldly sense? Do they put themselves first or others first? Do they walk the extra mile for others? Are they humble and do they practice humility in everything they do? Do they live that which they teach? Do they truly put everything and I mean everything, of an inner and outer nature including all relationships, on the "Altar of GOD"? Do they truly put GOD above all else? Do they fully realize how much their own relationship to themselves and their own psychology affects their relationship to GOD and other people! The last question I will ask is, if they went through the "Job Initiation" and everything, and I mean everything, was immediately taken away (this includes health, money, family, fame, fortune, power, romantic relationship, children, and I mean everything), how would this person respond? Would they put GOD first? Would they remain righteous in GOD? Would they keep their peace of mind? Would they get angry, upset and or depressed?

My Beloved Readers, these are the true Spiritual tests of the Spiritual path to see if one is truly demonstrating God! It is not the fame, all the lectures, being a channel, being a world famous Spiritual teacher, having all the Spiritual knowledge, having psychic abilities, having millions of students, being a Master Healer or famous Spiritual scientist, being a Master Meditator, or being blissed out on joy and love, being a Spiritual leader, or running a major Spiritual center, that will determine your God Realization! I am not saying these things are not important, along with all the other examples I have listed in this chapter. They are all important. However, my Beloved Readers (please listen to this), it is even more important what you are demonstrating when you are not on stage, not giving a lecture or workshop, not doing Spiritual leadership, not doing a channeling session, not doing a psychic reading, not doing a healing session, not doing service work, not meditating, not reading, not writing, not doing your Spiritual practices, and not running your Spiritual center!

Are you staying balanced and integrated within your three minds and four bodies? Are you staying out of your negative ego at all times? How are you treating all the people around you? Are you treating each person you meet, even if it is a stranger, like an incarnation of God? Are you treating your maid like you would Buddha or Jesus? If you are seeing life with your Christ eyes this is the appropriate way to live! It is the small things and the daily things that are most important. Treating your employees right! Remaining unconditionally loving to everyone at all times as well as completing all your Spiritual projects and service work! Maintaining a proper relationship to your spouse! Treating everyone you meet as God! Most importantly, demonstrating all your Spiritual beliefs and Spiritual principles in your earthly life every moment with no excuses, even if you are doing Spiritual service work. Do not let your negative ego say that because you are doing Spiritual service work and working on some world-famous Spiritual project that Spirit and the Masters want you to do, that you don't have to be balanced in your three minds and four bodies, and maintain your Spiritual/Christ/Buddha consciousness at all times! Just because you are doing all the Spiritual service work and world famous Spiritual projects doesn't mean you can then forget about demonstrating God in your daily life every single moment and in every single interaction with another individual! If you don't do this, this will be hypocrisy, lack of integrity, lack of consistency between levels, and lack of honesty with self, and you will not be God! Regardless of what we are doing we must keep all levels together! We must keep the big picture and the little picture together simultaneously! We must practice what we preach on every level of our being at all times, with no rationalizations or excuses! I do not mean to be judgmental in saying what I am saying here, I am just attempting to say that we all be "devastatingly honest" with self! I am speaking here in this Spiritually impassioned fashion, for I say to you, my Beloved Brothers and Sisters, do we truly want to Realize God, or do we want to realize some illusion or misperception of what God is? I know all of you, my Beloved Brothers and Sisters, for I know myself! We are all one and we are all made of GOD! I know with all my heart that you want true GOD purity as much as I do! Let us not settle for anything less then total and complete 100% God purity! Let us not settle for anything less than total and complete 100% God Realization! Let us not settle for anything less than total and complete 100% demonstration of God on every level of our being at all times! I know you are exactly like me and that all you want is GOD! So let us in this moment totally and completely 100% rededicate our lives to demonstrating God every moment of our lives in all the ways that we have been talking about in this chapter, not just in all the big ways but even more importantly in the daily way we live our lives and with all our relationships of all kinds. Let us totally and completely 100% rededicate our lives to "Demonstrating God and Integrated Ascension" every moment regardless of what Spiritual work or Spiritual projects we are focusing on, and to treat all people regardless of their Spiritual evolution, Spiritual status, worldly success or socioeconomic status as the Gods they are, whether they realize it or not! Let us now make a total and complete 100% dedication to treat every stranger as the Brother or Sister and God Being they are! Let us totally and completely 100% rededicate our lives to demonstrating and practicing all that we believe Spiritually, and to put it into practice every moment of our lives!

So let it be Written! So let it be Done!

CHAPTER 29

How to Utilize the Unbelievable Power and Abilities of the Holy Spirit

One of the great untapped secrets of the Universe which lightworkers and people of the Earth have not taken full advantage of is the incredible power, love and grace of the Holy Spirit. Now, when I bring up the Holy Spirit, I am not saying here that you need to be a Christian. I personally am a Christian, a Buddhist, a Hindu, a Jew, a Muslim and a follower of all Spiritual paths and mystery schools and no one religion, mystery school or path. To me, they are all one. This, again, is the Path of Synthesis, my friends. This I know in my heart of hearts, and soul of souls of the living, breathing existence of GOD, Christ, and the Holy Spirit. I know and believe in this, just as I recognize in the same way the existence of the Buddha in Buddhahood, and the Atma in Hinduism, YHWH in Judaism and the Kabbalah, and Allah and the Prophet Mohamed in the Muslim faith.

I do not just believe in the existence of the Holy Spirit; I know the Holy Spirit. It is interesting to me that so many people in the New Age Movement work with the inner plane Ascended Masters, the Archangels and Angels, the Elohim Masters, the Christed Extraterrestrial Races, their Mighty I am Presence and Monad, their Higher Self, and their Soul, but very rarely do I hear people talking about the Holy Spirit.

In some ways the Holy Spirit is the ultimate Spiritual Master, for it is the aspect that GOD created right out of Himself to, in essence, be the "Answer" to all our challenges and lessons in life. It is wonderful to go to the Ascended Masters, the wonderful Archangels, and the Elohim; however, you can also go directly to GOD, and the voice of GOD is the Holy Spirit.

When we pray to GOD, the Godhead does not come Himself, but rather has divided Himself into three aspects. This is the Trinity of GOD, GOD being the Godhead or the Creator of everything at the 352nd level of Creation. GOD is in part unfathomable, and yet on another level is also quite personal. We think of how big our Universe is or how big the Melchizedek Universe is on a multidimensional level. Well, consider that GOD is made up of an infinite number of universes. It is true that we are made in his image. However, there is one big difference. GOD created us; we did not create GOD! This is why *A Course in Miracles* says that "awe" is an appropriate response to GOD, but not an appropriate response to a fellow inner plane Ascended Master, no matter how high their evolvement. The proper response to a very evolved inner plane Ascended Master is "respect." It is the respect for an elder Brother or Sister, but not awe. Awe is only appropriate for GOD, who is unfathomable, but is also incredibly personally knowable.

At the annual Wesak Celebrations I do Ascension Activation Meditations where GOD actually participates. Many think that GOD should be kept separate. However, this is illusion; it is possible to have a direct personal relationship with GOD. There are many kinds of relationships to GOD, the most profound being the state of "Revelation."

Now the second aspect of the Trinity is the Christ, which is the intermediary, so to speak, between GOD and His Creation. What many lightworkers and people do not realize is that there are many levels to the Christ. When Jesus realized the Christ two thousand years ago, he was realizing it on a Planetary level. What you must realize is that there is also a Solar level to the Christ, a Galactic level, a Universal level, a Multi-Universal level and a full Cosmic level of the Christ.

The initiation process, of which, in truth, there are 352, takes you through all of these to fully realize the Christ in the fullest sense of GOD, at the highest possible level. No one on Earth has done this. The most evolved realization of Christ on Earth is His Holiness the Lord Sai Baba in India. He is demonstrating on Earth the realization of the Christ at the Universal level. He has not, however, realized the Multi-Universal Christ or the Cosmic Christ status of a Cosmic Ascended Master. He is, however, the most advanced realization of the Christ the Earth has ever known.

Lord Maitreya, who is head of the Spiritual Hierarchy, holds the position of being a Galactic Christ for our planet. Master Kuthumi is preparing to take over the position in the Spiritual Government of the Planetary Christ, which is a Galactic-level realization.

I want to make it clear here that no one can skip levels, and if you think you can this it is the negative ego talking. Everyone must go through the initiation process through each level, demonstrate their Divinity, and serve at each level before advancing. Demonstration of GOD on an ongoing basis and service at each level is the key. So as we evolve we come to know and realize greater and greater levels of the Christ. The Master Jesus is working on fully realizing the Galactic Christ at a very high level, along with Master Kuthumi and a great many of the other well-known Ascended Masters of our Planetary Hierarchy. In their initiation processes, they have not yet begun the realization of their initiations of becoming a Universal Christ. Most lightworkers on Earth are focusing on realizing the Planetary Christ.

So, as we see here, it is also possible to have a very close relationship to the second aspect of the Trinity, which is the Holy Christ Presence. I am not talking about Jesus here, for he is just one man who realized this integration and unification on a Planetary level. Since his life as Jesus two thousand years ago, he has also done so on a Solar level and on a Galactic level. He is still in a state of evolution through the 352 levels of initiation as well. The most important point here is that it is 100% possible to have a continuing ongoing personal relationship with the Holy Christ Presence, which keeps expanding as we evolve spiritually.

The third aspect of the Trinity is the Holy Spirit. The Holy Spirit is an aspect of GOD that He has placed within us, as the answer to all our problems. In truth, all problems are created by the negative ego or separative mind. All answers and solutions come from the Holy Spirit. The Holy Spirit speaks for the "Atonement" or the "At-one-ment." To atone means to undo. Of the many profound gifts of the Holy Spirit and the infinite wisdom, knowledge, love and power it possesses, the most profound ability it has in my humble opinion is its ability to undo past mistakes and negative interactions and situations.

My beloved Brothers and Sisters, listen very closely to what I am about to share with you, for in my humble opinion, this is one of the most profound esoteric secrets of GOD's infinite Universe, which has unbelievable importance and significance in your life. The Holy Spirit has the ability to atone for, or stated more clearly to "undo," the ramifications of any mistake that you have made in your life. The Holy Spirit can not only undo it in your subconscious and unconscious minds and auric field, it can also undo the effects that your mistakes may have caused to other people or other situations.

My Beloved Readers, I cannot tell you how many times in my life, when I have made a mistake or even when I didn't make a mistake, and I have gotten myself into some sticky situation, that I have called on the Holy Spirit to undo the causes that have gotten me there. I have called on the Holy Spirit to undo health lessons. I have called on the Holy

Spirit to undo mistakes I have made and the negative results that came from them. I have called on the Holy Spirit to undo negative actions with people, even when the negativity was coming from someone else and not me. I have called on the Holy Spirit to undo situations in my life that need fixing. I have called on the Holy Spirit to undo literally everything that is not going 100% according to my preferences. Again, it is funny, a lot of lightworkers are so busy on calling on the Masters and Angels that they forget that they can call on GOD and the Trinity of GOD and especially the Holy Spirit.

The Holy Spirit has powers and abilities that are so multidimensional and Cosmic in nature that, in truth it, would be impossible to explain how the Holy Spirit is able to do what I am telling you. All I know is that the Holy Spirit can and will do this for you if you ask. There is no situation in life that it cannot undo or rebuild if you call upon it. There is no situation in life that it does not have the answer for. Definitely continue calling on the Ascended Masters, the Saints, the Archangels and Angels, the Elohim Masters and the Christed Extraterrestrial groups such as the Ashtar Command and the beloved Arcturians. However, do not forget to call on the Holy Spirit. The Holy Spirit is the ultimate Cosmic Master that GOD has placed inside of you to be the answer to all your challenges and lessons, and the ultimate power in the Universe to undo obstacles in every aspect of life. This applies to the physical level, the etheric level, the astral level, the mental level, and the Spiritual level. There is not one time in my life that I have called on the Holy Spirit and it has not been able to do as I requested. As long as your requests are sincere and pure, and are not negatively ego motivated, it will help you and it is literally the arm of GOD. Do an experiment and try out what I am saying and see if every word I have told you is not the truth!

With GOD's help, the help of your own Mighty I Am Presence and your own Higher Self, the Ascended Masters' help, the help of the Archangels and Angels, the help of the Elohim Masters, the help of the

Christed Extraterrestrial Races, the help of your own personal power and will, the power of your own subconscious mind which can be utilized through creative visualization and creative affirmations, and the help of GOD, Christ and the Holy Spirit, how can you fail? If you utilize in your life all of these levels of power, love, and wisdom there is no force in GOD's infinite Universe that can stop you!

There are in truth, only two voices in life; the loud, irrational, unloving, separative, fear-based voice of the negative ego and lower-self, and the "still small voice within" of unconditional love, forgiveness, grace, omnipotence, omnipresence and omniscience. As you learn to deny and quiet the negative ego mind and learn to think and feel only from your Christ/Buddha mind, which is the mind of the Holy Spirit, you will live and move and have your being in GOD's Grace, Grandeur, and Love at all times. If ever you begin to slip out of this "Holy Instant" on any level, call upon GOD, the Masters and the Holy Spirit for help, and the infinite Love, Power and Wisdom of GOD's infinite Universe will come leaping to your aid! There is no problem, challenge, or lesson on any level that GOD, the Godforce and the Holy Spirit cannot solve to bring you peace of mind.

Your job, my Beloved Readers, is to be joyously vigilant for GOD and His Kingdom against the negative ego, and to deny any thought not of GOD to enter your mind. If you do this, there is only one other voice that will hence be present, and this is the sweetest voice of all Creation. It is the Voice of GOD, also known as the Holy Spirit!

CHAPTER 30

The Incredible Importance of Organization and Making Spiritual Lists

This might seem like a strange title and/or concept for a chapter! My Beloved Readers, do not underestimate the importance of this chapter, for it holds within it a real key to inner peace and success! The first thing I do and the last thing I do every day in my life is organize! Life has become extremely complex. We have personal lives, relationships, friends, family, employees, businesses to run, Spiritual leadership responsibilities, planetary world service responsibilities, and all kinds of earthly responsibilities. We now have the Internet, faxes, e-mail, cell phones, pagers, and Websites. The world, in truth, has become a very small place. The more one moves into Spiritual Leadership, the more responsibility that will be placed on one's shoulders. As the saying goes, "Much is given and much is expected"!

Remaining right with self, right with GOD and the Masters, and right with all the different kinds of relationships, can become a complicated business. It is essential to realize that our thoughts create our reality! So, it is essential to remain extremely organized. If one does not remain organized, one is going to feel overwhelmed. I learned a little secret early on in my life, which I am sure you all have learned as well! No matter how much work I have to do or how behind I am in my work, if I just make a list of all the things I have to do "I feel better"! Since our thoughts create our reality, the act of organizing causes us to feel better! Even if I don't even do the work on any given day, if I just organize what I have to do I feel better!

I have worked out other smaller organization tools, such as circling the most important things to get done. Of course, my favorite thing of all is crossing things out as I get them done! Sometimes I use different color pens to signify really important things. I am also very big on making lists. I have my Daily Lists, and Secondary Lists, which are things to do in the future but not right now. I have my Wesak Lists. Adding to all the normal responsibilities, I have the added responsibility of not only running the Academy, but putting on a yearly Wesak Celebration event for two thousand people. I am in charge of every aspect of this event. People come from all over the world. You can imagine the details. I never feel overwhelmed, for I have a whole system of lists. Everything that needs doing just goes into its appointed list. Every morning I go over the lists and prioritize what is most important to get done that day. Then, I type out on my computer all my lists for my employees and volunteers. At the end of the day I make my new lists for the next day, and so when I am through with work I feel totally on top of things. As hot ideas come to me in the course of relaxing in the evening, I will make a quick note to add them to my various lists.

The advantage of writing things down on these lists is that I do not have to try and remember anything, so my consciousness stays free and clear to be creative and receive inspiration, guidance, and direction. It allows my consciousness to sparkle with creative ideas and sparkling potentialities. It also allows me to really keep track of details. Nothing is lost. It allows me to "Pursue Excellence" at a very refined level, which I enjoy! It also allows me to always feel on top of things, which is a very energizing feeling! It allows me not to get stressed no matter how much Spiritual leadership and planetary world service is on my plate.

I also work into this organization time for myself, if I need it. Sometimes I might need to journal about certain issues, or I might need to do some attitudinal healing or journal programming. Sometimes I need to make other types of Spiritual lists for the purpose of Spiritual or psychological healing. For example, occasionally I make a Gratitude List. A Spiritual list of my victories. A Spiritual list of why I love life! A Spiritual List of why I feel happy! Since our thoughts create our reality, you would be amazed how doing something like this gives one a shot in the arm, so to speak! I have never ever heard anyone talk about the importance of making Spiritual Lists.

One of the three most important Spiritual qualities, in my opinion, are Spiritual Purity, Clarity and Integrity, in everything one does! This cannot be achieved if one is all disorganized. Even the ability to remain in unconditional love at all times and to master one's thoughts and feelings requires a certain type of organization of the mind. If you want your outer life to be together you have to keep your mind and emotions organized and together. It is very important in life to pay attention to detail. I am amazed how many people I meet do not. They let things slide! I believe one of the absolute keys to Spiritual and worldly success is to pay attention to every thought, every word, every feeling, every piece of energy, and every deed! As the great Hermetic Law states, "As Within, So Without. As Above, So Below"! If you want your outer life to be successful your must make your inner life immaculate on every level. You must make sure your every thought only serves GOD and Christ/Buddha consciousness. You must make sure your every feeling and emotion only serves GOD and Christ/Buddha consciousness. You must make sure every use of your energy only serves GOD and

Christ/Buddha consciousness. You must make sure every physical action you make only serves GOD and Christ/Buddha Consciousness! You must make sure that every word you speak only serves GOD and Christ/Buddha consciousness! If you really want to be successful Spiritually, Psychologically, and in a Physical/Earthly sense, you must strive to be "immaculate" at all times in how you use your energies. If you make a mistake it is fine, of course, and, of course, this is going to happen. Part of being "immaculate" in all that you do is being aware of what you do, making the appropriate attitudinal adjustments, and of course forgiving and unconditionally loving yourself when you do make a mistake. This means being focused, conscious and vigilant at all times. To maintain a flawless character and immaculate nature Spiritually and psychologically takes enormous attention to detail in an inner and outer sense. Most people give in to automatic pilot, and are constantly letting the subconscious mind, their desire body and/or the negative ego take them off course!

So, I think you can see how important it is to stay inwardly and outwardly organized. Part of staying organized is developing a strong work ethic. Taking care of business! Not procrastinating! I have trained myself to do just the opposite. My tact is to do all the hardest jobs first, and the ones I do not like to do the most first, so I have the wonderful feeling of having them all done and I have the rest of the year to work on projects that I enjoy more. This takes a lot of responsibility and stress off me as well! Part of this also has to do with developing a strong "Will", and or "Personal Power"! This helps to get work done, even sometimes when you don't feel like it or are a little tired!

Every morning I get up and go to my computer and get all organized on every level (Spiritually, Psychologically, and in a Physically/Earthly sense), and then I start my day, and the organization and clarity I have provided myself allows me to work at lightening speed, and to work with the love and joy that every day should ideally be filled with!

Since our thoughts create our reality, if our mind is disorganized we are going to have disorganized feelings and emotions. If our mind is disorganized our energies are going to be a little chaotic. If our mind is disorganized our behavior is going to be a little chaotic. If our mind is disorganized our life is going to be chaotic.

One of the keys to inner peace is the ability to compartmentalize certain things in your mind!

For example, if something is bothering you, you must have the ability to put it in a compartment or on the shelf so your present moment is not interfered with. I personally find this ability to organize my Spiritual life, Psychological life, and Physical/Earthly life in balanced manner makes me much more clear and efficient in everything I do, and also allows me to be much more loving and joyous, for I feel on top of things even though I have an astronomical amount of work to do in my life and accomplish way more than the average person. The ability to be organized allows me to channel and write in a very organized manner. Most of the books I have written are all first drafts. The work just comes out organized because my consciousness is organized. This is also what has allowed me to write as many as five to seven books a year! Most people take three years to write one!

Another advantage of writing things down and keeping lists is that you don't forget. I have so many creative and channeled ideas that are constantly flowing through me, and if I didn't write them down I would forget them. This attention to detail is to take advantage of every little nuance of creative and sparkling potentiality. This attention to detail and striving to be "immaculate" in everything that one does establishes an integrity in your person. You do not fudge. You hold to your Spiritual and psychological ideals! That greatly helps in manifestation, for your entire being becomes this incredible magnet of attraction for this "Immaculate Spiritual/GOD/Christ/Buddha ideal! It allows the Superconsicous/Conscious/Subconscious to all work in perfect integration and harmony. It does not allow for victim consciousness.

When you are organized you are asserting yourself against life, instead of letting life attack you! It allows you to remain in self-mastery at all times, as well as unconditional love and Christ/Buddha consciousness.

Now I must add here, I am not suggesting that you become neurotic about this, otherwise the next chapter I write will be on the importance of learning to "flow"! Most people flow more than organize! This is why there is a need for this chapter! The interesting thing about this process of learning to become organized is that once you learn how to do it, it becomes a habit! Even though I am incredibly busy and have an enormous amount on my plate, I can organize myself some evenings and/or mornings in just five minutes or less. So I am not talking about being neurotic here. Sometimes it can take longer if there is an avalanche of work to do! What I am basically saying here is that once you get your system set up, then it kind of takes care of itself. Many people use the "organizers" you can buy in a store, or organizing software, which is fine as well. Being the maverick that I am, I developed my own little system, which I have described. Having developed a lifestyle of being a little more organized, I could go months without organizing and still feel organized within my consciousness. For I have learned how to file things away in my own mind and to keep my consciousness organized, which is essential to do, otherwise one cannot maintain a constant state of inner peace.

I would be remiss to say as well, there are also times in life to just flow! To go on vacations and to just do what you feel like doing! This does not mean, however, giving in to your lower-self and overindulging your desire body. A person who really has mastered the art of flowing remains in self-mastery and the "Tao." Spiritual, Psychological, and Physical Mastery and Attunement is maintained, and the there is no giving in to the negative ego or lower-self. This is what I call staying attuned to the Spiritual Flow, not the subconscious flow that is disconnected to Spirit.

I personally find that my ability to organize and stay on top of things is actually what allows me to flow and be spontaneous. If one is out of control and run by the negative ego and negative emotions, one cannot really trust oneself to let go and be spontaneous. It is when self-mastery has been achieved, in service of a Spiritual ideal, that one can then be free to let go and be spontaneous, and for comes out then stems from an "Integrated Psychospiritual System"!

One other very interesting thought and understanding about this process of keeping organized and making Spiritual lists is that, ironically and paradoxically, what this actually helps you to achieve is to keep a "quiet mind or not think"! This is something most people in this world and even a great many lightworkers do not know how to do. Their minds are always racing. One of the things that causes them to race is all these things that are in their mind, which if organized and written down would not bother them or cause them to have to think. So, in truth, what I am really saying here is that this little extra time to consciously think in an effective manner has the real purpose of helping you to quiet your mind and to not think. It is not good for the mind to always be racing and thinking. It is not good Spiritually, for it blocks inspiration and Spiritual guidance from coming through. It is not good mentally, for it will just cause you to become mentally fatigued and cause a mental cloudiness to come over you. It is not good emotionally, for it will not bring you inner peace, joy or bliss! It is also not good for you etherically, for it keeps the third chakra and sixth chakra overactivated and overstimulated. This can cause underactivity in other chakras. The overstimulation or understimulation of these chakras affects the under or overstimulation of the glands connected to these chakras. On a physical level, overthinking is not good, for it has a deleterious effect on the liver, which is the organ in the body that has to do with planning. Thinking also affects the kidneys, spleen, pancreas, and entire digestive system. It also affects the pituitary gland and adrenal gland. Too much thinking or the wrong type of thinking can cause adrenal exhaustion.

So, what I am really recommending here is to take this small amount of time to develop an organizational system, and then take a little time each day to organize your inner and outer life so your mind can be programmed to have a more natural state of being quiet and calm, instead of always going in a state of overwhelm, survival, or, at times, crisis.

Therefore, when I publicly speak at Wesak for two thousand people, I never have any fear whatsoever! I feel right at home, like I am talking to one person. I can be spontaneous and say whatever is on my mind on the spot and everything always seems to come out very well, because it stems out of self-mastery and an integrated psycho/spiritual/physical system. I humbly share this, not for any egotistical reasons, but to share this most profound insight, that self-mastery and an organized mental/emotional/physical system can allow you to truly be flowing and spontaneous in a most enjoyable and charismatic way! This will not take place unless what has been talked about in this chapter has been mastered and achieved first, in a balanced and integrated manner!

It is my hope and prayer this short discourse on the importance of organization and Spiritual lists in an inner and outer sense has been useful to you, and has been put into the proper perspective of appropriate yin and yang, and/or masculine/feminine balance!

CHAPTER 31

Finding Your Point of Balance

This is a most fascinating subject that I have really been looking forward to writing about. Everyone has their unique point of balance in all aspects of life. It is very important in life that everyone speaks only for themselves, and never tries to impress their point of balance on another person.

Let me begin here by giving some examples on a very foundational level, and then I will build upon this. Let us begin with your physical diet. You may love to eat broccoli and pasta and lots of salads. You may also love tofu, and like to eat bee pollen for extra energy along with yeast tablets for extra B vitamins. This all sounds wonderful. However, do not take the next step to think that your diet is how everyone should eat, even if you are a trained nutritionist. What is good for one person can be poisonous for another. In the above example, bee pollen might give another person hives, and this other person may have a yeast infection and taking yeast would be the worst thing in the world. This other person may need to cook their food rather than eat raw food. They may have an allergic reaction to tofu. I had a friend who had terrible stomach pains and it turns out she had an intolerance to tofu. There is no such thing as healthy food. Every person's body elemental is different. You may tell me that eating an orange is good for you. Well, I tell you an orange may be poisonous to other people. The same thing applies to supplements. You may take a supplement that you swear by. However, energetically another person might be completely vibrationally intolerant to that substance. Normal nutritionists, who are not tuned into energy and true communication with the body elemental, do not really know what they are talking about. Dairy products, which are good for one person, may cause an allergic reaction for another. The best way to figure out your diet is to use a pendulum and ask the body elemental what it really wants. In my experience, most foods people eat the body doesn't really want on an energetic level. The mind will tell you, oh, this is a great supplement or this is great food, but, if you really communicate with your body, I think you would often be very surprised as to its true food desires. Many people get very self-righteous about diet and lay all kind of food trips on other people, and I highly recommend lightworkers to not let the negative ego do this. Every person has his or her own unique point of balance. I was very blessed for over 25 years to work with a psychic nutritionist, who could directly communicate with the body elementals, and I was amazed at how different nutritional books and guidelines were as compared to what my body really wanted. After working with this woman for many years, I began communicating with my own body elementals in a very refined manner, and the diet that I live on most nutritionists would say is impossible. Yet, it is the perfect diet for me and gives me tons of energy, and by the grace of GOD and the Masters, I do not get sick.

There are other people in this world that actually live on light. What would a nutritionist say about that? Living on partial light is part of the transformation my body has gone through, so I do not receive very much food.

One's diet is governed by one's type of work, ray structure, astrological horoscope, spiritual development, health lessons, body type and unique nutritional needs.

This dietary nutritionist told me many stories of people with life threatening health problems that were given death sentences by the medical profession, but recovered by eating only what the body wanted. In one case, the man was only able to eat millet and one vegetable for an entire year and nothing else, and had a complete recovery. I don't recommend this diet to everyone, but for this person's unique point of balance that was what was required. For another person, a diet like this would completely poison them. Fasting might be good for one person and terrible for another. Being a vegetarian may be ideal for one person and eating meat for another person may be the right thing. Do not be self-righteous on this point and claim you can speak for every person on planet Earth. Just for the record books, the Dalai Lama eats meat because of a past case of hepatitis. I happen to be a vegetarian myself. However, I would never claim to think that I had all knowledge of the body elementals and the needs of every person on Earth.

Let us now take this concept of finding your point of balance and apply it to physical exercise. For one person, jogging might be great, for another person it is too jarring. One person might like yoga and another swimming. Some gurus and spiritual teachers do not need physical exercise because there is so much spiritual current running through their bodies. Some people get their exercise through their daily work life.

It is important to understand that GOD didn't create everybody the same. Every person has a different Monadic Ray and Soul Ray. Some people were born to be mystics and some, occultists. Some people were born to do physical work, and some people spiritual work. Some people were created by GOD to be artists, and others, scientists. For some people, reading books is very important, and for others it is not as necessary. For some people working sixteen hours a day is their point of balance. For another person working part-time is their point of balance.

It is not possible to write a book and say this is what everyone should be doing, because this would just be one person laying their trip on everyone else. Be more concerned in life with finding your own point of balance. There are many people in this world who are run by the negative ego and are very self-righteous, and go around telling people how everyone should follow their point of balance. This is illusion, and nothing more than a massive ego trip. Be vigilant against the negative ego if it ever tries to do this.

People's points of balance are greatly affected by their physical health or lack of it. A person's point of balance is also enormously affected by their spiritual development. The more advanced you become spiritually, often the more unconventional some of your habits may become.

Also, what must be factored in here is that people's points of balance are constantly changing. For example, I used to be a long distance runner, and in the current phase of my life this would be an enormous waste of time and take me away from all service work I am doing. What is good one moment, 10 years later can be exactly the opposite. This reminds me of the saying, "One man's meat is another man's poison."

Another example of this might be a person who is having physical health lessons. The self-righteous egotistical person will say that this person is doing something wrong or they would not be feeling this way. What this self-righteous, egotistical person does not realize is that the spiritual person may be on an extremely accelerated ascension path, and the physical health lesson may be nothing more than the bodies adjusting to an extremely accelerated ascension process!

For some people, having an active social life is their point of balance, and for another person it may be living in the Himalayas in a Buddhist monastery.

This issue of finding your own point of balance as your Mighty I Am Presence, Higher Self, and the Holy Spirit guide you to find is extremely important. I guide you to follow the beat of your own drum, so to speak. Do not compare yourself with others, but rather trust your own inner guidance. Most of all do not let your negative ego tell you that the point of balance you have found for yourself is the point of balance everyone else should follow.

Every person is at a different state of evolution, which also greatly affects one's point of balance. This is why it is often dangerous to make hard and fast rules. The purpose of this chapter is to encourage each of you to fully trust your own inner guidance and find your own point of balance in every aspect of your life. This chapter has also been written to help lightworkers and people of the Earth to be more compassionate and accepting of other people, and to not judge others so quickly until you have walked in their moccasins.

May each one of us find our own point of balance in every aspect of our lives, and learn to love and enjoy the diverse colors and kinds of flowers in the different gardens of the Earth.

CHAPTER 32

The Importance of Occasional Spiritual, Mental, and Emotional Body Maintenance and Upgrades

I love all the different tools and techniques I have written about in my books that I have come up with myself in the process of my own personal transformation and work with clients. As the saying goes, "Necessity is the mother of invention"! I have always been one to follow the beat of my own drum, so to speak, and never followed any kind of conventional path! I use what I find works and am always coming up with methods and tools that help in this process. The insights and tools I share in this chapter are another series of these tools and techniques.

Every once in a while I feel a need for what I call a "Spiritual, Mental, Emotional and Energy Body Maintenance and Upgrade"! It is sometimes after a grueling service work period or busy time in my life, where lots of lessons were going on. It is sometimes after having to deal with a few or a lot of unclear people and/or my own thinking and feeling to be raised to a higher level. I have come up with two ways for doing this upgrade and both work equally well and have slightly different effects but in a similar manner!

The first way I do this is to just start writing in a journal or typing on my computer in a type of free-flowing manner. I will start typing, and basically list as I am talking to myself all the reasons why I feel good! I will start with things that are going on this day or the previous day that I feel good about! Then I will go over all the different areas of my life. I will just write in this free-flowing manner, very fast, why I am feeling good Spiritually. Why I am feeling good mentally and emotionally! Why I am feeling good physically! Why I am feeling good about my service work and business. I will write why I feel good financially! I will write why I am feeling good about my relationships! I will do kind of a free-flow overview of every aspect of my life! If I don't feel good about a certain area, I will keep writing about it until I come up with a type of battle plan and/or perspective to make the area feel good! If there are any points of unclarity or confusion, I will make sure I am clear on them. I will also use this time to get organized. I usually do the organization part first, before I begin the free flow writing so I feel really organized as I begin!

My Beloved Readers, I would highly recommend trying this. I sometimes do this if I am a little tired, and it also has the effect of energizing me and get-ting my chakras spinning. This is also what I do to stimulate my enthusiasm a little bit if it is not 100% full force! I actually do this quite often, sometimes just for a little while. Usually it is at the very beginning of my day, and sometimes at the very end of the day. It is also a way to tap back into myself! It is a little bit like positive self-talk or even a little pep talk to myself! It is a time to get things in perspective if anything is out of perspective. Perspective is one of the absolute keys to effective living, for our thoughts create our feelings, emotions, and reality! This simple little process keeps me in a state of personal power, unconditional love, inner peace, enthusiasm and joy all the time. It sparks a lot of creativity! I have done this enough times that this has become my "baseline," and anything else but this does not feel right and I immediately can do this process and it will always bring me back to it. Somehow, the process of writing or typing helps one focalize or concentrate better. Also, the act of writing this down has a greater effect of programming the subconscious mind!

The second tool I use that has a very similar effect but is slightly different in structure is that I have a Spiritual List of all the reasons why I feel good about my life and myself! It is a typed list of about twenty pages of all the reasons, on a Spiritual, mental, emotional, physical, earthly, professional, business, social, and every other level one could think of, why I really feel good about myself and my life! Every once in a while when I feel the need, I either read over the list or type the list over! Or consolidate the list to the main reasons on it. This has the most unbelievable affect of raising one's feelings and emotions. The mind and feelings are sometimes a funny thing. A person could have a million reasons why they are the happiest man or woman on Earth, but over time because of the business of life or certain earthly lessons, the mind begins to forget. Doing this process reminds me metaphorically like taking a plug and sticking it back into my Spiritual socket. It reminds me of incredible things that I know or think about myself, and/or that have happened in my life, and I just go over the list and remind myself of them. By the time I am done with this process, which can actually be done very quickly, I am the happiest most grateful man on Earth. I feel that doing this also has the effect of cleaning my aura. For, my entire aura becomes filled with all these positive thoughts and feelings that I have just reminded myself about. It is like the saying goes, "Is the glass of water half empty or half full?" It is all how you look at it. Part of this process also may involve listing all the things you have to be grateful for!

I sometimes look at doing these processes as taking my inner car in for a 30,000-mile tune-up, or 50,000-mile tune-up, or 70,000-mile tune-up. Just as a car needs maintenance occasionally, so do your Spiritual, Mental, Emotional, Etheric and Physical vehicles! The process of using both of these Spiritual tools goes over all the vehicles in all the bodies and makes sure they are all running on high octane Spiritual fuel, and makes sure everything is oiled, greased, washed, purified and cleansed properly. If any part of my car or vehicle is not working properly, I work with my attitudes, thoughts, and even prayers, as part of this process, to GOD and the Masters, to get it in perspective so I am asserting myself towards self and life and self and life are not victimizing me! When I am done with one or both of these Spiritual tools, I feel like a new man and completely transformed! Almost born again, for I have, in a sense, reaffirmed my Godself on every level! My vehicles are singing with love and joy and are filled with light and love and backed with 100% personal power and the full power of GOD and the Godforce! I feel totally Spiritually and Psychologically resurrected by the power of my own thoughts, feelings, affirmations and prayers! No matter what is going on with me and what Spiritual tests or lessons I am about to face, I feel 100% totally and completely ready to handle them! I feel filled with joy and sparkling with the potentialities. Sometimes in the free-flow writing I also write about the things I am looking forward to doing and working on! This adds even more to the positive energy field, for the mind overflows and sparkles with all the creative potentialities life holds! I have just given myself the supreme overall affirmation process and pep talk to lead me to Spiritual victory in whatever I am currently focusing on at this time! My Beloved Readers, I think you are now getting a total understanding and feeling for how the process works!

I cannot emphasize enough how doing this Spiritual list process, and the other more free-flowing one, can help you feel in almost a Spiritual ecstatic state all the time! I have programmed myself over time for this to be my natural state! This is why I never feel Spiritually weary in life and why I never seem to feel Spiritually fatigued! I keep my attitude and emotional body in this extremely positive Spiritually plugged-in state! At this stage of my life, I don't even need to do these things very often, and actually don't for it has become a natural part of me! Earlier in my life, when I did not have the level of self-mastery and evenmindedness to the degree I have now, I needed to do these things more. This is the ideal, to make this a Spiritual habit! It is nice to know, however, in the back of my mind, no matter what happens in life, that I can always go back and do these things, and I know that no matter what is going on in my life I can work with myself in this manner. I always get back on the up and up, so to speak, and feel unbelievably great by just working with my attitudes, feelings and Spiritual victory list.

My Beloved Readers, trust me, try this, you will be absolutely amazed at how incredibly effective these Spiritual, and Psychological tools are!

CHAPTER 33

Walking Through Life in Other People's Moccasins

One of the most important lessons in the process of transcending negative ego/fear-based thinking is the ability to transcend the selfishness, self-centered-ness and narcissism of the negative ego separative mind. The negative ego mind is only concerned with self. It sees itself as just a physical body completely separate from GOD, life and all other people. It sees itself at war and competition with other people. The negative ego lives in a reality of being better than everyone else or worse then everyone else. It is hence prone to jealousy, comparison, judgement, attack thoughts, and conditional love.

Now, the Spiritual/Christ/Buddha consciousness is just the opposite. It sees you as being a Son or Daughter of GOD or Spirit, inhabiting or incarnating into a physical body for the purpose of Spiritual growth and service in this planetary mystery school called Earth. Recognizing your identity as Spirit and not just a body, the Spiritual/Christ/Buddha Mind recognizes that, in truth, you are one with GOD, one with your Brothers and Sisters, and one with all Creation! It recognizes that you are in a process of evolution, fully realizing this truth at a Planetary level right now, and that in time you will evolve through the Solar, Galactic, Universal, Multi-Universal and Cosmic realities until you fully Realize the truth. It is fully recognized, however, that although you have not fully realized this oneness yet, it remains an inherent truth of your being! You are one with GOD, your Brothers and Sisters, and all Creation!

The negative ego sees you just as a physical body that will die, and Spiritual/Christ/Buddha consciousness sees you as an eternal, immortal spirit living in your current physical body of which you have had many this most probably being your last one!

Almost everything in this society trains us to see life through the personality and negative ego, rather than the Spiritual/Christ/Buddha consciousness and the Soul or Mighty I Am Presence. Our training from our parents teaches us this, school teaches us this, and our peers, television, magazines, movies, psychologists, counselors, and, to a certain extent, even religions all teach us a great deal of negative ego thinking. Unfortunately, so does the entire field of psychology, and a great many aspects of the New Age Movement.

The process of undoing all this negative ego/fear-based thinking and changing it to the Spiritual/Christ/Buddha thinking is one of the hardest and most difficult aspects of the Spiritual path. As Sai Baba says, the definition of GOD is, "GOD equals man minus ego"! The negative ego pervades how we are trained to respond emotionally and act physically. It is the model by which all our heroes and heroines are based upon. Our entire society is based on negative ego structures. Our economy is based on competition and dog-eat-dog mentality. Our educational systems are devoid of Spirituality and Soul. So are our prison systems, the media, the legal system, the political system, and the list goes on. The most difficult area to cleanse is our motivations. Many people think they are being Spiritual. However, if you examine their true motivations at the very core of their being they are still of the negative ego. Much of the channeling in the New Age movement is filled with negative ego and glamour. How could it not be, when the people doing the channeling have not yet purified and cleansed themselves of negative ego in their own consciousness? This is not a judgement, just a simple statement of truth. It is impossible to channel clearly if one's consciousness is not clear. The same applies to teaching, healing, science, clairvoyance, telepathy, clairaudience, psychic readings, or any other form of service. This is why learning to cleanse, undo, and purify one's consciousness of negative ego thinking and feeling is one of the most important, if not the most important of all, Spiritual practices of the Spiritual path. Unfortunately, it is probably also the least understood. It is quite complicated, and although the negative ego thought system is quite delusionary, illusionary, and insane, do not underestimate its ability to deceive, seduce, tempt, and delude. Its original premise is inaccurate, so everything that comes after it is inaccurate as well. Although this is the case, it uses the full power and creativity of the mind to support its delusionary and illusionary belief system. Since our thoughts create our reality and our thoughts cause and create our feelings, emotions, behavior, energy and what we attract and magnetize into our lives, you can see the havoc it can cause. All channeling, psychic abilities, Spiritual teaching, healing, and science is filtered through our conscious and subconscious minds before it comes out. You can see why Religion and the New Age movement are so filled with glamour, illusion, and maya as well! You can also see why so many lightworkers are taking a tumble down the Spiritual Mountain and/or are falling from grace. You can also see why so many forms of psychology and Spiritual study are fragmented and not integrated and just slivers of the truth, which their proponents think are the whole truth.

It is for these reasons and many more that this book has been written. This book has been written in conjunction with my other books *Soul Psychology, How To Clear The Negative Ego*, and *Integrated Ascension*, to take an in-depth look at all the intricacies of Spiritual psychology and the differences between Spiritual/Christ/Buddha thinking and negative ego/fear-based thinking, in order to purify, cleanse and undo this mental and emotional illusionary thought system from our being!

Now, everything written in this chapter so far has been the foundation for that which I wish to speak about next, which is the title for this chapter, "Seeing Life Through Other People's Moccasins"! One of the most important states of consciousness and/or Spiritual abilities to develop in life is to transcend this inherent selfishness and self-centeredness of the negative ego, and to be able to see life through the eyes and heart of another person! The most appropriate Spiritual quality or qualities that might describe this are "Compassion" and/or "Empathy." I am not talking here about going to the other extreme and taking on another person's pain, for that does not serve them or you. I am, however, speaking of having compassion for another person's consciousness, reality, and sometimes pain and suffering. To truly see life through another person's moccasins, one first must truly love and care about other people. This is not hard when you recognize that each person you meet, in truth, is an incarnation of GOD. Each person you meet is a God being! Each person you meet in truth is the Christ and the Buddha, even if they have not fully realized it yet or even if they do not know it yet. This is the truth of their being! Every animal, plant, and mineral is an incarnation of GOD as well. Every person is literally our Spiritual Brother and Sister in a much greater Spiritual family. Every person we meet is a fellow Son and Daughter of GOD. Hence, every person we meet is a "Holy Encounter"! Christ meeting Christ! Buddha meeting Buddha! Spiritual Being meeting Spiritual Being! God meeting God! Since, in truth, we are one with all our Brothers and Sisters and all Creation, another person's suffering is, in truth, our own suffering! For, in truth, there are not many separate beings, there is only one being and that is GOD. We all share one identity in GOD!

If your right hand were sore, would your left hand say I don't care? If your stomach is upset, does your spleen say who cares I am out for myself? Is a cell in your leg in competition with a cell in your arm? This, my Beloved Readers, is how absurd it is for all people to not get along and not care about each other. We all are one Being and one body. It is just a matter of what set of glasses you are wearing. Are you seeing life through the negative ego's glasses, or are you seeing life through God's glasses?

For this reason, take time to really get out of your self when communicating with others and to really "listen" to what they have to say. Put aside all the negative ego's agendas and selfish concerns. Fully remember that this is God you are speaking to. This is a "Holy Instant and Opportunity" to really get to know, understand and feel into another God being and fellow Brother and Sister in Spirit/Christ/Buddha. Fully remember at all times that you are not working and serving just for your self, you are working and serving for GOD. The reason you are doing this is that this is who you really are. Why just serve the illusionary fence that is your physical body, when that is not really who you really are? We all are so much more than that. In truth, we are all Creation. We are and have everything. We are literally one with GOD! The law of the mind, however, is that our thoughts create our reality. So if we think we are just a physical body, living in an infinitely small reality, this is not true, but you will live in the delusion of your own thought creation. You will live in your own negative hypnosis. You can wake-up any moment you chose to. It is just a matter of "changing your perspective"! As the saying goes, "Change your perspective and you change your life"! "As a man or woman thinketh so are they"! "You are what you think"! As *A Course in Miracles* says in its introduction, "Nothing real can be threatened, nothing unreal exists, herein lies the Peace of GOD"! So, all one's faulty thinking has not changed the truth of your being. It is just a matter of waking-up from a bad dream. You do not blame yourself when you wake-up from a bad dream at night. In the same manner, you can just wake-up from the bad dream you sometimes fall into in a waking state, which is caused by thinking with your negative ego mind instead of your Spiritual/Christ/Buddha mind. It is really that simple. The truth has always been the same. That will never change. It is just a matter of when your thinking will align with this truth.

Once you do this, then truly listening and caring for your Brother and Sisters is not just an act of charity, or a sacrifice your negative ego is willing to make. It is a sincere, genuine caring and interest that comes from the depth of your being!

Once this initial step is made, then truly listen to what your Brother and/or Sister has to say, free from projecting onto them all your beliefs and your personal reality. Take the interest and time to truly hear and feel what they have to say. Have compassion, for they are a part of you and you are a part of them. You are both a part of GOD talking to each other. God is talking to God! Take the time to really hear and understand how this part of God experiences reality. You must remember that GOD created every person differently. Each person has a different ray structure, mission, purpose, astrological configuration, numerology set up, past life history, earthly background, cultural and religious background, Spiritual line of evolution, Spiritual background and GOD structure. By truly putting your feet in their moccasins you will truly learn about GOD and hence you will learn about yourself. We are all inherently the same, but because we each have a different mission and purpose in GOD's infinite universe there are slight configuration differences. This is why it is so important to not expect everyone to be exactly like you. Just as you don't expect a rose to be like a daisy. Flowers are all inherently the same, yet it is so wonderful to explore, sense and experience the beauty and profundity of each one. By truly learning to see life through another person's moccasins, you will learn much about GOD and much about Self and they will learn much about you! Take time to experience reality as they see it, not as your negative ego wants you to see it. This is not to say that you can't share your thoughts, feelings, ideas, suggestions and even guidance and direction. I am just saying do it free of the negative ego attachment, projection and selfishness that feels a need to make everyone be exactly like your self. Fully listen and explore their entire reality to make sure that you are not inflicting your point of balance on the person you are dealing with. So many people in Religion, the New Age movement, or people in general give "pat answers"! We have all heard the saying, "A little knowledge is a dangerous thing"! People are often like an evening newscast, laying out Spiritual sound bites that they have read in a book or heard in a workshop that have no relationship to what is really going on. People make quick judgments, or Spiritual discernments that 90% of the time have nothing to do with what the other person is going through, but the self-righteous negative ego thinks it does for they read it in some Spiritual book or heard it from some channeling, or at a workshop. Some of the most insensitive, self-righteous, negative ego-run people I know are actually so-called religious and/or New Age people. They are often more opinionated and self-righteous with their New Age beliefs than the average person you might meet on the street! We all know people like this! We are all bigger than this. Let us all not only be aware of this, but also be vigilant against the much subtler forms of negative ego projections, advice, judgements and even Spiritual discernment. Just because you call it Spiritual discernment instead of judgement, or share it in a loving way, doesn't make it accurate. As you can see, we are getting into a more in-depth study of Spiritual psychology here. Before giving advice, fully listen to what the person has to say. We know how complicated the physical body is. There can be a thousand different reasons why a person has a headache or sore throat or any other given symptom. Deluded lightworkers go around giving pat answers like there is only one reason for any symptom. All it is showing is how run by the negative ego they are. The same is true of psychological issues, and Spiritual issues. The Spiritual, Psychological, Physical, and Earthly issues of life are all extremely complex. Before giving advice, suggestions, guidance and direction, truly listen to the complexity of the infinite factors that make up the profundity of this glorious God Being you speak and communicate with. Avoid the negative ego's need to be a know-it-all, or to have all the answers. What every person needs most of all is love! Knowing that someone is truly willing to take the time to listen and truly genuinely care! Knowing the complexity of life on all these levels, be very Spiritually discerning about the advice you give. Make sure you truly understand everything that is going on. The negative ego is often more concerned with giving the answer before it has even really heard the problem. The negative ego doesn't care, for it doesn't inherently care about the person, it just cares about hearing what it has to say and making everyone like itself. We are all bigger than this.

In conclusion and summary, take the time to fully get to know on every level this precious fellow God Being that GOD has brought before you this day. By doing so in a way and manner that transcends negative ego consciousness and fully embraces Spiritual/Christ/Buddha consciousness, it is not only the other person who will be Blessed but you as well will be Blessed. For you will learn much about the nature of GOD and the nature of your Self, for all is One!

CHAPTER 34

The Seven Rays and Chakras and the Importance of Making Decisions from an Integrated Perspective

One of the most important aspects of becoming a Self-Realized Being and being successful in all areas of one's life deals with the process of making decisions. The ideal is to make all your decisions from a full spectrum prism perspective integrating all seven rays. A great many lightworkers have not been trained in this work, and often tend to emphasize one ray over another, which can skew or cause an imbalance in their decision making process. Let me explain here what I mean.

Although every person has one specific ray that characterizes their Monad, Soul, personality, mind, emotions and physical body; the true ideal is to become a master of all the rays. A person may have a different ray structure for each of their bodies, but one should not strive to only embody one's ray structure. One should strive to be a master of all seven rays.

If a person overemphasizes the First Ray then the decisions they make will be based on achieving power and political gain. There is nothing wrong with this as long as this serves Spiritual power and political concerns, not negative ego power and political gain. We see the corruption of this in our Government, with many political leaders making decisions for power and politics to serve the negative ego and not the Spirit.

If someone is overly identified with the Second Ray, which is love/wisdom, they may make all their decisions to serve love and harmony but be unable to integrate the proper balance of personal power, and consider the political implications of the decisions they are making. The word "political" here is not a negative word. In our government and society it has become a negative word because of how much political corruption and negative ego usage of the First Ray there is. A positive Spiritual use of a political decision might be, for example, having a party and inviting a certain family member to keep the peace in the family, for if you did not a big emotional explosion would take place. Intuiting this in advance, you make a political decision to take this action, which in the bigger picture is a much better move even though your personal feeling in the moment might be that you do not have a preference for this. Second Ray overidentification may bring someone to making decisions only out of how they feel, rather than out of their intuition or mind. The ideal is to integrate all three. All decisions should, in truth, integrate all seven rays to come to a balanced perspective.

The first person might make their decision out of power and political rightness but may not make it out of unconditional love and/or achieving oneness and harmony. The person who is overidentified with the Third Ray will make their decisions out of "Active Intelligence" which is out of a mental place that considers the physical action. For example, they make a decision not just out of the feeling of being Spiritual, but out of how this Spiritual feeling translates into actually physically helping self and others. The Second Ray person might only consider the feeling of love and not how this love translates to physical service. I am again reminded of Sai Baba's famous quote, "Hands that help are Holier than lips that pray"! The Third Ray is also concerned with business. So the decision making process would consider, how does this decision affect my business? The Second Ray person would be more concerned about how this affects their Spiritual education and the Spiritual education of others. The First Ray person only sees the political implications.

Are you beginning to see that each of these are like "lenses" we see through?

The Fourth Ray person is interested in beauty and harmony. All decisions will be made out of more artistic and aesthetic concerns. Here we have the artist and musician. They are not concerned with power or politics. They may not even be concerned with love/wisdom and active intelligence. They see through the lens of artistry and aesthetics. You can see why many artists have a difficult time making it in the world. They are not integrated in their decision making with the other rays.

The Fifth Ray focuses on Spiritual science. So this type of person will look at the decision making process through the lens of a scientist. Hopefully, a Spiritual scientist and not just a materialistic one. The danger here is also that if the other odd-numbered rays are integrated, the decision may be too rational and not include the Second Ray heart, the Fourth Ray artistic concerns or the Sixth Ray devotion.

The sixth ray is devotion and idealism. All the rays have Spiritual and negative ego usage or application. Devotion and idealism is a beautiful thing if applied Spiritually and in a balanced way. However, if someone is too devotional and idealistic this can be a limiting lens as can all the rays. Their decisions become focused on devotion to a Spiritual teacher, guru, or ideal. If this ideal is not integrated and balanced, you can see the problems it can cause.

The Seventh Ray Person is focused on ceremonial order and magic, freedom, transmutation, alchemy and economics. For example, the Seventh Ray person may make their decisions out of a desire for freedom, but may miss the power, love, active intelligence, artistic, scientific and devotional concerns.

So you see, my friends, from this very simple discussion, how all decision making must consider all seven lenses in an integrated and balanced fashion to make sure you are making the right decisions. This is how GOD and the Masters make decisions! This is called decision making from a full spectrum prism perspective. Karma and/or wrong decisions are often made because the person is unconsciously seeing through one or two Ray lenses and doesn't realize it. This occurs extremely often in life among most people, including lightworkers and is not a judgement of any kind. It is just a good lesson to examine right now to not make decisions too impulsively and to make sure you are embodying a "Seven Ray Decision Making Process"!

Now, to add to this a little more, people make decisions out of overidentification with their chakras. A person overidentified with their First Chakra will make their decisions out of survival and/or fear. If they are underidentified, they make decisions because of a lack of groundedness, or lack of connection to Mother Earth. The Second Chakra person may make decisions out of sexual or overemotional reactions or responses. Or they may make decision out of a lack of emotional response if underidentified with this chakra.

The Third Chakra-identified person may make their decision out of, again, personal power or a mental response, or lack thereof. The Fourth Chakra-identified person may make their decision out of love, but, we all know there are different types of love. Is it a Spiritual and integrated love? If not, we have all heard of the book, *Women Who Love Too Much*. Perhaps they are too Fourth Chakra-identified and too Second Ray, which causes imbalanced decision making. If the person is too Fifth Chakra-identified, the decision process might be based on a desire for communication. Have you ever heard of people who process and communicate too much in an almost obsessive manner? Under-identification can cause one to make decisions based on avoidance of proper communication.

The person overidentified with the Sixth Ray may, again, make decisions too much out of a mental focus not considering the Earth, emotional concerns, power concerns, heart concerns, communication concerns, or Transcendent concerns. Underidentification will cause the reverse to take place.

The Seventh chakra is the center of truly transcendent and religious concerns. This is beautiful, but again, so are Earth, survival, emotions, mind, heart, communication, and integration. All must being considered.

So, my Beloved Readers, I think you can see that decision making is a tricky business. In truth one must trust one's intuition, one's heart, one's mind, one's feelings, one's instincts and one's physical body to come up with the proper decision. One must do this in an integrated and balanced manner.

If your Spiritual practice is astrology, then all the houses of the horoscope must be considered, for each is a lens and can be over or underidentified! The same can be said of the Tree of Life! Are you over or underidentified with one Sephiroth over another? Or are you integrated and balanced and seeing life from the full Cosmic Tree of Life? Are you making decisions from just a Planetary lens, or a Solar, Galactic, Universal, Multiuniversal and Cosmic Perspective?

Are you making decisions out of all the 12 major Archetypes, or just seeing life through one or two? Are you seeing life through all the cards of the Tarot Deck, or from a limited and fragmented perspective?

My Beloved Readers, are you getting a sense now of the Full Spectrum Perspective that GOD and the Masters make decisions out of? This is really not that complicated, once you develop Spiritual mastery in an integrated manner. Then the decision making process can occur automatically and very quickly. This chapter has been written to make sure you have done your Spiritual and psychological homework to develop yourself in these different areas, so that every time you make a decision, automatically the full integration of your entire being is being brought into the process. It is also to ensure that you do not have any blind spots, or over or underidentification in your Spiritual philosophy and psychology! Once you become an Integrated Spiritual Master you will be able to trust your intuition, heart, mind, feelings, instincts and physical body, for they will all be working in an integrated and balanced fashion, and they will give you instantaneous and accurate guidance. This will be true as long as you also have done your Spiritual and psychological homework to release all negative ego/fear-based thinking and feeling and to only think and feel from your Spiritual/Christ/Buddha mind and perspective. As Sai Baba says, the definition of GOD is, "GOD equals man minus ego"!

CHAPTER 35

How to Overcome Spiritual, Mental, Emotional and Physical Fatigue

One of the lessons a great many people and lightworkers are dealing with is Spiritual, Mental, Emotional and Physical fatigue. My inner guidance has asked me to write a chapter on this subject to help people and lightworkers remain highly energized on all levels, at all times. I will begin here by explaining what causes these levels of fatigue, and what lightworkers can do to reverse this process and have it never return.

The number one reason why people feel fatigued is not from a physical level, it is from a psychological level. The number one reason for fatigue is that most people, and that includes lightworkers, do not fully own their personal power at all times. When you don't own your personal power at full strength, it drains your energy battery.

The second reason is that people are not fully demonstrating self-mastery over their mind and emotions, which causes them to be victims of themselves and of life instead of Masters and causes of their reality.

This completely drains one's energy battery. Instead of mastering life, life beats down the individual.

The third reason people get exhausted is they don't love themselves and forgive themselves for their mistakes.

The fourth reason people get exhausted and fatigued is they think too much with their negative ego mind instead of interpreting life from their Christ/Buddha mind. This completely debilitates one's energy system because the mind has too many negative thoughts, and hence creates and builds too many negative feelings and emotions.

All these aforementioned psychological lessons cause one to not be right with self and right with GOD. This causes untold numbers of conflicts and imbalances in relationships, which again totally drains the energy body.

All the negative thoughts and emotions also debilitate the physical organs and glandular system, which creates even more fatigue.

The fifth reason why people get fatigued is they do not psychospiritually protect themselves properly each morning to start their day. This causes them to be victimized by other people's negative energy and to be hypnotized by other people's negative suggestions. It also allows other people to become the computer programmers of their emotional life. This is incredibly exhausting and debilitating to the energy body.

The sixth reason people get fatigued is they do not pray enough. They do not realize the incredible powers that GOD, Christ, the Holy Spirit, the Ascended Masters, Archangels and Angels, Elohim Masters, and Christed Extraterrestrials can bring to bear on a daily basis. They get fatigued because they try to create life themselves, instead of co-creating life with GOD and the Masters. Each person must cause their own reality, but part of doing this effectively is constantly calling on GOD and the Masters for help in everything.

The seventh reason people get fatigued is they don't do enough positive affirmations and visualizations along with attitudinal healing. Every time something doesn't go your way, one should always do a prayer, affirmation, visualization, or attitude adjustment to bring that situation back to the perfected state. This way, one's consciousness always remains in a state of healing the situation in an assertive manner, which keeps one incredibly energized.

The eighth reason people become fatigued is that they allow themselves to be run too much by the emotional body, instead of recognizing that one's thoughts create one's emotions. Once one sees and demonstrates this self-mastery over the emotional body by learning to cause and create only positive Christ/Buddha emotions, they will become much more energized. This incredibly energizes the etheric and/or energy body as well as the subconscious mind.

The ninth reason why people get fatigued deals with the physical level. A great many people use too many artificial stimulants for energy. In the short term this helps. However, in the long term it exhausts the physical body. Artificial stimulants should be used in emergencies only, not on a regular basis. People also do not eat a good diet with enough vegetables and protein. This, over time, will deplete the physical body chemically and nutritionally.

The tenth reason for fatigue is people do not get enough physical exercise on a regular basis, which makes the body very sluggish. They also do not get enough fresh air and sunshine. People must also be sure to get enough sleep and not overwork or underwork. They must also take time for play and recreation.

The eleventh reason why people get fatigued is they have not found their Spiritual service work, puzzle piece, and Spiritual mission. Too many people work at jobs that do not have meaning for them and/or they do not have the proper attitude of service at that job. When one takes the attitude of Spiritual service in whatever job they are doing in life, then work becomes joy. As the Master Jesus said, "True pleasure is serving GOD." I personally can't wait to get up every morning. It doesn't matter what kind of work I have to do. To me work is incredibly enjoyable. If someone gave me a billion dollars I would be doing the exact same thing. When one finds one's Spiritual mission and service work, then every thought, word, and deed becomes energized because you are doing it to serve GOD and one's fellow Sons and Daughters of GOD.

The twelfth reason people get fatigued is another physical one. People eat too much food. Too many people live to eat instead of eating to live. Most people do not need half the food they are eating. The body does not require seven course meals. The improper combining of foods and eating too much drains one's energy and makes one tired.

The thirteenth reason people don't have as much energy as they want is that they do not fast often enough. Some kind of fast once a week or once a month for one to three days will do wonders for the body's energy level.

The fourteenth reason people do not have enough energy is they do not drink enough water. The drinking of water will keep your body clean and free of toxins.

The fifteenth reason people do not have as much energy as they would like is that they do not spend enough time in nature and connecting with the Earth Mother. Enormous sustenance and energy can be acquired from remaining grounded and connected and attuned to the Earth. It must be understood that energy can be gained from the Earth, from a proper psychology, and from Spiritual levels. It is essential to take advantage of all three. If any one is rejected or disconnected, it will have a short circuiting effect on the other levels.

This is why I call the sixteenth key to becoming more energized "Integrated Ascension." It is essential on your Spiritual path to integrate Spirit in a balanced manner in all four bodies. The doing of this will have a very energizing effect on your entire system.

The seventeenth key to energizing your system is to not eat too much sugar, junk food, processed food and food with too many chemicals and preservatives. The doing of this just fills the body with too many adverse chemicals and toxins. Sugar on occasion is fine, but too much will toxify the body and facilitate the growth of bacteria and viruses, which are depleting to the immune system and the body's energy system.

The eighteenth key to becoming more energized is to not be a workaholic. This is because pushing yourself too hard will, over time, exhaust your adrenal glands. The adrenals will then be pulling energy from the other glands and organs.

The nineteenth key to energizing your system is stopping your bad habits such as smoking, too much alcohol, and other lower-self addictions. These over time can drain the body of energy.

The twentieth key to energizing your system is to cultivate the psychospiritual quality of enthusiasm. One should ideally be enthusiastic at all times. This is the use of personal power with the emotional body engaged. Your feelings and emotions lie within the subconscious mind, which is the real storehouse of energy within your being. When you own your personal power with feeling and enthusiasm, this activates the subconscious storehouse of energy.

The twenty-first key is to be sure to breathe. Most people do not breathe enough. They take breathing for granted, hence they do not breath deeply enough. When you breathe in fresh air, you are breathing in Prana and Vital Force. This Prana and Vital Force is then stored in the etheric body for later use. This is also why aerobic exercise is essential. Breathing also allows more oxygen into the cells, organs, and glands, as well as the blood stream.

The twenty-second key to having more energy is to supplement your diet with extra, natural food sources, vitamins and minerals. I am not going to list all the possible supplements one can use, for I leave that up to your own intuition and personal knowledge. This is essential in our society because of all the pesticide use and low grade food we eat, and because of a lack of relationship to the Nature Spirits, Nature Devas, and Elemental Kingdom. If we worked with these kingdoms more, our food and vibrational frequency would be at a much higher level. This is why nutritional supplementation is a good idea for most people.

The twenty-third key to energizing your system is to always be optimistic and never be pessimistic. Pessimistic thoughts and feelings will deplete your energy. Optimistic thoughts and feelings will energize your system. Most people do not realize the incredible effect our attitude and feelings have on our energy system.

The twenty-fourth key to energizing your system is to ask GOD, Christ, the Holy Spirit, your Higher Self, your Mighty I Am Presence, the Ascended Masters, Archangels and Angels, Elohim Masters, and Christed Extraterrestrials for more energy. It sounds simple, but it really is that easy. The key to life is asking. "Ask and you shall receive." Ask for more energy and GOD and the Masters will give you more energy. Why rely on artificial stimulants when you can rely on GOD, the Masters, your personal power, your positive attitude, the power of your subconscious mind, the laws of the physical body, the Earth, and the Earth Mother, to energize you? You can even ask the Earth Mother to give you energy through your feet chakras so you will be receiving energy from Spirit and the Earth, and you will be creating it yourself through your personal power, self-mastery, and causal mental attitude.

The twenty-fifth key to energizing your system is to remain focused on your path of ascension and God Realization at all times. Keep your attention always focused on GOD and your Higher Self. Never allow yourself to give in to your lower-self desire. If you do, just forgive yourself, learn the lesson, move forward, and do not look back. The higher and more advanced you become in your initiation level and path of ascension, the more light you will carry in your Light Body, which of course, is more energizing. The higher your initiation level, the more electrical frequency you will hold and the more energized your system will become. The higher your level of initiation the more you will fully embody your Mighty I Am Presence, which is also incredibly energizing. If you demonstrate your Spiritual path in an integrated and balanced way, your entire 12 body system will become an absolute "Lightening Rod" of energy on a Spiritual, Psychological, and Physical/Earthly level.

The twenty-sixth key to energizing your system is to not overindulge in sex, but do not necessarily underindulge either. This is not to say that you need sex for energy, for the path of celibacy can actually build energy and build what is called in the East "Ojas." This is sexual energy that is brought up the Chakra Column to build Brain Illumination. This might be called Brain Orgasm! I bring up not underindulging in sex only because sexual involvement does not have to be energetically depleting if done properly. If done too much or with lack of love, it can be. It can also be depleting if done with the wrong people. So it is not sex, it is how sexual energy is used. Tantric sexuality can also be incredibly energizing.

The twenty-seventh key to energizing your system is to hang around people and form friendships with people who are energizing. Also be sure to never give your power to others, and to be unconditionally loving towards others at all times!

The final key to be energized at all times is to, in every situation of life and every moment of life in thought, word, and deed, always choose GOD instead of ego. Every moment of our life we are confronted with this choice. It occurs with every thought we think, every feeling we create, every action we take. Every time you choose GOD you will become reenergized. Every time you choose the ego, your energy will drop a bit. The nice thing about this process is that everything is forgiven and everything is a lesson, so in the next moment you can always rechoose GOD again!

CHAPTER 36

Star Wars:
A Modern Day Spiritual Paradigm

One of the most popular series of movies in the history of the film industry has been the Star Wars movies by George Lucas. One might ask what it is about these movies that has caught the imagination and spirit of so many movie goers? The special effects are certainly wonderful, but there have been other movies with great special effects that have not been nearly as successful. So what else could be the reason? In my humble opinion, the true fascination and success of this series is the profound spiritual paradigm that pervades the story and the dialogue.

The story is really the journey of every disciple and initiate on Earth. In the movie this was portrayed by Luke Skywalker and his sister Leia. The movie told the story of his training in becoming a Jedi Knight. In real life every soul on Earth is going through a similar training to become a Self-Realized being and/or Ascended Master. Luke trains with his teachers Obi Wan and Master Yoda. These were, of course, his

Spiritual teachers. One of the main themes of all of the movies was the concept of "The Force." It pervades all things and binds all things together. This, of course, is the GOD or Spiritual component of life. When Master Yoda told Luke not to get seduced by the dark side of "The Force" this was indeed a very true statement. It is a perfect metaphor for the way life really is. The dark side of "The Force" is, of course, the seduction of the negative ego, fear-based, separative, lower-self aspect of life. Master Yoda also told Luke not to give in to his anger and fear, or it would take him on a path to his ultimate destruction. This is indeed a true statement, for anger and fear are the two sides of the negative ego that must be transcended to fully realize GOD. This is why Sai Baba has said, "GOD equals Man minus ego." The *Star Wars* movies are the story of Luke's Spiritual path from discipleship, to becoming an initiate, and then finally becoming a full-fledged Jedi Knight or Spiritual Master. We see how Obi Wan many times appeared to Luke from the Spiritual world after he physically died. At the end of the third film, *Return of The Jedi*, we saw Obi Wan, Master Yoda and Luke's father Darth Vader appear again from the Spiritual world in their Light Bodies.

So, the *Star Wars* movies show the battle between the forces of the negative ego and the forces of Spirit and the Jedi Knights and/or Ascended Masters. The Emperor, Darth Vader for a while, and in the newest film Darth Maul were all initiates of the negative ego side. The term "initiate" is being freely used here; however, it is not the same meaning as "initiate" of the inner plane Ascended Masters. In real life, this indeed exists. There are beings on the side of the negative ego that have formed their own hierarchy for purposes opposed to GOD and the inner plane Ascended Masters. This movie is depicting this battle, so to speak. In our modern society, we call this the battle of Armageddon. It is a battle that is going on within each person, a battle that is going on in our world, and a battle that is occurring on the inner plane. Every person who incarnates into this world must learn to master their lower-self and become their Higher Self. Every person in this world must learn to master fear and become unconditional love. Every person in this world must learn to master separative thinking and learn oneness thinking and feeling. Every person in this world must learn to transcend the negative ego thought system and selfishness, and evolve their consciousness to think and feel only from the Melchizedek/Christ/Buddha consciousness. To do this one must become right with self and right with GOD. One must first become right with self and GOD before one can be effective and successful in all outer endeavors. In the *Star Wars* movies, this was beautifully depicted when Luke had that experience of having to battle the image of Darth Vader in his own consciousness, before he would be ready to fight the real Darth Vader. This is true in real life, for every disciple and initiate on the Spiritual Path must master what is esoterically called "The Dweller on the Threshold." "The Dweller on the Threshold" is the conglomeration of all the glamour, maya, illusion, and negative ego within one's being. In essence, everyone must win the battle of Armageddon within self first before one can help the world and other people to win this battle.

Han Solo is the more worldly third dimensional figure who is not as Spiritually advanced as Luke was. Although he was more self-centered, in the end his Spiritual nature came through, as he came back to save Luke, and joined the battle to fight the Empire. These types of selfless acts, which put selfless desire before selfish desire and greed, touch a deep Spiritual chord within people.

Another aspect of these films that touches a very deep Spiritual chord are the bar scenes in the movies showing all the different types of extraterrestrial beings. These scenes are not only entertaining, but they are also true in real life. Our material universe is filled with extraterrestrial life, and not all extraterrestrial life looks like the beings on this planet. The higher parts of ourselves know this and relate to this movie because of the more full spectrum prism consciousness of the true nature of our galaxy and universe. Adding to this, there have actually been extraterrestrial battles for planets and sectors of our galaxy and our universe. Some of the *Star Wars* movies related very much to the actual Orion Wars that really did take place. Again, a higher part of us knows these facts. Many of us have had incarnations on other planets and in different types of bodies. Many of us have had contact with ETs on subtle and not so subtle levels in this lifetime. So the *Star Wars* movies are not only a perfect symbol for each person's Spiritual path, they are also a symbol and representation for our universal and galactic extraterrestrial heritage and brothers and sisters.

At the end of the movie *Return of The Jedi*, Luke has his final battle and confrontation with Darth Vader, who used to be a Jedi Knight but was seduced by the negative ego side of "The Force." This reminds me very much of the true story of Lucifer, who was an Archangel, however got seduced as well by the forces of the negative ego. In the story, once Lucifer was turned, he had a first lieutenant in the negative ego side by the name of Satan, who was assigned to Earth. Satan was an angel who was turned to the negative ego side. It reminds me very much of the most recent film and the relationship between the Emperor and Darth Maul. Anyway, in the final battle scene, Luke is fighting Darth Vader, but part of him is hoping that Darth Vader will rechoose his allegiance to "The Force." When Luke will not give in to his anger and fear, and will not join the Emperor's allegiance as an apprentice and destroy Vader, the Emperor steps in to kill Luke with his negative energy. Darth Vader, Luke's earthly father, now has the great existential choice to keep his allegiance to the Emperor, or save his son. In the film, his conflict is beautifully depicted, and in the end the forces of compassion and love win out as Darth Vader picks up the Emperor and throws him into the "plasma core abyss." This, of course, also touches a very deep Spiritual core in all movie watchers, for we each have a choice every moment of our lives, whether to choose GOD or negative ego. No matter how much negative action we have taken in the past, there is always the possibility and potential for redemption. This reminds me of the story of the Prodigal Son or Daughter who is always welcomed home by GOD.

This whole theme of redemption and forgiveness also touches a very deep spiritual chord and truth within movie watchers. The final culmination of this teaching is seen at the very end of the movie with Obi Wan, Master Yoda, and even Darth Vader now in his light body, having joined the other Jedi Knights and inner plane Ascended Masters as they watch the celebration.

So, my Beloved Readers, the *Star Wars* movies are, in truth, a modern day fairy tale that perfectly depicts the Spiritual path of every soul on Earth and their material galactic and universal heritage. In conclusion, strive to become, every moment of your life, a Jedi Knight. Take hold of your light saber, which is much like the sword of Lord Michael, and take a stand for GOD, unconditional love, service, and goodness. I close this chapter by saying, "May the Force be with you, always!"

CHAPTER 37

How to Resolve Conflict

One of the most important understandings and skills in one's spiritual path is the ability to resolve conflicts in yourself and your relationships. It is of the highest importance to resolve conflicts within self as quickly as possible. This is necessary to remain in a state of personal power, self-mastery, and decisiveness. Too many conflicts in your conscious and/or subconscious mind begin to drain your energies over time. It is possible to put a given conflict on the shelf for a little while and still remain in total personal power and self-mastery. For that matter, you can do this with a lot of conflicts within self, or with other people, and still remain in total personal power, self-mastery and decisiveness. It is better, however, to resolve them as quickly as you can. The fastest way to do this is to pray for guidance, and sometimes the guidance will come very quickly. Most times, however, what I find most beneficial is to write out my conflict on a piece of paper. I list all the pros on one side, and all the cons on the other side, and then I intuitively compare them. The act of writing them down is enormously clarifying. Ninety-nine percent of the time I can resolve all my conflicts in this way. Once in a while I need to sit a little longer with a conflict if it is something really big, to make sure I am making the right decision. I usually ask GOD and the Masters for extra help at these times. I always make it a big priority to resolve my conflicts so they never drain my energy. Part of owning your personal power is being decisive. Indecision will cause unclarity; sometimes it is better to make the wrong decision than no decision at all, so as to not live in what I like to call the "twilight zone."

Conflicts with People

One of the most important understanding and skills to develop in one's Spiritual path is the ability to resolve conflicts with other people in all types of relationships. The first principle in developing this understanding and skill with people you have a close personal relationship to is loving, open, honest communication of your thoughts and feelings. This should be done in a calm, rational, unconditionally loving manner.

Principle number two is the importance of avoiding arguments and attack thoughts and feelings when there is a difference of opinion.

Principle number three: Always state your thoughts and feelings as "This is my personal opinion" and "personal perception." At all costs avoid being self-righteous even if in your heart you know you are right.

Principle four: When bumping into differences of opinion and perception, frame the situation as "Let's agree to disagree."

Principle five: Always frame the discussion in a "win/win" manner instead of a "win/lose" perspective.

Principle six: Take time to listen and really hear what the other person has to say, even if you disagree with where they are coming from.

Principle seven: Strive not to be overly emotional and strive to remain as calm, objective, evenminded, and rational as possible.

Principle eight: Frame your communication in the words "this is the lens that I see it from and you are seeing it from a different lens." This honors the other person's lens even if you disagree with it.

Principle nine: Pray to GOD, the Holy Spirit, the inner plane Ascended Masters, your Angels, and your Mighty I AM Presence for help in resolving the conflict before beginning communication. This can be done inwardly or openly with the other person as is appropriate.

Principle ten: If you find your communication is becoming heated and both of your negative egos are becoming too involved, I highly recommend stopping all communication, but to say to the other person that your observation is that both of your negative egos and emotional bodies are becoming too engaged and you strongly prefer to end this discussion for now and continue it when both of you are more calm.

Principle eleven: Before entering into communication, even a day or more in advance, ask the Holy Spirit to undo the conflict on the inner plane and in each person's subconscious and conscious program. Also, ask the inner plane Ascended Masters and Angels to heal the situation on the inner plane. This will actually get a lot of the work of resolving the conflict completed before you ever start communicating consciously and verbally.

Principle twelve: When going into communication to resolve conflict always keep in mind the proverbs "Do I want love or do I want to be right?" "Do I want GOD or do I want my ego in this situation?" and "Do I want Love and Peace or conflict, fear and attack?"

Principle thirteen: Before beginning your communication to resolve a conflict, make a list on a piece of paper of all the key points and how you want to frame them so they will be more likely to be received in an open and non-defensive manner.

Principle fourteen: Go into the communication with your full personal power, unconditional love, attunement to GOD and Golden Bubble of Protection so you can respond instead of react.

Principle fifteen: If the other person starts getting angry, attacking or coming from their negative ego, don't catch their psychological disease. Set a better example. It takes two to have a war, and if one person engages in one and the other person doesn't, it can't happen.

Principle sixteen: Be the first to apologize and admit your mistakes. This may be one of the most important principles of all. I find most people and most lightworkers being way too interested in defending their egos than striving for egolessness which is the true nature of GOD. Start your communication out by admitting your mistakes and apologizing for them before ever mentioning the other person's mistakes. This will throw the other person completely off guard, and will set the tone for a Christed communication rather than an ego battle.

Principle seventeen: Be the first to forgive no matter how much you have been wronged.

Principle eighteen: Choose your battles carefully, for there are certain battles that are just not worth fighting.

Principle nineteen: Always remember, there is a time to talk and a time to be silent, and sometimes the best form of communication is silence. Honesty does not mean you have to say everything. True mature honesty means you say what is appropriate, as GOD would have you say it, to gain maximum results in a Spiritual and Earthly manner.

Principle twenty: Do not be attached to your opinions or to an outcome, or for that matter to material results. For example, sometimes it might be necessary to sue someone who has committed a crime, and this is okay from a Spiritual perspective as long as it is done in unconditional love. Sometimes, however, one must weigh whether the material gain is worth the psychological stress and spiritual results. Sometimes the creation of harmony in the long run is more worthwhile than the material gain.

Principle twenty-one: Strive to set the example of achieving a selfish-selfless balance. If there is any question about this, always choose the selfless path.

Principle twenty-two: Always remember, the purpose of life is to live in unconditional live, oneness, peace, and harmony with GOD, Light and your Brothers and Sisters. Remember, every situation of life is a Spiritual test to see if you will choose GOD or ego. Every situation of life is a Spiritual test to see if you will choose love and oneness, or fear, attack and separation. The true purpose of this conflict is to see if you can demonstrate GOD/Melchizedek, Christ/Buddha consciousness in how you deal with it. Remember at all times that GOD, Christ, the Holy Spirit, the Ascended Masters, your Angels, your Higher Self, and your Mighty I AM Presence are watching your every move.

Principle twenty-three: Also remember that the person you are in conflict with is an incarnation of GOD, is a Son or Daughter of GOD, is the Christ, is the Buddha, is the Atma, and is the Eternal Self, in truth. Treat them as such even if they are not demonstrating it.

Principle twenty-four: In some communications to resolve conflict it is possible your lesson may be to just practice humility and humbleness. Or, as the Master Jesus said, "To turn the other cheek." It is always important to intuitively and psychically "psyche out" the conflict. If the person is so defended that communication serves no purpose and will just make things worse, then why do it? Sometimes the lesson might be just forgiveness.

Principle twenty-five: Be more concerned about learning your lessons than teaching other people their lessons. Leave that to GOD.

Principle twenty-six: Always remember, if you do not resolve conflict and you hold onto karma in relationships, you may have to incarnate again in a future lifetime to work it out. In your next life they may be your father, mother, brother or sister, so get real clear about what your priorities really are. Let go of material attachment and put your Spiritual life and inner peace first.

Principle twenty-seven: Sometimes it is much better to resolve a conflict through writing rather than direct verbal direct communication. You can communicate in writing in a very thoughtful, clear and concise manner in a non-emotional way, and you are guaranteed to be listened to and not interrupted. This may take a little longer, however, in this day and age with e-mail and fax machines it is often even a better way to communicate. This must be left up to your intuition.

Principle twenty-eight: Most of all do not get into an ego battle with the other person. This is the creation of Karma. Look at the example the Master Jesus taught in his life. Look at the example Mahatma Ghandi taught, and he freed an entire nation doing it.

Principle twenty-nine: It must be understood, and this is of the highest importance, that most people on Earth are totally run by the negative ego. It also must be understood that most lightworkers have not been trained in the difference between Christ/Buddha thinking and negative ego thinking. It also must be understood that even a great many of the Spiritual leaders and teachers in the New Age movement, consciousness movement, and religion have not been trained in this understanding. It also must be especially understood that there are very few souls on Earth who are truly what I call "pure" in the highest Melchizedek/Christ/Buddha sense. To be "pure" means to be truly the embodiment of GOD in the purest sense, Spiritually, Psychologically and in a Physical/Earthly sense. There are very few souls on Earth who are truly egoless in their every thought, word, deed and motivation. This is not a judgement, just a spiritual fact. I bring this up because it is your job, my Beloved Readers, to set this Melchizedek/Christ/Buddha pure example. This does not mean that you have to be a doormat. This does mean that you must be the highest embodiment of love/wisdom/power and egolessness. Egolessness does not mean that you are not allowed preferences or opinions or loving spiritual observations and discernments. It does mean, however, that these aspects of self must be shared and utilized with extraordinary Divine unconditional love, and Spiritual and psychological wisdom. I share these things because it is essential for you to know and understand that you will have to be the one to set the better GOD example. It will be you who will have to apologize first. It will be you who will have to forgive first. It will be you who will have to practice Humility and nonattachment. It will be you who will have to demonstrate egolessness because it is just about guaranteed that the other person won't.

Principle thirty: In my humble opinion, I would rather lose an argument, lose material gain, be seen as the loser of the disagreement, and still have unconditional love, oneness with GOD, inner peace and harmony than the opposite.

Principle thirty-one: In some situations the lesson to resolve a conflict is really to just, in written or verbal form, apologize and list and admit your mistakes without speaking in the slightest about the other person's lessons or being concerned if they win, learn anything, or are taught any lesson. What is most important is that you remain pure in GOD and that you learn your lessons. Very often, this type of selfless, egoless example will touch the soul and heart of the closed heart of the person you are dealing with, and they will respond in kind. Also, equally often they won't. Most people, again, are too ego-defended. It must be understood, however, that all karma is resolved within self. So if you learn your lessons and the other person doesn't, you are freed from the karmic situation and the other person will have to reincarnate to learn this lesson with someone else in a similar situation, and you will have been liberated from this situation and from the need to reincarnate.

So again, looking at the life of Master Jesus, there were many of a limited third dimensional perspective that believed he lost by allowing himself to be crucified and killed. The truth is, however, he gained full realization of his Christed nature by what he did and became one of the most loved, well-respected and famous people to ever grace the Earth. It is each our Spiritual mission and purpose to set the highest Melchizedek/Christ/Buddha example in each of our interactions with our Brothers and Sisters.

So in conclusion, my Beloved Brothers and Sisters, use every conflict as a Spiritual challenge, test, and Spiritual opportunity to practice the Presence of GOD and Godliness. By doing this you will not only help yourself Spiritually, you will also be giving yourself unconditional love, oneness and inner peace. You will also be setting a wonderful example to your Brothers and Sisters, for it is very rare on this Earth that individuals resolve conflict in such a Godly manner. By doing so as well, you will have brought unconditional love, oneness, and peace into the world. How can we have peace between nations, if we do not know how to create unconditional love and peace between ourselves and our Brothers and Sisters when conflict arises? Each of these conflicts are just mini Spiritual Tests, Spiritual challenges, and Spiritual opportunities to practice this.

So in all conflicts and situations of life, it comes down to, do I want GOD or do I want my ego in this situation? Do I want unconditional love or fear and attack? Do I want oneness or do I want separation? My Beloved Readers, the choice is yours! The paradoxical nature of life, however, is perfectly stated in the Biblical verse, "Seek ye the Kingdom of GOD and all things shall be added onto thee." Those that choose GOD and the Path of Egolessness may at times look like they are losing from the limited third dimensional perspective. This is illusion of course. The truth is, you have gained and Realized GOD in that moment and series of moments. In the long run you will not only Realize GOD, which is the greatest gift of all, but your egoless, selfless example will bring to you material gain as well. For the Bible verse ends with the words, "All things shall be added unto Thee"! This may not happen in that particular situation. However, in the bigger picture choosing the Path of Ego and selfishness will only cause you ultimately to lose money and material wealth, and not gain it. Choosing GOD and unconditional love in this manner will allow you to "Gain the Whole World and not lose your own Soul." For does not the Bible also say, "So what if it profiteth a man to gain the whole world, but lose his own soul." My Beloved Readers, the consistent choice to choose your soul and spirit every moment of your life, and especially when conflicts arise, will bring you a Spiritual, psychological, and earthly wealth that "Passeth understanding"!

CHAPTER 38

The Issue of Temptation

The whole issue of temptation is a very interesting subject. The first question we must ask is, What is temptation? My Beloved Readers, as you all know there are two ways of looking at life and only two. You can interpret life from a Spiritual/Christ/Buddha/Higher-Self perspective, or you can interpret life from a negative ego/fear-based/lower-self/separative/self-centered perspective. When we interpret life and make all our choices from the Christ/Buddha perspective, we are realizing GOD in every thought, word and deed.

When we choose to follow the thought system of the negative ego and lower self we become out of tune with our Realization of GOD. In every situation of life there is an appropriate choice and an inappropriate choice. Your own Mighty I Am Presence, your Higher Self, and the Holy Spirit, also known as "the still small voice within," will tell you what thought, what feeling and what action are appropriate in every situation for you to manifest and demonstrate. As *A Course in Miracles* says, there are no neutral thoughts. Every moment of your life you are choosing GOD or you are choosing negative ego. The key to proper living is to choose GOD every moment of your life. This is why being conscious and Spiritually vigilant at all times is so important. Too many people in life live on automatic pilot, not realizing the degree to which the negative ego and its illusionary thought system are running them.

So again I ask, What is temptation? Temptation is the negative ego trying to steer you away from the straight and narrow path. Temptation is the negative ego's inappropriate thinking and misinterpreting reality. Temptation is the negative ego trying to get you to indulge in negative emotions. Temptation is the negative ego trying to pull you into your lower-self, whereas your Mighty I Am Presence and the Holy Spirit will always guide you to remain in your Higher Self. Temptation is the negative ego trying to make you take the low road where GOD would always have you take the high road. Temptation is the negative ego trying to make you indulge in lower-self, carnal sexuality, where GOD would have you use sexuality only in service of unconditional love and in an appropriate and non-overindulging manner. Temptation is the negative ego trying to make you follow the path of hedonism and overindulgence and pleasure seeking. GOD would guide you that there is a higher purpose to life than just pleasure seeking. Temptation is the negative ego guiding you to indulge in bad habits where GOD would guide you towards self-mastery, Self Realization, and moderation in all things. Temptation is the negative ego guiding you to pollute your body, mind, feelings with things not of GOD, where GOD would guide you to maintain purity of consciousness on all levels.

In Christianity, they would refer to temptation as stemming from the Devil or Satan. In truth, there is no horned creature inside of you or outside of you. This is nothing more than a symbol for a psychological process, one which is called the negative ego, separative thinking or fear-based thinking. This is why it is so important that every person on Earth be on a strict mental diet. This is the key to Self-Realization, success, happiness and inner peace because it is our thoughts that create our reality. In Hinduism the negative ego would be called illusion or maya. In Western esoteric teachings it would be called glamour.

When temptation occurs, the key is to pull your attention away from it. This can be done in your consciousness and/or by partaking in a different physical action. It can be done through doing a positive affirmation or visualization. It can be done through immediately praying and asking GOD and the Masters for help. It can also be done by beginning to repeat the name or names of GOD or one of the mantras of GOD. It could also be done by just telling it to go away. It is always a process of denial and affirmation. What is also helpful is if temptation begins to occur physically, do something else like go get some physical exercise or watch TV It is true that an idle mind is the devil's workshop. The key to successful living is to keep your focus and attention always on GOD in thought, feeling, and action. When you make a mistake and give in, forgive yourself, learn the lesson and don't make a big deal about it and just go forward. I am not giving you permission to make mistakes, but what I am saying is mistakes are part of the Spiritual path, for everyone will make them whether they like it or not. As I have said many times "Perfection is not, not making mistakes. Perfection is not making conscious mistakes." In other words, unconscious mistakes will always happen. The key is, when you become conscious that you are indulging in the negative ego and/or in temptation, just stop without judgement and with for-giveness. GOD does not expect perfection even consciously. Even if we consciously give into the negative ego or temptation, it is not the end of the world or a crime. It is just a mistake and mistakes are okay. We are just all striving to be as God-like as we can on all levels. So, the Spiritual path, in truth, is like climbing a mountain where you take three steps up and two steps back. Five steps up and three steps back. Once greater mastery is obtained, you will be able to move more quickly up the mountain and make fewer mistakes, but occasional mistakes will always occur and this is okay. The key is to just become conscious as quickly as you can, and once conscious, make the choice to own your power and stop the process. You must own your personal power. A lot of people have consciousness, but they do not have personal power. They are victims, they are conscious of it, and this makes it even worse. A true Spiritual Master has consciousness and 100% personal power, wisdom and unconditional love to enforce his or her conscious discernments.

Some people make the mistake of becoming aware they are giving in to temptation and then the negative ego says, "You have already made a mistake and totally blown it so you might as well just continue." My Beloved Readers, I would suggest that this is not, in truth, the best path to follow. It is not necessary to compound a smaller mistake with a bigger one. All is forgiven by GOD and the Masters; the key is forgiving yourself. I have always loved the lesson in *A Course in Miracles*, "My Salvation is up to me." GOD has already given us everything, the question is will we give GOD to ourselves. We do this by choosing to not give into the negative ego and temptation, and if we do, to forgive ourselves, unconditionally love ourselves and learn from our mistakes.

It is my great hope and prayer that this brief discussion on the nature of temptation has brought some light and understanding to this most interesting and important subject!

CHAPTER 39

Negative Ego and Lenses

This chapter and concept is a revolutionary new understanding that is incredibly important for our transition now into the New Millennium and Seventh Golden Age. You all know by now the importance of learning to think, interpret, and see life from your Melchizedek/Christ/Buddha mind rather than your negative ego/separative/fear-based mind. You will feel and act in life according to how you think. There are only two choices in life, you think and interpret from your Higher-Self perspective or your lower-self perspective. From love or from fear, from separation or from oneness. From GOD's perspective or the negative ego's perspective.

Language and how we word things is extremely important. Sometimes people use words that they think are spiritual but are actually very judgmental. One such example in Buddhism is calling people ignorant. To me this word has kind of a judgemental tone. It is always important, however, not only to look at the word but the person's intent behind the word. One person can use a word and be unconditionally loving, while another person may use the same word and be judgmental. The semantics, tones, and meaning of words is a science unto itself.

His Holiness Lord Melchizedek has shared with me a most profound insight and tool for language and better communication in this New Millennium and Seventh Golden Age. Melchizedek shared with me that it is very important in life to develop a full spectrum prism consciousness that allows one to see life through all the lenses of a prism. When looking at a prism, we all know there are thousands of lenses that one can look through. Melchizedek told me that there are a great many people who see life through a very limited and fragmented prism or lens. He went on to say humorously that there are many people who see life through the lens of a fly.

Some people see life through the lens of being a parent, some a doctor, some through their parental upbringing, some through their race, some through their religion, and some through a particular psychology or philosophy. The list of possible lenses that people see through and often remain stuck in is infinite.

In my books, I have tried to present a full spectrum prism lens that allows one to see life from as large a spectrum prism as possible. This is why I have called the entire series "The Easy to Read Encyclopedia of the Spiritual Path."

What Melchizedek has shown me is that this whole concept of under-standing the lenses that people see through is a way of creating what might be called much clearer communication and understanding between people, and a way of preventing ego battles and polarization between people.

Fundamentalist Christians, for example, will say that anyone who doesn't see life from their lens or perspective is run by Satan. This, of course with no judgement intended, is the height of polarization and, in truth, egotism.

A New Age person might say that someone who doesn't see things the way they do is run by the negative ego, fear, or separative thinking. Now in many cases this might be true. However, in some cases this may create some polarity and ego battles that do not necessarily need to happen or should hap-pen. This is where the concept of lenses comes into play!

Instead of telling to someone or speaking about someone that they are always being run by their negative ego, fear or their lower-self, in some cases it might be more appropriate to frame the situation as this person is just seeing life from a certain lens. There are situations in life where it is not really the negative ego, but is rather just a certain perspective that person is taking. This differing perspective may be a result of cultural differences, religious training, the country they grew up in, sexual preference, or socioeconomic considerations to just name a few of the, again, infinite possibilities. By framing the situation, or sometimes even the ego battle or polarity differences in a given discussion, as that both people are just seeing the situation, through a different lens, it takes the issues of polarity, ego battles and who is right or who is wrong out of the discussion. Sometimes this understanding tool and insight is very helpful in arguments, heated discussions, and even in fights that take place. By framing the situation as that both people are just looking at the situation from a different lens, both people can let go of the argument not feeling judged with both people being right and hence having a Win/Win situation.

We have all heard the saying, "In matters of taste there is no dispute." This would be another example of people seeing things through a different lens.

The saying, "Beauty is in the eye of the beholder" also comes to mind If you look at a painting, one person may love it and one person may hate it. People are again seeing things through different lenses.

Another relevant saying is, "One man's garbage is another man's gold." The more we can transcend ego battles, polarity, and win/lose consciousness, the better. The more we can create communication that is based on "I'm okay, you're okay" instead of "I'm okay and you're not okay," the better. I think you can see where this understanding of framing things as lenses can be an extremely helpful tool and understanding!

In conclusion, my Beloved Readers, strive to see life from as wide and large a full spectrum prism as possible. Doing this will accelerate your spiritual growth, enrich your life and help you to understand self and others. I humbly suggest that the reading of my entire series of books is one method or tool of accelerating this process if you are interested. By understanding all religions, all spiritual paths, all mystery schools, all forms of psychology, and the best teachings of the past, present and future, we are able to get a brief glimpse of the lens, or, I should say more accurately, the full spectrum prism perspective of GOD, who sees through all lenses of the prism in a balanced and integrated manner. Although realistically we may never achieve the totality of this ideal, it is possible to get a glimpse and to also begin to see life not just from a Planetary perspective, but also a Solar, Galactic, Universal and Cosmic perspective. It is my sincere hope that this most profound insight of His Holiness Lord Melchizedek, in the way and manner I have explained it, will be useful to you and enrich your life!

CHAPTER 40

The Importance of Clarity, Pursuing Excellence, and Immaculateness in Everything You Do!

The foundation of all Spiritual work is the "God Clarity, Immaculateness, and Pursuit of Excellence" that you maintain every moment of your life and on every level of your being. This point cannot be emphasized enough. What will manifest in your outer life is the Clarity, Pursuit of Excellence and Immaculateness, or lack thereof in your consciousness. Many on the Spiritual path do not hold themselves to the high standard and high calling of really trying to be God, be the Christ, be the Buddha, and be a Son or Daughter of GOD on Earth. This means monitoring every thought to make sure that it is a GOD thought and not a negative ego thought. This means monitoring every feeling and emotion to make sure is stemming from your Spiritual/Christ/Buddha consciousness and not your negative ego/fear-based/separative consciousness. This means monitoring and being vigilant over every word you speak, recognizing the power of the spoken word. This means monitoring and being vigilant over your every action and behavior to make sure your every movement is representative of the Most High GOD! This means using your energy and energies only in the most Spiritual and Sanctified manner!

This means keeping your word as GOD keeps His Word! This means maintaining the highest level of integrity and honesty in everything you do, with yourself and with others. It means striving to be absolutely egoless and selfless at all times! When it is right to be Spiritually selfish, it means to make sure that you are really being Spiritually selfish and not egotistically selfish. This means being devastatingly honest with self, and examining your every motivation for everything you are doing and to constantly check yourself to make sure your motivations are not coming from a selfishly motivated place! It means being able to admit your mistakes to yourself and to others when necessary. It means being willing to apologize for your mistakes! It means to put GOD first and not have false gods before him in a psychological sense (like power, fame, greed, and lower-self desire).

This means every moment of your life trying to practice the presence of God and to practice living like an Integrated Ascended Master on Earth. It means truly unconditionally loving and caring about people. It means being truly compassionate! It means sticking to your Spiritual and psychological ideals on every level no matter what the circumstance! It means doing this even when you are physically exhausted, stressed out or overwhelmed. It means walking the extra mile for a Brother and Sister. It means being "Faithful unto death so you may receive the Crown of Life"!

It means not fudging on your Spiritual and psychological ideals ever. It means really keeping your priorities in order! It means living like a God Being on Earth while simultaneously not putting yourself above others, but instead doing it with humbleness and humility. It means not giving into temptation. It means striving to live a life of perfection, but when you do make mistakes, forgiving yourself, and forgiving others and always being unconditionally loving and nonjudgmental to self and others. It means keeping your inner life as clean and organized as your outer life! It means not fudging on any level just because you are tired. It means demonstrating the same immaculate ideal on a Spiritual, Psychological, Physical/Earthly, Social, and Business level, and on every other level you can think of.

It means not giving into your lower-self and lower-self desire. It means manifesting a flawless character to your highest ability every moment of your life. It means recognizing that mistakes and adjustments are okay and part of every person's life. It means, however, learning from your mistakes and trying to not repeat them again. It means keeping the highest Spiritual and psychological standard you can keep, and sticking to it and not compromising where you are not supposed to. It means being more focused on learning your own lessons and letting GOD teach other people how to learn theirs. It means not being lazy or procrastinating. It means making choices and standing behind them. It means maintaining absolute Mastery over your thoughts, feelings, emotions, subconscious mind, negative ego, inner child, lower-self desire, energies and physical body at all times in service of GOD, unconditional love and balance! It means balancing Heaven and Earth and feminine and masculine energies at all times. It means most of all maintaining GOD Purity in every aspect of your life, every moment of your life!

It means striving to maintain clarity in your consciousness at all times so your subconscious mind and negative ego thinking cannot slip in to sabotage your manifestation. It means not being self-righteous, a know-it-all, or opinionated, and being open to continually learning and refining your being. It means treating others who are not at your level of Spiritual, psychological and physical/earthly development with the utmost kindness, generosity, and compassion. It means never judging another who does not hold the "Immaculate Standards and

Demonstration" that you keep. It means not only being 100% clear about what your Spiritual and psychological ideals are, but having the personal power and dedication to demonstrate them every moment at the 100% level, not just know you have them. It also means being consistent on a superconscious, conscious, and subconscious level and physical body level, so that all three minds and the physical body are consistent with each other. It means to dedicate your life to being of total service to your Brothers and Sisters as your main purpose for being here. It is to hold to your Spiritual ideal of being an "Integrated God Realized Being" and never wavering for a moment in your demonstration of these ideals to the very best of your understanding.

It means to always be open to learning more, refining your process, and making subtle adjustments to be even more God like. It is to strive to resolve all conflicts or any confusion within yourself as quickly as possible so the "base-line" of your daily consciousness is always clear and on top of things! It is to not give in to the line of least resistance and the indolence of the subconscious mind. It is to not give in to all the rationalizations and excuses of the negative ego and lower-self to not do what you are supposed to do. It is to get back on the saddle when you fall off, and not indulge in self-pity or self-indulgence when you get knocked off or fall off the wagon, as you invariably will at times. It is to look at every moment of your life as a Spiritual test and to try and pass every Spiritual test to the best of your ability. It is not only to try to pass every test, but to help others to the best of your ability to pass their tests. It is to never compete or compare with others, to never give in to fear or separation. It is to treat every Brother and Sister as God, for that, in truth is who and what they are! It is to recognize there is only one being in this infinite universe and that is GOD, and we all share the same identity with Him! It is to fully know and understand that "To Have all, you must Give all!" To hold back from a Brother and Sister your unconditional love and complete generosity of spirit and everything you have is to hold it back from yourself! Your Brother and Sister in truth, are your mirrors. If you see anything but the Christ and unconditional love, no matter what their level of consciousness or even negative ego disturbance factor, you are in truth just seeing yourself. That which you hold back from a Brother and Sister you will hold back from yourself! It is okay to make Spiritual discernments, but do so from unconditional love, still recognizing that all you meet are still Sons and Daughters of God even though they may not be acting like it. Practice every moment of your life the "Holy Encounter," that every interaction with a Brother and Sister is Christ meeting Christ, Buddha meeting Buddha, God meeting God! If this is not how you are seeing every Brother and Sister, then, with no judgement, you are not seeing correctly! To be a Son or Daughter of GOD is to see with innocent perception. It is to see each person as the God Being they are, but to also see with Spiritual discernment simultaneously. This is when your Third Eye will become more completely and fully open! This is the balance you must seek! Love your enemies! Turn the other cheek! Live a life of personal power, self-mastery, unconditional love, active intelligence, harmony, spiritual science, devotion, freedom, defenselessness, harmlessness, unconditional love, compassion, gentleness, forgiveness, nonjudgmentalness, tolerance, patience, evenmindedness, and equanimity. Be the Light! Be the Love! Be God! Be Christ! Be the Buddha! Be crystal clear and precise in your every thought, word and deed! Pay attention to detail! GOD is in the details! Pursue excellence on every level of your being! Be immaculate in your Spiritual and psychological ideal and in your demonstration of this ideal on a Spiritual, psychological and physical/earthly level!

CHAPTER 41

Integrated Ascended Master Romantic Relationships and the Issue of Women and Men Who Love Too Much

There is a well-known book that I have never read called *Women Who Love Too Much*. What is unique about this chapter is that where almost all books on the subject of relationships are written from a personality perspective, I am going to give you the Soul, Monad and Ascended Master perspective on this issue. I am also going to include men in the subject of "loving too much," for this is not something that only happens to women. It can happen just as easily to a man! I am also going to write from a lightworker's perspective, which adds a whole other dimension and set of variables to this issue. It is very interesting for me to write chapters and articles. For, the way it works is, that I am inspired with an idea or inspiration for a chapter, but I never know exactly 100% for sure what I am going to say. I have an initial basic idea, but once the process starts the mixture of my own creative juices begin to flow and the process of channeling Spirit and the Masters also begins to occur. Because of my psychological training as a Ph.D. in psychology, and a licensed Marriage, Family, and Child Counselor, as well as Spiritual teacher, each chapter is also like a very complicated and intricate puzzle that is my Spiritual assignment to explain and unravel in very easy to understand and practical language. It is also my job to explain the subject in a very comprehensive manner, so all aspects and lines of thought and understanding are covered. So, what I am trying to explain here is that there is always a little bit of an excitement and Spiritual challenge for me in writing any chapter and I feel it now starting this chapter. It is like having an initial inner vision, and in the process of writing the chapter the full vision is revealed! This is actually a very exciting and enjoyable process for me as well. The skill and artistry for me comes in seeing if I can humbly create and channel a "Masterpiece Understanding" of this chapter's topic for my Beloved Readers! This is a very enjoyable, exciting, fun process for me, for I never know how a chapter is going to turn out. I am usually surprised at what comes pouring out and at many of the intricacies that are explored that I was not planning to get into. If I can really do this entire process properly and create this "Masterpiece of Understanding" on the given topic that has been given to me and I have chosen to do, then there is this tremendous feeling of accomplishment and Spiritually euphoric type of feeling I receive. When I am done, each chapter reverberates through my being for a period of time, which is another added benefit if I can really do it right! My goal in writing each of my books is to humbly write each chapter as one of these "Masterpieces of Understanding" on the subject presented. What also happens is I get on a real Spiritual high when I am in the flow of writing a book and I am able to write many such "Masterpieces of Understanding" in a row. I honestly share this in a very humble way, and I am writing this almost as an artist would share before beginning a work of art that he or she has been looking forward to doing for a very long time. I only bring this up to share with you the excitement, Spiritual attunement, and psychological state of consciousness I am in when beginning this chapter! Even though I have now completed 27 volumes in my Ascension Book Series and Easy to Read Encyclopedia of the Spiritual Path, I always marvel at the fact that each time I start a new chapter it feels like my first! It is this excitement and anticipation that is the state of consciousness that best attunes me on all levels to write the "Masterpiece of Understanding" I am attempting to write. For some reason, I felt inwardly guided before writing this chapter to share with you my inner process as an author and channel, to let you, my Beloved Readers, share in my inner process as well, so in a sense I can join you more fully and we can unfold and experience this chapter together. This is to create a greater sense of unity, oneness, and attunement between I and you, my Beloved Readers. Now that this unique perspective has been shared of my experience as the author in writing this chapter, we have a much greater sense of attunement to officially begin. Now that we are fully attuned with each other, I am ready to officially begin!

At first glance at the title of this chapter, a Spiritual person might say, "How can a person love too much, I thought this was the purpose of life to love?" This is of course true, but it must be understood that there are two kinds of love. There is Spiritual/Christ/Buddha love and there is negative ego/fear-based/addictive love! Most people on Earth have not been fully trained in Spiritual psychology; it is not taught at home, in schools, churches and temples, though it should be. It is as important as studying math, spelling, science, or anything else. It is really the Spiritual and psychological science of being right with self and right with GOD, hence right with other types of relationships including romantic!

So let us take out the "magnifying glass and microscope," so to speak, and examine why women or men love too much! It occurs for two initial reasons. The first is because the individual is not fully right with self and whole within self. Secondly, it occurs because the person is a little cut-off from their Spiritual life and doesn't realize it.

Let us start on the psychological level first, or the issue of being right with self. If a person does not first off fully own their 100% personal power, they will seek this power often in another person. Secondly, if a person does not fully love themselves, then they will often seek to find this love in another person rather than find it within self first. Thirdly, if a person is not feeling whole within self, they will seek their wholeness in another person rather than first finding wholeness within self. This might be called a father/daughter or mother/son relationship and/or an addictive relationship, rather than a preferential relationship. This could also be described as a mutually dependent relation-ship, rather than a mutually independent relationship. Then fourthly, there is the issue of what is called attachment versus preference. As Lord Buddha taught in his Four Noble Truths, "All suffering comes from attachment and wrong points of view"! The ideal, from a Spiritual perspective, is to never have attachments in life to anything or anyone and only to have super strong preferences. Addiction is another word for attachment!

The nature of a preference attitude is that if it is taken away you still remain happy. Whereas with an attachment, if something outside of you is taken away you become unhappy. When you are attached, happiness instead of being a state of mind becomes something outside of self. Also, the nature and law of life is that which keep "you become" specifically attached to, ultimately will repelled from your life, so it is better to learn this lesson the easy way, instead of the hard way of having life take it away before you have let go of your attachment attitude and changed it to a preference. These are the main issues on a psychological level for why this happens. Now let us look on a Spiritual level, which has rarely, if ever, been looked at on this issue!

From a Spiritual perspective, the reason this issue of women or men loving too much occurs is that the person is either cut off from their Spiritual life, or misunderstands how to translate their Spiritual life into a proper psycho-spiritual understanding. If the person is cut off from their Spiritual life, then it is straightforward. All that energy that first should be going to become right with self and right with GOD, which in truth are the two most important relationships in your life, is sublimated into another person instead of into self and GOD first. This can happen in one of two ways. It can happen on a psychological and Spiritual level, or just on a Spiritual level. If it happens on both then the addictive love will be even more pronounced and serious. If it is just the Spiritual level that is cut off, it still is addictive but just not quite as addictive. If it is both, then one's personal power, lack of self-love, lack of wholeness, dependence, attachment, and all one's cutoff Spiritual life are channeled into another person. Metaphorically, that other person has become God, though the person who is addicted would not of course think of it in that way, but that is what has happened, in truth. That which you put first in life is your God!

So, sublimation has taken place. This means energy that was meant to be used in establishing a right relationship to self and a right relationship to GOD and the Masters has been sublimated or re-channeled inappropriately into a primary romantic relationship!

There are people who somewhat self-actualize themselves on a psychological level and establish their personal power, self-love, and wholeness to a certain extent and are neither completely attached nor dependent, but are not that Spiritual. They are still susceptible to this form of addictive love, for even if they have a somewhat right relationship to self, they still are cut off Spiritually, so this cutoff relationship to GOD will be sublimated or inappropriately channeled into a romantic relationship. What we are seeing here is that there are degrees and/or types of addictive love.

Now let's take this discussion one step further. Then we have the lightworker who totally believes in GOD and the Masters and Angels, or is involved in traditional religion and is very religious. They totally believe in GOD. However, even though this is the case, they are right with GOD and the Angels and/or Masters but not right with self. This is enormously common in religion and in lightworkers. They are more advanced Spiritually than they are psychologically. This is actually more the norm in the New Age Movement. People tend to be more right with GOD than they are right with self. Although they believe in GOD, they don't fully own their personal power or fully love themselves, don't feel fully whole within self, do not fully control the negative ego, and are still very much attached and dependent. This type of person is very susceptible to this type of addictive love.

Then, the fourth type of lightworker or religious person is one who very much believes in GOD and the Masters and Angels and is on their Spiritual path. They also do a lot of work on themselves psychologically, and may have a good deal of personal power, self-love, wholeness, independence, and a certain degree of preference rather than attachment. In this last type there is still a lack of understanding or proper alignment. They think they are fully together Spiritually and psychologically on this issue, but they are not. For they are still not fully putting their right relationship to self and right relationship to GOD before a romantic relationship. They are still running somewhat with the mass consciousness programming that so pervades our society. They in essence believe their right relationship to self and right relationship to GOD should come first and strive for this, yet they are not achieving it. This is not because they are not sincere or not trying, but rather because they are still a little bit out of alignment psychologically and Spiritually. The purpose of this book has been to fully put you back into full chiropractic alignment on a Spiritual, psychological and physical/earthly level. Each chapter has been specifically designed to "shift your consciousness," and remove blind spots and limiting lenses that are preventing you from fully realizing what it means to put your relationship to Self and relationship to GOD first before any and all relationships no matter what. So this type of person is totally trying to do this, and in most cases think they are, but they have not fully realized the full scope and scale of what this means. There are a great many lightworkers who fall into this category as well. I honestly and humbly say to you that if you fully read this book and my book *Soul Psychology,* that this can be easily and fully corrected! I am sure this chapter has already given some extremely important insights, shifts, and chiropractic mental and emotional adjustments, to fully help many achieve this state. This fourth level, however, is the most advanced and one that has really never fully been talked about ever before in any book on romantic relationships I have ever seen. The first three levels can be fully realized by reading this chapter and then making any needed adjustments in your consciousness. This fourth level is the one for advanced lightworkers who are even in successful romantic relationships in the highest sense of the term, but still have is a little bit of addictive love programming left. In taking this in-depth study of this issue, I am taking it from the very beginning level to the most advanced. I am attempting to teach all lightworkers not only how to achieve full Self-Realization, Ascension, Integrated Ascension, and God Realization within self, I am also attempting to teach you and show you how to do it in relationship to another! There are many gurus, for example, who claim to be Self-Realized or God Realized on a Planetary level. However, if you put them in a romantic relationship they would be totally dysfunctional. Interesting lesson, is it not? I am taking this issue now to the very highest ideal. Here is a new concept that has never been discussed before on Earth. How to realize an "integrated ascended master romantic relationship! How about that! This is what I am trying to teach you now! This is extremely powerful and profound! It is a revolutionary new concept and under-standing!

I will now try to share a little bit more to try and explain what this is and how this works. This chapter can help you make all the adjustments needed to fully master this understanding and lesson, to the very highest level, just by reading it. However, I am not just satisfied with this. I want to take you one step further to help you "polish your diamond" to such a degree that "full realization of integrated ascended master romantic relationship consciousness" can be achieved! So listen closely!

To achieve this highest degree of consciousness on this lesson, you must be 100% right with self and right with GOD, entering into and while being involved in this romantic relationship. We are going for the perfected ideal now and this is for advanced lightworkers and all seekers of truth. Some light-workers have mastered this lesson at the 60% level. Some at the 70% level. Some at the 80% level. Some at the 90% level. We are now going for 100% mastery of this lesson, so your diamond is not only fully polished within self, but is also fully polished in how you are involved in your romantic relationship. Just because you are right with self and right with GOD within self, doesn't mean you have mastered all lessons of a romantic relationship. This, my Beloved Readers, is a whole other set of lessons to learn. As has been said in many Spiritual books, it is easy to Realize God in a cave, but Realizing God while living in the marketplace and being involved in relationships, the horizontal plane of life, and romantic relationships is the ultimate Spiritual test! If you really want to "polish your God Realization diamond" then get involved in a romantic relationship and maybe even have some children! This will really "polish your diamond," I think you will all agree!

So let us now examine under our magnifying glass and microscope how we can take this lesson of "realizing integrated ascended master romantic relationships" to its very highest level! The first principle is that you must put your right relationship to self and right relationship to GOD first, before any romantic relationship, 100% of the time. This does not take away from love, it adds to love. It is when you don't do this that unconditional love will be lost. It sounds paradoxical but true. When you don't remain 100% right with self and right with GOD as I have been describing in this chapter, what happens is that at whatever percentage you lost self-mastery on this issue, that is the amount of addictive love you will have! This leads to the negative ego/fear-based/separative mind slipping in, which will create addiction, attachment, separation, judgment, fear, abandonment issues, rejection issues, resentment, anger, irritation, impatience, intolerance, unhappiness and so on. It is only, and I mean only, if you are 100% right with self and right with GOD that you can stay out of this stuff and remain clear! When you are right with self and right with GOD, you have your full personal power, self-love, wholeness, mutual independence, preference rather than attachment, bubble of protection, and lack of ego sensitivity, you are not judgemental and critical, you don't take things personally, and you are not prone to feeling rejected or abandoned. You have, in essence, cleared the negative ego thought system and feelings within self, which really allows you to be a clear mirror for your partner. When your partner gets off-kilter you don't take it personally. If they occasionally judge or get angry it just slides off like "water off a duck's back." You respond instead of react. You remain centered and have compassion. You realize an attack is really fear and a call for love! When you are right with self and right with GOD you see through the eyes of love. Everything is a Spiritual test and lesson! Every moment is a choice between GOD and negative ego! Every moment is a choice between unconditional love and conditional love. Every moment is a choice between forgiveness and holding grudges! Every moment is a choice between judgment and unconditionally loving Spiritual discernment. To mistreat your partner is to mistreat God, for your partner is an incarnation of God!

My Beloved Readers, every moment is an opportunity to practice the Presence of GOD! Every moment is an opportunity for you and your partner to see that what is going on has nothing to do with anything outside of self, or anything really to do with each other, but is first a Spiritual test for both of you to see if you both can keep things in proper perspective.

When you are right with self and right with GOD, it doesn't even matter if your partner doesn't even learn their lessons, for you are not interested in being their teacher and forcing them to learn their lessons. That is negative ego. When you are right with self and right with GOD, all you care about is learning your own Spiritual and psychological lessons to the best of your ability! It is your preference that your partner learns their lessons, but you are not attached!

When you are right with self and right with GOD, your happiness is 100% within yourself and not within your partner. You cause your own reality by how you think. You cause your own feelings and emotions, and you are not a victim of your partner! You are not attached; you have super strong preferences, so you cannot suffer. Hence there is no fear of rejection or abandonment. You are not destroyed if they leave, for you are right with self and right with GOD first, which is exactly why they don't leave. You are not possessive or jealous, for your relationship is based on trust! You communicate what is on your mind in a calm, rational, loving way! You state your preferences to your partner. However, if they are not met, you are still happy! Happiness is a state of mind, and is not based on what your partner does. Sex is a preference and not an attachment. You are not moody for you are right with self and right with GOD, so you don't let your emotional body, astral body, mental body, negative ego, desire body, lower-self and subconscious mind run you.

You not only see through the eyes of love, you see through the eyes of Christ. You see through the eyes of Buddha. You see though the eyes of humbleness and humility. When attacked, it just slides off your bubble like "water off a duck's back"! When you respond, you respond calmly and ration-ally in unconditional love. Since everything is a Spiritual test, sometimes you may turn the other cheek. You respond appropri-ately to every situation. Since your relationship to self and relationship to GOD comes first, and you are seeing through your Christ/Buddha consciousness, you are mastering the "Art of Love"! You are also balanc-ing the God/Goddess energies by being in this relationship! It is helping you to more fully refine this balance within you! You are never self-righteous in this state, or holier-than-thou, for that would be negative ego parading as Spiritual. Everything is shared as your own personal opinion, Spiritual observation, Spiritual discernment and preference.

You agree to disagree in unconditional love! You pray together before having a heavy discussion and ask for GOD and the Masters to help! You hold to your Spiritual and psychological ideals above all else, which keeps you centered. When your partner gets physically sick, you don't catch it for you maintain your strong physical immune system. You set a better example because you are maintaining your right relationship to self and right relationship to GOD! When your partner gets psychologically or Spiritually sick, you maintain your strong psychological and Spiritual immune system and you don't get it. You maintain your right relationship to self and right relationship to GOD! You set a better example! You take the high road! You do this not out of negative ego, you do this out of genuine Christed compassion, love and caring!

Being right with self and right with GOD, you live to serve and live to please, give and help! It doesn't matter if you do a little more of the chores. You state your preferences and whatever happens, happens. Things are meant to be or not meant to be! Your happiness is not affected! You feel so good about yourself and so filled with GOD that your cup runneth over. All you want to do is give off this abundant and overflowing love. You are constantly buying your loved one flowers, and gifts, writing sweet notes, telling them how much you love them, giving them affection and hugs, giving them compliments, raising their Spirits, supporting them, and helping them to be God! You are helping them to be right with self and right with GOD as well, if you can, and if they are open to it. If not, be quiet and just demonstrate the example, for this is a greater teacher!

It is because you are this way, and so whole and complete within self and so right with GOD and the Masters and Angels, that your loved one loves and appreciates you so much! Your relationship is based on total trust and integrity so there is never anything to fear!

You can fully share your full love and all your feelings and emotions because you are fully secure in your right relationship to self and right relation-ship to GOD. There is never any competition, for all you both care about is God Realization for self and each other and for everyone in the world. Both of your Spiritual paths come first, that is a given. This adds to build even more love! Both of your lives are dedicated to service! You share a GOD life together! You apologize for your mistakes when you make them. You admit your mistakes even if your partner doesn't. You never ever engage in an ego battle. When you start getting overemotional or become too passionate or heated, you stop talking. You learn within self, and with each other and don't repeat you mistakes. You communicate often but don't overprocess. You work many things out within self for they are your lessons to learn. You are constantly making attitudinal and emotional adjustments to keep the romantic relationship in the "Perfect Tao."

My Beloved Readers, you set such a Spiritual/Christ/Buddha example on all levels in such a humble and egoless way that your partner can't help, of course, to love you tremendously, respect you, and also learn from you! They will begin to take on your energy pattern of being right with self and right with GOD! It will have to be that way for you will not allow yourself to do anything else. You can't! You couldn't even if you wanted to for this "is" your Spiritual path. You are not doing this for your partner, you are doing this for yourself so you may Realize God. If you don't do this, you will not be Realizing God, every moment you choose not to. GOD is the only purpose of existence! GOD is the only reason we have incarnated! GOD is who we are! We each are incarnations of God living in a physical body! A romantic relationship is in truth God having a relationship with God! Christ having a relationship with Christ! Buddha having a relationship with Buddha! The Eternal Self in a relationship with the Eternal Self!

My Beloved Readers, as I tune in fully, I know and sense the final chiropractic Spiritual, mental, emotional, and energetic adjustment has been achieved! What I am trying to show you is that to fully realize this "Highest Ideal of an Integrated Ascended Master Romantic Relationship," it is all perspective!

This chapter has now fully realized its purpose! I humbly suggest the "Masterpiece of Understanding" has come! You can fully see and understand now what you need to do to fully transcend all addictive love at the 100% level! You now fully see and understand what attitudinal and emotional adjustments you need to make to now "fully achieve 100% integrated ascended master romantic relationship status in your present romantic relationship!" It does not matter if your relationship partner is not perfect, for no one on Earth is. We are all apprentice Gods in the process of realizing God fully on all levels. Each person is at a different level and is working on different lessons on different levels. All that matters in this moment is not what your partner is doing. All that matters is what you are doing! Do not focus on your partner's lessons for that is not your business. That is between your partner and GOD! Your lesson is to be more focused on your lessons! By your good nonattached, preference-type example, they will learn quickly! For you now have a map and you know what to do! It could not be clearer or made easier to understand!

You are now being Spiritually challenged in a most loving and gracious way by Spirit and the Masters to take this most profound step and fully realize what it means to "fully 100% realize the ideal of being a fully integrated ascended master in your romantic relationship at all times!" It is no accident you are reading this chapter! It is now time to take your romantic relationship to this next level of God purity and God refinement! You are now being Spiritually challenged in the most loving and gracious way, by Spirit and the Masters, to take this next step in your Spiritual evolution, and strive to demonstrate this most noble and highest of Spiritual ideals at the 100% level to the best of your ability! Mistakes are okay and, of course, part of the process! You will get the hang of it quicker than you think. In the shortest amount of time it will become a Spiritual habit to stay in this state of consciousness at all times. It only takes 21 days to cement any new habit into the subconscious mind!

My Beloved Readers, in final conclusion, if you can maintain being in a right relationship to Self and right relationship to GOD in a romantic relationship, I humbly suggest, and the Spirit and the Masters acknowledge, you are making very excellent progress on your path to full God Realization!

CHAPTER 42

The Negative Ego and the Path of Initiation and Ascension

Recently I have had some extremely interesting insights concerning the transcendence of negative ego consciousness and the path of initiation and ascension. In the beginning of the spiritual path, almost by definition, pretty much everyone is controlled by the negative ego to varying degrees. Most people, as they evolve on their spiritual path and initiation process, begin gaining more self-mastery over their thoughts, emotions, physical body, subconscious mind, inner child, and negative ego. There are some examples of people, as I have mentioned, who complete their initiations, but have still not mastered their emotional body and control of the negative ego.

One of the insights that I have had of late that the Masters have guided me to write about here is, that even though a great many lightworkers fundamentally work with this process and seem to be practicing it, they do not have a total 100% grasp of the intricacies of maintaining this state of consciousness under more difficult or stressful circumstances.

The second insight and spiritual observation I have had is that I am see-ing an enormous number of high level initiates and even ascended beings actually going backwards in this process. It almost seems, the higher they go in their initiation process the more negative ego there is. I have observed an enormous number of high level lightworkers actually "fall" spiritually. The number of lightworkers I have seen this happen to is so great, that finally it has really gotten my attention.

In the past couple of days, I have been meditating upon this most curious paradox. Why would so many high level initiates be filled with so much negative ego, and be manifesting so much corruption, and actually falling from grace in many cases?

The guidance I received is absolutely fascinating! In the early stages of the spiritual path, lightworkers tend to be more humble and less ego-tistical because they have not achieved their ascension, or completion of their seven levels of initiation. In most cases, they have not come into their full professional success. They have not also come into their full Spiritual leadership. They also have not come into their full planetary world service. They are also open to learning and still see themselves as students as well as teachers. At this stage they are also very open to receiving guidance from the Masters. With all these factors in place, the negative ego is kept somewhat under control. The deceiving factor here, however, is that it is not a control of true self-mastery, it is more a con-trol of outer circumstances.

What I see very clearly now, and what is fascinating, is that the reason high level lightworkers are manifesting more negative ego as Masters than they were as students is that they never really learned the lesson completely of how to transcend negative ego consciousness, even though it appeared at face value that they had. I humbly suggest to you, my Beloved Readers, that this is incredibly pervasive. I cannot tell you how many Spiritual leaders, Spiritual teachers, channels, and even friends I have seen fall into this scenario. It is almost shocking seeing extremely high level lightworkers, who have some incredible abilities and knowledge, fall into such degrees of self-aggrandizement and negative ego corruption.

Let us now take a look at why this happens. The reasons are multifaceted. First, once a person achieves their ascension or passes their seven levels of initiation, they think they are a full Spiritual master and this goes to their heads.

Second, their own egos and other external channels fill their heads with all kinds of grandiose spiritual ideas about how great they are.

Third, for the first time in their life, they taste success and are making large amounts of money and this goes to their head.

Fourth, they taste Spiritual leadership and power over others and this goes to their head.

Fifth, they taste fame and public recognition, this acts like a drug to the negative ego, and the person goes a little crazy.

Sixth, the person, having moved into Spiritual leadership and planetary world service, has enormous responsibility and stresses, and where there is a character flaw, this begins spilling out. When they were under no stress and did not have this level of responsibility, it was easier to keep this hidden.

Seventh, by claming they are a Spiritual master, when in truth they are not, because they have not in most cases achieved the Integrated Melchizedek/Christ/Buddha consciousness, they have invoked a Spiritual lesson. By this, I mean if you claim you are a spiritual master, then you are invoking from the universe tests to prove this. Most lightworkers are more developed in their Spiritual body than they are in their psychological body. This means they are ill-equipped to deal with all the lessons that have come.

Eighth, if you put yourself out as a Spiritual master in Spiritual leadership, wherever there is a character flaw, your students will find it.

Ninth, the expanded Spiritual leadership and world service brings forward an enormous amount of having to deal with people, employees, students, and fellow Spiritual leaders, and in truth, one has to be a master communicator and master psychologist to deal with all the lessons that come.

Tenth, all the aforementioned people that you now have to deal with have all kinds of negative ego issues themselves, personality quirks, personal agendas, neediness and even psychological disturbance. The newfound Spiritual leader must deal with all this stuff and is very often ill-equipped or not ready to do so, and this brings up all their psychological issues and material.

Eleventh, the new found Master and Spiritual leader then has to deal with all the jealousy, competition and personal attacks that come with fame and public recognition. Other lightworkers who feel less worthy or run by their own negative ego, always attack and judge those on the top to try and feel good about themselves. They do not realize that the only way to inner peace is to transcend both sides of the negative ego. Newfound Spiritual masters are not often ready to deal with this stuff and do not have a thick enough skin.

Twelfth, the newfound spiritual and professional success has the negative ego go on a massive aggrandizement trip. As the Bible says, however, "After pride cometh the fall"!

The Masters are also guiding me here to share three last points as to why there is sometimes more negative ego the higher lightworkers go on the Spiritual path. The thirteenth reason is that many lightworkers, once believing they are a Spiritual master, stop their Spiritual and psychological practices. They think they don't need them anymore. They are in essence stopping the practices that got them to the place of being a Spiritual master. This is always a bad sign.

The fourteenth point is that the person believing they are a Spiritual master believes they do not have to keep their Spiritual vigilance because they are a master. Spiritual vigilance, in truth, needs to be kept up no matter how involved you become, and this applies even on the inner plane.

The fifteenth reason why there is often more negative ego the higher most lightworkers go is that as they come into their self-mastery, power, wisdom and love, there is a negative ego tendency to think "I am an Ascended Master and I do not need the Ascended Masters anymore," or "I don't ever need to channel guidance anymore." There is nothing wrong with choosing not to channel or do as much channeling if that is what you want. However, there are some lightworkers who do this out of negative ego corruption. This causes a lack of attunement to the Masters, a false pride, and reliance upon the personality instead of the Masters, which often causes even more negative ego and corruption.

The sixteenth reason why there is often more negative ego in light-workers the higher they go is that, in the beginning, they were open to receiving knowledge because they saw themselves as students. Now that they see themselves as a master, the negative ego closes the door to learning and often tends to corrupt the channeling, for the channel thinks it knows better than the Masters. In the beginning, there was a certain innocence and openness. The person now wants all the acclaim and does not want to share it with the Masters in a co-creative relationship. The person also often thinks that they are at the level of the inner plane Ascended Masters, which is an illusion as well. On one level, it is true, but one must also remember that the inner plane Ascended Masters are evolving also. So, we may become Planetary and Solar masters, but they are now working on a Galactic level of realization or higher. So, in truth, there is always more that can be learned from the Masters. All the negative ego cares about is false pride, so it blinds itself to this fact.

Conclusion

My beloved readers, these sixteen points of consideration, which I am sure you can all fully see and understand, show us that some of our fantasies about the Spiritual path and becoming an Ascended Master are not exactly as we had imagined.

When a person is a student and doesn't have all this responsibility, the Spiritual path is a lot easier. The key lesson here is that in becoming a Spiritual master and moving into Spiritual leadership and planetary world service, you will be tested by GOD and the Masters unmercifully. If you are not an "Integrated Melchizedek/Christ/Buddha" on all levels and at all times, even under the most extreme tests and lessons, the universe will quickly show you this.

This is why when people claim to be at a certain level of initiation, or claim to have famous pasts lives, or claim to have certain siddhis or powers, or give a great channeling, or write a book, it means nothing. The true test of one's spirituality comes in one's demonstration of GOD on a daily and moment-to-moment basis. The true spiritual test of whether you really are an "Integrated Melchizedek/Christ/Buddha" will come when you achieve realization and success. Can you still resist the negative ego, even when you have this level of power, fame, success, money, Spiritual leadership, Spiritual students, Spiritual status and position? If you can keep your true Melchizedek/Christ/Buddha consciousness and not give in to the negative ego on any level under these circumstances, only then are you truly a full-fledged Ascended Master.

So, my Beloved Readers, as the Bible says, "The Spiritual path is a straight and narrow path." My Beloved Readers, you would be amazed how many lightworkers do not pass these tests. I am flabbergasted at how many high level lightworkers I know and see on a daily basis who are becoming corrupted.

My Beloved Readers, I share these things with you as a fellow Spiritual brother and friend to Spiritually challenge you to retain your purity, selflessness, humbleness, humility and egolessness even when Spiritual success is fully achieved. This is the true test of the Spiritual path. Be aware of this in your own path, and be more Spiritually discerning of others who make claims about them-selves.

If you thought that once you passed your seven levels of initiation and ascension that everything would get easier, I am here to bring a word of enlightenment on this matter. In some ways, this is true, but in other ways, the Spiritual path actually becomes much more difficult. As the Masters told me, which had a very profound effect on me, "Much has been given and much is now expected." If you want to accelerate your Spiritual growth, that is wonderful, but be prepared to take on the responsibilities that come with the grace that is given!

The choice to take on this Spiritual responsibility will accelerate your Spiritual growth a million fold. It will be molding fire, which will help you to fully become an "Integrated Melchizedek/Christ/Buddha"! It will bring you fulfillment and love beyond your wildest dreams and expectations. The main point, however, is to at all costs retain your Melchizedek/Christ/Buddha purity, egolessness, selflessness, humbleness, and humility. Do not give in to the temptations and false gods the negative ego has to offer you. Can the false gods of the negative ego compare to the true Realization of GOD? Every moment of your life you have a choice between GOD and the negative ego. No matter how high you go on your Spiritual path, this choice remains. My Beloved Readers and friends, ever "be joyously vigilant for GOD and His Kingdom!"

CHAPTER 43

The Development of Purity

After unconditional love, my single most favorite Christ/Buddha quality is purity. As I stated in a previous chapter, it is one of the rarest qualities on Earth. Earth life can be a very tough school and the lessons of Earth life and the meanness and cruelty of others makes it hard for one to maintain their innocence and purity of character. So when I say purity, what does this mean?

To remain pure means that one loves GOD to such an extent and to such an attunement that no matter how mean or cruel people are and no matter how tough the lessons of Earth life are, one holds to their unconditional love and faith, trust and patience in GOD. It means one holds to their Christ/Buddha consciousness at all times, no matter how high the degree of momentary defeat or how high is one's Spiritual and earthly success. Purity means that one's love for GOD and one's attunement to GOD is so great that the temptations, glamour, and false GOD's of the negative ego hold no interest.

The development of purity means choosing the path of selflessness at all times. It means never giving in to an attack thought. It means admitting your mistakes when you have made them no matter what the circumstance. It means never giving up, and holding to unconditional love and one's Spiritual ideals at all times. It means always being the one to apologize when an ego battle has been entered into. It means you are the first to forgive others and self. It means being constantly vigilant against the negative ego and ever more so the more success you achieve on all levels.

My Beloved Readers, I cannot tell you how many lightworkers and even friends I know, who cannot admit their mistakes. It is absolutely mind boggling to me to see how defended most people are.

Purity means when you get into an ego battle with another and are becoming aware of it, having the courage to stop although the other person hasn't. Purity means apologizing and admitting one's mistakes even if the other person won't. Purity means forgiving and unconditionally loving your enemy.

Purity means maintaining humbleness and humility. Purity means truly having compassion for other people's suffering and being willing to do something about it. Purity means sticking to your Christ/Buddha ideals even when you don't feel like it. Purity means walking the extra mile for your Brother and Sister even when you're tired. Purity means sacrificing everything at the altar of GOD. Purity in its larger sense means always choosing against negative ego thinking and emotions and always choosing the Christ/Buddha thoughts and emotions regardless of the circumstance. Purity means never giving in to the negative ego's need for power, greed, fame, vanity, false pride, overindulgence in sexuality, hedonism, to name a few of the tests of the Spiritual path. Developing purity means never attacking or striking back psychologically although you have been attacked. Purity means learning to be silent. Purity means never giving in to being judgemental or critical while still maintaining Spiritual discernment. Purity means saying nothing if you have nothing nice to say. Purity means not gossiping or engaging in ego battles. Purity means not competing with others. Purity means always being the peacemaker and establishing harmony, oneness, and love in all situations. Purity means sticking to your ideals in thought, word, and deed, even when alone and even when physically tired and/or exhausted. Purity means not giving in to temptation.

Purity means recognizing that in every moment of life, one is choosing between GOD and ego, and given this fact and awareness, always choosing GOD.

Purity means applying GOD's principles and ideals on all levels, and not being lazy in application on any one level, which includes the physical. Purity means having faith and trust in GOD even when the physical plane has not yet manifested one's prayers. Purity means not giving in to anger, upset, and depression when things don't go according to your preferences. Purity means not giving in to negative emotions, even when you're tired. Purity means stopping yourself in the middle when you find the negative ego and negative emotions have taken over.

Purity means that you remain the same person no matter if you become the most famous person in the world in a Spiritual and earthly sense, or if you live in seclusion and have a very small sphere of influence. A person of purity keeps a love for GOD foremost in their mind and heart and even though they may do great Spiritual work and service for the planet, their consciousness maintains this innocence and pure love and is attracted to none of the glamours, illusion, maya and false GOD's of the negative ego and overidentification with third dimensional reality. The development of purity means looking at everything that happens in life as a Spiritual test and lesson to practice the presence of GOD. Purity means being able to flow with whatever comes down the pike and with whatever changes take place, even if they do not reach your preferences at times and to say "Not my will but Thine O Lord, thank you for the lesson."

The development of purity means being steady and evenminded every day, and not being prone to extreme highs and lows and manic depressive application of Spiritual principals. Being pure means maintaining self-mastery and discipline at all times in service of GOD and unconditional love. Purity means striving for balance at all times. Purity means leading a simple life even though you may have enormous global responsibilities. Purity means paying attention to detail, recognizing that in the details is GOD made manifest on Earth. Purity means maintaining joy at all times as well as maintaining an optimistic rather than pessimistic attitude.

My Beloved Reader, it is when all these attitudes and qualities are made manifest that a person demonstrates true unconditional love and purity. My Beloved Friends, strive at all times to maintain your purity and to not succumb to the corruption, negative ego, glamour, illusion, maya of the lower-self and fear-based reality. This will take enormous consciousness and vigilance on your part, however the gift and fruit that you will attain is greater than any gift or item you will find in this world. I again leave you with the words of the Master Jesus who said, "Be ye faithful unto death and I will give thee a Crown of Life"!

CHAPTER 44

The Heavenly Ideal versus the Real World

This is a most interesting chapter, for it is about a most interesting balance and integration that many lightworkers have gotten confused about! This confusion has given rise to the negative ego causing a great deal of sabotage in lightworkers' lives as well! I repeat again that the Spiritual path is really quite complicated in many ways. It is quite fascinating to watch how the negative ego has woven its delusionary web not only into religion but the New Age Movement as well!

To begin this discussion, there are teachings from Masters, prophets, and channels and in books like *A Course in Miracles* and many others that tell us we each are the Christ, the Buddha, the Eternal Self, the Atma and so on! The Bible says we are made in the image of GOD! The Bible also says, "Ye are Gods and know it not"!

Now on the other side of the coin, there is the real world perspective, which sees what it sees and calls a spade a spade! If the real world perspective sees corruption, negative ego contamination, dark energy, and even evil the person calls it for what it is! So which is the truth? Is every person the Christ, in truth, as *A Course in Miracles* states, or are there negativity, corruption, and negative ego contamination going on? Which is it? Are we Gods or not? Are we Christs or not? The answer is, both are true! Every person is God, is Christ, is the Buddha, is the Eternal Self, and is the Atma, but it is also true there is all this other negative ego and imbalanced stuff as well. So the question is, how are we supposed to see ourselves, and how are we supposed to see others? The answer is, we are supposed to see both simultaneously!

It is of the highest importance to see each person as God and the Christ, for that is their true identity even if they have not even stepped onto their Spiritual path. This is true even if they are a mass murderer! Every person is God! Every person is the Christ! We don't have a choice in this because GOD created us, we didn't create ourselves! This is the rationale for always being unconditionally loving! Everyone is deserving of unconditional love no matter what they have done, are doing or will do, because they are God, and the Christ, in truth! The problem is, many books like *A Course in Miracles,* which is one of my favorite books in the whole world, actually can kind of foul people up if they don't interpret and integrate the teachings properly. *A Course in Miracles* is a book written from the lens of the heavenly ideal, not from the real world! So do you see where the confusion comes in? It is not that it is untrue for every word is true. It is true from the lens of the heavenly ideal but not from the lens of the real world. If this balance is not understood, you can see the havoc the negative ego can create with this one. Now on the other side of the coin, other Spiritual teachers and books focus from the perspective of the real world, seeing all the glamour, maya, and illusion going on but not recognizing the heavenly ideal! Also, there is so much imbalance and faulty thinking within people, that unless you are really holding an "immaculate perception" it is quite easy to forget about the Heavenly Ideal! In this world it is very easy to focus on the "form" level rather than the "essence"! The key, however, to God Realization and integrated ascension is to see both! If you don't hold this "Innocent Perception" towards self and others, there is the danger of losing unconditional love! This is especially true when coming across really corrupt, negative ego-driven, and really evil people!

Now there are corollary issues that are related to this, which the negative ego has distorted because of not understanding it. One is the issue of judgment versus Spiritual discernment. There are many that think that we should never even have discernments, that any time you observe negativity it is a judgment. So they try to blind themselves to seeing any negativity. This sounds very strange, I know, to many of you, yet you would be surprised how many lightworkers are totally confused on this point. There are others who judge, which means they are discerning with no unconditional love! Both of these are the negative ego. To blind yourself to the existence of evil is a prescription to be run by it! To blind yourself to not being allowed to have Spiritual discernments is also a prescription to be totally run by the negative ego! To judge others with "Innocent perception" or unconditional love for everyone, no matter how evil, is a prescription to be totally run by the negative ego! The proper integration comes in allowing yourself to have Spiritual discernments and observations while simultaneously seeing each person as God and the Christ, and only making these observations through the heart and unconditional love!

Now, another interesting issue of negative ego corruption and contamination stems from this misunderstanding that I call the "Pollyanna consciousness"! This is where everything is love and light, and again, there is no evil, or dark brotherhood, or black lodge, or negativity. The person refuses to look at it, see it or acknowledge it as a potentiality within self or manifesting in others. The Pollyanna philosophy is a prescription to be taken over by the darker side!

One other interesting corollary of this issue that has also caused much negative ego corruption is the confusion between the heavenly ideal and the issue of Realization. Books like *A Course in Miracles*, which again I absolutely love, and is one of my favorite books in the whole world now that I understand the lens it is written from, states that we each are the Christ and nothing can ever change that. Now, massive numbers of lightworkers have misunderstood this to think they are God Realized or Christ Realized! The negative ego will distort any Spiritual teaching to make it feel good about itself! I hate to burst this bubble, but this is illusion and more negative ego corruption. It is not that what *A Course In Miracles* is saying is not true, for it is the truth. The confusion is that many lightworkers are interpreting it from the wrong understanding and lens. What is being said is true. We are the Christ regardless of what we have ever done, are doing, or ever will do! This is true for everyone. Yet simultaneously it is also true that no one on this planet has Realized GOD! To Realize GOD one must pass 352 levels of initiation. There is no one on this planet except for Sai Baba who has incarnated at a higher level than the fourteenth initiation at this time of the year 2000. I hope this puts the issue of GOD Realization into proper perspective! Although we each are the Christ, in truth, GOD created the infinite universe and set it up that evolution was part of the plan. The process of evolution did not occur because there was a fall. Even if all Sons and Daughters of GOD never misused their free choice, and had never eaten of the Tree of Good and Evil or thought a negative ego/fear-based/separative thought, they would still have to evolve through the 352 levels of initiation. Isn't that interesting!

So those who interpret *A Course in Miracles* to mean they do not have to do anything for they already are the Christ have taken a truth, but have confused the process of evolution with this truth! Every being in GOD's infinite universe has been a part of this evolutionary process. It was just part of the Divine plan. Every being must go through this evolutionary process and demonstrate Godliness and

Spiritual/Christ/Buddha consciousness at each level before being allowed to graduate and move to the next! This is what the initiation process is about! So if someone thinks they can just say to themselves, I am the Christ and I always have been, are, and will be, and they are God Realized, with no judgment intended they have been deluded by their negative ego. Isn't the negative ego tricky in how it has infiltrated New Age teachings? It is amazing to watch! It changes form like the AIDS virus! So the proper perspective is that each person is God and is the Christ, always has been, is now and always will be regardless of all factors, but there is an evolutionary process you have to go through, and the law of karma does exist, and if you do not do all the things discussed in this book you are not going to Realize God!

Now, those who claim to be God Realized, or Self Realized, as we see in all their advertising, are usually as I have said before fifth, sixth, or seventh degree Initiates. They are confusing Planetary realization with Solar, Galactic, Universal, Multi-Universal and true GOD Realization! Spiritually impressionable lightworkers believe these claims. Again, most of these people are not only 345 initiations away from God Realization, they are also more often than not totally unintegrated on the psychological level and very often on the earthly level as well. Their realization is a Planetary one on the Spiritual plane only! In trying to give them a little bit of the benefit of the doubt, they just do not have a full understanding of how vast and infinite GOD really is and that true God Realization is a process of mastering the Spiritual, psychological, and physical/earthly levels in a balanced and integrated manner. From reading this book you can now see how much goes into just the psychospiritual level, let alone the Spiritual and earthly level. If you would like to learn what goes into the Spiritual level of GOD Realization, read my books, *The Complete Ascension Manual, Beyond Ascension, Cosmic Ascension*, and *The Golden Book of Melchizedek: How To Become an Integrated Christ/Buddha in This Lifetime, Revelations of a Melchizedek*

Initiate, Ascension Activation Meditations of The Spiritual Hierarchy, How To Teach Ascension Classes, The Ascended Masters Light The Way, and *The Ascension Names and Terms Glossary!*

If you would like to know how to develop physical/earthly God Realization then read my books, *Manual for Planetary Leadership, Your Ascension Mission, The Golden Keys To Ascension and Healing, Hidden Mysteries, The Soul's Perspective on How To Achieve Perfect Radiant Health, Empowerment and Integration of The Goddess!* All these books are available from the Academy! You will find this information at the end of this book!

To know and Realize God on a Spiritual, psychological and physical and earthly level in a balanced and integrated way and manner is the greatest feeling in the world! Every thought, word and deed becomes filled with joy and bliss!

It is my sincere hope and prayer that this relatively short but most important chapter on the difference between the heavenly ideal and the real world, and all the corollary issues of how the negative ego can create illusion and delusion if these most intricate balances are not understood, has been useful to you!

CHAPTER 45

GOD Realization, The Spiritual Path, Humbleness and Humility

As you can see from reading and studying this book, the path to true "God Realization" and "Integrated Ascension" is not an easy one! There are an enormous number of Spiritual tests that come at every level. There are an enormous number of Spiritual aspects to mastery! There are unbelievable psychological tests to master! There are an unbelievable number of physical/earthly tests to master! Then there is the even bigger test of integrating all three levels in perfect harmony and balance!

Then come all the Spiritual tests of Spiritual leadership and planetary world service! And then there are all kinds of relationship tests: romantic, family, friends, business, professional, acquaintances, students and impersonal! The second that one thinks they "have it together" is when they are most in danger! The second a person lets down their "joyous vigilance" they are in danger! The second the slightest element of "false pride" enters in they are headed for a fall!

From reading this book you can see that the real foundation of the work is the psychological level! In truth, it is easy to build light quotient or invoke activations. That is simple! In that sense, initiations are relatively easy to pass! From reading this book you can see how "incredibly complicated" it is to maintain perfect balance and integration psychologically! You can see how incredibly seductive and manipulative the negative ego/fear-based/separative mind is! You can see how every time you catch one act of deception, sabotage, and delusion, it will rationalize, change forms, become slippery, and change forms again! You see how many subtle balances there are to keep on the Spiritual path, including balancing the: Three-Fold Flame, Seven Rays, the 12 archetypes, three minds, feminine and masculine, Heaven and Earth, the twelve houses of the Aodiac, all the archetypes of the tarot cards, and the 12 Sephiroth of the Tree of Life, parenting the inner child, controlling and quieting the mind, mastering one's feelings and emotions, transcending all lower-self desire, not going on automatic pilot, taking proper care of the physical body, not being taken over by power, fame, or money, properly using sexuality, mastering money and business, properly integrating the God/Goddess energies, learning to own your personal power and self-mastery at all times, being a master and not a victim, changing all attachments to preferences, practicing the presence of God at all times, looking at everything as a Spiritual test and lesson, integrating and mastering Earth energies, manifesting your Spiritual mission on Earth, being Spiritual in the marketplace, balancing the horizontal and vertical, reprogramming the subconscious mind, staying in control of the subconscious mind at all times, staying out of hypnosis, staying pure in God at all times, always being honest with self, developing an efficient perception of reality, remaining in the Tao at all times, making all the daily attitudinal, emotional, energetic, physical and earthly adjustments one needs to make to remain in the Tao, keeping your seven chakras balanced and integrated, passing all your 12 levels of initiation, building your Antakarana, transcending all glamour, maya and illusion, having self-love and self-worth, keeping your golden bubble of protection up, keeping up all the Spiritual, psychological, and physical practices, maintaining self-discipline, practicing of meditation, building your light and love quotient, maintaining your main psychological quotients and/or flawless character, admitting mistakes and apologizing, not falling into blind spots, mind locks, or limited lens seeing, maintaining full spectrum prism consciousness seeing at all times, fulfilling your Spiritual mission and puzzle piece, staying on top of all the lessons of Earth life, living only in unconditional love, transcending all fear-based/separative thinking and feeling, transcending all negative feelings and emotions, getting proper diet and physical exercise, dealing with Spiritual mutation, remaining in integrity and honesty with self and others at all times, determining and fulfilling your puzzle piece, demonstrating prosperity consciousness, using Spiritual discernment, maintaining a good Spiritual, mental, emotional, etheric, energetic, physical, environmental and social diet at all times, maintaining one's point of balance, dealing with negative ego-run people, balancing and integrating the four bodies and three minds, integrating the Four Faces of GOD, properly integrating the 72 Subquotients of GOD, taking care of family, fulfilling all one's earthly responsibilities, properly caring for students, meeting family obligations, building you Light Body, dealing with health lessons, dealing with chronic health lessons, the Job Initiation, living in this world but not of this world, maintaining a strong Spiritual, psychological, and physical immune system, remaining physically grounded, fully integrating and grounding one's Higher Self and Mighty I Am Presence into one's four-body system and Earth life, achieving physical ascension, cleansing all physical impurities and subtle toxins from the physical body, cleansing and undoing all subtle mental and emotional toxins from the mental and emotional body, bearing one's cross, removing all negative implants and elementals, achieving 352 initiations to truly achieve GOD Realization and become a Cosmic Ascended Master, not just a Planetary Ascended Master, attuning to the Earth Mother and the Nature and Devic Kingdom, avoiding all the corruption, glamour, and contamination of the negative ego mind on the Spiritual path, being truly egoless in the sense of transcending all negative ego thinking and feeling and changing it to Spiritual/Christ/Buddha thinking and feeling, integrating the 12 levels of initiation into one's four body system, not letting negative ego belief systems, subconscious programming and personal agendas contaminate one's channeling, doing Spiritual teaching, psychic work, healing, writing, and Spiritual science work, being careful how one uses the power of the spoken word, practicing self-inquiry, self-introspection, and truly knowing oneself, avoiding lower psychism, paying one's rent to GOD on all levels, dealing with attack and criticism, properly integrating one's feeling and emotions without being a victim of them, properly integrating one's conscience, not giving in to temptation, resolving conflict, forgiving self and others, releasing all anger, releasing all worry and fear, dealing with psychic attack, developing appropriate self-boundaries and boundaries with others, learning to turn the other cheek, loving your enemies, differentiating truth from illusion, remaining right with self and right with GOD at all times, integrating all the Ascended Master teachings, learning to be, integrating multidimensional communication, dealing with death, working with your dreams, dealing with the slippery slope syndrome, properly processing life, staying organized, truly learning compassion and innocent perception, seeing life from other people's moccasins, knowing/learning who am I, why am I here, and where am I going, seeing life only through the eyes of love, pursuing excellence on all levels all the time, paying attention to all the details of life on all levels, parenting, inner Spiritual parenting, recognizing the Spiritual ideal but still having Spiritual discernment, not being judgemental but still maintaining unconditionally loving Spiritual discernment, not getting caught up and confused by all the nonintegrated, fragmented

Spiritual leaders, Spiritual teachers, channels, Spiritual scientists and psychologists who have different and opposing beliefs, philosophies and perspectives that are not all integrated, truly realizing the words: "GOD equals man minus ego," last but not least, truly realizing "Integrated Ascension"!

My Beloved Readers, this chapter is being written to once and for all put fully into perspective the incredible complexity, subtleness, and intricatenesss of the Spiritual path. It is so incredibly easy to delude oneself. It is so incredibly easy to fall into one's negative ego. It is so incredibly easy to fall asleep. It can happen in the twinkling of an eye. It is so easy to take a tumble down the Spiritual mountain. My Beloved Readers, it is so incredibly easy to "Fall from Grace"! It happened to Lucifer and he was an Archangel! It is happening right and left to religious leaders, channels, Spiritual teachers, and Spiritual scientists, right in front of our eyes. Some lightworkers see and some don't. Why don't they see all of what is going on? The answer is contained within the pages of this book. You cannot see in others that which you have not come to see and understand as aspects and/or potentialities within self. I humbly suggest to you that this book has opened your Spiritual, psychological, and earthly/physical eyes to a great many subtleties that you may have not been focused upon within self and others. Some of these things may have been occurring within you, and some of the potentialities, but by reading this book, you have learned by grace instead of karma. This is the real purpose of this book. To nip this stuff in the bud! Don't think for a moment that it cannot happen to you. If you do, it is the negative ego reading this book, not you! Isn't that an interesting thought.

You don't think this happens. Most lightworkers don't read the book; it is the negative ego that reads. As they are reading the negative ego is saying, "I mastered that in the Spring of '72!" "I don't need this, for I already have mastered all this psychological stuff!" All I can say is, "After pride cometh the fall"! On the other side of the coin of the negative ego, it is saying, "I am not worthy!" "I am not deserving of this!" "This is too much, I will never achieve this!" "This is only for really advanced light-workers, not for me!"

My Beloved Readers, the negative ego's game is to be better than every-one else or worse than everyone else! The negative ego's game is to be superior or inferior! This is why I recommend in this moment to do what Fritz Pearls, who invented Gestalt psychology, said, which is to "Laugh the Top Dog/Under Dog specific thought complex off the stage!" I humbly and unconditionally lovingly state that I do not agree with everything that Fritz Pearls taught or did, but this particular statement I think is quite a brilliant way of describing the need of the moment. It is only when we transcend the negative ego, as all great Spiritual masters have taught throughout the ages, that true God Realization, God purity and God honesty with self and others can be achieved! It is only then that we can achieve a balanced, integrated, and efficient perception of reality and ourselves. It is only then that we will not see life through the dark tinted glasses of the negative ego!

My Beloved Readers, as we see from this Spiritual list, the Spiritual path is incredibly complex. Even if we can achieve a sense of balance and integration among all these aspects and issues, which indeed is of course possible, and is indeed the purpose of this book, one can lose it at any moment. Never forget this. This may be the single most important thing I have said in this entire book. It is so important I am going to say it again! "At any moment, no matter what level you are at, a Planetary Ascended Master, a proclaimed Self-Realized Being, an Avatar, an Archangel, an Elohim Master, a Christed Extraterrestrial, a Solar Master, a Galactic Master, a Universal Master, a Multi-Universal Master, or a Cosmic Ascended Master, one can always lose it." Why is this? This is because GOD gave us free choice and all it takes is one moment of automatic pilot, one moment of becoming unconscious, one moment of losing your personal power, one moment of not being joyously vigilant, one moment of not being centered, balanced and integrated in one's consciousness, to start heading down the wrong path again!

So first we see how incredibly complex and hard it is to achieve Self-Realization and/or Integrated Ascension! Now secondly, we are seeing how incredibly easy it is to take a tumble down the Spiritual Mountain and/or fall from grace! I share this not to create any fear, for that is not necessary or appropriate. I share this to "Spiritually Challenge" you to remain in your personal power and Spiritual joyous vigilance at all times, and to not give in to any sense of false pride! I cannot tell you how many Spiritual leaders, Spiritual teachers, Spiritual channels, Spiritual psychics, Spiritual scientists, Spiritual healers, Spiritual authors, and Spiritual friends take a tumble down the mountain, and a great many of them fall from grace. Not a single one knows that it has happened! This is the incredible power of delusion, deception, glamour, illusion, and maya of the negative ego! Don't think for a second that it cannot happen to you! If it can happen to an Archangel, it can happen to you! As Master Yoda said in the *Star Wars* movie, "Don't underestimate the power of the dark side of the Force!" and "Do not give in to your anger or your fear!" The single most important Spiritual lesson of the Spiritual path is learning to transcend negative ego/fear-based/separative thinking and feeling, and change it to Spiritual/Christ/Buddha thinking and feeling! This is the key to being able to remain in unconditional love at all times and the key to keeping your Three-Fold Flame of love/wisdom/power, seven rays, and all the other things I have mentioned in this chapter in perfect balance and integration!

If all this were not enough to keep us humble and filled with humility, what I mentioned about there being 352 levels of initiation to achieve true GOD Realization should help to reinforce this point as well! My Beloved Readers, there are all these lightworkers in the New Age movement or in the world claiming to be Self-Realized. Claiming to be God Realized beings. Claiming to be Avatars! Claiming to be fully Realized Ascended Masters! Claiming to have completed their nine trillionth initiation and forty millionth chakra! Claiming to be the full embodiment of this cosmic being or that one. Claiming to be a saint! Claiming to have completed all 352 levels of initiation! Claiming to be not only a Planetary Ascended Master but also a Cosmic Ascended Master! Now, I am not saying it is not ever appropriate to share certain information given to self by Spirit and the Masters. I am just saying here that one must be very careful about making claims of being fully GOD Realized! There are 352 levels of initiation to achieve full GOD Realization! There is not one being on this planet except for Sai Baba who is even beyond the fourteenth initiation as we begin this New Millennium. Most of the people who are making these claims of being Self-Realized are fifth, sixth and seventh degree initiates and are not even psychologically or earthly integrated. It is almost a joke with no judgment intended! My Beloved Readers, do you think all these people making these claims are keeping all the things I have mentioned in this chapter in perfect integration and balance? To be honest, most of them probably have not even heard of half the concepts! So half the time these claims are made, it is the negative ego who is making them! The other half of the time it is Spiritual leaders or teachers who mean well, but are seeing life from a very limited lens and do not really understand in the slightest what true God Realization is, or they would not make such claims. So all I am saying is be very careful about the claims you make, or the claims you see others making, for 99 out of 100 times they are "hot air and limited lens seeing" and nothing more! It is the negative ego's need to feel good about itself, and with no judgment intended, a lack of a "Full Spectrum Prism Consciousness" of what true GOD Realization really means on a Spiritual, psychological and physical/earthly level! I see so many lightworkers getting sucked up and seduced by all this negative ego and limited lens claims, that most of the time they do not even begin to properly address all the psychological or physical/earthly lessons of life, let alone the full totality of one's Spiritual life. This was one of the many reasons I have written this book!

This chapter has been written to bring home with a "Sledgehammer" to all lightworkers the importance of seeing the incredible complexity of the path of God Realization on a Spiritual, psychological, and physical/earthly level and the tremendous need to be incredibly humble and filled with humility at the true glory and splendor of GOD!

Many are claiming GOD Realization when the truth is, "GOD is Unfathomable!" Even when we become fully integrated Ascended Masters, and complete our 352 levels of initiation and become "Cosmic Integrated Ascended Masters," GOD is still Unfathomable! My Beloved Readers, this is because GOD is infinite and contains everything! GOD also continues to grow and expand as well! GOD continues to experiment, create and expand the glory and profundity of His kingdom! So even when we are official Cosmic Ascended Masters at the 352nd level of Divinity, there will always be another level of refinement, purification and expansion to realize!

If GOD is a ten-inch ruler, the most advanced being on this planet is not more than an inch or two up the ruler at most. The inner plane Ascended Masters who are our teachers of the Planetary Hierarchy are not more than three or four inches up the ruler at most. So you see how ludicrous a great many of these claims lightworkers, Spiritual leaders and teachers are making really are! This chapter is given in total unconditional love, humbleness, and humility for the purpose of stressing the importance for lightworkers to see the incredible complexity of the Spiritual path on all levels, and to emphasize the importance of being and demonstrating the utmost humbleness and humility in our daily lives. Forgiven the perspective that has been laid out in this chapter, how could we be anything else? It is only the negative ego and limited lens seeing that could cause us to be any other way!

So my Beloved Readers, rejoice in the humbleness and humility, for even though the path to God Realization is quite complex Spiritually, psychologically, physically/earthly and in an "Integrated Ascension" sense, we must under-stand that we are made in the "Image of GOD"!

We are each incarnations of GOD! We are each Sons and Daughters of GOD! We each are the Christ, the Buddha, and the Eternal Self! We are each in a sense "Apprentice Gods" learning to become like our Spiritual Father and Mother! The Spiritual path is extremely complex. However, GOD has given us the tools and understanding to achieve all that has been stated and more if we have the proper dedication and a pure heart! In understanding the incredible complexity of the Spiritual path and learning to be humble and manifest humility, we, in truth, are really on the way to fully realizing this Spiritual ideal of becoming a "God Realized Being and Integrated Ascended Master"!

As I have come to like saying at the end of many of my chapters, So let it be Written, So let it be Done!

CHAPTER 46

The Seven Faces of GOD

It is very interesting to watch where the Spiritual path becomes a little fragmented or disintegrated. I have spent much time in many of my books clearly showing how this is taking place in many areas of the Spiritual path and psychological levels. One of the real interesting places where this is occurring place, that is not one of the more obvious ones is in regard to Spiritual seekers relationship to GOD, The Spiritual Hierarchy, the Christed Extraterrestrials, the Consciousness or Psychological Movement, traditional religion, the environmentalists, and the atheist. In this chapter I will approach this from a personal and impersonal point of view. I will begin with the personal perspective first.

There are a great many people on the Spiritual path who by definition believe in GOD, and their entire focus is on GOD, and this is fine. A great many do not first realize that there are different aspects of GOD within their being that can be focused upon. There is GOD the Creator. There is Christ and the Holy Spirit. There is each person's own Higher Self, and then their own individualized Mighty I

Am Presence or Monad. GOD is on, so, in truth, it does not matter who or where you focus upon; however, in truth, there are different kinds of attunements to GOD one can make. When people in traditional religion think they are having a relationship to GOD the Creator, in reality they are communing with their own Higher Self. This is not a judgement, or statement of anything wrong, it is just a point of fact. Sometimes lightworkers get focused on one aspect of GOD, and do not take advantage of, let's say for example, the incredible powers of the Holy Spirit, because they just focus on the Mighty I Am Presence. Some might not cultivate a relationship to GOD the Creator. In other religions, they might just focus on Brahma, Shiva, Vishnu, Allah, or Yahweh, or in the case of Buddhism on no GOD at all. I recommend cultivating a relationship to all the different aspects of GOD, although, in truth, they function as one.

Now lets take this discussion a little further. A great many on the Spiritual path focus on GOD but do not focus on the Spiritual Hierarchy. This Hierarchy would be all the prophets, saints, and masters who have graduated and achieved liberation from the wheel of rebirth and are on the inner plane now still helping and working with the planet. Most of traditional religion completely ignores all this help. Occasionally a few are honored, usually the founders of that religion and maybe their family, and a small lineage of prophets that followed. The entire Spiritual Government of this planet is ignored, as is the entire Cosmic Hierarchy of inner plane Ascended Masters who govern the Solar System, Galaxy, Universe, Multi-Universe and entire Cosmos.

Then it is also not understood that their GOD created three lines of evolution. There is the Ascended Masters, but there are also two other lines, which are the Archangels and Angels, and then the Elohim lines of evolution. The Elohim are not even recognized as having a line of evolution and are almost completely ignored. They are the Creator Gods, and connected with the thought attributes of GOD. The Archangels and Angels being connected more with the feeling tones of GOD. It is interesting how some people worship GOD, which is obviously good, but ignore often all three lines of evolution which could greatly help in their Spiritual journey and path. Then there are those who attune to the Ascended Masters, but ignore the Angels. There are those who focus on the Angels but ignore the Ascended Masters. There are those who focus on the Ascended Masters and Angels, and ignore the Elohim. My Beloved Readers, there are even those who focus on all these Celestial beings and forget about GOD, Christ the Holy Spirit, the Mighty I Am Presence and the Higher Self. This may be hard to believe but is true. Some people just get into GOD. Some people get focused on the Cosmic Hierarchy of Celestial beings. I am recommending staying connected to both groups and all three lines of evolution for the highest understanding and Realization of GOD.

Then there is another group that is into the Extraterrestrials. This is interesting for there are two groups in this camp. There are those who are involved that are not connected to their Spiritual path, and those that are. It is hard to believe that you can be involved with Extraterrestrials and not be Spiritual, but I assure you it is true and there are enormous numbers of people who fall into this category. Then there are others who are more Spiritual, who focus on such groups as the Arcturians and the Ashtar Command, which are two of the more Spiritual Extraterrestrial groups. There are many Extraterrestrial groups that are borderline, and many that are not Spiritual at all. The level of Spirituality in the Extraterrestrials begins to fall off from here. I personally love the Extraterrestrials, but I myself remain more focused on the Arcturians, Ashtar Command and Venusians for my personal discernment is that the level of Spiritual clarity begins to drop off from there. I am not saying that other Extraterrestrial groups are not Spiritual, but just that these are the most advanced ones, and I try to keep my attunement more on them, although I am interested in all Extraterrestrials. Although it must be understood that they are not all

Christed races and there are some extremely negative ones, so people must be very careful and discerning. Ninety-five percent of the Extraterrestrials are quite positive in nature. The ones who are doing all the abducting are not.

So, we have those that focus on the Extraterrestrials who are not Spiritual, but almost more science fiction oriented and/or materially interested. And we have those who are Spiritually attuned to the Christed races of Extraterrestrials, who can help an enormous amount on one's Spiritual path. Then we have those that focus on the Extraterrestrials but reject the Ascended Masters, Angels, and Elohim. Then we have those that focus on the Ascended Masters, Angels, Elohim and Christed Extraterrestrials, but do not focus as much on GOD, or any combination of the above.

Adding to this mix then, we have what I am going to call the Consciousness Movement and/or Psychological Movement. There are enormous numbers of people who are more psychologically centered and are interested in therapy, traditional forms of psychology, and personal growth, but are not really Spiritual. I call this "personality level" forms of psychology and personal growth. It is good that they are interested in growing and should be commended for that, but they have not really awakened to their Soul, Spirit, and GOD, yet. A great many people get involved with my work through the psychological lens, another large group through the Ascended Masters and ascension lens, another large group through the GOD lens and another still through my work in the Extraterrestrial Movement. My work, being of a synthesis nature, appeals to all four groups because of the cutting-edge nature of the work in all four areas. Others still come into the work through its focus on religion and the integration of all the religions, and showing the strengths and weaknesses of all the religions. Others still, come into the work through the focus on physical healing, environmental consciousness, political consciousness, and social consciousness. Others still come into this work through intense Spiritual, psychological, and earthly suffering from former atheistic perspectives, because their personal suffering from disobedience to GOD's Laws on all levels has caused a type of "dark night of the soul," which has allowed the "still small voice within" to get through the defenses to guide them to the integrated, easy to understand, practical, intuitive, scientific, and comprehensive answers they seek. In truth, it is a fascinating process to watch. This is why I encourage all my readers to become "Masters of Synthesis and Integration"!

It is fascinating to me how everyone who comes into my work has a different favorite book. Some love the psychological books, some, the ascension books, some, the GOD-focused books and chapters, and others, my books on Extraterrestrials. I call the process of integrating all four aspects, "seeing life from a Full Spectrum Prism." It is very easy in life to get focused on certain lenses. There is no judgement in this, and at times it is even appropriate as long as you don't get stuck in the lens and lose sight of the big picture. In my work I have attempted to write an easy to understand, yet incredibly comprehensive encyclopedia of all four lenses, and show how they are all interconnected and one. They are, in a sense, another understanding of the Four Faces of GOD, and each one is essential to a complete understanding and realization of the nature of GOD.

It is amazing to me how many New Age Spiritual people are cutoff and completely unclear on the psychological level, which eventually leads to a corruption of all their Spiritual work if this is not focused upon and corrected. It also amazes me how many Spiritual New Age people are cutoff from the Christed Extraterrestrials and Extraterrestrial Movement as a whole. I am amazed at how many people are into GOD but not the Masters, Angels and Elohim. I am amazed at how many people are into these Celestial beings and begin to forget about calling on GOD in His various forms and aspects. Then I am amazed how many people who are into the Extraterrestrial stuff are not Spiritual, and often not even psychological. I do not share this as any type of judgement, but just as a point of Spiritual observation as another example of the fragmentation and disintegration that takes place among seekers. I recommend that you become a Master and be attuned to all four levels.

The fifth group is religion. This group is focused on GOD, but not the inner plane Ascended Masters and not the Elohim, connected a little with the Angels, cut-off usually from the Extraterrestrials, and cutoff from the psychological in a true understanding of what Spiritual psychology is. They also completely reject the New Age Movement, and the teachings are often too dogmatic and rigid, and are too contaminated with misinterpretation. Religion is still of great value, do not get me wrong. There is much corruption, misinterpretation and glamour in the New Age Movement as well. There is, however, much more openness, and less self-righteous and opinionated views. There will always be the different religions and this is good. Eventually they will learn to not all compete with each other and see they are one, in truth, and come from the same Source, and see that all paths lead back to GOD. So, here in traditional religion we see another lens that is better than no GOD at all, but sees life through a very limited prism consciousness.

One other group that could also fit into this understanding is what I would call the Environmentalist Movement. This is a more recent movement; however, a great many are focused on this. This is a group that is not necessarily focused on GOD, the Celestial Hierarchy, Extraterrestrials, the Consciousness or Psychological Movement, or religion. It is hard to believe but true. These people are more focused on the environment, with possibly Green Party affiliation, and on saving the trees, saving the animals, upholding earthly social causes, saving the rainforest, preventing animal cruelty, fighting to save the ozone layer, and stop the greenhouse effect, and cleaning up pollution on Mother Earth, to name just a few. They are to be congratulated for their work in this area. What is fascinating is that they are often not GOD inclined, not into the Celestial Hierarchy, not psychologically focused, not into religion, yet they love the Earth and are more environmentally, socially, or politically motivated. They are more earthly focused in their lens. This might be termed the Sixth Face of GOD. One cannot truly Realize GOD unless one grounds their Spirituality into their physical bodies and onto the Earth. The ideal is to bring Heaven to Earth and to fulfill your Spiritual mission on Earth and get involved with Earth life and love Earth life.

If you do not love the Earth and do not love Earth life something is missing. I am not saying Earth life is the easiest thing, for it is not. However, learning to love the Earth and be happy on Earth is one of the most important lessons we are all here to learn.

What is absolutely fascinating as well, is to see that those who are focused on GOD are often completely cut-off from environmental, political, and social concerns. New Age people into the Ascended Masters are so focused on Celestial beings, that they are often cutoff from environmental, political and social concerns on Earth. They are more interested in Heavenly Realms, which I hate to tell you is not right! Extraterrestrial people are not necessarily concerned with environmental, political or social concerns, and neither are psychological people in terms of their actions. Atheists could probably care less, being by very definition probably more self-absorbed.

After this we have the atheists or the hedonists who do not believe in GOD, the Masters, Angels, Elohim, Extraterrestrials, psychology, personal growth, and religion. With no judgement intended, they are the worse off. They see life from a totally materialistic, third dimensional love, seeing life only through the intellect and often though a lens based on a science of materialism completely cutoff from their inner senses. In truth, they are still Sons and Daughters of GOD, and are on their Spiritual path. They just don't realize it. They see life through one-tenth of a Full Spectrum Prism and are stuck there. The Atheist may still have some moral code, but it will be based on a personality level theory. The Hedonist lives to just enjoy life and does not recognize any purpose to living. For deeply religious or Spiritual people, it is hard to believe anyone can live an entire life not believing in GOD, when GOD is all that exists. This, my Beloved Readers, is the delusionary potentiality of the negative ego/fear-based/separative/lower-self mind that runs an enormous number of people in our world. Their purpose becomes one of pleasure seeking, power, greed, sex, material possessions, and the completion of temporary and impermanent goals that have no eternal or immortal consequence or meaning. All these Souls will eventually wake-up; it is just a matter of time. The suffering they will bring upon themselves by being not right with self, and not right with GOD, will cause them ultimately to seek truth. This is not GOD or the Masters doing this to them, this is they bringing it upon themselves, for we all live under the "law of cause and effect" and karma of our thoughts, feelings, energies and actions.

So, in conclusion, on a personal and collective level we see that GOD, the Cosmic and Spiritual Hierarchy of Celestial Beings, the Extraterrestrial Movement, the Consciousness and Psychological Movement, religion, the environmentalists, and political and social activists are, in truth, all one. They are all aspects of GOD, and to fully Realize GOD one needs to integrate and synthesize all of them for the most complete understanding of GOD Realization. It is only when we get focused in one lens, which is a beautiful lens, but still only one lens, that we see that we are missing a whole other lens of GOD that is equally beautiful and equally beneficial and important to a complete understanding.

Now, some people of course may focus on two out of six, or three out of six, or four out of six. I am not including here the Atheist group who, of course, are a part of GOD, but in truth are not something to be integrated, where the other six are. My Beloved Readers, is it not fascinating how individuals and large groups of individuals around the globe become too focused on one lens of life and miss the Full Spectrum Prism picture? If you truly want to Realize GOD at the highest level, open your mind, consciousness, heart, thoughts, feelings, words and actions to all these levels, for then you will truly see life as GOD sees life, from a point of unity, integration and oneness!

CHAPTER 47

The Spiritual Science of Blind Spots, Mind Locks, and Lenses

In my humble opinion, this chapter is an extremely cutting-edge understanding in the field of Transpersonal Psychology, Soul Psychology, and Spiritual Psychology. It is something I have not written about before or seen in any other book I have ever read. It is the Spiritual science of blind spots, mind locks, and lenses. As you all know, we don't see just with out physical eyes, we see with our mind. How can one hundred people see any given event take place and every one will have a different version? How can it be at a jury trial that twelve people hear the facts yet there can be so much conflict as to whether the person is guilty or not? How can half the population think O.J. Simpson was innocent and the other half believe he is guilty? How can half the population of any given country belong to one political party and the other half to another? How can millions of people become susceptible to cults, when it is so obvious to others how corrupt certain individuals and organizations are?

My Beloved Readers, the Spiritual science of blind spots, mind blocks, and lenses is a most fascinating psychospiritual science. To begin this discussion let us look at the basic masculine/feminine balance. If a person is too feminine and too overidentified with their emotional body and right brain, then they will automatically develop enormous numbers of blind spots in their masculine side. They will have extremely poor Spiritual discernment. They will likely be very weak in business and mathematical areas. They will likely be very child-like and have blind spots in being more adult and impersonal. They will also have a great many blind spots to the negative ego's thinking, because when the emotional body is too in control, the negative ego automatically becomes the programmer.

On the other side of the coin, if someone is too masculine and identified with the mind, they will have blind spots to the appreciation of heart energy and feeling energy. They will have blind spots in romantic relationship functioning. They will have blind spots to their own criticalness and judgementalness.

If a person is too Heavenly, they will have blind spots as to how to function effectively on the Earth plane. If a person is too earthly and too grounded, they will have blind spots to proper development of their Spiritual life.

The same thing can happen in relationship to the Seven Rays. If a person is more identified with the First Ray of Power, then they will have blind spots in development of their Second Ray of Love/Wisdom. If a person is highly developed in the arts or Fourth Ray, they often have blind spots in relationship to the Fifth Ray of Spiritual Science. If a person is highly developed in the more "feeling" Rays, two, four, and six, which are Love/Wisdom, Harmony, and Devotion, then they often have blind spots in Rays one, three, and five. Rays one, three and five are Power, Active Intelligence, and Spiritual Science. The same is true in a reverse sense.

The same is true in Carl Jung's theory of types. He suggested there were four types of people: intuitive, thinking, feeling, and sensation function. People are often strong in one or two types, and weak in the other two. If one is intuitive and thinking, one tends to have blind spots in their feeling and sensation function. Sensation function is the focus on one's five physical senses. Some people focus on this, others do not think it is important. The same is true of all these types. The ideal of course, is to integrate all four types in a balanced manner. If one is too thinking and logical they will have blind spots in understanding their own feeling nature, and in understanding the feeling nature of others. If one is very intuitive they often have a hard time being grounded and really working practically with the Earth. People who are overidentified with their sensation function often have a hard time accessing their intuition and higher Spiritual nature.

If you are identified with the collective programming of Earth's history, then you will have a hard time understanding and appreciating the Goddess energy. If you are overidentified with the Goddess, the reverse is true.

The same concept of blind spots applies to astrology. If you have a lot of "water" in your horoscope you may have blind spots dealing with "air." If you have a lot of "fire" you may have blind spots with "earth," and vice versa.

An unbelievable key principle in understanding the Science of blind spots is, that which you cannot see within self you cannot see within others either. If you are not in control of the negative ego within yourself you will not be able to discern the negative ego in others. If you are run by the emotional body within self, you will not be able to see this happening within others. The same is true of the mind and/or Spirit. So from this profound statement and understanding, you can see how important it is to develop one's self Spiritually, psychologically, and in a physical/earthly sense. Otherwise, you will not be able to see those same undeveloped aspects within others. What most people do is attract to themselves those people that have the same imbalances they have. This has a reinforcing effect on their imbalanced psychology and/or philosophy. The only people they get feedback from are people with the same imbalances.

Let us now take this discussion a little bit further, to professions. A Spiritual psychologist sees a great many things others do not see because of their training. An artist sees a great many things that others do not see in the realm of beauty. A psychic sees many things that others do not see. A channel sees many things that others do not see. A clairvoyant sees many things that others do not see. An energy healer sees and feels many things that others do not see or feel. A gardener sees a great many things that others do not see. A Spiritual scientist sees many things that others do not see. I could go through hundreds of other professions, which would add to this list. The key question now is, what does this show us? Because of our training and focus in this life and past lives, we see through that which we have been trained in, and we have blind spots in areas we have not been trained in. This is why it is to our benefit to strive to be as integrated and balanced in all the rays, astrological signs, elements, types, the four bodies, numerology, tarot, the archetypes, professions, and lenses.

The twelve major archetypes are an example. If we are overidentified with one or more archetypes then we will have blind spots in the other archetypes. This is why it is to our benefit to be integrated in all twelve major archetypes. The same is true of the cards in the tarot deck.

Now let's take this discussion of blind spots even further. To understand GOD Consciousness it must be understood that GOD sees life through a full spectrum prism consciousness. All of the aspects in this chapter GOD sees through simultaneously. If we are going to be like GOD, we must do the same in the development of our God Consciousness. This is why I recommend to people to follow a path of "Synthesis" and a more eclectic path. This is why I have written a thirty volume "Easy-to-Read Encyclopedia of the Spiritual Path". Every form of psychology, every Spiritual path, every mystery school, every guru, every well-known channel and/or Spiritual teacher, every religion, and every well-known Spiritual text is a different lens of GOD. When we identify with one or study only one, we have blind spots to other forms of worship. GOD sees through all lenses, not just one or a few. I have written these books to help my readers to develop a more full spectrum prism consciousness and to help remove blind spots within self, and hence, in how they see others and their world.

In speaking before about professions, even though you may make money in one profession, this does not mean that you cannot become a Master Spiritual Psychologist, Channel, Healer, Author, Intuitive, Psychic, Gardener, Business Person, Economist, Environmentalist, Spiritual Teacher, Political Expert, Minister, Artist, Spiritual Scientist, Counselor, and so on. Most of us have had hundreds of past lives with different professions, and training on both the inner and outer plane, so this is not as impossible a task as you might think. I know at different times in my life that I have focused my development in all these areas and more. Wherever I have an undeveloped aspect in any area mentioned in this chapter, I work on developing it and this increases my full spectrum prism consciousness and removes more blind spots.

Which country you are born into and where you live is another lens. GOD sees through the cultures of all countries. If you have only lived and studied one culture, you will have blind spots to other cultures and belief systems. This is why it is a good thing to travel and to study other cultures and even speak other languages.

Another lens and blind spot is the color of our skin or ethnic background. We do not realize how we are programmed into seeing life through our particular skin color and ethnicity. This carries a whole set of belief systems that may or may not be true. If you are white in skin color, try talking to someone living in an African body and really see and experience how different their reality is. This is why it is a good thing to expand one's consciousness of ethnicities.

One's socioeconomic upbringing will also create a lens and corresponding blind spots that will limit your full God consciousness. This is why it is also a good idea to break out of this lens and pattern within self, and to communicate and commune with people with different experiences in this regard.

Now, there are many more lenses that we have been programmed to be locked into. I call this phenomena with any of the above mentioned issues or the ones I am about to mention "mind locks." A mind lock is when we get stuck in a certain aspect, lens, or belief system and don't realize it. We are hence locked in and only seeing life through a very small number of lenses, rather than all the lenses GOD sees through.

In truth, every belief system is a lens and potential mind lock. Do you identify with being a Republican, Democrat, or Reform Party member? This can be a mind lock and limited lens that blinds you. Your emotions can be a mind lock and your mind can be a mind lock. The negative ego can be a mind lock. Any given subpersonality can be a mind lock. Any given habit can be a mind lock. Any belief system that you have been given by your parents, teachers, ministers, rabbis, counselors, psychologists, friends, grandparents, workshops, lectures, past life programming, or childhood programming are all singular lenses, potential glamour, illusion, maya, blind spots, and potential mind locks.

Now I realize that this chapter can be a little humbling, for how many people in this world have developed themselves in all these areas and hence released themselves from these blind spots, mind locks, and limited lenses of seeing life. Melchizedek, the President of our entire Universe, told me that most people see life through the lens of a fly. He was not being judgmental, he was just contrasting his full spectrum prism consciousness of being responsible for an entire universe to that of most people on Earth, who see life from such a fragmented, unintegrated, and limited lens perspective. This humbling process I spoke of at the beginning of this paragraph is good and is a healthy humbleness and humility, which is one of the steps in achieving true God consciousness. Our negative egos always want to tell us how together and evolved we are. I am amazed at how many people in the Spiritual Movement go around claiming to have fully Realized GOD. Not only have they not Realized GOD in a Cosmic sense, they have not even realized GOD in a Planetary sense, a psychological sense, or a physical/earthly sense in becoming an integrated Planetary Ascended Master. 99.99% of the time it is their negative ego talking, and more glamour, illusion, and maya. Even most of the inner plane Ascended Masters who we are familiar with, have only Realized GOD two inches up a ten inch ruler in the true infinite nature of GOD. Hence, with no judgement intended, you see how comical and delusionary these claims are.

My Beloved Readers, even being Spiritual can be a mind lock and can enormously limit your perception if you are not properly integrating the psychological and physical earthly level. Many on the Spiritual path are overidentified with the Celestial realms and are not doing their psychological and physical/earthly homework. This is a blind spot and mind lock, as well as a limited lens, through which one is seeing and experiencing life within self and in others.

It is interesting to me how a great many people each have a favorite book in my Ascension book series and they are all different. This is because of the different lenses people are coming from. For example, some people approach my work from a psychological lens. Some people approach my work from a Spiritual or ascension lens. Others still, approach it from a more grounded physical/earthly lens.

In conclusion my Beloved Readers, the key to removing blind spots, mind locks and limited lenses is to follow a Spiritual path in life that I call "Integrated Ascension," and/or becoming an "Integrated Melchizedek/Christ/Buddha." This focus on integration, balance, and synthesis in all things will allow you to see from a more full spectrum God prism consciousness, and hence remove the blind spots, mind locks, and limited lens seeing that will come from not doing so. It is an approach of being a well-rounded individual. It is an approach of being a Renaissance man or woman. It is an approach of being whole and complete within self and within the true nature of GOD.

The last thing I wish to say to conclude this chapter is, that the vision I have laid out here to remove blind spots, mind locks, and limited lens seeing is a big one. The number one most important thing to do to keep your priorities straight and to make this process work is to master your mind, feelings and emotions, subconscious mind, inner child, and lower-self desire and to most of all learn to transcend negative ego/fear-based/separative thinking, and learn instead to think from your Melchizedek/Christ/Buddha mind. This is essential, for even if you develop yourself in all the areas I have mentioned in this chapter, the negative ego will corrupt the entire process and keep you blinded for it will have you use all that you have gained for the wrong purpose. You will be as blind as ever and not realize it, for this is the delusionary and hypnotic nature of the mind. To avoid this blind spot, mind lock, and extremely limited lens, be joyously vigilant against the negative ego at all times. Never forget that in every moment of your life in your every thought, word, and deed, you will be continually Spiritually tested as to if you choose GOD or negative ego in that moment. My Beloved Readers, work on this lesson first, and fill in the rest in the process of your life, and then you will be on the right track. What I have shared in this chapter, and the perspective I have put it in, is the "God Formula" for most quickly and efficiently removing your blind spots, mind locks, and limited lens seeing, and achieving God consciousness and a full spectrum prism consciousness in the specific vein this chapter is focused upon!

CHAPTER 48

Spiritual Tests

One of the most important understandings of the entire Spiritual path is the understanding that Earth is a Planetary mystery school, and that every single thing that happens in life is a Spiritual test. Planet Earth is a Spiritual school to teach Souls to become "Integrated Ascended Masters and/or God Realized Beings." Every single thing that happens in life is a teaching, lesson, challenge, and opportunity to grow. Most people do not realize, or they forget, that each and every moment of our lives we are being Spiritually tested. Every thought we think is a Spiritual test. As Edgar Cayce said, "Thoughts are things." A Course In Miracles states in its lesson book, "There are no neutral thoughts." What this means is that every thought that enters your mind from within or without is of GOD or is of the negative ego. Every thought that you think stems from the Christ/Buddha Consciousness or lower-self consciousness. Every thought you think stems from oneness or separation. Every thought you think stems from Love or fear. All day long, even when we think, sleep, or dream, thoughts are coming to us from within and without. Every single moment of life is a Spiritual test to think only GOD Thoughts.

The same is true, my Beloved Readers, with every feeling and emotion you create. This is a Spiritual test. Your attitude, perception, interpretation, and belief system cause your feelings and emotions. This is an indisputable fact and a law of the universe. We each cause our reality by how we think. If we think with our Melchizedek/Christ/Buddha mind, we will create only Spiritualized, positive feelings and emotions. If we think with our negative ego/fear-based/lower-self mind, we will create negative feelings and emotions. Every moment, even when you are by yourself, is a Spiritual test to see if you can keep your emotional body in a God consciousness and positive state at all times.

Every word you speak, every moment of your life is a Spiritual test. Are your words coming from the negative ego or are they coming from the Heart of GOD? What is the mental motivation of your words? Are they sourced from the selfish, self-centered negative ego, or were they motivated from true God consciousness? What is the feeling tone of every word? Is there any attack energy, anger, or criticism, or do they carry the feeling tone of unconditional love and nonjudgmentalness?

My Beloved Readers, every action you take, no matter how small or infinitesimal, is a Spiritual test. Is that action coming from and motivated by GOD and God consciousness, or by negative ego and separative/fear-based consciousness? Is that action adding to your Spiritual path or decreasing it? Is that action a waste of time or a good and balanced use of your energy?

My Beloved Readers, every use of your energy, no matter how small and infinitesimal is a Spiritual Test. Is your energy helping self and others, or hurting self and others? Is the use of your energy adding to your Light Body or decreasing it? Are you wasting energy or are you using every particle of your energy for a greater Spiritual purpose, for Love, for balance in a larger perspective and for healing self and others? Every moment of your life is a Spiritual test to see if you can use your energy to only serve GOD and not to serve the negative ego, fear, the lower-self, lower-self desire, the carnal self, separative thinking, and victim consciousness.

My Beloved Readers, in every situation of life there is an appropriate response and an inappropriate response. Every moment of life is a Spiritual test to learn to respond appropriately from the way GOD would have you respond. Who gives us the guidance on how to respond? This guidance comes from our Higher Self, our Mighty I Am Presence, the Holy Spirit, and our own Melchizedek/Christ/Buddha ideals that we have taken on consciously and programmed into our subconscious mind. Every moment of life is a Spiritual test to see if we can respond in a balanced manner instead of an imbalanced manner.

Every interaction with another person is a Spiritual test to see if we can remain in unconditional love, forgiveness, nonjudgmentalness, patience, service, oneness, and egolessness at all times. Every interaction with an animal, plant, or mineral is a Spiritual test to stay in harmony with GOD and His three lower kingdoms.

Now, my Beloved Readers, what happens if we do not always pass these Spiritual tests? The answer is nothing, in the sense that everything is forgiven and everything always remains in unconditional love. Mistakes are positive not negative, and every mistake can be turned into a positive if you gain the "golden nugget of wisdom" from that mistake. GOD always forgives, and it is just necessary for each person to forgive themselves. I will add here, however, that every moment of life is a Spiritual test and Spiritual opportunity to Realize GOD or not Realize GOD. When you think a negative thought, you lose your Realization of GOD on the mental plane in that moment. When you allow yourself to feel a negative emotion, you lose your Realization of GOD in that moment on the emotional plane. When you behave inappropriately, you lose your Realization of GOD in that moment on the physical plane. Now, it is important to understand that it is impossible to never make a mistake. It also cannot be emphasized more emphatically that mistakes are positive and part of the learning process. So the Spiritual path for everyone is up the mountain five steps, and down four, up three down two, up three down one. I will say, however, that the more overall integrated Spiritual mastery you gain, the fewer mistakes you will make and the quicker will be your Spiritual progress. The nice thing about GOD is that He always welcomes His Sons and Daughters home like the Prodigal Son, no matter what they have done in past lives, or this life, as long as they are willing to change their ways. One does not have to be perfect to evolve. If you truly want to Realize GOD, at the highest level, however, then you must be unbelievably "joyously vigilant" over what you are causing and creating on every level I have mentioned in this chapter. Every time you allow yourself to slip and give into the negative ego or lower self there is no judgement from GOD, but you will have lost your opportunity to Realize GOD in that moment. You all know how much better it feels to Realize GOD every moment on all these levels. You also know how terrible it feels to be out of harmony with GOD and out of harmony with Love. It is also important to understand that the continual positive choices on your part to continually Realize GOD on all levels will build your Love Quotient, Light Quotient, and Power Quotient. It will also speed up your initiation and ascension process. It will also cleanse your karma. Every right choice speeds up your path to total God Realization and is creating and cementing good habits into the subconscious mind. It is also helping the planet and helping your Spiritual Brothers and Sisters, for all minds are one. It also helps your Brothers and Sisters in an outer sense by demonstrating Melchizedek/Christ/Buddha consciousness at all times. If you are truly responding appropriately at all times, then your entire life will be a selfless path of service as well. You will not need to be selfish that often, because you are whole and complete within self and are one with GOD in your Realization in each and every moment. Hence, every bit of energy on every level of your being can go to loving and serving others. Once God Realization is achieved on a Spiritual, psychological, and physical/earthly level, one's only purpose to be on Earth is to serve. In doing this, one needs to stay balanced and integrated and to enjoy one's life. Within this context, one's total joy in life is to serve, because "true pleasure is serving GOD." Never forget your Brothers and Sisters are incarnations of God as well, even if they do not realize it.

True Spiritual testing does not take place just when things are going well. True Spiritual testing of an individual takes place when emergencies, crises, stresses, and attacks occur. Anyone can pass Spiritual tests living in a cave or never leaving their house. The true test of a Spiritual master is to get involved with Earth life and relationships with people of all kinds. This is where the true testing occurs. Can you stay out of your negative ego and remain in the Christ/Buddha consciousness when raising children? Can you stay out of your negative ego and in the Christ/Buddha consciousness in a romantic relationship? Can you stay out of your negative ego and in the Christ/Buddha consciousness with family members, extended family, parents and in-laws? Can you stay out of your negative ego and in the Christ/Buddha consciousness with your boss, business partners, business associates, and/or employees? Can you stay out of your negative ego and in the Christ/Buddha consciousness with fellow Spiritual leaders, Spiritual teachers, lightworkers, and Spiritual competitors for clients or students in your field or profession? Can you stay out of your negative ego and in the Christ/Buddha consciousness when people attack you, get angry with you, or judge you fairly or unfairly? Can you stay out of your negative ego and in the Christ/Buddha consciousness if someone slanders you publicly or professionally? Can you stay out of your negative ego and in the Christ/Buddha consciousness if someone steals a large sum of money from you? Can you stay out of your negative ego and in the Christ/Buddha consciousness if your spouse or relationship partner doesn't want to have sex? Can you stay out of your negative ego and remain in the Christ/Buddha consciousness if your spouse or relationship partner is in a bad mood and emotionally off-centered and is taking it out on you? Can you stay out of your negative ego and in the Christ/Buddha consciousness if you or others around you are making tons of mistakes regardless of if they are large or small? Can you stay out of your negative ego and in the Christ/Buddha consciousness watching the news, watching opinionated politicians and/or reporters, or reading the newspaper? Can you remain in the Christ/Buddha consciousness when physically sick or during extended chronic health lessons? Can you stay in the Christ/Buddha consciousness when someone you are close to passes on to the Spirit world? Can you remain in the Christ/Buddha consciousness during a traffic accident or when getting a ticket? Can you remain in the Christ/Buddha consciousness during a messy divorce or fight with your partner? Can you remain in the Christ/Buddha consciousness and out of the negative ego when someone is holding a grudge against you? Can you remain in the Christ/Buddha consciousness and out of your negative ego when everything is taken away in your life like Job in the Bible? Can you retain this Christ/Buddha consciousness during a natural disaster such as a major earthquake, hurricane, tornado, flood, or fire? Can you retain your Christ/Buddha consciousness and stay out of your negative ego if you lost all your money, had a divorce, your physical health broke down, and you lost your job?

My Beloved Readers, these are the true Spiritual tests. Can you live in the "marketplace," be fully involved in earthly life and relationships of all kinds, and keep your Spiritual mastery and balance? This is the true test of a full-fledged Ascended Master and God Realized being! It must be understood that 100% perfection is not required to pass these tests. Some of these would be extraordinarily difficult. Mistakes are positive and we do not want to practice any kind of negative ego perfectionism that expects us to be perfect at all times and never make mistakes. This is impossible and unrealistic. The main purpose for this exercise is to just be clear as to what the ideal is, and to strive for it. Going through an exercise like this can be a preparation for maintaining the proper attitude and perspective when lessons like these come. This is a blueprint, in a sense, for the potential Spiritual lessons and tests people on Earth often face. My Beloved Readers, I highly recommend setting your attitude and perspective now, almost like programming your conscious and subconscious computer, so you will not be knocked off-balance when these things do happen, and you are mentally and emotionally prepared to respond from your Christ/Buddha mind to the best of your ability. Again, perfection is not required. You can actually achieve ascension by balancing only 50% of your karma. The key point, however, is the more you can learn these lessons, the more you can Realize GOD psychologically in that moment. So, Earth is a school to practice in. There is no such thing as death, and we are allowed to come back as many times as we need to learn all these lessons and other ones on the Spiritual path. My suggestion, however, is to take advantage of this incarnation and aim as high as you can on a Spiritual, Psychological, and Physical/Earthly level to Realize GOD on all levels. By doing this we not only help ourselves, but help others as well.

Now, my Beloved Readers, there is one more series of Spiritual tests that are the most severe of all, and where most lightworkers and initiates "miss the mark and do not pass." The Spiritual tests I speak of here are when a person or lightworker moves into a position of leadership and/or Spiritual leadership over others. What I am speaking of here is when a person has become a master of some degree and has become successful in an inner and outer sense. They have lots of clients and students. They may have become very financially successful and also may have become very famous. They may hold positions Spiritual Leadership in the world. They may have very large followings. They may be in positions of great worldly and Spiritual power over others. They may give extremely large workshops, seminars, and classes, maybe on television, and radio, be authors, and be in newspapers and magazines. My Beloved Readers, I think you get the picture. It is now that the true Spiritual testing begins. If you or others have made it through the first two lists, now the real Spiritual Testing begins. Does the power the person now has go to their head? How do they treat others? How do they treat those not in their league? How do they treat their employees? How do they treat people who call them on the phone? How do they deal with other Spiritual leaders? Do they let the fame go to their head? What are their true motivations for doing what they are doing? Do they put GOD before money? Do they put GOD before fame? Do they put GOD before power? Do they have sex with all their students? How do they react when criticized? Do they practice what they preach once they are off the stage and out of the limelight? How do they react if someone tries to take away their position of power, fame, or money? Are they the exact same person they were before they were graced with this power, fame and wealth? Are they on a path of true Christ/Buddha conscious-ness or has self-aggrandizement taken over? Has their channel remained clear or has it been corrupted by negative ego? Have they truly retained their GOD purity and egolessness or have false Gods and symbolic idol worship of negative ego attributes taken over? How do they treat their students or disciples? Is their true motivation to fully empower their students or is it always to retain their position of author-ity? Do they truly put everything on "The Altar of GOD"? Have they allowed their channel or teachings to become clouded by personal, self-ish agendas? Do they have Spiritual ambition or negative ego ambition? Is the focus of their work about themselves or about GOD and the Masters? Do they co-create with other Spiritual teachers and leaders, or are they islands unto themselves? Are their books, channelings, and teachings focused on telling you how great they are, or really on selfless service? Are their teachings continuing to be balanced on a Spiritual, psychological, and physical/earthly level, or has the negative ego begun to fragment and create lack of balanced integration in the teachings? Do they continue to maintain mastery over their mind, emotions, behavior, lower-self desire, inner child, subconscious mind, sexual energy, and energy in general, or have they let down their standard now that they have achieved their ascension, seven levels of initiation and have climbed to the top of this particular planetary mountain?

My Beloved Readers, these are the true tests of the Spiritual Path. Most people have a hard time passing the second list in this chapter. Many Spiritual leaders reach this third level or list before they have mastered the second list. Even those who have mastered the second list, in my Spiritual observation, do not always pass the third one. The Bible speaks of the Spiritual path being "a straight and narrow path." In my Spiritual observation as a Spiritual leader, Spiritual teacher, and Spiritual psychologist, most do not meet this high mark and high calling. The usual cause is that they are more developed in their Spiritual Body than they are in their Psychological Body. Lack of proper mastery and integration of the psychological level will always ultimately corrupt the Spiritual level. You cannot live on the second floor of a building when the first floor is falling apart or has become corrupted. My Beloved Readers, in all humbleness and with absolutely no judgement in my heart, I cannot tell you how many Spiritual leaders, Spiritual teachers, Spiritual channels, Spiritual scientists, and Spiritual friends that I have seen fall from grace and become corrupted. It is mind-boggling! It is why the inner plane Ascended Masters have asked me to focus so much work on the concept of "Integrated Ascension." Spiritual leaders, channels, Spiritual teachers, and lightworkers are achieving their ascension and seven levels of initiation, but are not integrated. When the true Spiritual tests in lists two and three come, they are not able to pass them. The most amazing thing is that even though they are falling from grace, corruption of the negative ego is happening on a massive scale, and they are even tumbling down the mountain Spiritually because of this corruption of the negative ego, they do not have the slightest awareness that they have fallen. This is the extraordinary delusionary nature of the mind and the negative ego. They are in a negative hypnosis and realize it not. The main cause of this is not because they are bad people, for there is no such thing. They just have not received the proper psychospiritual training before moving into such positions of Spiritual Leadership and power. I have said this over and over, and I will say it again. The world does not need more channels. It needs more trained Spiritual counselors and teachers who can train large numbers of people around the world how to master their mind, emotions, body, and behavior, and most of all master the negative ego thought system and replace it with the Christ/Buddha thought system. If this lesson is not learned all Spiritual practices will ultimately become corrupted. This statement is not meant as a judgement, but just as a simple statement of truth. The negative ego has infiltrated and contaminated religion. It also is to a great extent infiltrating and contaminating the New Age Movement. Lightworkers must be aware of this and have great Spiritual discernment within self and in regard to others.

In conclusion, be Spiritually discerning as to the Spiritual leaders, Spiritual teachers, channels, authors, healers, and Spiritual scientists you work with. There are good ones out there. Make sure they are meeting the "higher calling and true mark" of a true Spiritual Master. The lesson is not to be judgmental, but it is to be Spiritually discerning. This Spiritual quality needs to be much more developed in lightworkers.

In final conclusion, my Beloved Readers, strive for the highest level you can of "Integrated Spiritual Mastery and GOD Purity." It is indeed a rare quality in this world. This chapter is meant to give you the "Divine Blueprint" and road map of the Spiritual tests you will face and need to pass to truly become an "Integrated God Realized Being." Be forewarned that the negative ego thought system is incredibly tricky, slippery, and seductive. It is going to take a 100% effort on your part, and you are going to have to claim and cultivate an enormous amount of "Joyous Vigilance and true GOD Purity" to pass all of these Spiritual tests. Half the battle is having the "Blueprint" and knowing what the Spiritual tests are. My Beloved Readers, the rest is up to you. Do not settle for false Gods and idol worship of paltry gifts as power, fame, money, and sex. If certain things come to you, so be it, and thank GOD for it, but do not make a false God out of these things. GOD has given you the understanding and abilities to master and learn these lessons. All that is required of you is great Spiritual focus and dedication. This chapter has been written to make you aware of the Spiritual tests that are present in your life and that may be coming. This chapter has also been written to "Spiritually Challenge" you, in this moment, to dedicate your life and every ounce of your energy on every level of your being to becoming the "Highest and Most Pure Integrated God Realized Being" you can, in service of GOD on all levels, every moment of your life! This, my Beloved Readers, is the "Noble Calling and Mission we have all Incarnated to Fulfill"!

CHAPTER 49

The Three Levels of Integrated Spiritual Growth

There are three levels of integrated Spiritual growth that each person on Earth must master to truly achieve God Realization. These three levels are: the Spiritual Level, the Psychological Level, and the Physical/Earthly Level. The Spiritual or Heavenly Level of God Realization deals with building one's Light Quotient and Light Body, Love Quotient and Love Body, and Power Quotient and Power Body. This Spiritual level also deals with the anchoring, activation and actualization of your Higher Chakras eight through three hundred thirty. It also deals with the anchoring and activation of your Higher Bodies. Some of these are: The Anointed Christ Overself Body, The Zohar Body of Light, The Higher Adam Kadmon Body, The Lord's Mystical Body, the activation of The Electromagnetic Body, the activation of The Epi-Kenetic Body, the activation of The Gematrian Body, The Overself Body, The Paradise Son's Body, The Elohistic Lord's Body, The Monadic

Body, The Causal Body, The Buddhic Body, The Atmic Body, The Logoic Body, The Cosmic Astral Body, The Cosmic Mental Body, The Cosmic Buddhic Body, The Cosmic Atmic Body, The Cosmic Monadic Body, The Cosmic Logoic Body, The Light Body of Metatron, The Light Body of Melchizedek, The Light Body of The Mahatma, and The Light Bodies of the entire Planetary and Cosmic Hierarchy, to name a few.

The Spiritual or Heavenly level of growth also deals with one's ability to channel, pray, meditate, and co-create with GOD, Christ, the Holy Spirit, your own Mighty I Am Presence, your Higher Self, the inner plane Ascended Masters, the Archangels and Angels, the Elohim Masters, and the Christed Extraterrestrials. The Spiritual or Heavenly level of growth also deals with the creation and establishment of one's Antakarana back to one's Monad and back to Source. This level also deals with many of the other forms of Spiritual practice such as chanting, repeating the names of GOD, and reciting mantras, to name a few. It also deals with the process of completing your Twelve Levels of Initiation and the fine-tuning of your Intuition and Inner Guidance. Lastly, it deals with the cleansing and integration of all your Soul Extensions from your Oversoul (Higher Self) and Monad/Mighty I Am Presence!

The Psychological Level of Spiritual Growth

The Psychological level of Spiritual growth is a totally unique level and must be mastered in its own right. Spiritual practices will not help you achieve psychological mastery. Most lightworkers on this planet are much more developed in their Spiritual Body than they are in their Psychological Body. This often leads to massive corruption of the Spiritual Body later on the path if is not corrected. The psychological level is the foundation of your entire Spiritual house. The reason for this is that your thoughts create your reality, and hence this level of Spiritual growth enormously affects the Spiritual and Physical/Earthly levels.

The Psychological level deals with key core issues such as: (Owning your personal power, self-love, self-worth, your bubble of protection, Christ/Buddha thinking rather than negative ego/fear-based thinking, balance, integration, transcending lower-self desire, proper parenting of the inner child, reprogramming the subconscious mind, mastering the subconscious mind, mastering and properly integrating your feelings and emotions, developing your inner Spiritual higher senses, letting go of attachments and replacing them with preferences, balancing your Three-Fold Flame of Love, Wisdom and Power, becoming a cause of your reality instead of an effect, balancing your Four-Body System, balancing and integrating your Conscious/Subconscious/Superconscious minds, integrating and balancing the Seven Rays, removing implants and negative elementals, learning to make appropriate choices at all times, and developing your psychic abilities, to name a few.

The importance of developing a healthy and balanced psychoepistemology is one of the most important aspects of the Psychological level. A person's psychoepistemology is the paradigm, philosophy, and/or belief system that filters all other thoughts. For example, if a person believes their feelings and emotions are the most important thing to the neglect of their mind, intuition and physical body, then they are not going to have a right relationship to self. This imbalanced psychoepistemology will cause them to be a victim of their feelings and emotions and to be psychologically and Spiritually off balance in every-thing they do. It will also imbalance all relationships with other people, for one cannot be wrong with self and right with others.

The same is true with someone who is overidentified with the mind, intuition, or physical body. The only proper healthy psychoepistemology is to be integrated and balanced in all four aspects.

Another example of an unhealthy psychoepistemology is someone who does not understand the difference between negative ego/fear-based/separative thinking and Melchizedek/Christ/Buddha thinking. These are the only two ways of thinking in the world. That is why Sai Baba says, "GOD equals man minus ego." We must transcend negative ego thinking and only think with our Positive/Spiritual mind. That is why the Bible says, "Let this mind be in you that was in Christ Jesus." Most people in this world including lightworkers have not been trained in this understanding. This is why we see so much corruption and glamour in the world and in the New Age Movement. Not having this understanding causes one's psychoepistemology, how one filters their reality to be off center. Sai Baba has said that seventy-five percent of one's Spiritual path is the process of self-inquiry. Self-inquiry is the process of how we filter all our thoughts, feelings, emotions, and the content of one's consciousness from within and without every moment of one's life. If one does not have a healthy, balanced, well-integrated psychoepistemology or belief system that filters one's reality properly, it will cause an off-kilteredness, which will cause an imbalance in every aspect of one's life. If one doesn't know that one should be Spiritually vigilant against negative ego thoughts and emotions at all times and doesn't know to replace them with Christ/Buddha Spiritual thoughts and feelings, do you see the problem that this will create? Most people in this world do not have the slightest idea what the negative ego/fear based/separative thought system is, as it relates to the Christ/Buddha thought system. This being the case, they end up being run by the negative ego. This is why so many people in this world are lacking in happiness, inner peace, self-love and/or self-worth, successful romantic relationships, career success and with financial success, to name a few.

When one develops a healthy psychoepistemology and/or Spiritual philosophy for properly filtering their reality, they then develop "The Midas Touch." The reason for this is that a healthy, balanced, well-integrated Spiritual philosophy and psychoepistemology allows one to be right with self and right with GOD. One cannot be right with any other relationship in life if one's relationship with self is not right first. The science of developing a proper psychoepistemology is the key to learning how to properly deal with all the thoughts, feelings, impulses, desires, intuitions, subpersonalities, instincts, inner child impulses, energies, and sensations arising from the subconscious mind and our physical bodies every moment of our lives. It also allows us to deal properly with all these aspects coming towards us from the outside world. An unhealthy psychoepistemology causes us to not filter all these energies properly, as GOD would have us process them. The slightest improper processing will cause a negative reality to manifest on a thought, feeling, or Physical/Earthly level if you are not vigilant, clear and centered every moment of your life.

So the most dangerous imbalanced psychoepistemology you can have is not understanding the importance of keeping the negative ego thoughts, feelings, emotions, and behaviors out of your consciousness, and only allowing yourself to manifest Melchizedek/Christ/Buddha thoughts, feelings, emotions, and behaviors. The lack of this key understanding on the Psychological level has corrupted more people in this world, and more lightworkers, Spiritual teachers, Spiritual channels, Spiritual scientists, and Spiritual leaders than you'd ever want to know. No matter how advanced you are Spiritually and no matter how good a channel or Spiritual teacher you are, and no matter how famous you are, if you have not done your homework on the Psychological level, your entire Spiritual program will become corrupted over time. It is like a cancer that spreads behind the scenes over time to every aspect of life within and without. It corrupts the channeled information, it corrupts the Spiritual teachings, and it corrupts one's motivations. Even if one has controlled it somewhat, when the true Spiritual tests come, when a person moves into Spiritual leadership, power, and control over others, fame, success, and money, to name a few, that negative ego cancer that was not nipped in the bud begins to spread. That slightly imbalanced psychoepistemology pours forth. It is like a dam with a crack. As soon as the big Spiritual tests come and there is more stress, and the ego has tasted power, fame, money, and sex, the crack in the dam becomes a major breach and gaping hole. I share this metaphor as a warning to lightworkers to be "Spiritually vigilant" against the negative ego. The number of lightworkers, Spiritual teachers, Spiritual channels, and Spiritual scientists, I have seen fall and become corrupted and contaminated by negative ego and glamour is astronomical. I say this with no judgement intended. I do say it with Spiritual discernment for those who have the eyes to see and the ears to hear.

Another psychoepistemological blind spot is the over or underidentification with the God/Goddess balance. Usually this manifests as a disownment of the Goddess aspect within self, and hence the inability to appreciate it within others.

Another psychoepistemological blind spot is having too much fire, air, water, or earth in one's horoscope and psyche. People end up seeing through one lens and disowning the other aspects or being slightly imbalanced, which then of course affects one's psychological and spiritual vision of oneself and their world.

Another potential psychoepistemological imbalance is being overidentified with mastery to the diminishment of love. For some, mastery is more important, and for others, love is more important. In truth, both points of view are psychoepistemological imbalances. A person who is just interested in love to the exclusion of power will make tons of mistakes all over the place and be very flighty in their energy. The person identified with power over love will be very efficient and masterful but will often lose the unconditional love connection and be prone to being angry and too critical and judgmental. Both sides of this coin are a pitfall and trap. These again are the first two Rays of GOD and they both must be balanced.

Another psychoepistemological trap is being too masculine or too feminine. This may manifest as being a workaholic or too much of a hedonist. It can also manifest as being too serious and/or playful and fun loving at inappropriate times. It is also essential to cultivate the emotional body properly, and part of this is having enthusiasm and passion, and not being too detached to properly integrate the feminine side.

Another psychoepistemological pitfall and trap is to be overidentified with the parent and/or child. The ideal is to identify with the adult and integrate the parent and child in their appropriate balance.

Another imbalanced psychoepistemology or Spiritual philosophy is lightworkers being highly Spiritual, but not knowing how to properly parent their inner child. Another common imbalanced psychoepistemology is people not realizing and being able to demonstrate that their thoughts create their feelings and emotions. Another imbalanced Spiritual philosophy is a person or lightworker flowing with the content of their consciousness rather than choosing it every moment of their life. Another imbalanced example is someone who does not realize that the subconscious mind has no reasoning and that they have to be the master of it at all times. Another common imbalance in a person's belief system is they don't realize that they need to be the master of their thoughts, feelings and physical body at all times. Another common imbalanced psychoepistemology is the overidentification with Heaven/Earth. This is extremely common. Another example might be the overidentification with one of the Rays instead of being balanced in all the Rays. Another example would be the overidentification with one of the twelve Major Archetypes to the neglect of the proper integration of the others. Another example is the overidentification with one of the Astrological Signs to the neglect of the others. Another classic example is the identification with a traditional form of psychology that does not fully integrate the Soul or Spirit. Another example is a Spiritual philosophy that is highly Spiritual, but not integrated on the Psychological or Physical/Earthly level. One other extremely common imbalanced psychoepistemology is people who try to balance negative ego thinking and feeling with Christ/Buddha thinking and feeling. They do this because they think they have to be balanced in everything. It is true that you want to be balanced in self and in life. The one thing you do not want to balance is negative ego consciousness versus Christ consciousness. Said another way, you don't want to balance Spiritual consciousness and fear-based/separative consciousness. Said one last way, you don't want to balance lower-self consciousness and Higher Self consciousness. Because of lack of psychological training, lightworkers get the crazy thought in their mind that the positive and negative should be balanced, and/or the light and dark should be balanced. Boy, does the negative ego love this psychoepistemology. My beloved readers, you would be amazed at how many lightworkers fall into this one. This is like saying love and fear should be balanced. Unconditional love and conditional love should be balanced. Forgive-ness and holding grudges should be balanced. Christ and Satan should be balanced. Anger and love should be balanced. Lower-self desires and Higher Self desires should be balanced. Judgementalness and nonjudgmentalness should be balanced. I think you can see how absurd such a philosophy is, and I tell you, it is the height of negative ego corruption. Adopting such a philosophy will not only manifest massive amounts of negative energy in yourself and your life, but it will also cut you off from your Higher Self and Mighty I Am Presence. There are only two voices in the world in truth. These are the voice of negative ego and the voice of Spirit. Do you really think these should be balanced? A great many confused lightworkers will tell you so. The nature of the mind is, "Argue for your limitations and they are yours." Listening to counselors, psychologists, marriage and family counselors, and social workers that are steeped in traditional psychology confuses many people. They have not realized their own Soul or Monad, yet are counseling people. This is called "personality level psychology" and 99 percent of the books on the market and in colleges and universities are steeped and stuck in it. I do not say these things as judgement, but rather I bring forward the light of Spiritual observations and discernments to help you avoid the pitfalls and traps of the negative ego. Be discerning as to the Spiritual teachers, channels, psychologists and counselors you choose for yourself, for very few are well-versed in Soul and Spiritual psychology as opposed to Traditional psychology or personality level psychology. Another common psychoepistemology is that similar books, counselors, and teachers will tell you that negative feelings and emotions are good. My beloved readers, "Argue for your limitations and they are yours." From the perspective of Soul and the Holy Spirit, they are not good and they are not necessary. Personality level psychology teaches victim consciousness. This school of thought does not have a clue that it is thoughts that create one's reality. Negative ego feelings and emotions come from negative ego thinking. Stop thinking from your lower-self/fear-based mind and they will disappear. Start thinking from your Christed, Higher Self mind and you will have Christed, Higher Self, positive feelings and emotions. Your anger and upset does not come from any person or situation outside yourself. It is coming from your interpretation, perception, and negative ego belief system. So, in this chapter today we are busting the negative ego's corruption of psychology. The negative ego has entered every field of Earth life including Religion and the New Age Movement. Today's discussion in this section was to explore its corruption and contamination of traditional psychology.

My beloved readers, in conclusion, as we can see the list of imbalanced psychoepistemologies is infinite and complex. This is why it is incredibly important to do your homework on the Psychological level and not just focus your energies on the Celestial realms, inner plane Ascended Masters and Angels, and Spiritually esoteric knowledge and information. I cannot tell you how many lightworkers, Spiritual leaders, Spiritual channels, and Spiritual teachers have become corrupted and contaminated by negative ego and imbalanced psychoepistemologies from focusing too much on the Spiritual level, and not enough on the Psychological level as well as the Physical/Earthly level.

Each one of these potentially imbalanced psychoepistemologies I have mentioned causes the individual to see life from not only an imbalanced and slightly skewed state of consciousness, it also causes one to have a slightly imbalanced and skewed relationship to GOD and the inner plane Ascended Masters and Angels. You cannot be wrong with self and right with GOD and the Masters. Being wrong with self will cause imbalance in every aspect of your life including your relationship to GOD and the Masters. This is an indisputable law and fact of the mind. It is a mathematical equation. I share these insights in this clear manner so there is no room for the negative ego to seduce and manipulate you into its corruption and its illusionary web of deceit.

It also must be understood that every time you buy into one of these potentially imbalanced psychoepistemologies, it limits your Full Spectrum Prism Consciousness that GOD would have you see from. GOD would have us see life from thousands of lenses simultaneously. Each lens being an aspect of our integrated and multidimensional nature. Each time we buy into an imbalanced psychoepistemology we see life from a smaller and smaller prism. Most people on this Earth see themselves and life through an extremely limited prism. Instead of seeing themselves and life through the Full Spectrum Prism of GOD, they see themselves not through a prism but through an extremely small number of lenses. The illusionary nature of consciousness, the mind, and the negative ego thought system will cause these people to believe that they are totally centered and clear, and they will most often believe that they are God Realized. This is at least what they tell themselves and advertise to others. When one is caught in these imbalanced psychoepistemologies, they do not realize they are seeing life from an extremely small number of lenses. The negative ego tells them they are totally clear, and clearer than anyone else is. This again is the delusionary nature of the negative ego. Do not underestimate its powers to seduce and take you over. The first second you do underestimate its powers, you will be its next victim. Very few in the world are able to escape its seduction, manipulation, and deceit. It takes enormous honesty and GOD Purity to not let it take you over for a whole lifetime. Some do it for awhile, however as soon as they think they have mastered it is in truth when they lost it. As the Bible says, "After pride cometh the fall." Let this be a warning to us all. No matter what level of Spiritual, psychological, and physical/earthly development, and no matter what level of initiation, Spiritual leadership, success, fame, or fortune, one must be "ever vigilant for GOD and His Kingdom." True GOD Purity through a whole lifetime is something rarely seen in this world. This section of this chapter is a "Spiritual Challenge" to each of you, my beloved readers, to strive to hold this ideal. Mistakes are okay for they are just lessons. If you fall for a moment or a brief period of time, for-give self, learn the lesson and get back on your "Spiritual Horse." As you do so, be ever more determined and Spiritually vigilant to retain your "Purity in GOD."

One more interesting insight into these three levels of growth is that the physical body grows automatically. If an adolescent drinks and smokes too much, and never psychologically matures, they will still physically grow, although their physical growth could be slightly stunted. Spiritually, if a person focuses on the light and continues to do Spiritual activations they will continue to Spiritually grow, even if they have chronic health problems and are undeveloped and immature psychologically. The psychological level is slightly different however, because it does not grow automatically as the physical body does. Just because a person physically grows into an adult, it doesn't mean that they are psychologically one. Just because the Spiritual body achieves Ascension and/or the Seven Levels of Initiation, doesn't mean the psychological self is evolved in the slightest. I know above and beyond seventh degree initiates who have achieved their ascension initiation and are some of the biggest egomaniacs I have ever met. I have met others in this category that are absolute victims of their emotional body. I have met ninth, tenth, and eleventh degree initiates who have been completely taken over by power and greed. I have met others who are filled with imbalanced psychoepistemologies and are run by the negative ego thought system. So just because the physical body grows and the Spiritual body may be growing, this says absolutely nothing about psychological level of development. The physical body and Spiritual body, once you get tapped in, can grow and evolve almost automatically. This is not true of the psychological body.

An enormous number of people on this Earth, including a great number of lightworkers, are still stuck in an adolescent level of psychological development. An enormous number of Spiritual leaders, Spiritual teachers, Spiritual counselors, and Spiritual channels are extremely run by the inner child the second they get offstage. There are an enormous number of ways that this adolescent psychology manifests. Some are victims; some are too run by the emotional body, some are too run by the negative ego, some have bizarre psychoepistemologies. The list is endless, for there are infinite numbers of ways that the negative ego can distort and create illusion. Always remember that for every thought the negative ego has, the Holy Spirit and the Christ/Buddha Consciousness has an opposite thought and attitude. Whatever your problem or dilemma, the Holy Spirit and Christ consciousness can help you find a way out. GOD did not create the negative ego, people did. It is the misuse of free choice. So the key point here is that GOD and the Masters cannot help you develop psychologically, and your physical body cannot help you. They cannot create a healthy psychoepistemology for you, for this is a by-product of your own thinking, and GOD, the Masters, and the Angels cannot control your mind, your feelings and emotions. This is your job. So being an adult psychologically, and becoming a Master psychologically, will only happen when a person takes responsibility for being the cause of their reality, and becomes the Master of their thoughts and emotions, and develops a healthy, well-balanced psychoepistemology and/or Spiritual philosophy on all levels. On the Psychological level there is no free ride. Building Light Quotient is easy, it is just a matter of calling it in from the Celestial realms. Physically feeding the physical body is easy, and the physical body will grow even when we abuse it and feed it junk food. My Beloved Readers, the real "nuts and bolts" of the Spiritual path is the Psychological level. It again is the foundation of your Spiritual "house." If you do not address this level properly it will totally corrupt the Spiritual work you have done and it will make the physical body ill over time. Too many lightworkers are fragmented in their Spiritual growth. Too many lightworkers are falling into the glamour of the Celestial realms and not doing their psychological homework. Because of this, a new term has had to be invented called "Fragmented Ascension." This would seem to be paradoxical. How can you ascend and achieve the Seven Levels of Initiation and still be completely fragmented, have imbalanced psychoepistemologies, and be run by the negative ego? My beloved readers, unfortunately this is happening and it is happening en masse. It is for this purpose that the inner plane Ascended Masters have guided me to write this chapter.

Strive with all your heart and soul and mind and might to develop a psychoepistemology that is centered, balanced, and well-integrated as GOD, the Holy Spirit, your Higher Self, and your own Mighty I Am Presence would have it be. I humbly suggest that reading some of my other books on these subjects might help you refine this process a bit. The books I recommend are *Soul Psychology, How To Clear The Negative Ego, Integrated Ascension, The Golden Book of Ascension, The Golden Book of Melchizedek, Ascension and Romantic Relationships,* and *The Golden Keys To Ascension and Healing.* I have great faith and trust in you, my Beloved Brothers and Sisters, to learn these lessons and to be "Pure in GOD." The main problem in this world is not that people or lightworkers are bad or have any negative intent. It is more a matter of not having the information and proper integrated Spiritual and psychological training they need, to avoid these traps and pitfalls. It is to this humble purpose that I have written this chapter and this series of books. It is my humble hope and prayer that you, my Beloved Readers, will find that the information and tools are useful, and will help you to accelerate your path to true God Realization.

Physical/Earthly Spiritual Level

This third and final level of Spiritual growth deals with the physical/earthly level. Now we have already established that the physical body will grow physically into adulthood no matter how evolved or unevolved one is Spiritually, psychologically or physically. Again, if an adolescent smokes cigarettes and drinks too much alcohol and doesn't get enough exercise, that can stunt one's growth but will not stop one from growing into an adult physical body. What a lot of lightworkers do not realize is that there is an evolutionary process for the physical body as well. One aspect of this is having a healthy physical body. If the physical body is ill or chronically ill, it makes learning one's psychological and Spiritual lessons more difficult. So part of evolving the physical vehicle is eating a good diet, setting physical exercise, fresh air, and sunshine, drinking lots of pure water, getting enough sleep, not taking recreational drugs, balancing work/play, affirming, visualizing, and praying for good health and help from the Masters for maintaining this state.

Besides the health of one's physical body there is also the issue of bringing light quotient, love quotient and power quotient into the physical vehicle itself. The process of ascension, in truth, would be better termed "Descension." For the ideal is to fully ground one's Mighty I Am Presence and Light/Love/Power bodies fully into the four-body system, which includes the physical vehicle. We are meant to become embodiments of GOD in our physical bodies on Earth. We are also meant to physically ground all the Higher bodies I mentioned in the first section of this chapter from the Spiritual realm into the four body system (Spiritual, mental, emotional, and physical). We are also meant to anchor all of our 330 chakras into the physical body. So just because one has passed their Seven Levels of Initiation, it does not mean they have fully integrated these initiations into their mental, emotional, and physical bodies. People are allowed to pass their initiations when it is accomplished in the Spiritual body. This is very gracious and generous of GOD to allow this to happen. Once we pass these initiations it is then our job to make sure that we have fully integrated them into all four bodies, this includes the physical.

Another aspect of evolving the physical vehicle is building one's immune system Spiritually, psychologically, and physically. This is done first by mastering the Spiritual and psychological level. This is so because every negative thought and/or negative feeling and emotion, and every piece of negative energy is a toxin to the physical body, just as pesticides would be on a physical level! When you learn to master the Spiritual and Psychological levels this will greatly help your physical health and immune system. This is also true because the subconscious mind runs the physical body. When it is out of control and run by the negative ego it will do havoc to the physical vehicle. This is the case because it operates like a computer. It has the intelligence to create perfect health or cancer, or any other illness. It doesn't have the reasoning however to know which one to create. It needs a computer programmer, which is you, to tell it what to do. There is a natural intelligence in the body that does move towards perfect health, however, it can be short-circuited by giving too many negative ego orders to the subconscious mind.

The other key to evolving your immune system is removing all the physical toxins from your physical body. Your cells, organs, and glands store toxins even from childhood. These toxins also come from environmental pollution, the food we eat, the drugs we take, and electrical pollution to name a few. Some of these toxins are: pesticides, petrochemicals, heavy metals, bacteria, viruses, funguses, mercury from silver fillings, radiation from such things as color television, electrical pollution from the myriad of electrical appliances, phones, telephone wires, preservatives, junk food, recreational drugs, antibiotics, drugs given by traditional doctors, air, water, and Earth pollution, manufactured "dead food", lead paint, and dental and traditional medical x-rays to name just a few. Part of the evolution of the physical body is to remove all negative thoughts, feelings, emotions, energy, and physical toxins from its physical and etheric cells, organs, glands, tissues, and blood stream. This is a field of endeavor that traditional Western medicine does not have a clue about. Western medicine, although extremely useful, is the cause of the great many of these toxins by all the drugs they prescribe, x-rays, invasive tests and dyes they pump into the body for these tests. In the future energetic testing will replace this form of invasive testing.

The best way to remove all these toxins is through homeopathic medical care and herbal medicine. If you are interested in doing so I suggest you find a really good homeopathic and/or naturopathic doctor who can help guide you in a process of finding the right homeopathics to remove all these toxins. Never forget that GOD exists as much in the material universe as He does in the mental, emotional and Spiritual universe. Never forget the purpose of life is to bring Heaven to Earth.

When these processes that I have mentioned in this section are done, the physical vehicle will be filled with Light, Love, and Power. You will have tons of energy, you will hardly ever get sick, you will need much less sleep and your physical vehicle will be able to withstand enormous amounts of stress and not break down. Most of all, you will be filled with energy and vitality to fulfill your Spiritual mission on Earth.

The last and highest level of evolution of the physical vehicle is the process of bringing down and anchoring so much of GOD's and your own Mighty I Am Presence's Light, Love and Power into the physical vehicle, that a process of etherealization takes place in the physical body itself. In other words, the physical body becomes fused and integrated, in a sense, with the Light, Love and Power body; so the subatomic particles begin almost to take on the nature of a more ethereal-type body that is still very grounded and connected to the Earth Mother and one's Spiritual mission on Earth. The highest level and form of this evolutionary process is where at death, translation, or ascension, an individual can choose if they want to ascend the physical body as well. This means at death the physical body is translated into the Light and taken with you into the next dimension of reality that it is your destiny to magnetize and vibrate to. I need to say here that it is not required or even necessary to ascend the physical vehicle, for it does take some extra energy and training on the inner planes to do this. It is, however, every initiate's choice if this is something they want to pursue. One choice is not better than another, it is just a choice, an option.

In conclusion, on this topic of the evolution of the physical vehicle, I think you can see that a great many lightworkers ignore and abuse their physical bodies by improper care and nurturing. They have a faulty belief that their physical bodies and even the Earth have nothing to do with their Spiritual evolution. They put all their energies into the Spiritual level. Others put their energy into the Spiritual and psychological level and feel the physical body and Earth is not as important. This is illusion for all four Faces of GOD (Spiritual, Mental, Emotional, and Physical) are equally important. It is essential to do one's Spiritual homework to evolve all four Faces of GOD within self, and within one's service work outside of Self. The material/physical/earthly plane is one of GOD's seven Heavens.

The final aspect of evolving the Material Face of GOD deals with the evolution of not only the physical body of yourself, but also the physical body of GOD. In our case, this is the Earth Mother, our worldly civilization, and our solar system. Again, a great many lightworkers do not pay much attention to the Earth Mother, worldly civilization, politics, social issues, changing the world, and current events. They believe this has nothing to do with their Spiritual life. I am here to tell you that it has everything to do with Spiritual life, and one will not fully Realize God, or their own personal full-fledged integrated ascension, unless they integrate and realize the "Material/Earthly Face of GOD." You cannot hate the Earth and the earthly world or even ignore this process and fully achieve your personal ascension. GOD is realized through mastery of all four levels (Spiritual, Mental, Emotional, and Physical/Earth. The ignoring of any one level will be a blind spot and lack of Realization of GOD.

So let us now examine what the Earthly level of God Realization is about. It deals with taking care of the Earth Mother on a personal and collective level and not polluting and/or abusing her. It is to take responsibility on a personal level to do one's part in loving the Earth Mother and attuning to nature. It has to do with developing a relationship to the kingdoms of the Earth Mother (Animal, Plant, and Mineral). It has to do with developing a relationship to the Ethereal Nature Kingdoms (Nature Spirits, Devas, Tree Spirits, Elves, Gnomes, Salamanders, Undines, Sylphs, Fairies, Pan, and the Elemental Kingdom).

Evolution of the Earthly level has to do with grounding your physical service mission on Earth. A great many lightworkers have great visions, wonderful ideas, and great love and passion, but never do anything on Earth. Their Spirituality remains on a Spiritual, Mental, and Emotional plane and never grounds into and with the Material Face of GOD.

Evolution of the Earthly level also deals with learning to make money and not depending on others to support you. It also has to do with maintaining self-mastery over Earth life. This means cleaning your house, doing all your errands, personal hygiene, respecting earthly laws, and paying your taxes, to name a few. It also means not only loving the Earth Mother, but also loving "Worldly Civilization." This means caring about all the problems and inequities going on in the world, such as hunger, homeless people, child abuse, spousal abuse, gang violence, equal rights, education, racism, saving endangered species, animal abuse, the ozone layer, the destruction of our rain forests, and all the pollution and abuse mankind has done to the Earth Mother. My Beloved Readers, this is a wake-up call. Our Spiritual paths are not separate from these issues. These issues and many more are our Spiritual path. As Sai Baba has said, "Hands that help are holier than lips that pray." It is our job to create Heaven on Earth. Who is going to create a Utopian Society on Earth if we as the Spiritual leaders and lightworkers don't do it? We are the "Externalization of the Hierarchy." It is our mission to get involved with Earth life in the way and manner GOD has created us to fulfill our part in the "Divine Plan" of things. Each person has a puzzle piece to fulfill, and this means "getting your hands a little dirty" and in helping those on Earth less fortunate than ourselves. It is our job to change all the institutions of this world from negative ego-based institutions to Christ/Buddha based institutions. This applies to the political system, the legal system, social work, gardening, religion, the arts, the sciences, the economic system, business, psychology, education, traditional medicine, child care, and the list goes on and on. This also means becoming educated on all these issues and raising consciousness whenever you can. If you can't help physically or politically in certain areas then pray on these issues and make them a part of your meditations. Have compassion for your Brothers and Sisters in other parts of the world who are being abused and mistreated. Ignoring the earthly world and civilization is ignoring an enormous part of your Spiritual path. I am not saying here that everyone has to go to Washington and march or write to their congressman. What I am saying is everyone must do their part as GOD guides them to. You will not Realize GOD if you do not love the Earth Mother, and love our earthly world, and dedicate your life to being of service to both. To be perfectly honest, the Celestial realms can be like a drug or glamour to some people. They believe they are being Spiritual by ignoring Earth life, and in truth what they are doing is ignoring at least one quarter of their own God Realization, if not more. Jesus taught and set an example of living in the marketplace.

The purpose of life is not just to achieve liberation and check out as soon as possible. It is to love the Earth Mother, Earth life, and the Material Face of GOD so much that you want to remain on Earth and help her become the shining Fifth Dimensional civilization she is meant to realize on all levels. If you do not learn how to be happy on the Earth, in truth you have not fully learned your lessons in coming here. I am not saying that this is an easy school, and I am not saying that Earth life isn't difficult at times; however, GOD lives and is in all facets of the Material Universe. If we do not love the Earth and Earth life and take responsibility for serving her and helping her heal, then, in truth, we are not loving GOD fully. Remember, the Earth and the

Material Universe is one of GOD's Heavens and is GOD's physical body. We have just talked about the importance of evolving your own physical body and not ignoring and abusing it. If we are going to do this, then why would we ignore and abuse GOD's physical body? The microcosm is like the macrocosm.

Look at the example Mother Teresa set. She got her hands dirty. Look at how Ghandi transformed India. Look at all the schools and hospitals that Sai Baba has helped set up and develop. My Beloved Readers, do not just let your Spirituality live in the Celestial realm, or on the Mental and Emotional plane. Ground your Spirituality and ascension process not only onto, but also into the Earth, and Earth life itself. Ground your Spiritual mission onto Earth, and not just in some Spiritual visions and good ideas. Do not let your negative ego go on an ego trip of having to do some glamorous super large Spiritual vision that will, in truth, never manifest on the earthly plane. It is time to put our actions where our visions and thoughts are. It is time to put our money where our mouth is. The two thousand year Piscean cycle never made it to the earthly plane, and neither did very many lightworkers. The Aquarian Age and our new Seventh Ray Cycle are about grounding our Spiritual visions and good ideas on Earth. "Talk is cheap"! It is time for physical action and demonstration on the physical/earthly plane. GOD is from Missouri, which is the "Show Me" state. GOD, in truth, is from everywhere, but for this next two thousand year cycle, He is from Missouri. The Seventh Golden Age on Earth is the complete transformation of the Earth and our worldly civilization into a Fifth Dimensional society on Earth! Whatever profession or field of endeavor you are involved within the Divine Plan, it is time now to love the Earth Mother and our worldly civilization with all your Heart and Soul and Mind and Might, and to be about the "Father's and Mother's business" of healing and redeeming all aspects of our society for our children and grandchildren to come! This is the true Mantle of the Christ and Buddha consciousness that is now being placed on each and every person reading this chapter. This is the Spiritual leadership and Spiritual mission of planetary world service that is now being placed on your shoulders. It is not a heavy load, for all that is required is for you to do your puzzle piece and part. It is also not a heavy load because each of us as lightworkers and masters on Earth stand arm-in-arm and shoulder-to-shoulder in the "Great Work" of redeeming the Earth and worldly civilization. It is not a heavy load because GOD, Christ, the Holy Spirit, our Mighty I Am Presence, our Higher Self, the inner plane Ascended Masters, the Archangels and Angels, the Elohim Masters, the Christed Extraterrestrials, the Earth Mother, and Pan and the Nature Kingdoms, both ethereal and physical, will be helping us every step of the way! So let it be Written, So let it be Done!

CHAPTER 50

The Personality of GOD

We have here one of the age-old questions from the beginning of time, which is what is the Personality of GOD? If we can understand what the Personality of GOD is, then we would really have a Golden Key to how to Realize GOD on Earth. By the Grace of GOD and the inner plane Ascended Masters I will share with you just this in this chapter.

GOD's Personality is divided into three parts and seven parts. This is one of the reasons why the numbers three and seven are considered to be some of the holiest numbers. GOD is first divided into the Trinity of GOD, which of course is GOD, Christ, and the Holy Spirit, GOD being the Creator, the Christ being the Eternal Self we as the Sons and Daughters of GOD are in truth, but are in the process of Realizing, and the Holy Spirit, which is the Voice of GOD and the "still small voice within," which speaks for the Atonement or the At-One-Ment. The Holy Spirit is GOD's answer to every question and every problem. For every miscreation of the negative ego/fear-based/separative mind, the Holy Spirit is the antidote. The Holy Spirit speaks for the

Christ/Buddha consciousness, which of course is the opposite of the negative ego/fear-based consciousness. The Holy Spirit speaks for the Atonement, which is the undoing of all problems that come from separative thinking. It can help undo everything in your personality that is not of GOD. Most people, and even lightworkers, do not take advantage of the incredible powers of the Holy Spirit.

Now, we are made in GOD's image as the Bible says, so we are a Trinity as well. We are a Trinity made up of the superconscious, conscious and subconscious minds. Part of our lesson is to become as integrated as GOD is in His Triune nature. This is our first clue into the Personality of GOD.

The second clue into the nature of the Personality of GOD is to under-stand GOD's seven-fold nature. GOD's body is made up of seven Cosmic Dimensions, with each Dimension made up of seven subplanes or subdimensions in each of these Cosmic Dimensions. These Dimensions are called the Cosmic Physical, Cosmic Astral, Cosmic Mental, Cosmic Buddhic, Cosmic Atmic, Cosmic Monadic, and Cosmic Logoic. The Cosmic Physical Dimension is made up of seven subplanes by the same names as the seven Cosmic Dimensions, but are the subplanes of the Cosmic Physical Dimension.

This, however, explains the nature and structure of GOD's body but does not explain GOD's Personality. GOD's Personality is divided into seven parts as well. These are the Great and Holy Rays of GOD. GOD's Personality is divided into Power, Love/Wisdom, Active Intelligence, Harmony and Beauty, New Age Science, Devotion, and Freedom, Transmutation, Alchemy and Divine Structure. GOD's Personality is the perfect balanced and integrated synthesis of these seven attributes. This understanding is a Divine and sanctified gift and map from GOD and the Masters to help us understand the proper way to balance and integrate our own personalities and psychological selves.

GOD's Personality is first made up of Power. This is the Power to be the First Cause and creator of the infinite universe. It is the Power to completely cause His reality. It is also the Power and Will of GOD, rather than the will of the negative ego, lower-self, fear-based, separative mind. So, my Beloved Readers, GOD owns His Power, and is the embodiment of the Will of GOD and not the will of the negative ego, fear-based thought system. This is the First Great Ray of GOD and Creation.

The second aspect of GOD's Personality is Love/Wisdom. GOD is unconditionally loving at all times towards self and His Creation, and manifests and demonstrates this unconditional love with great psychological wisdom. This is the Second Great Ray of GOD and Creation.

The third aspect of GOD's Personality is Active Intelligence. This again is a form of wisdom, but it is not wisdom of the Heart, or wisdom in a psychological sense, it is a different kind of wisdom which is "wisdom to put GOD's consciousness into action." Without this third aspect of GOD's Personality nothing would ever get done in GOD's plan. We would have Personality/Power and Love/Wisdom, however without this third aspect of GOD's Personality, the Power and Love would never manifest on the Material Plane of GOD's reality. This is the Third Great Ray of GOD and Creation!

The fourth aspect of GOD's Personality is Harmony and Beauty. GOD is not only powerful, loving, psychologically wise/wise in action in Material Creation, but GOD is harmonious and completely attuned to beauty in every aspect of Creation, in the way GOD manifests his reality on the Material Plane of Creation. This is the Fourth Great Ray of GOD and Creation.

The fifth aspect of GOD's Personality is New Age Science. GOD is not only power, unconditional love/psychologically wisdom, wisdom in action, attunement to harmony and beauty, but GOD is very scientific in how He has created the infinite universe. Everything in GOD's universe is governed by laws and is very much in Divine order. It is possible to understand and master these laws and hence understand the nature of GOD on His various levels. This is why, in truth, Religion and Science blend perfectly together if properly understood. This is the Fifth Great Ray of GOD and Creation.

The sixth aspect of GOD's Personality is Devotion. God is not only all powerful, all loving, all wise, all wise in action on the Material plane, attuned to harmony and beauty, totally scientific, but is also filled with devotion and love for His Sons and Daughters of GOD and His entire Creation. GOD is the perfect balance of masculine and feminine, for GOD is totally scientific yet filled with love and devotion for His Sons and Daughters and all sentient beings. This is the Sixth Great Ray of GOD and Creation.

The seventh aspect of GOD's Personality is Freedom, Transmutation, Alchemy, Ceremonial Order and Magic. GOD is not only powerful, unconditionally loving, psychologically wise, wise in action, attuned to harmony and beauty, scientific, and filled with devotion, He is also the embodiment of freedom and is Divinely structured in the process to achieve this freedom. GOD is skilled in the process of how to transmute and transform energy from fear into Love. From lower-self into Higher Self, from Separation into Oneness, from negative ego into Christ/Buddha/God consciousness. This seventh aspect of GOD's Personality is very skilled at setting up structures and systems to help His Creation achieve freedom. Freedom from what? Freedom from glamour, illusion, maya, and negative ego thinking. As Sai Baba has said, "The mind creates bondage and the mind creates liberation." GOD is total freedom from limitation and from the negative ego fear based thought system. GOD knows how to set up structures to help lead His Creation back to freedom.

There is now one last aspect of GOD's Personality, which is that GOD's Personality is not just the embodiment of these Seven Great Attributes, but is also the "Perfect Synthesis, Balance and Integration" of these Seven Great GOD Qualities and Rays. My Beloved Readers, listen very closely to my following words. We are made in the "Image and Likeness of GOD." We too are made up of these Seven Great Rays. For the microcosm is like the macrocosm. "As within, so without. As above, so below." If we want to fully Realize GOD, then we too must become the perfect integration and balance of these Seven Great Rays. We must fully own our personal power, and surrender to GOD's Will and not the negative ego's will. We must learn to be unconditionally loving at all times to self and others. We must develop "active intelligence" to be wise in learning how to manifest our consciousness onto the earthly plane, and manifest our Spiritual mission on Earth, not just in our minds. We must learn to strive to be harmonious and attuned to beauty and aesthetics in all that we do. We must learn to be very spiritually scientific in all that we do, and learn to understand the laws that make up GOD's infinite universe. We must not only understand these laws, we must use these Great Laws to help our selves and others. We must cultivate devotion to GOD, to the Masters, to our fellow Brothers and Sisters in GOD, and to all GOD's Kingdoms, without giving up our personal power, yet still retain the total unconditional love. We must learn to set up Divine structure in our life and in the design of our society and world, which will ultimately lead to freedom for all. We must learn the process of Divine alchemy, transmutation, transformation, and Spiritual magic to change our world and ourselves from just seeing ourselves as people, to our true reality as Sons and Daughters of GOD living in physical bodies. Lastly we must learn to perfectly balance and integrate these Seven Great Attributes of GOD within ourselves and develop each of them to our highest potential. In this way we will become the living embodiment of the Mighty I Am Presence on Earth. In this way, we will become full-fledged Ascended Masters on Earth.

In conclusion, I just wanted to point out that we are all aware of the Three-Fold Nature of GOD, which has also been called the Three-Fold Flame of GOD. This has been called the Love/Wisdom/Power of GOD. My Beloved Readers, do you not see that this embodies these First Three Rays and attributes of GOD? It contains the First Ray of Power, the Second Ray of Love/Wisdom, and the Third Ray of Wisdom. Wisdom here is having two meanings. The psychological wisdom of knowing how to unconditionally love, and the wisdom of how to manifest

GOD's power and unconditional love on the Material Plane. These Three Divine Attributes are the Three Key Qualities that need to be perfectly integrated to Realize GOD. I bring this up for many have not noticed the relationship of the Three-Fold Flame of GOD to the First Three Rays of GOD, and I felt it was important here to make this relationship and tie-in. Add to the Three-Fold Flame of GOD the Four Remaining Attributes of GOD, and you have the Seven-Fold Nature of GOD and of your self as an incarnation of God. If you truly want a map of how to demonstrate GOD on Earth, my Beloved Readers, let this be your guide and "Divine Road Map" for how you Create, Manifest, and Demonstrate your own Divine Personality on Earth!

CHAPTER 51

The Glory and the Corruption of the Seven Great Rays of GOD

We have already established that the perfect integration and balance of the Seven Rays is the Personality of GOD. It is essential to understand that the Seven Rays, as with all things, have a higher and lower aspect. This is because the Rays, although created by GOD, can be misused and corrupted by the negative ego/fear-based/separative thought system. In this chapter I would like to go through each of these aspects of GOD's Personality and clearly explain the glory and the corruption that can take place when they are used purely and when they are corrupted by the negative ego thought system.

The glory of the First Ray is when a person owns their personal power 100% in total service of GOD and unconditional love. It is also the glory of surrendering to GOD's Will and not the ego's self-centered, negatively selfish will. The corruption of the First Ray is when a person owns their personal power to control, hurt, and manipulate others for self-centered, narcissistic, selfish gain, not recognizing their Brother and Sister or themselves as an incarnation of GOD. The corruption of the First Ray is also not surrendering to GOD's Will in all things and instead unconsciously or consciously following the will of the negative ego, lower-self, self-centered mind. The glory of the First Ray is its ability to own one's personal power at all times, but be able to surrender to GOD's Will simultaneously. The negative ego/fear-based thought system completely corrupts this understanding by having the person either own their personal power and not surrender, or has them surrender to GOD's Will and not own their personal power. Both are a corruption of the negative ego/separative/lower-self thought system. Hitler, Mussolini, and Stalin are classic examples of historical figures that misused and misunderstood the First Ray. In the Spiritual Movement, examples are those who are on a trip of self-aggrandizement, being better than everyone else is, and being a perceived as a Guru, and/or people who are constantly angry and attacking others.

The glory of the Second Ray is its ability to unconditionally love self and others at all times, and the psychological wisdom it brings to help one do this in all situations and with all people. The corruption of the Second Ray is, first off, the negative ego/fear-based thought system's distortion of having the person manifest conditional love rather than unconditional love. The negative ego thought system has one love under certain conditions and requirements. The second main danger and corruption is becoming overly flowery, sentimental, and loving and not having a backbone, so to speak. This might stem from not having enough of Rays One, Three and Five, which are a little more mental in nature, embodying power, intelligence, and science. The third corruption could be in becoming overidentified with the teacher or guru role, and not being able to step out of it, and being a know-it-all, since the Second Ray is that of education. In the First Ray, the danger would be in being too political and not speaking one's truth enough. In the case of overidentification with the Second Ray, it would be speaking one's truth too much, and not knowing how to be self-controlled, tactful, Spiritually discerning, and attuned to timing. I am also reminded of a book called *Women Who Love Too Much*. This would also be an example of the imbalance of the Second Ray. A person can become obsessed, addicted and co-dependent in relationship to love, and this is, in truth, a negative ego thought system distortion of the true Second Ray unconditional love GOD would have us learn.

The glory of the Third Ray is the Active Intelligence or Wisdom to put our God consciousness into demonstration and action on and in the material/earthly world, and not just on the Spiritual, mental and emotional plane. The corruption of the Third Ray could be an overintellectual nature and lack of proper integration of one's feelings and emotions. It could also be being run by the mind, instead of being the master of one's mind and learning how to quiet the mind when needed. It could also be overplanning and overthinking about one's mission, but never doing it. It could also be a preoccupation and overidentification on making money and business pursuits to the neglect of one's Spiritual life, because the Third Ray is associated with business. It could also be a corruption of negative ego business practices based on negative ego competition instead of Spiritual cooperation. It would be the negative ego controlling one's business practices that tells one to make a buck at any price, and it doesn't matter who you hurt in the process. This could be summed up, "So what that you gain the whole world and lose your own Soul."

The glory of the Fourth Ray is the creation of harmony, unity and oneness at all times with self, and in relationship to others and one's world. It is also the creation of the arts in the glorification and sanctification of GOD. This could come in the form of beautiful Spiritual paintings, beautiful Spiritual music, Spiritual architecture, Spiritual poetry, Spiritual dance, Spiritual opera, plays and theater, to name just a few. It could also be Spiritual movies, Feng Shui, and aesthetics in daily living. The corruption of the Fourth Ray on a psychological level would be the negative ego, fear-based thought system creating disharmony and conflict within self because of lack of proper integration and negative ego contamination. This conflict within self then would manifest in conflict with others, and lack of harmony with others. The Spiritual ideal of the Fourth Ray would be to create love, harmony, oneness and peace at all times and not disharmony, conflict, separation, attack and fear. On a professional level, the corruption of the Fourth Ray would be the lower self, carnal self, and negative ego controlling the creation and flow of the Fourth Ray. This would manifest as maybe a great deal of the rock music these days, with very negative and dark lyrics. It could be the creation of art with images that do not Spiritually uplift, but do the opposite. Instead of "music of the spheres" and music that spiritually inspires, it would be music that appeals to the lower-self and carnal self. I do not think that this needs much explanation to my readers. It would be movies that appeal to violence and pornography, and horror films, instead of films or multimedia that provide uplifting Spiritual inspiration. We all see how many movies are playing in movie theaters that we can't even imagine that anyone would ever want to go see. These filmmakers appeal to those individuals run by the lower-self, negative ego, and lower nature. When the consciousness of the masses rises enough to a more Spiritual/Christ/Buddha state, there will be no one who would even pay money to see these movies. Any form of art that is created from and panders to the lower-self and lower nature, and does not inspire and sanctify GOD by its beauty, is a corruption of the Fourth Ray of GOD.

The glory of the Fifth Ray of GOD is its focus on Spiritual New Age Science. On a psychological level, it is the use of the mind in a scientific way for the purpose of healing all aspects of a person and our society. The proper use of this Fifth Ray leads to cutting-edge scientific breakthroughs in Medicine, Psychology, Law, Gardening, Ecology, Social Work, Religion, and Business, to name just a few. In truth, the list is endless. Everything in GOD's universe is made up of laws; and by understanding and mastering these laws we can use them to help other people, our world, and ourselves. The corruption of the Fifth Ray could again be an overintellectual nature, which cuts off the feeling and intuitive nature if corrupted by the negative ego/fear-based thought system. It could also be a worship of science and the rejection of religion and Spirituality, thinking that everything in life has to be proven by a scientific study. Or it could be believing that nothing is real except what can be proven by scientific means, or that nothing is real except that which can be sensed with one's five physical senses. This is a complete perversion of Spiritual science. This is the negative ego controlling science and is not the Science of GOD. Another corruption might be the imbalanced view that Science and Religion or Spirituality do not blend and integrate perfectly together. Contrary to popular opinion, GOD is totally scientific and understandable, if one will also allow oneself to use one's intuitive mind and not just their logical mind. Another corruption of the Fifth Ray is focusing too much on what I would call the concrete mind, and not allowing oneself to tap into the abstract mind, the Higher Mind, and the Intuitive right brain mind. When the Fifth Ray is properly understood and utilized, enormous scientific ideas and inspiration will come not only from logical thinking, which is fantastic when used properly, but also from telepathic sources of knowledge on the inner plane. Cures for AIDS, cancer, and all the ills of our society can come. There is not one field or endeavor of life in which the Fifth Ray Scientific mind cannot prove useful. There is, in truth, a science for everything. There is even a Science for how to run an effective business, office, or home. The danger and corruption of the Fifth Ray can come in being overly scientific in an intellectual dry sense, and also living too much in the mental body and scientific focus and not smelling the roses and enjoying and experiencing life, not just thinking about it. Every Ray has this danger within its focus and lens; it is not just the Fifth Ray. Each Ray of GOD can be a blinder in a sense, if not balanced with the other

Rays. The corruption of the Fifth Ray in a professional sense is scientists doing animal experiments with no consideration or feeling for the animals they are experimenting upon. That is one example. Another example might be the focus on only third dimensional traditional methods as in Western medicine, and the inability to open up to the vast Spiritual technologies that are not so invasive and poisonous to the physical body. In psychology, the corruption is a science only focused on traditional psychology that does not even recognize or believe in GOD or the reality of the Soul. With no judgement intended, these people call themselves scientists and they are seeing life through one seventh of reality and calling it science. It is a science based on seeing life through blinders. True Spiritual science sees life through a Full Spectrum Prism lens utilizing all one's senses, not just the physical ones. Those are five of about fifty or one hundred we actually possess. For more information on this read my books *The Complete Ascension Manual, Integrated Ascension* and *The Golden Book of Melchizedek.* There are many more examples I could give of the corruption of science on a professional level; however, I think I have made my point here, and you, my Beloved Readers, can extrapolate how this process carries over to all fields of study. I would also highly recommend that you read my book *Manual For Planetary Leadership,* for a great deal of this book is an in-depth explanation of just this topic, and how this process has infiltrated all fields and aspects of our society and civilization. It is quite fascinating reading if you would like to see how this process carries on in other areas of Earth life as well!

The glory of the Sixth Ray is Devotion. This is embodied in the Master Jesus' commandment to "Love the Lord thy GOD, with all your heart and soul and mind and might, and to Love your neighbor as you Love yourself." The glory of the Sixth Ray is that it brings an enthusiastic unconditional love and Spiritual passion to one's relationship to GOD, the Masters, to family, friends, people, and life itself. It is essential in life to fully embrace the emotional body, and have total Spiritual passion, enthusiasm, and joy. The Sixth Ray brings this total devotion and idealism. The glory of the Sixth Ray is that it makes us strive also for the highest within us, and pursue excellence at all times. The corruption of the Sixth Ray is becoming overly emotional and letting one's emotions run away with you, and becoming victimized by them. It is also giving your personal power away to GOD, the Masters, a Guru, and/or other people. Another corruption and glamour of the Sixth Ray is putting Masters, Spiritual Teachers, and other people on pedestals. Another corruption of the negative ego fear-based thought system that distorts the pure Sixth Ray is being too idealistic to the point of being a negative perfectionist. One can become so idealistic that they can become almost dysfunctional or impractical. The other great danger and corruption of the Sixth Ray is lack of Spiritual discernment. These are the main things to watch out for in how the negative ego/fear-based thought system can distort the Sixth Ray of Devotion and Spiritual Idealism. The corruption of the Sixth Ray professionally is in the field of religion, where ministers of all faiths are taken over by faulty negative ego concepts and beliefs and the true religious doctrine becomes contaminated. We have seen this take place in all the major religions where their doctrine is preaching negative ego-based concepts and theology that has no relationship to what GOD, the Masters and Angels really believe. This is why so many people have left their religion, which is unfortunate, but they had no choice. This is why more people have been killed in the name of GOD than for any other reason, I believe. It is also why different religions compete with each other and why most religions, but not all of them, state that theirs is the only way to GOD, which of course is total illusion. It is also why there are so many false prophets, cults, and religious leaders being caught in scandal, as the negative ego and corruption ultimately becomes exposed.

The glory of the Seventh Ray is its emphasis on freedom and its ability to set up Divine structures and systems within self and society that lead to even greater freedom within self and within our society. The glory of the Seventh Ray is also the ability to use Spiritual magic in the form of transmutation and alchemy to transform misqualified energies into the purity and substance of GOD. The corruption of the Seventh Ray can come in many forms. It can come from the negative ego/fear-based mind's misguided understanding of what true freedom is. Many people think they are free but in truth they are not. As His Holiness the Lord Sai Baba has said, "The mind creates bondage and the mind creates liberation." Many people think they are free, but in truth they are being very much run by the negative ego, the emotional body, the mental body, the inner child, lower-self desire, and the subconscious mind. Another aspect of the corruption of the Seventh Ray by the negative ego/separative thought system is a misuse of structure. Either first not having enough, or on the other side of the coin having too much, where a certain amount of spontaneity and free flow cannot take place. There is a proper balance to find here. Another corruption and glamour is setting up structures for the wrong purpose and goals which are really of the negative ego and not of the Divine Plan. Another corruption and glamour of the Seventh Ray is the use of magic without Spirituality. This is very common, and is one of the first signs of a cult. Slick, fast-talking teachers, who have some magic or alchemical abilities, but whose their motivation, in truth, is totally governed by the personality, negative ego and lower-self. They are more interested in gaining power, fame, money and having sex with their followers than truly doing Spiritual magic to be of service. Lightworkers beware, for there are millions of teachers out there who fit into this category. A great many lightworkers are very naïve and Spiritually undiscerning, and are too easily impressed by magic that is motivated by impure motivations. Freedom is not giving free reign to one's negative ego, lower-self, inner child, and emotional body. This is not freedom, but being a victim. True freedom stems from total self-mastery of one's energies in service of GOD, unconditional love, and a balanced, integrated ideal. The corruption of the Seventh Ray in a professional sense comes in the form of the misuse of money. Money is, in truth, a Divine substance of GOD that is meant to be used as a means of helping self and others. The corruption of money comes in many ways. It can come in the form of greed and miserliness. It can also come in the form of spending it too freely and wasting money on lower-self frivolous purposes. The corruption can come in not valuing money, using it for a Spiritual purpose in life and not saving it in the appropriate balance. It can also come from not giving it away for needy purposes in a balanced appropriate manner when the time is right. Money is the energy we use to make changes in the physical/earthly world. One of the reasons the earthly/material world doesn't change as fast as it could is that most lightworkers do not have as much money as they would like. This is part of the development of the Seventh Ray; the ability to have prosperity consciousness and not poverty consciousness; to not be afraid of money. To see the making of large amounts of money as part of your Spiritual path. Money is not the root of all evil, as some would suggest. Money in and of itself is neutral. The negative ego fear-based thought system is the root of all evil. It is when the negative ego/lower-self/separative mind controls money that problems occur. It is every Son's and Daughter's of GOD right to have as much money as they can imagine. It is part of their lesson to learn how to make money, the key point here being the more money you have the more you can serve others. If you do not have money, then you become dependent on others to give you money. There are periods of time, of course, when this is okay and totally appropriate in everyone's life. In the long haul so to speak, however, the ideal would be that each person be responsible for themselves and be able to make as much money as they can, for the more you have the more you can give. The great corruption of the Seventh Ray professionally is the enormous number of people in our society who have money and greedily hold on to it. They do not help others or society, and they use their money as well to hurt others and prevent others from gaining. Be aware, my Beloved Readers, that the law of karma exists, and every "jot and title of the law is fulfilled." Those that misuse their money will ultimately lose their money. For the law of karma also extends over past and future lives. Part of the movement into this New Millennium and the Seventh Golden Age is the understanding that our planet as a whole is now moving into a Seventh Ray cycle from a previous Sixth Ray cycle. Part of the energy of this Seventh Ray cycle is to also now ground our Spirituality on Earth. For too long our Spirituality has been floating around on the Spiritual, mental, and emotional planes. In this New Millennium and Seventh Golden Age it is now time to create Heaven on Earth. It is now time to fully ground our ascension in our physical bodies and into and onto Earth life. It is now time for each person to fully ground their Spiritual mission on the physical/earthly plane. It is now time for lightworkers to become masters of money on all levels, and to help use and allocate the money in our government and economy to create the utopian Ascended Master society that is destined to be built in this Seventh Golden Age. The proper use of the Seventh Ray both personally and collectively holds a great key to the transmutation and transformation that now needs to occur along with all the other Rays as well.

The final glory of the Seven Rays of GOD which form the true Personality of GOD which is extremely important to understand is how these Seven Rays in GOD's Personality work together in perfect synthesis and integration. In a true full-fledged Ascended Master this is also the case, for the microcosm is like the macrocosm.

The true Glory of GOD is seeing how these Seven Rays work together in perfect harmony and balance within self and within society. In truth we have yet to see this take place within our society. In my next book, I am going to endeavor to explain how this can take place and I have been guided to call this book *The Divine Plan for the New Millennium and*

Seventh Golden Age. For our purposes here it suffices to say that, in truth, there is not that many, even on a personal level, who have learned to fully develop all Seven Rays, and to also integrate and balance them in daily living. This is one of the great signs of a true full-fledged Spiritual Master on Earth. For this is the Personality of GOD. More and more however, are beginning to realize this ideal. Many in the Spiritual Movement are focusing on the Spiritual or Heavenly level and gaining initiations and building their light quotient and light bodies, as well as communicating and working in the Celestial realms, and this is good. However, my Beloved Readers, if the Seven Great Rays are not balanced properly on the psychological level, true God Realization will not have taken place, no matter what your level of initiation is. True God Realization must be done on the Spiritual, Psychological and Physical/Earthly level. All three levels must be realized, not just the Spiritual level. If the Seven Great Rays are not developed and balanced within self and the lower aspects of self, and/or corruption of these Rays is not transcended, then enormous corruption of the Spiritual work people are doing will take place. Many will not like to hear this. However, if you are truly a lover of GOD then listen very closely to what I have to say. If the Psychological level of God Consciousness is not developed properly, and there is negative ego/fear-based distortion and corruption of these Rays, then this will color and affect all your channeling, Spiritual teaching, clairvoyant work, Spiritual vision, and relationships. For as I have said many times in my writings, the single most important relationship in your life is your relationship to your self. If you are not right with self, this will skew all other relationships including your relationship to GOD, the Masters, and the Angels. This is because your thoughts create your reality. You cannot have faulty thinking within self, and within your own personality and psychology, and expect this to not affect all the Spiritual channeling, teaching and healing work you are doing. Your relationship to your self, your relationship to your personality, your relationship to your psychology, your relationship to your own subconscious mind affects everything. It is the foundation of your Spiritual "House." How can the first floor of one's house be corrupt and the second floor be working fine? The second floor works through the first floor. It is not separate from the first floor. It flows through the first floor. All channeling, Spiritual teaching and Spiritual vision flows through one's subconscious mind, psychology, belief system, interpretations, perceptions, philosophy, and Spiritual psychology. You cannot separate them. My Beloved Readers, this is why it is absolutely essential to learn to balance these Seven Great Rays within your own personality and psychology. This is a weak spot among a great many lightworkers. These Seven Great Rays of GOD serve as a "Lens." It is also incredibly easy to get stuck in the lens of power, or love, or wisdom, or action, or art, or science, or devotion, or freedom, structure and magic. Even if your Monad and or Soul is under the influence of a particular Ray as incarnating Sons and Daughters of God are, it is absolutely essential that you learn to see from a Full Spectrum Prism Consciousness through all Seven Rays in a balanced and integrated manner and not through just one or a few. This takes great psychological work and focus on your part. We all know people who are too stuck in power, or are too stuck in addicted love, or too stuck in the teacher know-it-all role, or too stuck in art and can't function in life. We all know people who are too stuck in science and the intellect, or in devotion and idealism to a guru, and are blinded. We all know people who are too stuck in structure or lack of structure, can't deal with money, misuse magic, and do not know what their Spiritual freedom is. These are the same great pitfalls and traps of the Spiritual path. These are not all of them, but some of the main ones. Develop yourself most importantly in your personal power and in surrender to GOD's Will, Love/Wisdom, Active Intelligence, Harmony and Beauty, Science, Devotion and Idealism, and Ceremonial Order and Magic. It is essential we develop our selves in these Seven Great Rays, not only psychologically but also in the professional aspects of these Rays. I am not speaking here in the sense of taking on these professions, but being developed in them. Develop your political side, the Spiritual teacher side, your business side, your artistic side, your scientist side, your Spiritual leadership side, and your economic mastery side. Not only develop all these aspects, but also learn to not get stuck in each of their "Lenses." This is easier said than done, for it takes great psychological introspection and vigilance to not allow oneself to fall into these "Lenses." This is especially true because of the fact that each person's Monad and/or Soul is under the influence of one of these Rays. I am not saying here that one should deny how GOD created them and should not fulfill one's Spiritual mission under that theme, so to speak. But be balanced and integrated in all Seven Rays while under the influence of that theme.

Most of all my Beloved Readers, be aware of the negative ego/fear-based/separative/lower-self thought system and how it corrupts and creates glamour, illusion and maya in everything it touches if you allow it into your mind. Only allow yourself to think with your Spiritual/Christ/Buddha mind and not your negative ego/fear-based mind. Think with your "Love Mind," my Beloved Readers, and not your "Fear mind." There are only two ways of thinking in the world and everything stems from Love or from fear. Everything stems from the negative ego thought system or the Spiritual/Christ/Buddha thought system. It is the negative ego/fear-based thought system that creates the distortion and corruption of the Seven Great Rays. Be ever joyously vigilant against the negative ego. This, my Beloved Readers, is the "Road Map" to achieve true God Consciousness. There is no work more important on your Spiritual path than learning to properly master, develop, balance and integrate the Seven Great Rays in your psychology and personality, and to not allow the negative ego/fear-based thought system to enter your consciousness and corrupt your proper understanding of these Rays. It is also important to not get stuck in the "lens" of any one of these Rays, or this will become a negative ego distortion as well. This is the "Great Work" of the Spiritual Path. Continue the work you are doing on the Spiritual plane, but do your psychological and personality level homework for it is equally as important and, in truth, even more important, for the Psychological level is your Spiritual vision that colors your perception of the Spiritual level. To be a clear channel for Spirit you must be a clear and balanced psychological channel as well. Once you have mastered this, do not forget to also put equal attention to doing your homework on the physical/earthly level as well, for GOD is as much in your physical body and in the material/earthly world as he is in the Heavenly realms, mental realm, emotional realm or psychic realm. There are four Faces of GOD: Spiritual, Mental, Emotional, and Physical. To truly realize GOD all four must be mastered and equally honored. To not master, honor and sanctify the Material Face of GOD is to also disown the Divine Mother, the Earth Mother and the Goddess energies. For the Goddess energies are also intimately connected to the Material Face of GOD. Our true Spiritual mission is to become our Mighty I Am Presence on Earth in a very grounded and balanced manner. Our true purpose is to manifest our Spiritual mission on Earth and to get involved with Earth life. Our true Spiritual mission on Earth is to transform our civilization and society into an Ascended Master society and to create Heaven on Earth, not to achieve liberation and leave the Earth as soon as we can. We are all the Light/Love/Power bearers for the New Millennium and Seventh Golden Age. Let us now each take on the "Full Mantle of the Christ/Buddha/God Consciousness" in a balanced and integrated manner and be about the business of fully transforming our selves and our world into the true Glory of GOD!

CHAPTER 52

Practicing the Presence of GOD

The inspiration for this chapter came one day to me while sitting on my couch in our living room. It stems out of a Spiritual observation I have made on many occasions among many lightworkers and people on the Earth. It is such an important point I thought I would write a short chapter discussing this.

What I am speaking of here is the understanding that we all of course are very involved with our Earthly Life and Earthly missions. This is of course as it should be. For as we all know the purpose of life is to fully anchor and ground our Mighty I Am Presence fully into all our bodies which includes the physical, and help to manifest Heaven on Earth! So contrary to what a lot of lightworkers believe, the physical body and our Earthly Civilization is very important and is not just a means to gradu-ate and achieve liberation and escape the wheel of rebirth. GOD's Divine Plan is to truly create a Fifth Dimensional Society and Utopian Society on Earth in a similar reflection as to how they operate in

Heaven. So, learning to love the Earth and Earth life is one of the most important lessons of the Spiritual Path!

A great many lightworkers do not like the Earth, and the truth is they will not truly Realize GOD in all his Glory unless they also learn to Love the Material Face of GOD as well!

Now people who are not on a Spiritual Path have the opposite problem, and that is they are so attached to the Earth and material life they see no other reality but this. This is not a healthy perspective either.

The interesting thing, however, is even lightworkers who are often very Heavenly and Celestial in focus and even do not necessarily like Earth or Earth Life are often still very attached to Earthly things. It sounds like a paradox, however, in truth it is not. Let me explain! What I am about to explain here is universally common on the Earth. It is also something that although almost all lightworkers know this, they continually forget this in the heat of Earth life so to speak. What I am speaking of here is that our lives on Earth are incredibly complex. We have romantic relationships, family, friends, service work, businesses, Spiritual Missions, students and all kinds of Earthly projects and involvements. It is the nature of Earthly life that no matter how Spiritual or together we are, things still do not always go according to our preferences or attachments. Even though we all know that everything in our life is a Spiritual Lesson, Teaching, Challenge, Opportunity to Grow, Stepping Stone for Soul Growth, and Spiritual Test, in the heat of Earth life and our involvement with it we tend to forget. For example, when someone judges or attacks, we sometimes forget that this is a Spiritual test to see if we can stay in our Personal Power, Bubble and respond back with Unconditional Love!

When someone steals from us we forget that it is not really about what has been stolen, as much as how we deal with the situation, that is really important. Do we stay Centered? Do we Forgive? Do we become angry and judgemental? How attached are we?

Let's say we are working on a very important project and it falls through. Is the most important thing the Spiritual Lesson GOD is teaching you or is the project the most important thing?

When something happens to a family member, is the first most important thing the Spiritual Lesson or the family member?

If someone cuts us off on the road, is the most important thing the Spiritual Test and lesson, or anger at the driver?

If a person is having problems with their car, and the car mechanic is overcharging you, is this really about your car, and being cheated, or how you are going to Spiritually deal with the lesson?

The phone company screws up your bill and phone service for the 50th time. Is this about the Spiritual Lesson and Test you are being given, or the incompetence of the phone company!

A friend or business partner makes a mistake and costs you $200,000. Is this really about the money and the mistake this person has made, or how you Spiritually and Psychologically deal with it?

What I am basically saying here is, that even though we all know that everything in life is a Spiritual lesson and Spiritual Test, most lightworkers in the heat of Earth Life and the often severity of the Lessons of Earth Life, forget that even though Earth Life is important. The real purpose and meaning of it all is that everything, and I mean everything, that is happening is really not about what is happening outside of self. It is about how you are responding to all the disasters, catastrophes, negative egos of other people, mistakes of other people, incompetence of other people, and unexpected as well as strange and unexpected things that happen in life. Everything that happens, bar none, is just to see if you will respond and demonstrate from your Spiritual, Christ, Buddha mind, or if you will react from your negative ego/fear-based/separative mind. No matter how severe, dangerous or unexpected the lesson, this is always the case. What happens is that most people and most Spiritual people of all kinds get so involved with Earth life that they forget really what the main purpose of everything is about. They may be involved with Channeling, Spiritual

Teaching, Spiritual Study, or Healing, all day long, however, often when things happen during their daily lives, even in the Spiritual Projects they are working on, they forget the main purpose is not about what is happening physically, it is about maintaining one's Christ Consciousness. Even if it is a Spiritual Project or Spiritual Business and disaster has struck; it is not about the Spiritual Project or Spiritual Business. I am not saying it is not important to get these Earthly matters straightened out, for they are extremely important. However, the first most important meaning of what has occurred, no matter how disastrous, how negative, how big a mistake someone made, how big a screw-up occurred, how negative a person has been, it is still most importantly about if you are able to remain in your Personal Power, Self-Mastery, Centeredness, Unconditionally Love, Forgiveness, Nonjudgmentalness, Evenmindedness, Happiness, Joy, Patience, Tolerance, Defenselessness, Harmlessness, Egolessness, God Consciousness, Christ Consciousness, Buddha Consciousness, Spiritual Consciousness. The key point, no matter what you are involved with and no matter how important it is in an Earthly, or Spiritual Sense, is did you Respond from your God/Christ/Buddha/Spiritual Consciousness, or did you react from your negative ego/fear-based/separative/selfish/self-centered/attacking/judgmental/impatient/depressed/upset/ annoyed/ irritated/sad/intolerant/ consciousness? Now there is no judgement if you responded inappropriately, for this is just a lesson in which a golden nugget of wisdom needs to be learned, and forgiven. However, the key point is to not get so attached and even involved with the lessons of outer life and the Earthly world that you forget what the true meaning and purpose of what you have incarnated onto Earth for. It is not about all your Earthly involvement and projects as the number one priority. The number one priority is to "Practice the Presence of GOD"! Said in another way, to practice being God in every situation of life! The more extreme the lesson the better the opportunity to practice!

My Beloved Readers, the reason I have written this chapter is that it is so incredibly easy to forget this!

Every single book, magazine, radio show, person, teacher in school, parent, family member, friend, counselor, psychologist, social worker, movie, television show and aspect of Earth life will be demonstrating the exact opposite of this.

To live life from this perspective means that you have to put GOD first in every situation. Even if the whole world is being destroyed your first responsibility is to deal with your Spiritual lessons properly. Many people in this world are much more interested in correcting the perceived wrongs in the world and in other people then truly learning their own lessons.

Animal Activists throw red paint on people wearing furs. Is that learning their lessons? A Spiritual teacher gets angry and attacks a student. Is that really the Spiritual Teacher learning their lesson? They may think it is but it is not! An AIDS activist interrupts a person giving a speech and won't allow anyone to hear what this person is saying. Is this AIDS activist learning their lesson? It is not from a Spiritual Perspective. These are extreme lessons, but the same thing applies to each and every one of the things that are happening in your life every moment of the day.

When your child is going through the terrible twos, and you become impatient and angry, is that your learning your lesson? How do you deal with people who are incredibly unclear and who are always making mistakes? How do you deal with people who make royal screw-ups in incredibly important situations? How do you deal with people who you find out lie, cheat and steal? Do you attack, judge, gossip, defend, engage in ego battles, compete, and/or try to punish? As the Master Jesus said, "Judge not that ye not be Judged! He that hath no sin, cast the first stone! Do not try and take the Speck out of the eye of your Brother when you have a Beam in your own eye!" I have said this before and I say it again!

It is of the highest importance to remember we are being "Spiritually Tested" every single moment of our lives. Although what happens in our Earthly lives is very important, it is not as important as Practicing

Demonstration of GOD every moment of our lives first! This chapter is a gentle, loving reminder to put GOD first and respond in God/Christ/Buddha/Spiritual Consciousness and to then secondarily get your Earthly Life fully Mastered as well. Do this, however, only after you have made sure to master your Spiritual and Psychological lessons of learning to respond appropriately as GOD would have you respond.

One more last thought I would like to share on this subject is that in my experience when I chose to respond from God Consciousness and Spiritual/Christ/Buddha Consciousness first, not only do I have more inner peace and feel better about my self, I also very interestingly find that things on an Earthly level are more likely to turn my way as well. For if you are not responding from your God Consciousness then by Cosmic law you are responding from your negative ego/fear-based/separative consciousness and this will, in truth, only in the long run repel what you want. Any negative response is only going to cause a negative response from others. It is not about teaching other people lessons. It is about you learning your lessons, and demonstrating a better Christed example for others. It is not about indulging our negative egos or indulging our negative emotions and punishing people who deserve it. It is about doing just the opposite. It is about learning our lessons, and reflecting the Self Mastery, Self Control, Evenmindedness, Pure Unconditional Love, Sweetness, Kindness, Gentleness, Harmlessness, Defenselessness, Forgiveness, Egolessness and Nonjudgementalness of God to another. They will be so shocked at your response. For they have been trained to expect attack, criticism, judgmentalness, punishment, that they will be deeply Spiritually moved by your example and they will work 1000 times harder to correct their inappropriate response because of your Spiritual Example. So you not only get the Spiritual Benefit of learning your Spiritual lessons as GOD would have it be, but you get the added benefit of the Earthly situation more likely to turn around in your favor. Realistically however, there are times this will not be the case. In those instances, you will have the added benefit of living in God Consciousness, unconditional love, and inner peace even if the outer situation did not remedy itself in your favor. Plus, you will have set a Christed example to another. They may not have learned their lessons but that is not important. All that is important is that you have learned your lessons. They will have to reincarnate again on Earth to learn their lessons. You will be freed from the wheel of rebirth for you have learned your lessons. In every situation of life you must choose: "Do you want GOD or do you want your negative ego? Do you want unconditional love, or do you want attack and fear? Do you want the permanent or the impermanent? Do you want truth or do you want illusion? Do you want liberation and graduation or do you want to reincarnate?

This chapter is a gentle, loving reminder from a fellow Spiritual Brother to remain joyously vigilant on this point and to keep Earthly life in proper perspective because the forces of indolence of the subconscious mind, physical body and mass consciousness will be constantly pulling you to react from the emotional body and negative ego, instead of your true God Consciousness! You are now being reminded by Spirit and the Masters of this most important Spiritual Practice and insight which is truly one of the true golden keys to achieving God Realization in this lifetime!

CHAPTER 53

My Spiritual Mission and Purpose
by
Dr. Joshua David Stone

My Spiritual mission and purpose is a multifaceted process. Spirit and the inner plane Ascended Masters have asked myself and Wistancia (we've been married since 1998), to anchor onto the Earth an inner plane Ashram and Spiritual/Psychological/Physical/Earthly Teaching and Healing Academy! This Academy is called the Melchizedek Synthesis Light Academy! We are overlighted in this mission by Melchizedek, the Mahatma, Archangel Metatron, the inner plane Ascended Master Djwhal Khul, and a large group of Ascended Masters and Angels such as the Divine Mother, Archangel Michael, Archangel Gabriel, Sai Baba, Vywamus, the Lord of Arcturus, Lord Buddha, Lord Maitreya, Mother Mary, Quan Yin, El Morya, Kuthumi, Serapis Bey, Paul the Venetian, Master Hilarion, Sananda, Lady Portia and Saint Germain, and a great many others who we like to call the "Core Group"!

I have also been asked by the inner plane Ascended Master Djwhal Khul, who wrote the Alice Bailey books, and was also involved in the Theosophical Movement, to take over his inner plane Ashram when he moves on to his next Cosmic position in the not too distant future.

Djwhal holds Spiritual leadership over what is called the inner plane Second Ray Synthesis Ashram. On the inner plane the Second Ray Department is a gigantic three-story building complex with vast gardens.

The Ascended Master Djwhal Khul runs the first floor of the Second Ray Department in the Spiritual Hierarchy. Master Kuthumi, the Chohan of the Second Ray, runs the second floor. Lord Maitreya, the Planetary Christ, runs the third floor! When Djwhal Khul leaves for his next Cosmic position, I will be taking over this first floor of the Department. The Second Ray Department is focused on the "Spiritual Education," of all lightworkers on Earth, and is the Planetary Ray of the Love/Wisdom of God. What is unique, however, about the Synthesis Ashram, is that it has a unique mission and purpose which is to help lightworkers perfectly master and integrate all Twelve Planetary Rays, which is one of the reasons I love this particular Spiritual leadership position and assignment so much! For this has been a great mission and focus of all my work!

Wistancia and my mission has been to anchor the Synthesis Ashram and Teaching Academy onto the physical Earth, which we have done and are continuing to do in an ever increasing manner on a global level. Currently there are over 15 branches of the Academy that have been set up around the world! The Academy actually first came into existence in 1996! This we have been guided to call the Melchizedek Synthesis Light Academy for the following reasons: because of the Overlighting Presence of Melchizedek (our Universal Logos), the Mahatma (Avatar of Synthesis), and the Light (which is the embodiment of Archangel Metatron who created all outer light in our universe and is the creator of the electron!) These three beings, Djwhal Khul, and a very large Core Group of inner plane Planetary and Cosmic Masters help us in all this work.

I have also been asked by the inner plane Ascended Masters to be one of the main "High Priest Spokespersons for the Planetary Ascension Movement on Earth." I have been asked to do this because of the cutting-edge, yet easy to understand nature of all my books and work, as well as certain Spiritual Leadership qualities I humbly possess. In this regard, I represent all the Masters, which works out perfectly given the synthesis nature of my work. I function as kind of a "Point Man" for the Ascended Masters on Earth, as they have described it to me.

The Masters, under the guidance of Lord Buddha (our Planetary Logos), has also guided us as part of our mission to bring Wesak to the West! So for the last six years we have held a Global Festival and Conference in Mt Shasta, California for 2000 people. This, of course, honors the Wesak Festival, which is the holiest day of the year to the inner plane Ascended Masters and the high point of incoming Spiritual energies to the Earth on the Taurus full moon each year! We invite all lightworkers to join us each year from all over the world for this momentous celebration, which is considered to be one of the premiere Spiritual events in the New Age Movement!

The fourth part of my mission and purpose is the 30 Volume "Easy To Read Encyclopedia of the Spiritual Path" I have written. So far I have completed 27 volumes in this "Ascension book series." The Ascended Master Djwhal Khul prophesized in the 1940's that there would be a third dispensation of Ascended Master teachings what would appear at the turn of the century. The first dispensation of Ascended Master teachings was the "Theosophical Movement," channeled by Madam Blavatsky. The second dispensation of Ascended Master teachings was the Alice Bailey books, channeled by Djwhal Khul, and the "I Am Discourses," channeled by Saint Germain. My 30 volume series of books is by the grace of GOD and the Masters, the third dispensation of Ascended Master teachings as prophesized by Djwhal Khul. These books are co-creative channeled writings of myself and the inner plane Ascended Masters. What is unique about my work is how easy to read and understand it is, how practical, comprehensive, cutting-edge, as well as integrated and synthesized. Wistancia has added to this work with her wonderful book *Invocations To The Light*.

The fifth aspect of our work and mission, which is extremely unique is the emphasis on "Synthesis." My books and all my work integrate in a very beautiful way all religions, all Spiritual paths, all mystery schools, all Spiritual teachings, and all forms of psychology! Everyone feels at home in this work because of its incredible inclusive nature! This synthesis ideal is also seen at the Wesak Celebrations, for people come from all religions, Spiritual paths, mystery schools and teachings. The event is overlighted by over one million inner plane Ascended Masters, Archangels and Angels, Elohim Masters and Christed Extraterrestrials. Wesak, the books, the Academy and all our work embody this synthesis principle. This is part of why I and we have been given Spiritual leadership of the Synthesis Ashram on Earth, and soon on the Inner Plane as well. This also explains our unique relationship to Melchizedek, who holds responsibility for the "synthesis development" of all beings in our universe. Our connection to the Mahatma is explained by the fact that the Mahatma is the Cosmic embodiment of "Synthesis" in the infinite universe. This is also why the Mahatma also goes by the name, "The Avatar of Synthesis." Archangel Metatron who holds the position in the Cosmic Tree of Life of Kether, or the Crown, hence has a "Synthesis Overview," of all of the Sephiroth or Centers of the Cosmic Tree of Life! Djwhal Khul holds Spiritual leadership of the "Synthesis Ashram" on Planetary, Solar and Galactic levels for the Earth!" The Core Group of Masters that overlight our mission are again the embodiment of the synthesis understanding!

The unique thing about our work is that it teaches some of the most cutting-edge, co-created channeled work on the planet, in the realm of Ascension and Ascended Master teachings. This can be seen in my books: *The Complete Ascension Manual, Beyond Ascension, Cosmic Ascension, Revelations of a Melchizedek Initiate,* and *How To*

Teach Ascension Classes. Because of my background as a professional psychologist and licensed Marriage, Family and Child Counselor, I also specialize in some of the most advanced, cutting-edge work on the planet in the field of Spiritual psychology. In this regard, I would guide you to my books: *Soul Psychology, Integrated Ascension, How to Clear the Negative Ego,* and *Ascension and Romantic Relationships*! I also have humbly brought forth some extremely cutting edge work on the physical/earthly level in the field of healing, Spirituality and society, politics, social issues, extraterrestrials, Spiritual leadership, Spirituality and business, Goddess work with Wistancia, and, of course, the annual Wesak Celebrations. This can be found in my books: *The Golden Keys To Ascension and Healing, Hidden Mysteries, Manual For Planetary Leadership, Your Ascension Mission: Embracing Your Puzzle Piece, How To Be Successful In Your Business From a Spiritual and Financial Perspective,* and *Empowerment and Integration of The Goddess* written by Wistancia and myself, to name a few!

Adding to this, the eleven new books I have just completed and am completing: *The Golden Book of Melchizedek: How To Become an Integrated Christ/Buddha In This Lifetime, How To Release Fear-Based Thinking and Feeling: An In-depth Study of Spiritual Psychology, The Little Flame and Big Flame* (my first children's book), *Letters of Guidance To Students and Friends, Ascension Names and Terms Glossary, Ascension Activation Meditations of The Spiritual Hierarchy, The Divine Blue Print For The Seventh Golden Age, How To Do Psychological and Spiritual Counseling For Self and Others, God and His Team of Super Heroes* (my second children's book) and *How To Achieve Perfect Radiant Health From The Soul's Perspective*!

Currently I have completed 27 volumes in my "Ascension book series." Fourteen of these books are published by Light Technology Publishers. A new version of Soul Psychology has just been published by Ballantine Publishers (owned by Random House), which I am quite excited about as well! The other books are in manuscript form and I am currently negotiating with various publishers for publishing rights! My books have also been translated and published in Germany, Brazil, Japan, Holland, and Israel, and this process continues to expand.

Spirit and the inner plane Ascended Masters have told me that because of this unique focus, that what I have actually done in a co-creative way and manner with them is open a new Portal to God. This new portal opening stems out of all the cutting-edge Ascension Activations and Ascended Master teachings, the totally cutting-edge Spiritual psychology work because of my background as a psychologist and licensed Marriage, Family, and Child Counselor, and my unique ability to ground all the work into the physical/earthly world in a balanced and integrated manner. Spirit and the Masters have told me that this new Portal to God is on an inner and outer plane level, and continues to be built in a co-creative way with Spirit, the Masters, myself, and certain other Masters and High Level Initiates who are helping me on the inner and outer planes! I have Spiritual leadership, however, in spearheading this project, and it is one of the most exciting projects I am involved in.

In terms of my Spiritual initiation process, as I have spoken of in my books, I have currently now taken my fourteenth major Initiation. These are not the minor initiations that some groups work with, but are the major initiations that embody all the minor initiations within them. The Seventh Initiation is the achieving of Liberation and Ascension. The Tenth Initiation is the completion of Planetary Ascension and the beginning of Solar Initiation. The Eleventh Initiation being the first Galactic Initiation. The Twelfth Initiation being the first Universal Initiation from an earthly perspective. Having taken my fourteenth initiation, what is most important to me is that these initiations have been taken in an integrated manner," for, in truth, the Masters told me that they are not really into Ascension, which may surprise a great many lightworkers! The Masters are into "Integrated Ascension!" There are many lightworkers taking initiations, but many are not doing so in an integrated and balanced manner! They are taking them on a Spiritual level, but they are not being properly integrated into the mental and emotional bodies, or the psychological level. They are also not transcending negative ego/fear-based thinking and feeling and properly balancing their four-body system. They are also not integrating their initiations fully into the physical/earthly level, addressing such things as: Healing, Grounding their Missions, Finding their Puzzle Piece Mission and Purpose, Prosperity Consciousness and Financial and Earthly Success, Integrating the God/Goddess, Embracing the Earth Mother and the Nature Kingdom, Properly Integrating into Third Dimensional Society and Civilization in terms of the focus of their Service Mission. This is just mentioned as a very loving reminder of the importance of an integrated and balanced approach to one's Spiritual path. The grace to have been able to take these 14 major initiations and to be able to have completed my Planetary Ascension process and to have moved deeply into my Cosmic Ascension process; I give to GOD, Christ, the Holy Spirit, Melchizedek, the Mahatma Archangel Metatron, and the Core Group of Masters I work with. I have dedicated myself and my life in service to GOD and the Masters, and I have humbly attempted to share everything I know, have used and have done in my Spiritual path and Ascension process with all of you, my Beloved Readers!

Melchizedek, the Universal Logos, has also inwardly told me, that because of the Cosmic work I am involved with, that I have taken on the Spiritual assignment of being one of the "Twelve Prophets of Melchizedek on Earth." I am very humbled to serve in this capacity. For Melchizedek is the Universal Logos, which is like being the President of our entire Universe. In truth, all religions and Spiritual teachings have their source in Melchizedek and in the Great Ancient Order of Melchizedek. It is my great honor and privilege to serve GOD and Melchizedek in this capacity. This is something I have never spoken of before, although I have known of this for many, many years. I have been guided after all this time to share a little more deeply about my Spiritual mission on Earth at this time.

The Academy Web site is one of the most profound Spiritual Web sites you will ever explore, because it embodies this "synthesis nature," and is an ever expanding, living, easy-to-read Spiritual encyclopedia that fully integrates all 12 Rays in design and creation! This is also embodied in the free 140 page information packet that we send out to all who ask who wish to get involved and know more about our work! The information in the information packet is also available by just exploring the Academy Website!

We have also set up a wonderful Ministers Ordination and Training Program, which we invite all who are interested to read about. I am also very excited about a relatively recent book I have written called *How To Teach Ascension Classes.* Because I have become so busy with my Spiritual leadership and global world service work, I really do not have the time to teach weekly classes as I have in the past. I firmly believe in the motto "Why give a person a fish when you can teach them to fish"! In this vein the Masters guided me to write a book on how to teach people to teach Ascension classes based on my work. I humbly suggest it is a most wonderful channeled book that can teach you in the easiest way and manner on every level to teach Ascension classes in your home or on a larger scale if you choose. These classes are springing up now all over the globe and have been successful beyond my wildest dreams and expectations. When I wrote the book I was so involved with the process of writing it that I never fully envisioned the tremendous success it would have on a global level. Using this book and my other books, I have really done the initial homework for you, which can and will allow you to immediately begin teaching Ascension classes yourself. I humbly suggest that you look into the possibility of doing this yourself if you are so guided!

One other very interesting aspect of our Spiritual mission is something the Masters have been speaking to us about for over ten years which is what they described as being "Ambassadors for the Christed Extraterrestrials"! We have always known this to be true! This was part of the reason I wrote the book *Hidden Mysteries*, which I humbly suggest is one of the best overviews in an easy-to-read and understand manner, of the entire Extraterrestrial Movement as it has affected our planet. If you have not read this book I highly recommend that you do so. It is truly fascinating reading! My strongest personal connection to the Extraterrestrials is with the Arcturians! The Arcturians are the most advanced Christed Extraterrestrial race in our galaxy. They hold the future blueprint for the unfoldment of this planet. The Arcturians are like our future planet and future selves on a collective level. Part of my work, along with the Ascended Master Teachings, that I have been asked to bring through has been to bring through a more conscious and personal connection to the Arcturians, the Ashtar Command, and other such Christed Extraterrestrial races. This year's Platinum Wesak because of being in the year 2001, will have a special connection to these Christed Extraterrestrials, and we invite you all to attend for this reason and many others! I also encourage you to read my book *Beyond Ascension* where I explore some of my personal experiences with the Arcturians, and how you may do so as well!

Currently, behind the scenes, we are working on some further expansions of this aspect of our mission, which we will share at a later time! Wistancia has also been involved with White Time Healing, which is another most wonderful extraterrestrial healing modality that she offers to the public!

One other aspect of our mission deals with having developed, with help from the inner plane Ascended Masters, some of the most advanced ascension activation processes to accelerate Spiritual evolution that has ever been brought forth to this planet. In this co-creative process with the Masters, we have discovered the keys to how to accelerate Spiritual evolution at a rate of speed that in past years and centuries would have been unimaginable! This is why I call working with the Ascended Masters "The Rocketship to GOD Method of Spiritual Growth." There is no faster path to God Realization than working with the Ascended Masters, Archangels and Angels, Elohim Masters and Christed Extraterrestrials! What is wonderful about this process is that you do not have to leave your current Spiritual practice, religion or Spiritual path. Stay on the path you are and just integrate this work into what you are currently doing! All paths, as you know, my friends lead to GOD! This is the profundity of following an eclectic path and path of synthesis! I humbly suggest I have found some shortcuts! I share this with all lightworkers on Earth, for I love GOD with all my heart and soul and mind and might, and I recognize that we are all incarnations of GOD, and Sons and Daughters of this same GOD regardless of what religion, Spiritual path or mystery school we are with. We are all, in truth, the Eternal Self and are all God! There is, in truth, only GOD, so what I share with you I share with you, GOD, and myself, for in the highest sense we are all one! What we each hold back from each other, we hold back from ourselves and from GOD. This is why I give freely all that I am, have learned and have, to you my Beloved Readers, giving everything and holding back nothing! In my books and audiotapes I have literally shared every single one of these ideas, tools, and ascension activation methods for accelerating evolution that I have used and come to understand. My Beloved Readers, these tools and methods found in my books and on the audio tapes will "blow your mind as to their effectiveness,' in terms of how profound and easy to use they are! I would highly recommend that all lightworkers obtain the 13 Ascension Activation Meditation tapes I have put together for this purpose. Most of them were taped at the Wesak Celebrations with 1500 to 2000 people in attendance, along with over one million inner plane Ascended Masters, Archangels and Angels, Elohim Masters, and Christed Extraterrestrials, under the Wesak full moon and the mountain of Mt. Shasta. You can only imagine the power, love, and effectiveness of these Ascension Activation Meditation tapes. I recommend getting all 13 tapes and working with one tape every day or every other day! I personally guarantee you that these tapes will accelerate your Spiritual evolution a thousand-fold! You can find our about them in the information packets and on our Website. They are available only from the Academy! Trust me on this, the combination of reading my books and Wistancia's book, and working with these Ascension Activation Meditation tapes, will accelerate your Spiritual evolution beyond your wildest dreams and imagination!

One other extremely important part of my mission, which is a tremendous Spiritual passion of mine, is the training of lightworkers on Earth in the area of Spiritual/Christ/Buddha thinking and negative ego/separative/fear-based thinking! These are the only two ways of thinking in the world, and each person thinks with one, the other, or a combination of both. If a person does not learn how to transcend negative ego thinking and feeling, it will end up over time corrupting every aspect of their lives including all channeling work, Spiritual teaching, and even healing work! One cannot be wrong with self and right with GOD. This is because, as we all know, our thoughts create our reality! I cannot recommend more highly that every person reading this reading my other books: *Soul Psychology, The Golden Book of Melchizedek: How To Become An Integrated Christ/Buddha in This Lifetime*, and *How To Release Fear-Based Thinking and Feeling: An In-depth Study of Spiritual Psychology*! I humbly suggest that these three books will be three of the most extraordinary self-help books in the area of mastering Spiritual/Christ/Buddha thinking. They are extremely easy to read, very practical, and filled with tools that will help you in untold ways. The last two books I mentioned are only available through the Academy. Being a channel for the Ascended Masters and being uniquely trained as a Spiritual psychologist and Marriage, Family, and Child Counselor; as well as being raised in a family of psychologists, has given me an extraordinary ability to teach this material through my books in a most effective manner. The combination of my books on Ascension and these books on Spiritual psychology, along with Wistancia's book on the art of invocation, will literally revolutionize your consciousness in the comfort of your own home! The most extraordinary thing about all this work is how incredibly easy-to-read, and easy-to-understand it is. It is also incredibly comprehensive, completely cutting-edge, and totally integrated, balanced and synthesized. It contains the best of all schools of thought from the past, present, and channeled cutting-edge future understanding that is available now! I humbly ask you to trust me in this regard, and just read one of these books and you will immediately want to buy the others!

One other aspect of our work and mission is our involvement with the "Water of Life" and the Perfect Science products, for the healing of our physical bodies and the healing of the physical body of Mother Earth of all pollution in the air, water and earth. This is the miracle Mother Earth has been waiting for to bring her back to her "original edenic state" after so much abuse. This is not the time or the place to get into this subject in detail; however, I invite you to check out the "Water of Life" and the Perfect Science information in the Information Packet and on the Academy Website! It is truly the miracle we have all been waiting for to help heal Mother Earth!

One other aspect of our work and mission is a project that the Ascended Masters have asked us to put together on behalf of lightworkers and people around the globe. It is called the "Interdimensional Prayer Altar Program"! The Masters have guided us to set up in the Academy on the property we live on in Agoura Hills, California. We have set up a 'Physical Interdimensional Prayer Altar" where we will place prayers regarding the subject that people send in. In consultation with the Masters, Archangels and Angels, Elohim Masters and Christed Extraterrestrials, we have made an arrangement with them that all physical letters placed upon this Altar will immediately worked upon by these Masters. We have been guided by the inner plane Ascended Masters to create 15 Prayer Altar Programs in different areas of life that people can sign up for. For example, there is one for health and one for financial help in your Spiritual mission. There are 15 in total, and two-thirds of them are totally free. There are five or six that are more advanced Spiritual acceleration programs where written material is sent to you to work with in conjunction with these programs to accelerate Spiritual growth that are also placed on this Interdimensional Prayer Altar. All letters we receive by e-mail, fax, or letter, are placed on the Altar by myself or my personal assistant. It is kept 100% confidential and is an extremely special service provided by the inner plane Ascended Masters and Angels to help all lightworkers and people on Earth with immediate help for whatever they need should they desire assistance. Other examples of Prayer Altars are: Building your Higher Light Body, Extra Protection, Relationship Help, World Service Prayers, Help for your Animals, Prayer Altar for the Children, Integrating the Goddess, Integrating your Archetypes, Integrating the Seven Rays and working with the Seven Inner Plane Ashrams of the Christ, Integrating the Mantle of the Christ, Ascension Seat Integration, and Light, Love and Power Body Building Program! These Prayer Altar Programs have been co-created with the inner plane Ascended Masters as another tool for not only helping all lightworkers with whatever they need help with, but also as another cutting-edge tool to accelerate Spiritual evolution!

In a similar regard, the Masters have guided us to set up a Melchizedek Synthesis Light Academy Membership Program which is based on three levels of involvement: Stage One, Stage Two and Stage Three! Stage One and Stage Three are totally free. Stage Two costs only $20 for a Lifetime Membership with no other fees ever required. You also receive, free for joining, large colored pictures of Melchizedek, the Mahatma, Archangel Metatron and Djwhal Khul. It is not necessary to join to get involved in the work. This program has been set up by the inner plane Ascended Masters as another service and tool of the

Academy to help lightworkers accelerate their Spiritual evolution! When joining the different Stages, the Masters take you under their wing, so to speak, and accelerate your evolution by working with you much more closely on the inner plane while you sleep at night and during your conscious waking hours. The joining is nothing more than a process that gives them the permission to work with you in this more intensive fashion! Again, it is not necessary to join to get involved in the work. The Academy Membership Program is really just another one of the many fantastic tools and services the Academy has made available to you to accelerate your Spiritual, psychological and earthly/physical evolution in an integrated and balanced manner!

After completing my two new books, *The Golden Book of Melchizedek: How To Become An Integrated Christ/Buddha In This Lifetime* and *How To Release Fear-Based Thinking and Feeling: An In-depth Study of Spiritual Psychology*, I had a dream where I was being shown the different Spiritual missions people had. My Spiritual mission was the embodiment of the Holy Spirit. I was clearly shown how other people within GOD, Christ and the Holy Spirit, had missions of being more detached offshoots of the Holy Spirit, and continuing outward from there with all kinds of different Spiritual missions. However, mine was the embodiment of the Holy Spirit on Earth.

My Beloved Readers, I want to be very clear here that in sharing this I am in no way, shape, or form claiming to be the Holy Spirit. There is enough glamour in the New Age Movement and I am not interested in adding any more to it. What I am sharing here, which is being given to more clearly and precisely share my Spiritual mission and purpose, is that which I am here to strive to embody and demonstrate. The Holy Spirit is the third aspect of the Trinity of GOD. I have always greatly loved the Holy Spirit, for the Holy Spirit is like the "Voice of GOD"! It is the "Still, Small Voice Within"! When one prays to GOD, it is the Holy Spirit who answers for GOD. The Holy Spirit is the answer to all questions, challenges and problems. The Holy Spirit speaks for the

Atonement or the At-one-ment! It teaches the Sons and Daughters of GOD how to recognize their true identity as God, Christ, the Buddha, and the Eternal Self! In truth, there are only two voices in life! There is the voice of the negative ego and the "Voice of the Holy Spirit"! There is the voice of negative ego/fear-based/separative thinking and feeling, and there is the Voice of God/Spiritual/Christ/Buddha thinking and feeling! There is the "Voice of Love" and the voice of fear! There is the "Voice of Oneness" and the voice of separation!

I was given this dream after completing those two books because, I humbly suggest, this was the energy I was embodying while writing them and the energy that I am striving to embody at all times in my Spiritual mission and purpose on Earth. This is not surprising in the sense that this has always been my Spiritual ideal, and the dream was just an inward confirmation in that moment that I was embodying and demonstrating that Spiritual ideal in the energy flow I was in. This is what I strive to do in all my work; whether it be my Ascension Book Series, Wesak Celebrations, Teaching, Counseling, Videotapes, or Audio Tapes, to be the embodiment of a "Voice for God"! By the Grace of GOD, Christ, the Holy Spirit, and the Masters, I provide a lot of the "answers" people and lightworkers are seeking! I teach people how to "undo" negative ego/fear-based/separative thinking and feeling and show them how to fully Realize the God/Christ/Buddha thinking and feeling! I show them how to release and undo glamour, illusion and maya, and instead seek "Truth, as GOD, Christ, the Holy Spirit and the Masters would have you seek it"!

My real purpose, however, is not to just be the embodiment of the Holy Spirit on Earth, for I would not be embodying the Voice and Vision of the Holy Spirit if I just focused on this. The Voice and Vision of GOD, Christ, the Holy Spirit and Melchizedek is that of synthesis! This is the other thing I feel in the deepest part of my heart and soul that I am here to embody! So, my "trust and highest Spiritual ideal" that I am here to strive to embody is GOD, Christ, the Holy Spirit, the inner plane Ascended Masters, the Archangels and Angels of the Light of GOD, The Elohim Councils of the Light of GOD, and the Christed Extraterrestrials of the Light of GOD. I feel in the deepest part of my heart and soul, and what I try to embody every moment of my life is, "All that is of GOD and the Godforce on Earth"! In this regard, it is my Spiritual mission and purpose to strive to be the embodiment of the "synthesis nature of God on Earth"! This is why I have been given Spiritual leadership of the Synthesis Ashram and Academy on Earth, and future leadership of the inner plane Synthesis Ashram that governs our planet.

The other thing I strive to do in my Spiritual mission is to embody Spiritual mastery on a Spiritual, psychological, and physical/earthly level. What most people and lightworkers do not realize is that there are three distinct levels to God Realization. There is a Spiritual level, a psychological level, and a physical/earthly level! To achieve true God Realization, all three levels must be equally mastered! Another way of saying this is that there are "Four Faces of GOD"! There is a Spiritual Face, a Mental Face, an Emotional Face and a Material Face! To truly Realize God, all four must be equally mastered, loved, honored, sanctified, integrated and balanced! The Mental and Emotional Faces of GOD make up the psychological level of GOD. My Spiritual mission and purpose is to fully embody Spiritual mastery, and unconditional love on all three of these levels and in all Four Faces of GOD! In a similar vein, my Spiritual mission and purpose is to embody self-mastery and proper integration of all Seven Rays of GOD, not just one or a few. For the Seven Rays of GOD are, in truth, the true "Personality of GOD"! My Spiritual mission and purpose is to not only strive to embody all levels of GOD, but to also try and develop all my God-given abilities and Spiritual gifts on a Spiritual, psychological, and physical/earthly level, and in all Four Faces of GOD!

My Beloved Readers, all these things that I have written about in this chapter are what I strive to fully embody and demonstrate on the Earth every moment of my life, and is what I strive with all my heart and soul and mind and might to teach others to do as well!

As the Founder and Director of the Melchizedek Synthesis Light Academy along with Wistancia, I say with great humbleness and humility that it has been my great honor and privilege to share "my Spiritual mission and purpose in a deeper and more profound manner at this time." I do so in the hopes that all who feel a resonance and attunement with this work will get involved with the "Academy's Teachings" and all that it has to offer. I also share this so that all who choose to get involved might join this vast group of lightworkers around the globe, to help spread the teachings and work of the inner plane Ascended Masters. The inner plane Ascended Masters and I, along with the Archangels and Angels, Elohim Councils and Christed Extraterrestrials, put forth the Clarion Call to lightworkers around the world to explore this work, integrate this work, and become Ambassadors of the Ascended Masters, so we may at this time in beloved Earth's history bring in fully now the Seventh Golden Age in all its glory!

About the Author

Dr. Joshua David Stone has a Ph.D. in Transpersonal Psychology and is a licensed Marriage, Family, and Child Counselor, in Agoura Hills, California. On a Spiritual level, he anchors **The Melchizedek Synthesis Light Academy and Ashram,** which is an integrated inner and outer plane ashram that seeks to represent all Paths to GOD! He serves as one of the leading Spokespersons for the Planetary Ascension Movement. Through his books, tapes, workshops, lectures, and annual Wesak Celebrations, Dr. Stone is known as one of the leading authorities in the world on the teachings of the Ascended Masters, Spiritual Psychology, and Ascension! He has currently written more than 27 volumes in his "Ascension Book Series," which he also likes to call "The Easy To Read Encyclopedia of the Spiritual Path!"

For a free information packet of all Dr. Stone's workshops, books, audiotapes, Academy membership program, and global outreach program, please call or write to the following address:

Dr. Joshua David Stone
Melchizedek Synthesis Light Academy
28951 Malibu Rancho Rd.
Agoura Hills, CA 91301

Phone: 818-706-8458
Fax: 818-706-8540
e-mail: drstone@best.com

Please come visit my Website at:
http://www.drjoshuadavidstone.com